ASIAN STUDII
Southe

MW01235783

Fa Cathleen ; helping
Thanks for helping
me to think about
Islam in Indonesia
and elsewhere.
Bill

No. 29
LEADERSHIP AND CULTURE IN
INDONESIAN POLITICS

ASIAN STUDIES ASSOCIATION OF AUSTRALIA
Southeast Asia Publications Series

Titles in Print

Leadership and Culture in Indonesian Politics

R WILLIAM LIDDLE

Asian Studies Association of Australia
in association with

ALLEN & UNWIN
Sydney

First published in 1996 by
Allen & Unwin Pty Ltd
9 Atchison Street, St Leonards, NSW 2065 Australia
Phone: (61 2) 9901 4088
Fax: (61 2) 9906 2218
E-mail: 100252.103@compuserve.com

National Library of Australia
Cataloguing-in-Publication entry:

Liddle, R. William (Raymond William), 1938– .
  Leadership and culture in Indonesian politics.

  Includes index.
  ISBN 1 86448 196 X (Allen & Unwin).

  1. Political leadership—Indonesia. 2. Indonesia—
  Politics and government—1966– . I. Asian Studies
  Association of Australia. II. Title. (Series: Southeast
  Asia publications series; no. 29).

320.9598

Cover photograph courtesy of the Indonesian Embassy, Canberra

Typeset by Vera-Reyes Inc., Manila
Printed by South Wind Productions, Singapore

10 9 8 7 6 5 4 3 2 1

Contents

To Norman Shub, who asked me what writers do

PART ONE

Introduction
Leadership and Culture
in Indonesian Politics

The essays collected in this volume were written between 1984 and 1993. They reflect the two central concerns of my research on Indonesia during this period: explaining the longevity of the New Order, the authoritarian form of government through which Indonesia has been ruled since 1966, and discovering the factors that might shape political change in the future. They also highlight two themes that have become more and more pronounced in my work over the decade: the centrality of political leadership in bringing about both stability and change; and the importance of incorporating a resource-based conception of culture as a variable in political analysis.

oOo

The first concern grew out of a dissatisfaction with the way in which I and others had been writing about the New Order for nearly two decades. I began to study Indonesia in the late 1950s as a believer in the Wilsonian principle, revived at the end of World War II, that all peoples or nations had a right to self-determination, to establish independent, sovereign nation-states equal in international standing with the already existing nation-states of the West and Japan. I admired the successful struggles for independence of the nationalists in India, Pakistan, Burma, and Indonesia in the 1940s, and saw comparable processes occurring elsewhere in Asia and Africa in the 1950s.

Underlying the Wilsonian principle was an important assumption, that self-determination would be realised in the form of popular governance domestically as well as freedom from control internationally. Another way to put this is that I took representative democracy for granted as the normal form of government in the modern world, a world which was then

3

rapidly expanding beyond its previous Western base to include the newly independent states.

Most of these states did in fact become representative democracies at the moment of independence. Indonesia adopted a European-style parliamentary constitution, the Constitution of 1950, shortly after the transfer of sovereignty from the Netherlands at the end of 1949. Under this constitution, Indonesians enjoyed the same freedoms of speech, press, assembly and so on as citizens of democracies elsewhere. In anticipation of elections, political parties emerged and began to organise throughout the country. When national parliamentary elections were finally held in 1955, the 91.5% turnout of registered voters displayed vividly the extent to which Indonesians had become politically mobilised citizens of their new country.[1]

Unfortunately, Indonesian democracy was short-lived. In 1959, President Sukarno, in alliance with the army, decreed a return to the revolutionary Constitution of 1945, which enabled the executive easily to dominate the legislative branch. No elections were held during the brief period of Sukarno's Guided Democracy, which ended in the wake of the assassination of six top army generals in the early morning hours of 1 October 1965.

I first conducted field research in Indonesia from 1962 to 1964, in the municipality of Pematang Siantar and its surrounding district of Simalungun, located in North Sumatra province. My topic was the impact on national unity of a political party system organised partly along religious and ethnic cleavage lines. At that time Indonesia was no longer a democracy, but the old political parties were still in existence. I could compare their activities in the locality in the early 1960s, as I was directly observing them, with accounts by participants who had been active in the 1950s.

The theoretical focus for this research was supplied by modernisation theory, which was the social science scholarly community's first attempt at providing a conceptual framework within which to examine the changes then underway in the newly independent states. In particular, I wanted to explore two widely-held propositions: (1) that social and cultural secularisation and rationalisation were inexorably dissolving ethnic and religious loyalties within new societies like Indonesia; and (2) that the organisation of political party systems along such cleavage lines was regressive (in light of the secularising and rationalising movement of history), destabilising to new democracies, and disintegrative of new nations.

Both of these propositions seemed dubious to someone who had grown up in industrial western Pennsylvania, where a plethora of ethnic and religious groups had long contended for power more or less peacefully within the structure provided by the American two-party system. Indeed, this boyhood experience may well have both influenced my choice of research topic and biased my reading of the Indonesian situation.

In any event, after two years of total immersion in local Indonesian politics, I became convinced that both of the modernisation theory propositions were unsupported by my cases. Ethnic and religious cleavages in North Sumatra were not an aspect of some now-fading "traditional" past, but a modern twentieth century reality created initially by the actions of colonial administrators and Western capitalists and the reactions of local Indonesian communities. Moreover, the political party system organised in part along ethnic and religious lines had worked reasonably well at the local level during the democratic 1950s. It had accurately represented local sentiments without at the same time creating insuperable obstacles to resolving differences among parties in the local legislatures. Indeed, I concluded that the chief danger to national unity, at least as seen from my micro-level perspective, was not representative democracy but Guided Democracy. By denying the legitimacy of partisan representation of religious and ethnic cleavages, Sukarno had turned a boiling pot into a pressure cooker that was likely to explode.

My first studies of the New Order were conducted with the same pro-democratic assumptions. In some respects—notably foreign and economic policy—the right-wing Suharto certainly differed from the left-leaning (or at least left-sounding) Sukarno. In terms of political structure, however, they both headed non-democratic regimes that relied heavily on coercion to suppress the articulation of a wide range of political interests. Indeed, the Suharto government has a worse record on this score than its predecessor. Sukarno had banned Indonesia's second largest political party, Masjumi, had jailed some politicians and journalists, had allowed the communist party to intimidate and harass its opponents, and had attempted to enforce his own brand of ideological orthodoxy. Suharto and his fellow army leaders, on the other hand, in their first months in power allowed or encouraged the mass arrest and execution of hundreds of thousands of communists.[2] Coercion has continued to be a hallmark of the New Order government ever since.

By the late 1970s, however, two realities about the New Order had become visible even through my thick analytic lenses. The government was politically stable and economically successful. For more than a decade, despite my concerns about overheating pressure cookers, the government had never been in danger of being overthrown, either from internal conflict or from mass political mobilisation. The one partial exception to this generalisation was the Malari incident of January 1974, in which student protest combined with urban unrest and conflict between two generals vying for Suharto's favor, to produce a few days of riots and looting in Jakarta and the fall from grace of one of the generals.

The economic success of the New Order has been recounted many times. Confronted immediately by unpayable foreign debts, galloping inflation, and stagnant production, the new President Suharto turned for policy advice to the "Berkeley Mafia", a group of Western-trained University of Indonesia economists under the leadership of Professor Widjojo Nitisastro. The economists prescribed a set of conservative market-oriented policies for stabilisation and rehabilitation. This enabled them to win the crucial support of Western governments and international lending institutions for rescheduling payment of the old debts and obtaining new loans to restart the growth process. From the late 1960s to the early 1980s the Indonesian economy grew at nearly 8% per year.

From the beginning, the New Order's economic policy makers paid attention to distribution as well as growth. One of the government's earliest successes was in the rehabilitation of the rice economy. Farmers were provided with high-yielding hybrid seeds, fertilizer, and pesticides; irrigation systems were restored or constructed anew; storage facilities were built to maintain an "iron stock"; prices were set to provide incentives to farmers. By the early 1980s Indonesia was self-sufficient in rice.

In the mid-1970s, the government also began a series of local-level programs, many labelled INPRES (Presidential Instruction), designed to provide direct developmental assistance to provincial, district, and village governments and to create new infrastructure throughout the country. By the 1980s virtually all children had access to an elementary school, health centers had been constructed in every subdistrict, and new bridges and paved roads connected previously remote regions with urban market and administrative centers. By 1987, according to World Bank measures, the incidence of poverty had dropped to 17% from about 60% in 1970.[3]

Political stability and economic success gave me a new appreciation for the New Order government. While not democratic, it had certainly done far more to modernise Indonesia—to realise the populist goals of the pre-war nationalist movement and the developmental goals of the modernisation theory to which I subscribed—than had either of its predecessors, the representative democracy of the 1950s or the Guided Democracy of the early 1960s.

How had these achievements come about? When I started asking this question, in the late 1970s and early 1980s, the most popular explanatory paradigm being applied to the Third World (a classification that had by then replaced the earlier "new states" and "developing areas") was dependency theory. In its classic formulation, dependency theory argued that the failure of Third World economies to grow was a consequence of their exploitation by foreign capital. A modified version, called "dependent development", argued that strong Third World states, in alliance with foreign and domestic private capital, could enable economies to grow but would distort distribution, leaving small business people out of the system and impoverishing lower class workers and farmers.

The dependency paradigm obviously had little to offer a student of the New Order. It was true that foreign capital, especially in the form of loans but also as investment, and the Indonesian state were playing a major role in development. But that role was positive, in its impact both on growth and on distribution. Equally important, the dependency approach begged the critical political questions of who obtained the power to make and implement policy and how they did so.

I next turned to scholarly writing on the military and development, since the dominant organised political force in the New Order is the army. That literature also turned out to be unsatisfactory. Most of its findings were inconclusive, establishing only that some economies grew and others did not in Third World countries under military rule. Some scholars, pro-democrats like myself, seemed out to prove that defence budgets ballooned when armies took power. In New Order Indonesia, however, the military's portion of the national budget has not been large, and the defence budget has never been a serious political issue.

In the end, my principal analytical help came from the rational choice theorists Warren Ilchman and Norman Uphoff, who wrote *The Political Economy of Change* (Berkeley: University of California Press, 1969), and Robert Bates, author of *Markets and States in Tropical Africa* (Berkeley: University of California Press, 1981). I was also strongly influenced by the development economist Albert Hirschman. What I took from Ilchman, Uphoff, and Bates was not the rational choice paradigm itself, which begs too many questions about actors' motivations and preferences. Instead it was the focus on individual political leaders making choices to build and maintain support in varying situations of constraint and opportunity.

What I learned from Hirschman was his "passion for the possible," the conviction that politicians and other social actors face few constraints that can not be turned into opportunities. Many of Hirschman's writings explore blessings in disguise, unintended consequences of policy actions, supposed one-way sequences that turn out to work in reverse, and similar unexpected twists and turns of development. He has been a keen pricker of others' theoretical balloons, while at the same time constructing theories of his own, like *Exit, Voice, and Loyalty* (Cambridge: Harvard University Press, 1970) and *Shifting Involvements: Private Interest and Public Action* (Princeton: Princeton University Press, 1982), that incorporate his possibilist vision.

Combining these insights produced an approach that attempts to study politicians' choices in the context of an assumption of multiple and flexible opportunities to create, mobilise, and deploy political resources. This approach seems to me infinitely preferable to the sociological determinism—the overwhelming of the individual actor by cultural, social, economic, political, and institutional constraints—that has long dominated academic political science studies of the Third World.

Most of the chapters in the first part of this book examine New Order political stability and/or economic success as a product of political choices,

particularly those of Suharto. For example, Chapter One, "Suharto's
Indonesia: Personal Rule and Political Institutions," describes the New
Order political system as a steeply ascending pyramid of bureaucratic and
military power with the presidency at the apex, and shows how Suharto's
choices created it. It argues that the system displays signs of institutionalisation, or long term durability, despite the fact that it is still headed
by its founder.

This is not, incidentally, a conclusion that I am as comfortable with
today as I was when I wrote it. Elite politics since the mid-1980s have
been dominated by the maneuvering of Suharto to stay in power despite
advancing age and the maneuvering of others to force him to step down.
It is hard to discern in this behaviour any impact of constraints imposed
by institutions. I do continue to believe, however, that the army's monopoly of political resources makes unlikely any major changes in New
Order institutions in the immediate post-Suharto period.

Chapter Two, "The Politics of Shared Growth," attempts to move beyond
the standard model of authoritarian political systems, in which armed
force is the key political resource and coercion the chief instrument of
power. Through an examination of cases of conflict in rice and sugar
policy making, I argue that the New Order decision process is complex
and involves some elements of participation by groups outside the government. Participation is a political resource, utilised by groups outside the
state to gain a hearing for their demands and by Suharto to increase the
legitimacy of his government. New Order stability is thus in part a product
of outside-the-state participation.

Chapter Four, "The Relative Autonomy of the Third World Politician:
Suharto and Indonesian Economic Development in Comparative Perspective", is the most systematic statement so far of my case for leaders'
choices. The title is a play on the neo-Marxist concept, which I reject,
of the relative autonomy of the state. I argue instead that it is Suharto
the individual politician who is relatively autonomous, that is, able to
choose his own political strategy within relatively broad constraints.
Suharto's genius as a political entrepreneur, first in the mid-1960s and
then in moments of crisis since, has been his ability to see that a political
order based on military dominance, with himself at the head, could be
built and maintained with resources acquired through market-oriented
economic policies.

oOo

In my most recent writings, the focus moves from an explanation of the
longevity of Suharto and the New Order to a concern with what may be
coming next. There are two reasons for this shift in interest. First, Suharto
was 74 years old in June 1995. Like Ronald Reagan in the United States

or Deng Xiaoping in China, Suharto may well continue to dominate Indonesian politics into advanced old age. Nonetheless, the post-Suharto period is surely coming soon.

Second, I have been fascinated by the new "transitions" approach to the study of democratisation in comparative political science. Earlier research on the prospects for democracy in the developing world (my choice for a new classificatory term to replace the Third World, now that there is no Second World) tended to select large, abstract, long-term and hard-to-manipulate "democracy prerequisites" for analysis. Examples are a high level of economic development, a high level of literacy, urbanisation, and/or mass media exposure, a large bourgeoisie or entrepreneurial middle class, a predominantly civic culture of participant citizens, a long evolutionary sequence of steps toward democracy, and so on.

The new literature, by contrast, focuses more narrowly and concretely on negotiation processes among politicians, representing various types of constituencies, in the recent democratic transitions in southern Europe (Portugal, Spain, and Greece) and throughout Latin America. A major finding of this literature, to suggest the contrast with the older approach, is that politically divided military establishments in authoritarian regimes provide a critical opportunity for democratisation.

In the case of Indonesia, which meets few of the fundamental criteria for democratisation, the transitions approach is obviously more appealing. It also fits better the focus on political leadership I have developed to explain the longevity of Suharto and his choice of economic policy. Not least important, it provides me with a good analytical reason to return to the subject of democracy, which—to recall my Wilsonian values—I have long believed to be the most suitable form of government for a modern nation-state.

Chapter Six, "Indonesia's Democratic Past and Future", is my most systematic attempt so far at applying my ideas about political leadership, resources, and multiple and flexible opportunities for mobilisation and deployment of resources to the study of the prospects for democracy in Indonesia. It focuses directly on the vulnerabilities of the New Order, which had been given shorter shrift in my earlier research, and suggests ways in which those vulnerabilities can be exploited by would-be democratisers as Suharto's presidency nears its end.

There is a second theme, in addition to political leadership, that appears in many of these chapters. It is most fully explored in Chapters Five and Ten. That is a search for the proper place of culture in the study of Indonesian politics.

Culture is not a popular concept in mainstream political science just now. The concept of "political culture", coined in the 1950s, was defined as deeply rooted, long lasting mass political orientations, beliefs, and attitudes such as trust in others, deference toward authority, willingness to cooperate, and so on. An empirical connection was asserted between these orientations and popular political behaviour. A small scholarly industry developed that attempted to describe specific political cultures and to establish empirically links between culture and behaviour. A hypothesised connection between democratic cultures and stable democratic institutions was of particular interest. Political culture research eventually foundered because of its inability to persuasively demonstrate the existence of these causal links.

It is hard for the foreign scholar who studies Indonesia to reject the view that culture, broadly understood, has important influences on behaviour. The evidence of deep and long-lasting differences in values, beliefs, and ways of thinking about politics—for example, among ethnic and religious groups, between urban and rural dwellers, and even among military, bureaucratic, and intellectual subcultures of the national culture—is too apparent to ignore. Chapter Three, "Politics and Culture in Indonesia", originally written for a United States Department of State audience without previous experience in Indonesia, is an attempt to lay out some of these differences.

Indonesians themselves often make claims about the impact of culture on their politics. Perhaps their most frequent argument is that Javanese culture, characterised as collectivist, hierarchical, and deferential, suffuses national political life. To some, especially high government officials including President Suharto, this is a cause for pride in one's cultural distinctiveness, while to others it constitutes grounds for despair that Indonesia can ever become a democracy. Foreign journalists and documentary film makers, with their *wayang* (shadow play) cliches about manipulative political puppeteers, rely heavily on the idea that Indonesian national political culture is Javanist in this sense.

Another common cultural argument is that Islamic beliefs are a major source of national political cleavage and potential strife on fundamental issues of statehood. Devout Muslims, it is said, want a state that enforces Islamic law, while other Indonesians want the state to respect all religions but to give no preferential treatment to any one religion. Suspicion of Islam has long characterised the military subculture, but it is prominent throughout the non-devout Muslim elite and in the larger society as well.

My own current struggle to understand the role of culture in Indonesian politics (my 1960s Sumatran research was also in part about culture and politics) began with an observation about the connection between President Suharto's beliefs and his behaviour that is recorded in Chapter Four. Suharto almost certainly strongly adheres to the belief, deeply entrenched in national Indonesian culture from its beginnings in the late nineteenth century, that capitalism is individualistic and exploitative, a Western invention that is, in principle, antithetic to Indonesian ideas of collectivism, village cooperativism, and the all-protective state.

In the early to mid-1960s, because of the pervasiveness and depth of these ideas among Indonesians, not least in the ideologically collectivistic military, I did not believe it possible that a general as president would embrace, for the next three decades, the advice of Western-trained economists. The fact that Suharto did take the economists' advice led me, not to discard the idea of the role of culture in politics, but to attempt to reconceptualise it.

I now want to place the political analysis of culture in a framework in which the central focus of attention is the accumulation, mobilisation, and deployment of resources by social and political actors. Values, beliefs, attitudes, and ways of thinking about politics provide some of those resources and shape other resources in diverse ways. My point is not to deny that culture has an impact on behaviour, but rather to suggest that that impact is mediated and shaped by social and political action.

Any specific culture—Indonesian, say, or American—contains conflicting values, beliefs, attitudes and ways of thinking about politics. Indeed, some of these conflicting values and beliefs, like those of protestantism and Catholicism within Christianity, or liberalism and communitarianism within Western social and political movements, form distinctive subcultures within an overall cultural pattern. In the Indonesian case, one of the arguments of Chapter Three is that Javanism and Islam are subcultures of a larger modern Indonesian culture. Chapter Three and other chapters also demonstrate that both Javanese and Indonesian Islamic subcultures are themselves internally complex, containing several distinctive sub-subcultures.

In addition to its internal complexity, another important characteristic of any culture is that it changes over time. Some subcultural currents narrow and others widen, as rivers do when they flow from place to place. Even the central ideas of a culture change, as in the transformation of medieval into modern Europe. In Indonesia, it is widely believed today that the Islamic current has been expanding for the last half-century at the expense of the Javanist one.

What explains the emergence of particular cultures and subcultures, and the changes they experience over time? Structuralists, for example followers of the "classical" interpretation of Karl Marx's theory of history, assert that culture is a product of social or class structure, and cultural change is accordingly a product of social change.

In my view, there is an intervening variable between structure and culture, not taken into sufficient account by structuralists. That is the actions of individuals who accumulate enough resources to enable them to make a difference in the content of the patterns of values, beliefs, attitudes, and ways of thinking about politics in their societies. Differently put, culture is a historical product and cultural change a historical process, the result of individuals acting within the context of their time. Social structure, and a host of other factors, create constraints and opportunities for these actors, but they rarely if ever determine outcomes.

Path-breaking research along these lines has recently been conducted

by the sociologist Robert Wuthnow, who studied the role played by Martin
Luther, Voltaire, and Marx in the three great cultural transformations of
modern Europe: the Reformation, the Enlightenment, and the rise of
European socialism.[4] Wuthnow's book is about the problem of "articulation" in societal change. How does a new idea, which necessarily arises
in a particular social, economic, cultural and political environment, develop the capacity to transform that environment and become the cultural
foundation of a new society?
Wuthnow rejects answers to this question that stress either broad
conditions of social unrest or the need of rising social classes for ideological legitimation. In his view, "The interpretation that best fits the
evidence . . . is one that emphasizes the available supply of economic and
political resources."[5] The Reformation, the Enlightenment, and the rise
of socialism all occurred during periods of exceptional economic growth
that provided many of those resources.
The connection between economic growth and successful cultural
innovation in Europe was not, however, automatic. It depended on new
alignments among an enlarged number of political actors and on specific
features of the production, selection, and institutionalisation of new ideologies. In this latter process certain individuals played a key role:

> Luther, Voltaire, Marx, and their respective compatriots were able
> to formulate critical ideological discourse by thematizing certain
> features of their social environments, setting them in opposition to
> alternative visions of cultural authority, concretizing both by
> drawing on conflicts evident in the societies in which they wrote,
> and supplying figurations of behavior that mediated between
> present and idealized realities.[6]

Chapters Five and Ten in this volume attempt to develop a comparable
individual action-based approach to the study of culture and politics in
New Order Indonesia, which has also experienced rapid economic growth,
the emergence of new political and intellectual elites, and considerable
ideological ferment. Chapter Five, "Improvising Political Cultural Change:
Three Indonesian Cases" is a study of three prominent Jakarta-based
intellectuals: Nurcholish Madjid, a modernist Islamic thinker and writer,
who promotes religious tolerance; Goenawan Mohamad, essayist and long-
time editor-in-chief of *Tempo*, Indonesia's leading newsmagazine from
1971 to 1994, an individualist and democratiser; and Sjahrir, an economic
consultant and prolific commentator on economic affairs, who supports
free markets.
The ideas and resources of these three individuals are juxtaposed to
the dominant ideas in New Order Indonesian culture and to the resources
of the chief adherents to those ideas. The point of the analysis is twofold:
to assess the current state of what might be called Indonesia's "culture
wars";[7] and to help proponents of religious tolerance, individualism and

democracy, and free markets to figure out how to make their ideas more influential.

Finally, Chapter Ten, "*Media Dakwah* Scripturalism: One Form of Islamic Political Thought and Action in New Order Indonesia" examines in detail the current cultural and political conflict between two groups of Islamic modernists, the tolerant "substantialists" led by Nurcholish Madjid and the more militant "scripturalists" represented by the young editors and writers at *Media Dakwah* (Proselytising Medium), a monthly publication of the Dewan Dakwah (Proselytising Council), a prominent Islamic missionary organisation in Jakarta.

The central argument of the chapter is that the growth in acceptance of the substantialists' point of view over the past few decades and their apparent great influence in Indonesian Islamic and national life today is in part a result of the support they receive from the New Order government, with which they share some elements of a broad vision of the good society. Since the mid-1980s, moreover, they have served a more particular purpose. Suharto has found them a useful counterweight to armed forces opposition to his unwillingness to step down as president.

During this same period, other forces have been working beneath the surface political calm to strengthen the militants. These include economic development and the spread of mass education up to the tertiary level, which have created new constituencies for scripturalists as well as substantialists. In the upper class world, for example, university campus mosques are today dominated by the militants. Lower down in society, many groups left out or disadvantaged by economic change, like the urban residents whose homes are razed for development projects, consist of devout Muslims whose economic grievances may one day fuel a religious upheaval.

oOo

In the new century that lies just ahead, what will happen in the conflicts between the scripturalists and the substantialists, the statists and the free marketeers, and perhaps most importantly, the authoritarians and the democrats? I have, of course, no crystal ball, only an approach that says: pay attention to politicians and other public individuals acting in context. Assess the environment, domestic and international, from which they draw resources. Observe closely how they accumulate, mobilise, and deploy those resources, and how others react to them. Draw lessons from recent events elsewhere, such as the attempts to democratise in East Asia, which have been reasonably successful, and in East Europe, where the record is more mixed. Above all, believe with Albert Hirschman that the future remains open.

1. Feith, Herbert, *The Indonesian Elections of 1955*, Ithaca: Cornell University Modern Indonesia Project, 1957, p. 50.
2. Robert Cribb, ed., *The Indonesian Killings 1965–66*, Clayton, Vic.: Monash University Centre of Southeast Asian Studies, 1990.
3. *Indonesia: Strategy for a Sustained Reduction in Poverty*, Washington, D.C.: The World Bank, 1990, pp. xv–xvi.
4. Robert Wuthnow, *Communities of Discourse*, Cambridge: Harvard University Press, 1989.
5. *Ibid.*, p. 9.
6. *Ibid.*, p. 15.
7. The reference is to James Davison Hunter, *Culture Wars: The Struggle to Define America*, New York: Basic Books, 1991.

1

Suharto's Indonesia: Personal Rule and Political Institutions*

Strong political institutions have not been a hallmark of Third World governments. With few exceptions, colonialism in Asia and Africa left a legacy of only rudimentary governmental institutions and even less-formed political party and interest group organisations. In these structureless environments, personal rule has been the almost inevitable alternative. Strong individuals, typically supported by armies, installed themselves in presidential palaces (formerly the residences of governors-general, also originally installed by armies) and swept away the flimsy and hastily erected democratic scaffolding of late colonialism.

In his still influential *Political Order and Changing Societies,*[1] Samuel Huntington explained the widespread collapse of democratic regimes as the natural outcome of a situation in which the mobilisation into politics of large numbers of detraditionalised people placed too heavy a load of demands on fledgling governments. Praetorianism, the direct control of government by social forces unmediated by political institutions, was Huntington's label for the personal or military regimes that replaced Western-derived democracies. Civic polities, in which autonomous political institutions—that is, one or more strong political parties—predominate over social forces, could ultimately be established following one of two routes: a "within system" coalition of urban elites with the conservatively-led rural poor, which would enable the former to impose order on conflicts among urban lower- and middle-class groups; or the seizure of central power by a revolutionary opposition supported by radicalised peasants. The second alternative is clearly the communist model. The first—para-doxically, Huntington says—is initially highly traditionalising, because it

* First published in *Pacific Affairs* 58, 1 (Spring 1985), pp. 68–90.

is based on a conservative rural following. But the stability of an urban-rural conservative coalition buys time for a more thoroughgoing modernisation to take place. The gradual growth of the party system keeps pace with the emergence of newly-mobilised social forces, and the end result is a developed civic polity.

Writing several years before Huntington, David Apter also recognised the fragility of new institutions in Asia and Africa.[2] His focus, however, was on the role that an individual political leader might play in bridging the difficult transition from "traditional" to "modern" politics. Apter borrowed Max Weber's framework of three types of authority (traditional, charismatic, and rational-legal), and his hypothesis that charismatic authority could be a bridge to modernity. Ghana's first prime minister, Kwame Nkrumah, was the charismatic leader whose personal authority, Apter believed, would serve to bind the detraditionalising masses to the unfamiliar institutions of parliamentary democracy. In the event, of course, Nkrumah and Ghana travelled other roads, but that did not diminish the potential usefulness of Apter's insight.

Identifying the weakness of institutions and emphasising the kind of role that individual leaders might play were major contributions. But the larger context in which these ideas were put suffered from the *Zeitgeist* of the 1950s and 1960s scholarship about the Third World. For both writers, the generalised European experience was a template for Asia and Africa: praetorianism would give way to party-centred civic polity, defined in Western or Soviet terms, along paths replicating American, British, continental European, or Soviet history; European-style parliamentarianism was a genuine option, requiring only the appropriate values and skills on the part of the paramount ruler.

The nation-states of Asia have now been independent for thirty to forty years, those of Africa for fifteen to twenty-five. The cumulative political experience of these decades is sufficient to allow us to begin to look at leaders and institutions in more direct and concrete terms—not as avatars of Jefferson, Bismarck or Lenin, separation-of-powers, the *Beamtenstaat*, or the dictatorship of the proletariat, but as politicians and organisations with a life and history of their own. What has happened since the initial victory of strong rulers over weak institutions? Has a kind of stasis set in, with the original ruler or an equally personalist successor still in the palace? Or have institutions—perhaps of the Western sort (we are after all talking about nation-states whose leaders have "modernising" ambitions and who also look to the West for assistance and, in a complex way, approval), perhaps of a more homegrown variety—emerged and begun to spin webs of constraints around the arbitrary impulses of heads of state? What qualities of the society, culture, polity, and economy are responsible for either the maintenance or the transformation of personal rule?

If there are general answers to these questions, one way to find them is through careful assessment of cases. Indonesia's current New Order government is a useful starting point. One of the largest Third World countries, Indonesia is culturally and socially complex, like India, Nigeria, Pakistan, Bangladesh, the Philippines, and other large and middle-sized states. Its economic development strategy for the past two decades has been based on petroleum and foreign assistance plus investment, which suggest comparison with Iran, Nigeria, and even Mexico and Venezuela. Politically, it is an almost classic case of weak Western-imported institutions overthrown by a charismatic leader, President Sukarno, who was in turn toppled by the minister and commander of the army, General (now President) Suharto.

For Indonesians and other students of Indonesian politics, the value of examining the relationship between personal rule and institutionalisation in the current New Order period, which began in 1966, is obvious and relatively immediate. President Suharto is sixty-three years old and now in his fourth five-year term, which began in 1983. What kind of succession will Indonesia have? From one personal ruler to another, with unpredictable consequences for development and other public policies, as happened in the transition from Sukarno to Suharto in the mid-1960s? Or from one office-holder to another within an established set of institutions? If the latter, what specifically is the structure of the New Order government and what consequences does its institutionalisation have for policy continuity?

I shall argue for the following propositions. First, institutionalisation has begun to replace personal rule in Indonesia. Second, what is being institutionalised is the "New Order pyramid": a dominant presidency, a politically active armed forces, a decision-making process centred in the bureaucracy, and a pattern of state-society relations that combines cooptation and responsiveness with repression. Unlike the Huntington model, political parties, including the government's own *Golkar*, are not central institutions in this system. Third, the key promoter of institutionalisation in New Order politics is Suharto himself. His policies have been remarkably consistent and successful over two decades. By design and by accident these policies have created an identifiable pattern of political expectations, anchored in a powerful structure of interests, affecting present and future presidential, armed forces', and bureaucratic behaviour. Fourth, nonetheless, the level of institutionalisation is low and must be seen in the context of the continuing force of some elements of personal rule, including the absence of arrangements for choosing the next President, trends in the flow of important resources, principally oil, and doubts which have been raised about the president's abilities as a political manager. Fifth, on balance, we can expect a presidential succession with more policy continuity than change. Bitter memories, current success, the logic of the Suharto strategy, and the nature of the probable pool of presidential candidates all point in that direction. Sixth, though the New Order appears to have shifted from a system of personal rule to an institutionalised "presidential-military-bureaucratic complex," there is still much room for the idiosyncratic behaviour of an incumbent President to shake the structure. President Suharto has himself raised doubts along these lines from time to time, and the potential danger from an as yet unknown and untested successor is of course much greater. Conversely, the dominant presidency may also turn out to be a flexible instrument for responding to the new demands generated by continuing economic development.

The New Order Pyramid

The political structure of the New Order can be described as a steeply-ascending pyramid in which the heights are thoroughly dominated by a single office, the presidency. The President commands the military which is *primus inter pares* within the bureaucracy, which in turn holds sway over the society.

The Indonesian bureaucracy is powerful in two senses. First, the bureaucracy pervades society. In every city, town, and village it is the largest employer. Its schools unlock the door to the modern, supra-village world. Its health centres, banks, agricultural extension services and marketing agencies, religious affairs offices, and the requirement of personal identity cards make it for better and worse a daily reality which most Indonesians cannot escape. The scope and weight of this presence are comparable to communist countries, although they are part of a more deliberate, coherent, and ideologically self-conscious plan of social control, but not to the contemporary West, where private sector industrialisation and a culture of unrestricted social organisation have encouraged a plethora of alternatives to dependence on the state.

The bureaucracy also dominates government, in the sense that bureaucrats are the most powerful actors in most policy conflicts. Formally, the "broad outlines of state policy" (*Garis Besar Haluan Negara*) are determined by the People's Consultative Assembly, which meets once in five years and also chooses the President and Vice-President. The membership of the Assembly consists of all members of Parliament plus an equal number of delegates appointed to represent regional and other groups. Parliament members have been elected on three occasions, in 1971, 1977, and 1982.

Three political parties, the result of a government-sponsored "fusion" of the nine parties in existence for the 1971 elections, are now represented in Parliament: *PDI* (*Partai Demokrasi Indonesia*, Indonesian Democracy Party), which won 8% of the vote in the 1982 elections; the Islamic *PPP* (*Partai Persatuan Pembangunan*, Development Unity Party), 28%; and *Golkar* (*Golongan Karya*, Functional Groups), 64%. There are also ninety-six appointed members in the 460-seat body. *Golkar* is the government's party, an electoral vehicle given its present form in 1969 in order to deny a parliamentary majority to the other parties. Its seats are filled with men and women who have or have had bureaucratic careers or are in other ways connected to the bureaucracy. In Parliament and the Assembly, the *Golkar* delegations have never taken autonomous initiatives, but served instead as the sponsors of policies arrived at elsewhere in the government. Provincial and district legislatures are smaller copies of Parliament. *Golkar's* provincial, district, subdistrict, and village branches are run by—indeed, are virtually identical with—institutions of local government.

Within the bureaucracy, the Department of Defence and Security plays several unique roles. First, every regional capital has a military command with responsibilities extending to vigilance against internal subversion and many other activities on the borderline between military and civilian government functions. In the 1971, 1977, and 1982 elections, military officers typically held the key positions within *Golkar* at each administrative level. Second, officers are routinely appointed to civilian government positions through an agency in the Department of Defence created for the purpose. Of the current cabinet of thirty-seven ministers, fourteen have military backgrounds. According to a recent study, 52 of 106 sub-cabinet positions—secretaries-general, directors-general, and inspectors-general—are held by seconded officers.[3] In regional government, the armed forces fill about three-quarters of the twenty-seven governorships and a small majority of district headships. Third, Defence officials themselves play a role in resolving issues well beyond their normal sphere of responsibility. This is especially marked in foreign policy, but is apparent across a wide range of other issue areas as well. One example is the ongoing debate over the design of a Large-Scale Industrial Zone in Aceh, the north-westernmost province in Sumatra, recounted by Donald Emmerson in a recent article.[4]

Three types of institution monitor state-society relations in New Order Indonesia. One is the security apparatus of the Department of Defence and Security. The powerful *Kopkamtib* (Operational Command for the Restoration of Security and Order) is a permanent martial-law-like device within the Department that enables the authorities to arrest and hold indefinitely anyone whom they suspect of subversive activity. Legislative assemblies, described above, are a second institutional type. From the state's point of view, their principal function is to give the old political party leaders, and the masses they can still command, sufficient feelings of participation to stay in the system and help legitimise it, while at the same time denying them any real power to affect the outcome of important decisions.

The least researched and understood institutions in New Order politics are the corporatist and quasi-corporatist organisations and procedures that link government or one of its departments to particular segments of the population.[5] An important example is *Kadin*, the Chamber of Commerce and Industry, an organisation of businessmen that is currently pushing the government to give its members exclusive rights to bid for state contracts. Another is the *Majelis Ulama Indonesia* (Indonesian Council of Islamic Religious Teachers), created by the government to serve as a channel of communications between the state and Muslim organisations. Prominent Islamic leaders, though suspicious of government intentions toward them, have generally accepted appointments to the *MUI* at national and regional levels. A third example are the various *pembinaan* (from a verb root meaning to cultivate, develop, or construct) agencies in government departments, whose task is to "cultivate" relations with private organisations in their substantive areas. For example, the Department of Information has a *pembinaan* office which maintains liaison with the Indonesian Journalists' Association and similar private groups. In most cases, at least some members of these organisations seek a closer relationship with the government. Almost all of them have experienced government intervention in the election of their officers. Commonly, at the end of annual organisation congresses, a delegation is received by the president, who pronounces his blessing (*restu*) on the leadership and its policies.

The President is the decision-making hub of the New Order. There is no doubt that he is much more powerful than any other official. The number two man, Armed Forces and *Kopkamtib* Commander Gen. L. Benny Moerdani, is a personal loyalist, as is Lt. Gen. (ret.) Sudharmono, the head of the State Secretariat, the office through which the President controls the civilian bureaucracy.[6] All other officials are administrators and technocrats, including the cluster of economic policy advisers and implementers now header by Dr. Ali Wardhana, and such Suharto favourites as Adm. (ret.) Sudomo, former head of *Kopkamtib* and now minister of manpower, and the German-trained minister of research and technology, Dr. B.J. Habibie, who wields great power in the small but growing aircraft and other defence-related industries.

The Evidence For Institutionalisation

Huntington defines institutionalisation as "the process by which organisations and procedures acquire value and stability." Operationally, he suggests that the level of institutionalisation of an organisation or procedure can be determined by its adaptability, complexity, autonomy, and coherence.[7]

Using these criteria, much of the evidence for institutionalisation of the New Order pyramid is mixed or can be read two ways. The critical problem is that President Suharto, founder and leader of the New Order, is still in power. To what extent is the government's coherence a product of Suharto's firm hand, of "strong man" rather than "strong presidency" rule?

Is it a complex system, as suggested by the description in the preceding section, or a simple system "which depends on one individual"?[8] Are there any autonomous institutions? Is the presidency independent of the military, or the military of the presidency? Are either independent of Suharto as personal ruler? How autonomous is the whole system of its foreign backers? How adaptable are organisations and procedures that have endured since the late 1960s, but with many of the same leaders and little functional change?

While there are no certain answers to these questions, I think I can find some clues in the history of the New Order that argue, on balance, for post-succession continuity. They involve mostly the consistent implementation of a set of policies which have been so successful in creating and maintaining the pyramid that the question "Why would anyone who has a chance at replacing Suharto want to change the system?" seems to answer itself. My list of policies includes those directed against the organised political opposition, toward the building of performance-based support within the pyramid and between it and both domestic society and the Western world, and toward the creation of a legitimising political culture.

Repressing the Organised Opposition. The first set of policies chosen by Suharto was intended to create a political desert, an absence of organised opposition. On October 1, 1965, Major General Suharto, commander of strategic forces in Jakarta, struck back at a group of younger officers, in alliance with elements of the Communist party, who had in the early hours of the morning kidnapped and assassinated six senior generals. His actions were taken in the context of a highly personalised and "praetorian" political system, the Guided Democracy of President Sukarno, in which the army and the Communist Party were engaged in the increasingly intense and no-holds-barred competition for the succession.

To defeat the Communists, rid the armed forces of leftist sympathisers, and remove Sukarno (whose radicalism had driven him ever closer to the Communists in the early 1960s) Suharto chose a strategy which mixed policies appropriate to personal and institutionalised systems of rule. In the immediate aftermath of the assassinations, he created *Kopkamtib* with himself as commander on the basis of an order from Sukarno authorising him to restore security. On October 16 he was named minister and chief of staff of the army.

In the next few months, for the first and only time in the New Order's history, university and high school students in Jakarta and other cities and Muslim and other youth groups in the countryside were mobilised. Jakarta was awash in anti-Communist, anti-government demonstrations, and in the rural areas widespread killings and arrests of Communists began. On March 11, 1966, President Sukarno was manipulated into signing an executive order (since known as *Supersemar*, an acronym for Executive Order of 11 March, but also a reference to Semar, the most powerful god in Javanese shadow-play mythology) that granted Suharto broad powers, including the immediate banning of the Communist party. For the next year, until he was named Acting President by the Temporary People's Consultative Assembly in March 1967, *Supersemar* was the principal institutional foundation of his authority.

For the first few years of the New Order, *Kopkamtib* and *Supersemar* were used mainly against Communists and Sukarnoists. With the consolidation of Suharto's power in the late 1960s the mobilised youth and student groups also felt the new government's heavy hand, as did organised political Islam. In the political geography of 1950s and early 1960s Indonesia, Islam and communism represented the highest peaks—that is, the best organised, mostly ideologically coherent and most intensely supported political parties. *Masyumi*, the largest Muslim party (21% of the vote in the 1955 elections) and representative of the modernist wing of Indonesian Islam, had been banned in 1960 by Sukarno for complicity in regional rebellions. Its leaders now sought a rebirth of the party and alliance with the New Order. *Nahdatul Ulama* (which gained 18% of the 1955 vote), the party of traditional rural Javanese Islam, had a reputation for accommodation and opportunism (in contrast to the principled and "fanatic"[9] *Masyumi*) but was still an autonomous organisation with great mass strength.

Suharto's policies toward the student movement and politically organised Islam were and are complex, combining mild forms of repression (compared to the brutal treatment of Communists) with manipulation and cooptation. Student groups that demonstrated against the Suharto government were disbanded and their leaders arrested. More cooperative students joined a government-sponsored youth organisation and played a leading role in the formation of the government party *Golkar*. Modernist Muslims were at first allowed to form a new party, but were not permitted to elect old *Masyumi* activists to leadership positions. In 1973 all Muslim parties were coerced into forming the PPP. Though the PPP has continued to win over a quarter of the vote in New Order elections in 1977 and 1982, government policies of carrots, sticks, and direct intervention in internal party affairs have kept it ineffectual.

What evidence for institutionalisation of the New Order does this history provide? First, it is a chronicle of success. In contrast to the 1950s and 1960s, there are now no opposition parties with political resources sufficient to mount a challenge to the government. The Communist Party no longer exists within Indonesia in any form, and it is difficult to imagine its re-emergence given the continuing scope and penetration of military surveillance. Nor do the Muslims in the PPP represent a threat to the government. The party's first national congress, held in August 1984, was dominated by government-backed "leaders" and forced to succumb to presidential pressure to change its ideological foundation from Islam to the state philosophy of *Panca Sila*.

Second, the history of government-party relations indicates wide acceptance of repressive institutions within the New Order pyramid as a whole. *Kopkamtib* and *Supersemar* were of course created by Suharto as instruments of his personal power in the struggle against Sukarno and the Communists, and to some extent they remain such today. The state security network has also been closely controlled by the President himself, currently through Suharto's long-time intelligence chief, Armed Forces Commander Moerdani. Moreover, it has certainly been used, after the fashion of personal rulers everywhere, to ferret out dissent within the government. But the larger point is that these institutions have also furthered the interests of other components of the pyramid. Within the armed forces and the civilian bureaucracy there are individuals (one concentration of them, for example, is the Department of Religion, another is the state universities, and of course students—the next generation of members of the pyramid—are still a volatile group) who would prefer less repression; but there is no evidence that their numbers are large or their feelings intense. Nor do they have any clear conception of an alternative set of political institutions preferable to the New Order.

One piece of current evidence, although somewhat tangential to the issue of political repression, suggests its general acceptability. For more than a year army special forces teams have been use for summary executions of recidivists and other known criminals. The killings began in Yogyakarta, then spread to Jakarta and other cities, and have now apparently reached a total of over four thousand. A few journalists and intellectuals have tried to raise questions about the larger implications of this policy, which obviously must have presidential support, but (mostly bureaucratic) middle-class sentiment appears to be in favour of a rigorous war against what is widely perceived to be a sharply-rising crime rate.[10]

My third argument is more indirect. An important implication of the government's policy of flattening the landscape of political opposition is that since there are so few demands for participation only a low level of institutionalisation of non-repressive institutions is required. Karl Jackson has made the somewhat different but related point that demands for political participation in Indonesia are low because social mobilisation is low.[11] One should be careful about applying theories derived from a few hundred years of Western experience to contemporary Third World societies like Indonesia, especially in the light of the extensive mass political participation of the 1950s and early 1960s. But there is certainly a difference in the structure of interests and pressure of demands in an unindustrialised society like Indonesia's compared, for example, with a partially-industrialised one like the Philippines', where both business and working classes (but especially the former) are not so easily subdued.

Performance Legitimation. The positive interest-based support that the New Order receives has been built on a foundation of economic policies consistently applied for a decade and a half. On the supply side, these policies include relative (to the previous Sukarno government) openness to private foreign and domestic (especially Chinese) business, a strong emphasis on Western and Japanese economic assistance (currently running at well over US$2 billion per year), and a commitment to state, parastatal, and quasi-statal enterprises. In the all-important oil sector, which has consistently contributed half or more of national budget revenues (now at about US$20 billion), the Suharto government has used the state oil company *Pertamina* primarily as a collector of OPEC-determined dollars earned by foreign contractors. Of the total financial resources generated for the public and private use of the state and its officials, the budgetary component in 1984–85 represents about a forty-fold increase (in current dollars) over the 1967–68 budget year.

What has been done with this new-found wealth? There are essentially three mechanisms that have been used to convert it into political support. One is through allocations on the expenditure side of the budget. Government expenditures have been used to raise the salaries of officials and have created a vast panoply of projects, meetings, and special assignments to augment income further, lifting the civil service as a whole to a standard of living never before enjoyed in Indonesia. Budgetary allotments have also been used to benefit the public or substantial segments of it. Managed rice prices have been made possible by imported stockpiles, and kerose and other subsidies have eased the financial burdens of urbanites and the rural landless. Subsidised fertiliser, irrigation system rehabilitation and construction, miracle seeds, pesticides, and agricultural extension have helped land-owners. Several programs known collectively as INPRES (Presidential Instruction) have blanketed rural Indonesia with village construction projects such as roads and village-halls, schools, health centres, markets, reafforestation programs, and so on. The land-owning class has undoubtedly enjoyed disproportionately the fruits of these programs, but their impact has nonetheless penetrated society more deeply than any previous government effort.

Simple corruption—the misappropriation of state funds for private purposes—is a second source of New Order support. In the nature of things, there is no systematic evidence as to the extent of corruption and the amounts involved, but much gossip and several trials of small and medium-size malefactors. The government appears to walk a fine line between tolerance, which increases the incomes of some of its officials, and periodic crackdowns, which encourage the public to believe that the government is at least well-intentioned. A common rumour-mill estimate is that corruption takes away perhaps one-third of the development budget.

More important than simple corruption in maintaining the loyalty of subordinates is the elaborate network of government-business relations which centres on the role of the *cukong*, the Indonesian term for a Chinese businessman who is protected by a powerful official in return for a share of the profits. President Suharto and his family are connected with several *cukong*, most prominently Liem Sioe Liong, once a small businessman in Semarang and now reported to be one of the richest men in the world. Many high-ranking officials also head private companies, actually fronts for the *cukong*-owned businesses, which get lucrative state contracts. For example, about half of Indonesia's cement—millions of dollars of which are purchased for the various INPRES programs annually—is produced by the Liem interests.[12]

As in the case of simple corruption, we have no evidence of the amount or distribution of funds generated by the *cukong*. One characteristic of the system seems clear, however, and that is that President Suharto makes sure that joint government-private businesses of which he or one of his lieutenants disapproves do not prosper. Several prominent generals—among them Sumitro, the former defence minister, Ali Sadikin, former governor of Jakarta, and H.R. Dharsono, former commander of West Java's Siliwangi Division—have at one time or another felt the financial sting of presidential displeasure. On the other hand, it is generally believed that both corruption and the *cukong* system are organised in a way that distributes the benefits widely through the pyramid.

In what sense does performance legitimation institutionalise the New Order pyramid? Is it not just a simple—and, where corruption and *cukong* are concerned, cynical—matter of exchange of money and other valuable goods for political support? If the money dried up, would not the support turn into opposition? I have three answers to these difficult questions. First, performance legitimation must be understood in the context of repression of the opposition, which also legitimises the New Order pyramid for those inside it, and symbolic legitimation, the subject of the next section. In other words, performance can decline without a major impact on overall support as long as the other variables remain high. Secondly, to the degree to which performance is a complex, many-stranded system of benefits, it can be manipulated as effectively by Indonesia's third President as by its second. And the success with which it has been manipulated thus far is a powerful incentive to keep the mechanism running smoothly. Thirdly, the New Order leadership understands the relationship between squeaky wheels and grease, between the demands of powerful social groups and the need to respond to them. Apart from the suppressed groups described in the previous section, there appears to be a congruence between demand and supply. No groups of any significance are working to undermine the government's distribution system, only to get a bigger share for themselves.

Whether performance will continue to be a legitimating factor in the future is difficult to assess. An illustration of performance legitimation in practice, which also offers an interesting glimpse of the challenge which

the mixed fruits of success presents to future political management, is the
New Order's education policy.

Article 31 of the 1945 constitution states that "Every citizen has the
right to education," and "The government organises and implements a
national education system, to be arranged by law." As an instrument of
cultural and linguistic integration (from the third grade on, all instruction
is in the national language, *bahasa Indonesia*), political socialisation, and
economic development, education has received a high priority from most
Indonesian governments since independence. Only the New Order, however, has had the financial resources to make good on the constitution's
promise. Since the early 1970s, billions of *rupiah* have been invested in
education at all levels. The number of universities and other state tertiary
institutions has expanded, new buildings have been built, equipment has
been purchased, faculty have been sent abroad for training, and at the
same time the price of a higher education to the students has been kept
very low. The number and quality of secondary schools has also began
to improve in recent years, but the real push has been at the elementary
level, where tens of thousands of new schools have been constructed so
that virtually every child, even in the remote areas of Kalimantan or Irian
Jaya, now has access to a village school.

Several constituencies have been served by these policies. Most important are the civilian and military bureaucrats, whose children occupy
a disproportionate number of places in the subsidised universities. Muslim
and Christian interests have been catered to through the creation of state
Islamic education institutes at the tertiary level and subsidies to private
schools run by churches and other religious organisations. More prosperous Indonesians, including the better-off farmers, have benefited from the
greater availability of secondary schools and low university tuition. Builders,
cement manufacturers, textbook printers, and the bureaucrats who award
them contracts have all been enriched. Even the poorer Indonesians have
received an income increment from the presence of a village school which
charges (officially, at least) no fees. In terms of legitimacy and institutionalisation, however, the important point is that the government has responded
to an enormous hunger for education, at virtually every level of society,
with a consistently implemented set of policies that every year appear to
most Indonesians to go a little bit further toward satisfying the demand.

This very success, however, has led to new demands which in the next
decade may reverse the progress toward institutionalisation. So far, the
government has kept the number of places in state universities limited
and the graduation rate low in order to avoid creating a glut of over-
educated and under-employed young people. There has also been a tread-
mill affect—a continuing inflation of the market price of an education
(a process begun in the 1950s), so that while there are many more graduates
now than twenty years ago, the educational qualifications required for

most jobs have risen proportionally—a problem which the government has not tackled. And there are the inevitable failures in management of the present program, notably school buildings that collapse soon after they are built, and teacher shortages in many provinces. Most important, however, is the pressure being generated on the secondary and tertiary systems by the explosion of elementary school graduates. Though aware of the problem and attempting solutions ranging from the cosmetic (making the application process less traumatic) to the structural (a major investment in vocational education), the government appears to have painted itself into a very tight corner.

Symbolic Legitimation. The architect of the New Order had, in principle, three "great traditions" of political culture from which to choose in fashioning an ideology to support his system of government: the radical populism of Sukarno's Guided Democracy and of the Communist Party, the Islam of *Masyumi* or *Nahdatul Ulama*—both of which were rejected—and a set of ideas associated with the official class which we may label "bureaucratic populism".

The origins of bureaucratic populism are in the court ideologies of precolonial Java and some other islands, which were devoted to the glorification and aggrandisement of a hierarchical court culture and its ruling class. In the course of the twentieth century, this culture was linked first to the colonial ideal of bureaucratic service and then to the nationalist one of popular sovereignty. The central ideas of hierarchy and deference, of a class of rulers distinct from the people as a whole, remained but were legitimised as a kind of *noblesse oblige* or *kerakyatan yang depimpin oleh hikmat kebijaksanaan dalam permusyawaratan/perwakilan* (democracy led by wisdom and prudence through consultation and representation).[13]

If any single political party of the pre-New Order period can be said to have reflected bureaucratic populism, it was the nationalist PNI (the largest party in 1955, with 22% of the vote). The PNI was particularly strong in the territorial administrative service which staffs government in the regions and oversees elected village leaders. It was thus well positioned to exploit traditional attitudes of deference to authority, as well as to offer more interest-based rewards and sanctions in return for partisan support.

Beyond the special position of the PNI in the 1950s, it may be argued that a large proportion of middle and upper class Indonesians, of all parties and no party, most of whose livelihoods depend directly or indirectly on the state, have been at least tacit believers in bureaucratic-populist ideas throughout the independence period. Among radical populists, and Muslims, too, there have been and continue to be a good many closet bureaucratic populists.

In choosing bureaucratic populism, Suharto was thus tapping into a complex body of ideas with solid support among a probable majority of Indonesia's better-off urban and rural classes, and—false consciousness though it may be—even among a fair share of those whom the ideology requires to be deferential toward their betters. This was not immediately obvious at the beginning of the New Order, when the Suharto forces were for a time allied with Islam, or in the late 1960s when increasing repression of Muslims and students made the government look like a military dictatorship without domestic support of any kind.

In the New Order's first parliamentary election, in 1971, military-civilian hostility ran deep. *Golkar* was imposed by the military on the civilian bureaucracy, whose members were required to persuade their subordinates and the general public to vote for it. The party's electoral organisation in the regions was typically staffed by army officers and civil servants, with the former in the higher positions. The Department of Defence made it clear to its regional officers that the military was to be watchdog and enforcer of "Golkarisation." My field notes, taken from interviews in 1971 in Kulon Progo district, Yogyakarta, record feelings of frustration, helplessness, anger, and a very clear sense that "they" (army officers) were forcibly imposing their will on "us" (territorial civilian officials).[14]

By the third New Order election in 1982, civilians appear to have made their peace with armed forces predominance. Partly, this is a matter of not opposing an irresistible force, and partly it is a product of the material and status rewards described above. But with these benefits has also come a recognition that the New Order is indeed a *negara pejabat* or bureaucrats' state (an epithet frequently hurled at the government by its intellectual detractors), and that that is precisely their conception of what it should be.

In an attempt to strengthen his personal power and that of other components of the New Order pyramid, President Suharto has added two ingredients to bureaucratic populist ideology: a militant kind of constitutionalism, the attribution of an almost sacred quality to the constitution of 1945; and the legitimation of the armed forces' political role through development of the doctrine of *dwi-fungsi* or "twin functions." Both of these additions have contributed, largely unintentionally, to the institutionalisation of the system.

The constitution of 1945 is one of the continuities between Sukarno's and Suharto's versions of the Indonesian presidency. Sukarno from 1950 to 1959 was formally a figurehead president, trapped in the chief-of-state (as opposed to head-of-government) role prescribed by the European-style parliamentary constitution of 1950. His unilateral declaration on July 5, 1959 of a return to the revolutionary constitution of 1945 provided the ideological foundation for his subsequent domination of the legislative, executive, and judicial branches of government.

Suharto's reason for retaining the 1945 constitution appears to have been a desire to add democracy (and nationalism, since the constitution of 1945 is identified with the 1945–49 revolution) to his battery of legitimating props, which already included his role as national saviour on

October 1, 1965 and the grant of *Supersemar* from Sukarno. The way to become a constitutional President was to be elected by a People's Consultative Assembly whose members were chosen as prescribed in the constitution, a process that had not been followed since Sukarno's declaration. This in turn implied (though it did not actually require) a national election for Parliament.[15]

Perhaps paradoxically, the gap between words and actions in the implementation of the democratic provisions of the constitution has probably strengthened the institutional framework of the New Order while weakening the personal legitimacy of the President. All sophisticated observers of Indonesian politics recognise that Suharto's commitment is more to the letter than to the spirit of the constitution. The phoniness of *Golkar* as a democratic party, the manipulation of the other parties, and the government's unfair election rules and practices are as visible behind the screen as the Wizard of Oz. But the evidence of public debate in the Indonesian press indicates that these elements of a charade discredit the office-holder rather than the office. Elections have now been held three times. It is widely accepted that they are the appropriate procedures for choosing a President, which means of course choosing the directive force behind the whole political system. In the run-up to each election, the opposition parties, much of the press, university opinion, and even some military officers take positions in favour of more fairly conducted elections. It seems safe to argue that the election process, created by Suharto, now has a life of its own which he does not fully control and which will also constrain his successor.

The 1945 constitution also limits the President and the New Order by setting agendas or specifying the boundaries of debate on issues. A prominent example is the question of who is to share in and gain from economic development policy. Article 33, "Social Welfare," states that "the economy is to be organised as a common effort based on the family principle (*asas kekeluargaan*)." For much of the New Order period, the government's statist and capitalist economic policies have come under fire from those who interpret this article to mean that village-level cooperatives should be the most important production unit. While it is admittedly difficult to show how the government's policies have in fact been modified in response to these criticisms, the basic points are that the President strengthens the hand of his critics in this area by his passion for the constitution in general, and that two decades of debate based on Article 33 have made it a permanent feature of the economic policy-making process.

Suharto's second addition to bureaucratic populist ideology is *dwi-fungsi*, the doctrine that requires the armed forces to perform "twin functions" of national defence and a "positive socio-political role." If bureaucratic populism is the ideology of the New Order pyramid as a whole, *dwi fungsi* is a sub-set of ideas that justifies the subordination of the civilian to the military layer within the pyramid. These ideas include: the belief that the military has been the *juru selamat* (saviour) of the nation in moments of crisis, most notably against the Dutch from 1945–49, Muslim rebels in the early 1950s, regionalists in the late 1950s, and communists in 1948 and 1965; that it is the *pemersatu* (unifier) of a pluralist nation; the *pengayom* (protector, as a banyan tree protects with its shade) of an unsophisticated and easily deceived *rakyat* ("people," in the sense of the led as distinct from their leaders); and the *dinamisator* (driving force) of a people and economy that need to develop but have no source of political will other than the armed forces.

What is most remarkable about Indonesia's *dwi fungsi* is the extent of its acceptance in contrast to other Third World military doctrines. From Brazil to South Korea, Third World ruling militaries have never been able to legitimise the long-term possession of power. From the first day of the coup that installs them, military leaders typically promise an eventual return to civilian rule. Often, they are ultimately forced to make their word good, not least because of the shabbiness of their ideological underpinnings.

The difference in Indonesia is not so much that there is popular acceptance of *dwi fungsi*—the popular view is probably much more a combination of acceptance of bureaucratic populism plus widespread apathy, ignorance, and fear—but that the military itself believes so fervently in its mission. Why this is the case requires further research, but the army's origins as a self- rather than a civilian-government-created force during the 1945–49 period, its long struggle for internal coherence, the battles against a myriad of rebels, the absence of any democratic political cultural tradition, and its position after 1965 as the only organised, nation-wide political force in the country are all important variables.[16]

The relevance of *dwi fungsi* to institutionalisation is that it legitimises the armed forces as the *de facto* ruling party in Indonesia. Armed forces rule is not visible on a day-to-day basis. As in the United States, the Indonesian President governs without much consultation with, or direct accountability to, the leaders of his "party" hierarchy. Both organisations' critical functions is to choose the governors rather actually to govern. In the Indonesian case, there are no formal procedures comparable to primaries and conventions, but there is an unspoken consensus that the selection of a successor to Suharto will be made within the armed forces. This considerably reduces the prospect of uncontrollable anti-government mass political mobilisation should Suharto die or otherwise leave office abruptly.

Some Doubts and Questions

I have tried to identify the variables that add up to a case that the New Order is becoming institutionalised. A few nagging doubts and questions remain, however, that I would like to discuss briefly. One is the unresolvable question, raised earlier, whether in the final analysis the New Order is perhaps just Suharto's creation and may therefore disappear with him. There is, it must be admitted, considerable and continuing evidence that he makes all the key personnel and policy decisions. Prominent recent examples are his cabinet choices in March 1983 and an extended series of belt-tightening policy moves in response to the world recession and oil price and supply crises. If not placed in the framework I have tried to construct, this behaviour is certainly interpretable as that of an unconstrained personal ruler.

Second is the question of arrangements for the succession. A well-known characteristic of personal-rule systems is that the ruler never grooms an heir apparent, because as soon as the next ruler's identity is known power begins to flow to him or her. President Suharto has also been very reluctant in this regard, as witness the series of appointments of formal and informal seconds-in-command—vice presidents, ministers of defence, armed forces commanders—who, for one reason or another (usually ethnicity or religion), are not serious candidates for the presidency. When it is time to replace Suharto, what is the probability that the New Order pyramid will be destroyed as a result of a succession struggle? Most certainly, this will be a moment of great crisis, out of which could emerge a leader unlike Suharto. But two factors push strongly in the other direction: first is the special position of the military in the pyramid; second is the attention paid by Suharto and other senior officers to the care and feeding of the younger officers, in particular to their incorporation into the *cukong* system.[17] This may or may not achieve its primary purpose, which is to prevent a coup, but it will almost certainly result in a new president who understands how the system works and why Suharto stayed at the top for so long.

A third doubt concerns the relationship of performance legitimation to the other two variables. The New Order has, more because of OPEC than for any reason of domestic policy, had a greater supply of money and valued goods to dispense than any observer or its leaders themselves would have thought possible in the late 1960s. As in the question of whether Suharto is really just a personal ruler or not, it is ultimately impossible to know whether it has really been these vast expenditures of money that have made a stable New Order possible. There have, however, been two tests of the proposition which seems to confirm my conclusion that performance is only one aspect of New Order institutionalisation. These tests were the mid-1970s crash of *Pertamina*, which had overextended its commitments to domestic industrialisation and faced a massive debt repayment crisis, and the current world recession and oil crisis. Both of these events were met with economic policies that exacted costs from many New Order beneficiaries, including powerful generals and kerosine-burning Jakartans, and neither caused a ripple in the flow of political support to the government. A comparative perspective may be offered here: any correlation between oil and institutionalisation in Iran and Nigeria seems to be negative, suggesting that other variables account for the positive connection in the Indonesian case.

A final doubt has to do with the much-mentioned political astuteness of President Suharto. His skills have several times been called into question regarding two kinds of issues—repression of the opposition, particularly Islam, and his and his family's personal relationships with *cukong*, toward which there is both public hostility and perhaps within-the-pyramid anger and envy over the enormous wealth acquired by the Liem interests.

My response to the concern with repression is that the long record persuades me that, in combination with more positive incentives, it works. To the argument that collaboration with the Chinese is delegitimising, I would reply that the President personally may be damaged by over-involvement and over-exposure, but that *cukong*ism is an indispensable element in any viable system of rule in Indonesia today. Even if Suharto is overthrown, in other words, the *cukong* system will remain, though perhaps for a while in a more hidden form, alongside something very like the present New Order pyramid.

Conclusions

The arguments of this article support four related conclusions. First, there is clear evidence of the institutionalisation of the New Order pyramid. The complex strategy of repression, performance legitimation, and symbolic legitimation has created, and now sustains within and outside the political system, a solid base of support that is committed to the system itself and is likely to outlive Suharto. There are, to be sure, clouds on the horizon—institutionalisation is only at a low level, elements of personal rule remain, and the extent to which the government's support rests on its most uncontrollable variable, performance, rather then on the other two, remains unknown—but the sky overhead is blue.

My second conclusion is that a key explanatory variable for the degree of institutionalisation so far achieved is the skilful political management of President Suharto.

Foreign specialists and other observers of Indonesian politics have not been inclined to give the President much credit for his achievements. Moral outrage at repressive politics and inegalitarean economics has exacted a price in biased empirical arguments. These have taken two forms. One has been to engage in a certain amount of wishful thinking about the prospects for opposition politics. Marxists search diligently for the signs of a new bourgeoisie, proletarianisation, or peasant class consciousness; pluralists like myself have taken too seriously the capacity for organisational autonomy and continuing struggle on the part of the old political elites.

A second bias has been the tendency to look for explanations for the New Order's longevity that discredit the government. One favourite has been repression: the New Order stays in power because it treats opponents harshly. Another is oil: Suharto has bought his way to power through the budgetary and (especially) non-budgetary distribution of largesse. The conservative response to these liberal or left positions has been equally simplistic, maintaining that the level of demands is so low that stability is easy to achieve. I hope I have shown that each of these factors is present, but that none is a sufficient explanation and all must be seen in a larger context that includes an appreciation of Suharto the politician.

My third conclusion is that there appears to be a close connection between institutionalisation and policy continuity. Institutionalisation does not of course necessarily imply policy stability, as the example of the last thirty-five years of the People's Republic of China demonstrates with a vengeance. How much and what kind of continuity can we expect in Indonesia?

The New Order seems to me to present a paradox of strong presidential leadership and few policy options. Suharto's economic policies in particular have not strayed far from the rather conservative mixed-economy position of the dominant technocrats, though he was once tempted by the "industrialise-quick" schemes of oil-magnate Ibnu Sutowo,[18] and he now listens sometimes to his muse of high-tech, aeroplane-builder and Minister of Research and Technology Habibie. Why is Suharto an economic conservative, and will these reasons apply to his successor?

One insight into Suharto's economics is suggested by a recent comment of Albert Hirschman's that Latin American policy-makers have typically had a low propensity to defer to normal economic constraints.[19] Hirschman quotes the late Argentine President Perón's advice in 1953 to Carlos Ibáñez, then President of Chile:

My dear friend,
Give to the people, especially to the workers, all that is possible. When it seems to you that already you are giving them too much, give them more. You will see the results. Everyone will try to scare you with the spectre of an economic collapse. But all of this is a lie. There is nothing more elastic than the economy which everyone fears so much because no one understands it.[20]

Transposed to Indonesia, Perón's advice sounds very much like the economic philosophy of President Sukarno. Suharto's generation was traumatised by the consequences of policies based on that philosophy, and is not likely to repeat Sukarno's mistakes. Nor are its successors, partly because the Sukarno era is now deeply imprinted on institutional as well as personal memory, but also because the logic of performance legitimation will be so hard to reject. That logic requires careful attention to a complex balance of interests within the pyramid and between it and society. Careful attention in turn requires resources which can be best obtained by a continuation of the general policy line that has been followed since the late 1960s. Similar arguments can be made about continuity in other major policy areas, though examples like education suggest that serious challenges also await the next ruling group. The greatest danger to policy continuity arises, of course, from the concentration of power in the presidency. The next President may, for idiosyncratic and therefore unpredictable reasons, decide to defy or ignore the logic of performance legitimation or the Suharto strategy *in toto*. But if it is true that the next President will be a general, either from the senior generation or the younger officers, the prospect is very strong that he will be loyal, if not to Suharto personally, to the New Order pyramid as a system of rule. It should also be stated that a powerful and stable presidency with a substantial capacity for cooptation might be just the institution to meet the new opportunities and issues which will arise if the economy continues to develop even at the reduced pace of the very recent past.

My final conclusion is that Huntington's emphasis on the importance of one or more major political parties in managing the transition from praetorian to civic polity is probably misplaced in the Indonesian case. As is often true of social science theorising, Huntington may have identified a universal problem to which there are only unique solutions, or at any rate the solutions of the late twentieth-century Third World may be different from those of an earlier First and Second Worlds.

From the perspective of the mid-1980s, the strength of the party system in Indonesia in the 1950s and 1960s now looks like the by-product of weak government. There was a vacuum, and the nationalist elite rushed to fill it with parties based on whatever social and cultural groups had enough distinctiveness, solidarity, and intensity of demands to provide a constituency. But there was too little support in the culture for the procedures required to maintain a political system based on party competition. Instead, parliamentary democracy and then Guided Democracy became arenas in which a battle *à outrance* was fought among social forces with world views of radical populism, Islam, and bureaucratic populism. The victor was the army, under which Suharto's leadership quickly forged a coalition with the bureaucracy and then proceeded to create the distinctive—and almost partyless—pattern of state-society relations described above.

As one looks to the future, industrialisation (manufacturing is the fastest-growing sector in the economy) and the commercialisation of agriculture will inevitably produce new demands and pressures on the political system. But that system now seems to be on the one hand internally unified and confident of its repressive capabilities, and on the other sufficiently flexible and open for a major change in the institutions that monitor state-society relations to be unlikely. Instead, the New Order pyramid will continue to balance repression, responsiveness, and cooptation in such a way as to stay in control indefinitely—assuming, of course, that Suharto's successors are as skilful as he in strategy and tactics.

1. New Haven (Connecticut: Yale University Press, 1968).
2. *The Gold Coast in Transition* (Princeton, New Jersey: Princeton University Press, 1955).
3. John MacDougall, "Patterns of Military Control in the Indonesian Higher Central Bureaucracy," *Indonesia* 33: 1982: pp. 89–121.
4. "Understanding the New Order; Bureaucratic Pluralism in Indonesia," *Asian Survey*, XXIII:II: November 1983: 1220–41.
5. Dwight King is the pathbreaking scholar on this issue. See his "Indonesia's New Order as a Bureaucratic Polity, a Neo-Patrimonial Regime or a Bureaucratic Authoritarian Regime: What Difference Does it Make?" in Benedict Anderson and Audrey Kahin, eds. *Interpreting Indonesian Politics: Thirteen Contributions to the Debate* (Ithaca, New York: Cornell Modern Indonesia Project, 1982), pp. 104–16.
6. For a description of the emergence of a more institutionalised *kantor Presiden* (Office of the Presidency), see Mohtar Mas'oed, *The Indonesian Economy and Political Structure During the Early New Order 1966–1971*, Ph.D. dissertation, Department of Political Science, Ohio State University, 1983, p. 228ff.
7. Huntington, pp. 12–24.
8. *Ibid.*, p. 18.
9. There is dispute about the extent to which communist support in the villages was based more on conscious ideological and/or interest affiliation than on traditional factional and follow—the village-politics. See Rex Mortimer, *Indonesian Communism Under Sukarno: Ideology and Politics* (Ithaca, New York: Cornell University Press, 1974). My own view, admittedly influenced by direct observation of Communist Party mobilisation in the *évolué* plantation area of East Sumatra rather than Java, where most of the members and voters were located, is that there was considerable ideological sophistication among leaders and interest-based allegiance among members and followers. One can also question how deeply-rooted *Masyumi*'s support was, since its successor *Parmusi*, received only 5% of the vote in 1971. More important factors in *Parmusi*'s defeat, in my opinion, were the government's superior organisation and the exhaustion of an opposition spirit among modernist Muslims.
10. See *Indonesia: Extrajudicial Execution of Suspected Criminals, Document No. ASA-21/13/83* (Amnesty International, October 31, 1983).
11. "The Political Implications of Structure and Culture in Indonesia," in Karl D. Jackson and Lucian W. Pye, eds., *Political Power and Communication in Indonesia* (Berkeley and Los Angeles: University of California Press, 1978), pp. 23–42.
12. An account of the Liem family's meteoric rise is in the *Far Eastern Economy Review*, April 7, 1983, pp. 44–52. The Jakarta newsmagazine Tempo also ran a cover story on the Liems in its 31 March 1984 (XIV, 5) issue.

13. On the indigenous state, see: M.C. Ricklefs, *Jogjakarta Under Sultan Mangkubumi, 1749–1792: A History of the Division of Java* (London: Oxford University Press, 1974); Soemarsaid Moertono, *State and Statecraft in Old Java: A Study of the Later Mataram Period, 16th and 19th Century* (Ithaca, New York: Cornell Modern Indonesia Project, 1968); Clifford Geertz, *Negara: The Theatre State in Nineteenth Century Bali* (Princeton, New Jersey: Princeton University Press, 1980); and Benedict Anderson, "The Idea of Power in Javanese Culture," in Claire Holt et al., eds., *Culture and Politics in Indonesia* (Ithaca, New York: Cornell University Press, 1972), pp. 1–69. On the late colonial transformation, see Heather Sutherland, *The Making of a Bureaucratic Elite* (Singapore: Heinemann Educational Books, 1979). The Indonesian quotation is the fourth of the Five Principles (*Panca Sila*) of state doctrine.

14. See, also, my "Evolution from Above: National Leadership and Local Development in Indonesia," *Journal of Asian Studies*, XXXII:2: February 1973: 287–309.

15. The constitution states that "the People's Consultative Assembly consists of the members of Parliament plus delegates from regions and groups to be specified by law" (Article 2). The organisation of Parliament is also to be specified by law (Article 19). Since the 1959 declaration, however, it has been an unchallenged assumption that elections are the appropriate means to choose Parliament.

16. See Ulf Sundhaussen, *The Road to Power* (Kuala Lumpur: Oxford University Press, 1982). Salim Said is currently preparing a doctoral dissertation at Ohio State University that will explore the formation of the army's ideas about civil-military relations during the revolution.

17. Our most careful chroniclers of the appointments process in the Indonesian military are the editors of the journal *Indonesia*. Their "Current Data on the Indonesian Military Elite," *Indonesia* 36: 1983: concludes (p. 112) that "the President appears to have succeeded in achieving what was postulated as his main objective: handling the generational shift in such a way as to maximise his own power." This article and the series of which it is a part do not deal with the question of the officers' private economic arrangements.

18. A good account is in Hamish McDonald, *Suharto's Indonesia* (Blackburn, Victoria, Australia: Fontana, 1980), ch. 7.

19. "The Turn to Authoritarianism in Latin America and the Search for its Economic Determinants," in Albert O. Hirschman, *Essays in Trespassing* (Cambridge: Cambridge University Press, 1981), p. 105.

20. *Ibid.*, p. 102.

2

The Politics of Shared Growth: Some Indonesian Cases*

Overcoming the Pessimistic Politics of Liberalism and Marxism

Politicians and analysts who favour more egalitarian development policies in the Third World are at an impasse. Most of the current literature on the politics of what we might call shared growth, defined as economic development with widely dispersed opportunities to produce and consume, is trapped in one of two *culs de sac*. Mainstream or liberal scholars are committed to the idea of direct participation by the poor, organised in peasant and labour unions and political parties, while Marxists believe that shared growth is possible only after capitalism, by its very nature exploitative of the majority, is replaced by socialism. Neither group, however, holds out much hope that its solution will in fact be realised, at least in the near to medium term.

A typical example of the mainstream literature is the political scientist Francine Frankel's massive study of Indian agrarian policy since independence. Frankel argues that poorer farmers have lost at every turn because, despite ideological sincerity and elaborately conceived programs from the top, they have simply not had the resources to compete with entrenched regional and local power elites.[1] She issues a ringing call for the building of peasant organisations that transcend primordial cleavages, but given the history she presents it is difficult to see (as she freely admits) how that can happen.

On the Marxist side, the sociologist Peter Evans provides rich documentation of the resources used by multinational corporations, large domestic enterprises, and the state to dominate the Brazilian market-based

* First published in Comparative Politics 19, 2 (January 1987), pp. 127–46.

political economy, systematically shutting out small entrepreneurs and the urban and rural poor.[2] His analysis leads him to conclude that without fundamental restructuring of the socioeconomic basis of the political system significant policy change is impossible. Again, given Evans' and our best understanding of Brazilian politics, one cannot be optimistic about the prospects for such change.

Applied to contemporary Indonesia, these approaches also lead to an impasse. The precise form of President Suharto's New Order government, in power since 1966, has been a matter of considerable debate among scholars, but all agree that it is an authoritarian state with few opportunities for participation. Harold Crouch, for example, has compared Suharto's government to Weberian patrimonial polities in which "the government was able to rule in the interests of the elite without taking much account of the interests of the masses because the latter were poor, socially backward, politically passive, and kept in check by the regime's military forces. Politics thus took the form of a struggle within the elite itself, among rival factions and cliques that were concerned principally with gaining influence with the ruler who determined the distribution of the rewards of office."[3]

Benedict Anderson has offered three major interpretations of the New Order. In the late 1960s he called it a personalistic polity based on a Javanese mystical conception of political power as something tangible that must be physically possessed by the ruler. By the mid-1970s it had become a rightist coalition degenerating into a personal and military dictatorship. Today it is a "state-qua-state" whose interests are different from and indeed opposed to those of the Indonesian nation.[4]

According to the Marxist scholar Richard Robison, the New Order is "one fraction of a complex alliance embracing foreign and Chinese bourgeoisie; the urban technocrat/administrative/managerial class (the so-called middle class); and the politico bureaucrats." It "may be seen as a regime counter-revolutionary vis-à-vis both agrarian reform and economic nationalism."[5] Finally, my own most recent macro treatment of the New Order has characterised it as a "steeply ascending pyramid" of bureaucratic, military, and presidential power and emphasised the lack of participation by those outside the pyramid.[6]

None of these authors finds any signs pointing to the likely replacement of New Order authoritarianism with either a liberal or a radical government. Indonesia's experiment with parliamentarism was brief—from 1950 to about 1957—and there is now no powerful organisation or group committed to its return. The Communist Party, which once had nearly twenty-four million members in party and affiliated organisations, was brutally crushed in 1965 and 1966 and shows no sign of revival today. By most accounts, the state (or official class or ruling elite, as one chooses to label the power holders), supported annually by more than $12 billion (about 60% of the national budget) in oil revenues and more than $2 billion in foreign assistance, continues to grow in power relative to civil society. In these circumstances, what hope is there for development policies that benefit nonelite, nonofficial Indonesians? More to the point, are there political variables other than the organised participation of the poor called for by Frankel or the socialist transformation of Evans that might operate even under conditions of military and bureaucratic authoritarianism—to incline government toward more egalitarian policies?

I believe there are many but that they have not so far been discovered because political scientists are too caught up in the search for ways to transform rightist dictatorships into regimes more to our normative taste. An alternative course is to follow a trail blazed by the development economist Albert O. Hirschman. In his classic study of Latin American development policymaking, *Journeys Toward Progress*, Hirschman attempted to avoid the pessimistic politics I have described. "Political scientists," he argued,

> typically view good government as resulting from certain
> institutions and capacities such as an adequate bureaucracy, public
> participation in the governmental process, legitimacy, ability of a
> political elite to mediate conflicts and so on. Our inquiry, on the
> other hand, takes the existing political framework with its defects
> for granted and explores whether and how the weight and urgency
> of certain economic policy problems can nevertheless lead to
> constructive action. Our basic working hypothesis must be that,
> within rather broad limits, the existence of defects in political
> structure does not constitute an absolute impediment to progress in
> dealing with economic policy problems; by the same token, it is
> likely that problem-solving will under these conditions follow quite
> unfamiliar paths whose possible efficiency and hidden rationality
> we must try to appreciate. . . .
> How can good government arise out of bad, reform out of
> reaction and progress out of stagnation? . . . I attempt to answer
> these questions by avoiding the tempting device—or sleight-of-
> hand—which consists in discovering some "prerequisite," be it a
> resource base, a rate of capital formation, an elite, an ideology or
> a personality structure, that must allegedly be introduced before
> change can possibly assert itself. Rather, I am trying to show how
> a society can begin to move forward *as it is, in spite of what it is
> and because of what it is.*[7]

Unlike Hirschman in *Journeys toward Progress*, I will not focus on the impact of policy problems per se, although that is an implicit part of the story. My interest is in casting about for political factors that may operate to the advantage of economically and politically weak groups despite the presence of a highly stratified political system in which resources and power are concentrated in a few hands. Like Hirschman, therefore, I take the existence of the system for granted but believe it is possible to find variables that, while a part of the system, nonetheless work or can be turned against its basic tendency to concentrate wealth and power. Rice and sugar policy provide the data for this fishing expedition. As in most Asian countries, rice is the primary commodity in Indonesian agriculture and has been an important component of developmental policy in general. Sugar is a major consumption good and source of employment and has been the focus of much recent policy controversy. My findings are based primarily on six cases of policy conflict, three each for rice and sugar, as reported in the news, editorial, and opinion columns of the leading Jakarta daily, *Kompas*, in 1982 and 1983. This is supplemented by a more extensive reading of the Jakarta press and of the secondary literature on agricultural and development policy in Indonesia over the past decade.

To summarise at the outset, my conclusions are two. First, there is much more beneath-the-surface political activity in the New Order than the standard model of military and bureaucratic authoritarianism leads us to expect. To be sure, it is true (and amply documented below) that central government officials are the key agricultural policymakers today and that bureaucratic politics, that is, conflict among state agencies with different agendas and ambitions, has a great deal to do with decision outcomes. But the central state apparatus does not monopolise the policy process. Other significant—sometimes decisive—actors include local officials; organised and unorganised producers, intermediaries, and consumers; members of parliament; and the press and intellectual community.

Second, the "influence" that groups outside the top power holders exert on the decision-making process is often indirect or heavily dependent upon the perceptions, beliefs, and interests of insiders. Perhaps the most important mechanism by which the government responds to constituencies with specific interests is a kind of second-order or *anticipated participation*, meaning reactions to what officials anticipate to be the demands of particular groups because they recognise the actual or potential power of the group's political and economic resources. Anticipated participation explains much of the New Order's rice policy over the past two decades and also many of the government's actions in recent controversies in both rice and sugar.

A second mechanism, which appears at least twice in the cases, is *bureaucratic identification* with the interests of outside groups. This phenomenon is a familiar feature of Western politics, where it sometimes leads to outright capture of an agency by its clientele. Prime causes of identification are said to be the bureaucrats' need to mobilise external support for internal battles and a recruitment process in which government officials and interest group leaders frequently trade places. In New Order Indonesia identification has not led to capture because of the relative power of the state and weakness of interest groups. The causes of identification are less clear, though perhaps some limited mobilisation and recruitment of university experts (who tend to be profarmer activists) are both important factors in the agricultural sector.

A third mechanism, which appears only once, is the presence of *allies of convenience*, meaning a linking of the demands of a disadvantaged to those of a privileged group because of a coincidental congruence of goals or interests. For some of the poorest and least powerful groups this may be one of the only means to a better life. Unfortunately, it may also be one of the least predictable or manipulable by policy scientists or political activists.

A fourth mechanism, present throughout sugar and rice policy history and in recent cases but exceedingly difficult to isolate and evaluate, is the pressure, both external and internalised, of a *populist ideological tradition*. Marxists and the more hard-nosed brand of interest-and-resource balancing political economists are prone to dismiss cultural factors in general and ideological ones in particular as mere surface expressions of deeper structural forces. And it is certainly true that in Indonesia as elsewhere ideological pronouncements are an imperfect guide to locating the actual beneficiaries of any particular policy or program. Yet it is possible to argue that the formulation of policies and the settlement of disputes in Indonesian agriculture are affected by a populist rhetoric that induces the government to respond in an egalitarian direction when the balance of more tangible political resources would predict a different outcome. For the activist, the trick is to discover ways to raise the pressure and broaden and deepen its impact.

Rice

Rice is Indonesia's most politically sensitive agricultural commodity, a fact well known to the present leadership. New Order rice policy has been built in large part on a desire to please three constituencies: government officials, who receive rice as a part of their salaries; urban consumers; and rural producers.

The official class, which numbers over three million military and civilian government employees in a total population of 160 million, is the New Order's power base. It has been favoured in many ways, including frequent salary increases, perquisites of office, improved working conditions, expansion and upgrading of schools for its children, and a generally privileged position in society. But no benefits have been more fundamental than the monthly allotment of the rice staple plus the maintenance of steady and affordable market prices for rice and other necessities.

Because they constitute a large majority of the educated, politically conscious, and respected members of society, officials are a key source of support for any Indonesian government. In the New Order, their importance has been magnified by policies toward political organisation that deliberately limit participation by nonofficials in national political life and economic development policies that require an activist bureaucracy. No leaders of the two nongovernmental parties permitted to exist sit in the cabinet or hold powerful legislative positions. Their combined average vote in the national elections of 1971, 1977, and 1982 has been kept to just over 35% by the government's tactic of mobilising the bureaucracy in the form of a government party called *Golkar* (an acronym for *Golongan Karya* or Functional Groups). With all the facilities of the state at its disposal, *Golkar* has had no difficulty in piling up large majorities.

Urban, particularly Jakartan, consumers are a politically threatening force which must be placated with a regular supply of rice at a reasonable and stable price. Jakarta residents have on more than one occasion erupted over rising prices and shortages of food and other necessities. President Suharto and his lieutenants must remember very well the effectiveness with which they laid the blame for high rice prices at the doorstep of then-President Sukarno in 1965 and 1966. During the New Order, the only major challenge to Suharto's presidency, the student demonstrations and mass rioting in Jakarta from October 1973 to January 1974, may well be associated in the minds of central officials with the rice crisis of 1972–73.[8]

Finally, farmers are also a rice-related constituency to which the New Order has responded positively in terms of a combination of input subsidies, price increases, and infrastructural and organisational support that led to more than a doubling of the crop (from 10.8 to 25.5 million tons annually) between 1966 and 1984.[9] The reasons for this positive response are less concrete and direct than in the cases of government officials and urban consumers. Probably the most important element is demographic. Two-thirds of Indonesia's population is concentrated on Java, which has one of the most densely populated rural areas in the world. Because of the island's size, topography, and transportation system, movement between town and countryside is relatively easy and cheap. A massive shift to the cities of farmers unable to make a satisfactory living in agriculture would be a political and economic catastrophe that no government could survive.

Relations with external economic forces have also been a factor. If rice does not need to be imported, foreign currency is made available for other purposes (such as the purchase of agricultural and industrial production goods), and Indonesia is less dependent both on unpredictable world fluctuations in price and supply and on the good will of other governments. A third reason has been the need to demonstrate responsiveness to the interests of indigenous Indonesians—which virtually all rice farmers are—to offset a longstanding and now worsening image that the New Order's industrialisation policies favour domestic Chinese and foreign business.

Ideological pressures reinforce these structural and interest-based calculations. From the beginning of the mass-based nationalist movement in the 1910s to the war of independence in the late 1940s and the turbulent radicalism of the early 1960s, populism—the idea that serving the *rakyat* (people) is the whole purpose of leadership—has been the dominant theme of the political class and essential justification for its actions. A consistent subtheme has been that the *desa* (village) and its traditions are the source of Indonesia's deepest moral and spiritual values.

Economic policies that make farmers prosperous, keep them in the villages, and protect the country from foreigners without and within are obviously in keeping with this ideological tradition. Policies that are not, such as the reliance on foreigners in the urban business sector, are harder to justify both within the political elite and to other groups in society. These include not just the indigenous business class and others with a material interest, but also the intellectuals and journalists who are the guardians of Indonesia's conception of itself as a community. Their views in turn filter down to a population long exposed and at least partially attuned—as the government is well aware—to a populist conception of the role of government.

Though their priorities have shifted over the years, the principal elements of New Order rice policy have been apparent since the late 1960s.[10] They include strengthening the government's administrative capacity to buy and sell domestically, finding ways to purchase from abroad as cheaply as possible, and encouraging farmers to grow more rice. Underlying these policies has been a long-term commitment to self-sufficiency, achieved for the first time in 1984–85.

In the beginning, when the price of rice skyrocketed 300% in a single year, the government sought to increase its procurements through the creation of a National Logistics Command, now called *Bulog* (*Badan Urusan Logistik*, Logistics Board). In 1966, 640,000 tons were imported. Only 70,000 tons, too small an amount to have an effect on prices, were sold in the domestic market, however; the rest went to feed civilian officials and soldiers, the constituency whose support Suharto most urgently needed. In 1967, 350,000 tons were imported, 100,000 tons as PL 480 assistance from the United States, of which only 139,000 tons entered the open market. By 1968 the government was able to increase supplies enough both to feed its own employees and to bring down the market price significantly.

Since the mid-1960s, the only full-fledged rice crisis has been the 1972–73 doubling of the price, caused by poor harvests and exacerbated by weaknesses in the government's import purchasing power and domestic distribution system. That crisis was overcome by large quantities of United States' food aid and massive market injections. OPEC price hikes for Indonesia's petroleum exports (which now account for about 70% of foreign exchange earnings and nearly as large a proportion of national budget revenues) in 1974 and 1979 have given the government the means to import large amounts to prevent further crises. The United States has also continued to be a major supplier when necessary. (In the late 1970s, as demand for rice grew, Indonesia became for a few years the world's biggest buyer of rice on the international market.) Oil income has also been channelled by the government to *Bulog* to build a national network of storage facilities with a capacity of more than two million tons.

Programs designed to increase domestic rice production have been very successful in the 1980s after a slow start in the late 1960s and early 1970s. The policy package includes subsidies on inputs such as fertiliser and pesticides, cheap credit for the purchase of inputs (now being phased out), more intensive cultivation (use of miracle seeds, improvements in irrigation systems), and administratively set prices that were gradually allowed to rise and then have been maintained at world levels (benefiting both the farmer who receives the higher price and the government which does not have to subsidise the imported rice it sells on the domestic market).

Village-level cooperatives called KUD (*Koperasi Unit Desa*, Village Unit Cooperatives) have been a central institution in the government's domestic rice development program. The KUD are government created and financed bodies charged with buying rice for resale to *Bulog* (at a fixed profit to the KUD of about 8%) and maintaining a guaranteed floor price for farmers. The goals are thus simultaneously to assure a steady supply of rice to the government and to enhance farmers' incomes. KUD purchasing is expected to replace the network of (usually Chinese) intermediaries whose margins have traditionally been very large.

As its name hints, the KUD is also intended by at least some central government officials to play a larger role in rural economic life, becoming an autonomous organisation financed by members' dues and able to increase farmers' economic power through collective action. Some supporters of the KUD, in government and in the universities, see it as an institutional embodiment of a controversial article in the constitution which states that "the economy is to be organised as a common effort based on the family principle (*asas kekeluargaan*)."[11] Beyond rhetorical support, the top leadership's views on the long-term development of the KUD are unclear. In the short run, however, there is some evidence of an intent to make it the chief implementing instrument of most aspects of government agricultural policy in the villages.

A final element worth noting in this general survey of the principal features of New Order rice policy is a shift in the government's choice of incentives for increasing production from an emphasis on administrative programs backed by coercion to greater reliance on market-based inducements. Early *Bimas* (for *Bimbingan Massal*, Mass Guidance) production incentives programs in the late 1960s required all farmers in a targeted area to participate, while later versions permitted farmers to make their own decisions. During the 1972–73 rice crisis, heavy-handed government attempts to force farmers to sell at below the market price to the predecessors of the KUD were unsuccessful. Since 1973 positive incentives, such as raised floor prices and lowered *Bulog* quality standards, have been used almost exclusively. The growing number of defaults on agriculture loans, which apparently reflects the extension of the loan program to poorer farmers more prone to default, has also been handled not by attempts at coercion but by phasing out the program.[12] Nor have heavy sanctions been applied to resolve the more vexing problem of the many KUD which are in arrears on the loans they obtained to purchase rice from the farmers.

Three recent disputes over specific aspects of rice policy give us a closer look at the current structure of interests and power and the dynamics of the policy process. The first case shows among other things that rice farmers can win, the second that they may lose. The third explores the ideology behind government agricultural policies and its relationship to contending interests.

Case One: Bulog's Concern for Quality versus the Farmers' Floor Price

My first case is a mini-crisis that occurred during harvest season in early 1982.[13] One of *Bulog*'s concerns has been to increase the quality of rice it purchases, both for its ultimate market value and to accommodate the government employees to whom it is distributed. To that end the agency set at 5% the permissible level of immature grains (*butir hijau*) it would accept in rice purchased from KUD for the 1981–82 harvest. The KUD set a similar policy for their purchases from farmers.

In February 1982 reports from the villages, especially in Java, began to filter up to *Bulog* officials that a high percentage of the harvest was being rejected by KUD and bought by private traders at prices well below the floor price of Rp. 135 per kilo. Farmers in the government program and KUD officials were complaining that the five-percent limit was too low for the pest-resistant seed variety they had been given, which regularly yielded 9–14% immature grains.

On March 28 Bustanil Arifin, a retired general, long-term head of *Bulog*, and since 1978 junior minister for cooperatives, announced that *Bulog*'s depots on Java would for the month of April raise the acceptable level of *butir hijau* to 10%, when purchased from KUD "which do not cooperate with non-KUD."[14] On April 3, after meeting with President Suharto, Bustanil extended the new policy to all of Indonesia. He also reported the president's concern that the floor price be maintained and that the KUD system be strengthened by making it less burdensome financially for farmers to join.

On May 17, after a month of reports that farmers all over Java were selling their rice for as little as 50% of the floor price, the junior minister for food production, Achmad Affandi, announced that the government would buy all rice offered to it directly by farmers, at prices based on the floor price but adjusted for quality. "What is important," he said, "is to keep the floor price from falling."

This announcement was made in Semarang, the capital of Central Java, after a tense late night meeting reportedly ordered by the president between the central government's "food team" and provincial officials. Though closed to reporters, "through the window which was not covered by a curtain it was apparent that the meeting was being conducted in a very serious fashion." The food team had met earlier in the day with farmers who threatened that if they could not market the rice grown with government seeds they would switch to the better-tasting and more expensive (but lower yielding) *Cisadane* variety. The provincial officials may have been objecting to the policy of blanket purchases on grounds that they were unprepared to store or process large amounts of low grade rice.

The May 17th policy shift appears to have signalled the end of the crisis. The *Kompas* report indicated that its impact was in fact not likely to be very great since by that time most farmers had sold their rice to private traders, but that the earlier decision to raise the acceptable level of *butir hijau* had had a positive effect, pushing the market price closer to the floor price in many areas. Farmers' complaints, plus the sensitivity of some officials to those complaints, had clearly influenced the final policy outcomes.

Case Two: Intrabureaucratic Conflict and the Price Incentive

The second case is a brief dispute in late 1982 over the level of the KUD floor price for *gabah* (unhusked rice), which ended with a boost in the *gabah* price from Rp. 135 to Rp. 145 per kilo but also a simultaneous increase in the prices of two crucial rice inputs, urea fertiliser (from Rp. 70 to Rp. 90 per kilo) and pesticide (from Rp. 1,230 to Rp. 1,500 per litre).[15] The occasion for the decision was the approach of planting season, when farmers must decide whether to plant rice or some other crop. For most of the New Order, the policy has been to up the floor price each year as an incentive to farmers.

The chief protagonist of a price hike, at least in the public debate, was Mohamad Toha, national chairperson of HKTI (*Himpunan Kerukunan Tani Indonesia*, Indonesian Farmers' Association). HKTI is the farmers' wing of the state party Golkar, but (like its parent) has no substantial membership outside the state bureaucracy and is not generally taken seriously as a farmers' interest group. Nonetheless, Toha acquitted himself well as spokesperson for at least the one-fourth of Indonesian farmers who have enough land to be able to take advantage of the government's rice programs. Citing Central Bureau of Statistics figures, he argued that the urban-rural terms of trade in the 1980s have steadily turned against the rice farmer from a high of 109 in 1979 (using 1976–100 as the base) to a low of 87 in May 1982. Asked about the effect of a price increase on farm labourers and farmers who grow crops other than rice, he answered rather vaguely that it would lead to more work for all.

Toha's chief antagonist was the junior minister for food production, who presented complex arguments about balancing consumer and producer interests, the danger of inflation from a price increase, and the importance of other incentives such as input subsidies, credit, and intensification programs. In his view, the total current package of incentives was sufficient to maintain a satisfactory rate of growth in rice production. The real weaknesses in the rice sector, he argued, such as the lack of storage space, the absence of KUD in remote areas, and the rejection by KUD of substandard rice, could not be solved by pricing policy.

The decision to lift simultaneously the floor price of rice and the prices of pesticide and fertiliser inputs was taken at a meeting of the *Tim Harga Gabah* (*Gabah* Price Team) which included the chairperson of the National Planning Agency, the ministers of finance, agriculture, trade and cooperatives, and industry, plus the state secretary (whose job is to maintain presidential control over the bureaucracy) and the junior ministers for cooperatives and food production. An increase in input prices (that is, a reduction of government subsidies on these items) was apparently the position of officials whose responsibility is for the economy as a whole and who were concerned about the world recession and declining national budget revenues. In contrast, most agricultural officials argued for maintenance of the established pattern of an annual floor price increase. The outcome, probably a conflation of these two positions, was justified by the state secretary as a solution that would at minimum not reduce the net income of rice farmers.

A *Kompas* editorial the next day concluded that the farmers had lost this round. But, from a somewhat broader perspective, we can see that the farmers did not lack for supporters within the bureaucracy-dominated decision-making arena. Agricultural officials, perhaps in part assuming the mantle of farmers' representatives, and even the widely ridiculed HKTI exerted enough influence to at least maintain the status quo.

Case Three: Private Business, Cooperatives, and the State

My final rice case involves not a prolonged process in which various sides were able to air their views before a decision was made but rather *ex post facto* cries of distress from parties aggrieved by a ministerial decision.[16] The decision, taken by the minister of agriculture and cooperatives in February 1983, was to transfer, by stages beginning with the 1983 planting season, the distribution of fertiliser from the private sector to the KUD. The aggrieved parties, who did not speak up until late May, were the P2SP (*Persatuan Penyalur Saprotan Pusri*), the association of distributors of agricultural inputs from the state fertiliser company *Pusri* (Pupuk Sriwijaya), and *Kadin* (*Kamar Dagang dan Industri*, Chamber of Commerce and Industry).

The fertiliser case is revealing on two levels. One is the ideological context in which both sides framed their arguments. The economy the New Order is building, they agreed, will be based on three economic institutions—the state, the private sector, and cooperatives—each of which will play a major role. Spokespersons for P2SP and *Kadin* asserted that the fertiliser decision was not in the spirit of a balanced institutional development. "The duty of the Minister of Cooperatives," said the *Kadin* general chairperson, "is to develop cooperatives, but that doesn't mean he has to kill private business." According to the chairperson of P2SP, the proper role for cooperatives is as a price stabiliser, a weapon against private firms that get greedy and charge too much. "If cooperatives have no competition whatever, will they be healthy?" To which the newly appointed minister of cooperatives, Bustanil Arifin, replied—citing a host of figures—that cooperatives are by far the weakest of the three institutions and do not represent a threat to the private sector. (Left unsaid, but perhaps implicit in Bustanil's hard line, was his apparent belief that with the establishment in March of a ministry of cooperatives separate from the ministry of agriculture, plus the strong public backing of the president for greater cooperativisation, the institutional balance was about to shift.)

At a second level, the fertiliser case reveals the limited political autonomy or influence of private agricultural business, which is economically heavily dependent on the state. Members of P2SP, while formally private traders, are in fact licensed monopolists; they have exclusive agreements with *Pusri* for distribution rights in particular provinces. *Kadin*, Indonesia's largest business association, enjoys a quasi-corporatist relationship with the government. Most of its members (like its general chairman, Sukamdani Sahid Gitosardjono, a major fertiliser distributor and a relative of Mrs Suharto) have grown fat on state contracts. As a political interest group the agricultural business community has only two substantial political resources: the kickbacks it provides to officials and its indigenousness, which enables the government to point to it as evidence that New Order industrialisation policies are benefiting Indonesians as well as domestic Chinese. Organisations like *Kadin* and P2SP are thus, like the HKTI in my second case, real but distinctly lesser players in the agricultural policy game.

The discrepancy between the political power of private business on the one hand and the state on the other raises a question about the seriousness with which national politicians promote their tripartite ideology. Perhaps one way to approach the problem is to argue that they are serious but that their conception of a state-private-cooperative balance is corporatist rather than pluralist. State, private, and cooperative enterprises are given exclusive rights and responsibilities in particular areas of the economy by the central government, which then supervises and coordinates them.

Most indigenous private business persons seem to believe in this corporatist conception of their role (their success, after all, has depended upon acceptance of it). There is also very little support in academic and intellectual circles for more autonomy for business persons, who are believed to pursue their private interests exclusively (which means exploitation by those who possess capital of those who do not) while the state (ideally) promotes the public interest. Many voices, however, particularly among academics, favour greater power and autonomy for village cooperatives like the KUD, which are seen as another form of public interest group (on the assumptions that most villagers will join and that there will be internal democracy within the cooperative) that can serve as a check on business power."[17] Though autonomous cooperatives are not thought to be a threat to the state by academics, central government officials may disagree. In practice, in any event, they have not adopted programs that foster greater autonomy.

In conclusion, the three rice cases display a pattern of central state domination of policy making justified by a corporatist ideology in which weak and dependent business and cooperative sectors are regulated by the state, ostensibly in the public interest. Yet they also show a pattern of intrabureaucratic conflict over specific policies and their implementation that is closely linked to the often vigorous representation of farmer and other local and nonbureaucratic interests.

Sugar

For nearly a decade sugar has easily been the most controversial topic in New Order agricultural policy. More reports, interviews, and columns in *Kompas* and other newspapers and magazines have been devoted to it than to any other commodity, including rice. The cause of all this attention has been Presidential Instruction 9/1975, a major policy initiative that changed "the basic structure of the industry from one in which the mills grew cane on land rented in from smallholders to one in which the smallholders themselves took on the entrepreneurial role producing the cane on their own land."[18]

According to the Gadjah Mada University agricultural economist Mubyarto, the new policy was recommended by two British consulting firms hired by the department of agriculture. Their report "argued that smallholder farming promised to increase the area under sugar production, that it would improve the position of the farmers, and that it would help provide employment in rural areas."[19] While the annual rate of growth of production for the past several years had been above 5%, after decades of stagnation, domestic demand and therefore imports had been rising even faster. The success of the government's rice intensification program during the same period was also an incentive, both as a model for a new sugar program directed at individual farmers and because the rising value of the rice harvest had led to more and more complaints about low rents from the mills. In many sugar areas, the two crops are in direct competition for the best irrigated land.

Under the new program, called TRI (*Tebu Rakyat Intensifikasi*, Smallholders' Sugar Cane Intensification), farmers grow their own cane with seeds, fertiliser, pesticides, and credit supplied by the government. The local KUD are supposed to take the cane from the farmer to the government-owned mill, where it is crushed to produce refined sugar. The farmer is paid a percentage of the sugar from his cane calculated on the basis of the *rendemen* (sugar content) rate, that is, the higher the *rendemen*, the higher the percentage given to the farmer. *Bulog* buys all sugar produced by the mills at a fixed price. Though a stated purpose of the program is to free the farmer from the (colonial-tinged) inequity of a system in which he was forced to accept whatever rent the mill offered, a more fundamental element of compulsion remains. The government still decides, as it did in the mid-nineteenth-century cultivation system, which farmers' land will be allocated to cane each growing season.

According to Colin Brown and other recent observers, the TRI system has been at best a very limited success. Sugar production has grown but only because of increased hectarage. Yields per hectare have shrunk, in part because of extension of sugar cultivation to less suitable land but also because of inadequacies in the intensification program (generally regarded as much more poorly administered than its rice counterpart). Farmer hostility, based on the compulsory aspect of the program and the continuing income differential between cane and rice, has also been a major problem. Brown cites 1978–79 cases in which the net-profit differences were: Rp. 350,000/ha. for TRI sugar to Rp: 400,000/ha. for *Bimas* rice for a five-month season in West Java; Rp. 500,000/ha. for sugar to Rp. 1.35 million/ha. for rice in a TRI showcase district in East Java; and Rp. 480,000/ha. per year for TRI sugar to Rp. 900,000/ha. per year for three crops of a non-high-yielding rice in the Special District of Yogyakarta.[20] In 1982 the farmers' formulation in East Java, according to one account, was "one-two"—the price of one kilo of sugar should equal that of two kilos of rice of medium quality. By that measure the sugar price at Rp. 350 per kilo was about Rp. 50 too low.[21]

In many smaller ways, too, farmers have been at a disadvantage. The *rendemen* rate, for example, is calculated by chemists hired by the mills, and farmers assert that it is often put too low. The village power structure and local intermediaries find many ways to take advantage of farmers poor in capital, authority, and knowledge to lower their incomes still further. As Brown writes, often the farmer's land "is rented out, after the fashion of earlier years. In this way, the TRI farmer gets immediate access to cash income. . . . [but] in the absence of regulations governing the rental of land to the mills, rentals actually paid seem to be lower than if the old system had been maintained." Farmers who grow their own cane sometimes sell cheap to intermediaries before the harvest, a practice known as *ijon*. KUD officials or the heads (*ketua*) of farmers' groups (*kelompok tani*) organised to consolidate tiny and dispersed tracts of land for more efficient cultivation may serve their own rather than the collective interest. "Some farmers seem to have been reduced to the status of wage labourers on their own land, hired by the *ketua kelompok* and paid with TRI credit originally intended for them. In such cases, the *ketua kelompok* has taken on the functions of a contractor, managing the cane cultivation and enjoying the main benefits from it, but at minimal risk or cost to himself."[22]

Four generalisations about the politics of sugar policy are suggested by this history and by the more recent events I am about to describe. The first is that the structure of interests involved in the implementing of sugar policy on the ground is extremely complex and difficult for central officials to manipulate. Sugar mills, regional government and village officials, KUD officers, *ketua kelompok tani*, villagers with differing economic interests, private traders, and others all have many ways and means to frustrate Jakarta's policies.[23] This is further complicated by the number of agencies—seventeen by one count—responsible for TRI implementation.[24]

Second, the major beneficiaries of TRI are constituencies within the state bureaucracy; central government officials who are concerned with balance of payments problems and would like to see at least self-sufficiency in sugar production (achieved, perhaps only temporarily, in 1982–83); government domestic revenue collectors and budget planners, who have been successful in maintaining an originally Dutch-imposed excise tax on sugar, now the only one of the nine basic commodities whose prices are government-controlled to be so taxed;[25] and the state-owned sugar mills, most of which were operating at less than full capacity before TRI and are now bursting with cane.[26]

Third, producer interests are accommodated by government policymakers, but only within limits much narrower than in the case of rice. Accommodation may be seen in the initial decision to move away from the unpopular rental system, in an eleven-percent increase in 1980 in the price paid to farmers, and in policy changes designed to plug leaks that were being exploited by nonfarmers.[27] The principal narrow limit is the continuing existence of compulsion, which makes TRI very different from the rice intensification program. I have not seen an official explanation for the use of compulsion. It is probable, though, that central officials believe expansion of cane production is not feasible without it, given the apparent impossibility of raising refined sugar prices high enough to make cane cultivation economically competitive with rice.

Fourth, urban consumers, who presumably want stable supplies and low prices, are getting the former but not the latter. In 1983, the domestic ex-mill price was about twice the world price. TRI is thus a curious case of a policy that operates against both farmers, who would prefer to be growing rice or other crops, and consumers, who would prefer to be buying imported sugar.

Kompas articles in 1982 and 1983 suggest that current implementation of the TRI program is both confused and controversial. They also illustrate at least three of my four generalisations: the complexity and manipulative skills of local interests; state agencies as major beneficiaries; and responsiveness, in context, to farmers' demands. Urban consumers, however, are not being forced to make additional sacrifices.

Case One: Sugar Farmers versus the Mills, the Cooperatives, and the Provincial Government

The first of my three sugar cases involves widespread farmer dissatisfaction in Central Java during the 1982 crushing season. Crushing is a critical and sensitive event in the sugar production cycle because the *rendemen* varies greatly depending upon when the cane is harvested and how quickly it is crushed after harvesting. A delay of two days can make a major difference in the quantity of sugar produced and in farmers' incomes.

The proximate cause of much of the farmers' unhappiness was a bottleneck at several mills which claimed to be unable to crush all the cane being sent to them.[28] Gafur Mariadi, secretary of the *Bimas* development agency for Central Java, announced in early June that all mills would have to give priority to TRI cane and bump from their crushing schedules cane grown outside the TRI system, called TRB (*Tebu Rakyat Bebas*, "Free" Smallholders Cane).[29] The reason given was that planned rehabilitation had not been completed on schedule, so that several mills were either shutdown or only in partial operation. The initial *Kompas* article in a long string of reports estimated that 6,000 ha. of TRB cane would be crushed as a result of this decision and that some TRI cane would be crushed very late.

Gafur's announcement was followed by a flurry of scapegoating from mill officials, who blamed Japanese contractors for the delay, and much empty rhetoric from their superiors, officials of the state plantation companies that own the mills, who boldly declared that they were taking over the rehabilitation program. How rehabilitation could be completed on time to make a difference for the current crushing season was not explained.

More positively, plantation officials apparently made a serious effort to juggle crushing schedules so that as much cane as possible could be accommodated. But here, too, there was much confusion. A provincial government spokesman announced that some cane would be diverted to mills in East Java. A few days later, East Java officials expressed regrets that their mills could not absorb cane from Central Java.

Neither TRI nor TRB farmers were represented in this controversy by organisations of their own. What we know about farmers' views comes from interviews with journalists, who reported a pattern of opinion very much at odds with official explanations. The real problem, said many farmers, is not mills closed for rehabilitation. That is a cover for the practice of collusion between intermediaries and mill officials—the former buy up the rejected cane for a pittance (which the farmer accepts because he knows that his *rendemen* is declining) and bribes the latter to crush it quickly. An intermediary who bought up only 500 ha. of cane production in this way, according to *Kompas*, would clear about Rp. 250 million (in 1982 US$1.00 equals approximately Rp. 650).

A more concrete instance of alleged manipulation is the story of the brief rise and fall of KUD Makarti, a cooperative that was given the job of minimising the loss of TRB cane by coordinating delivery to the mills of all TRB farmers' output in the area around Pati district in Central Java. According to farmers' stories, however, KUD Makarti was abusing its authority to issue crushing permits by forcing farmers to sell to KUD officials as private individuals, who would then issue themselves the permits. Moreover, other KUD in the Pati area, it was charged, consisted of members who were also TRB farmers who took two-thirds of their assigned permits for their personal use.

Mardi Supriyo, chairperson of KUD Makarti, was given an opportunity to defend himself in a joint press conference with the junior minister for cooperatives Bustanil Arifin. Mardi accused the press of "lies, random attacks, and libel" and said that reporters had been bribed by the intermediaries whose business was taken away by his cooperative. "Before, the *tengkulak* [intermediaries] could freely buy TRB cane from the farmers and sell it to the mill. Every day there might be twenty trucks. But after KUD Makarti took over, they could only send two trucks." Despite Mardi's spirited defence and Bustanil's backing, the Central Java governor issued a new regulation instructing mills to accept TRB cane directly from the farmers.

Collusion involving officials at the provincial level was charged by farmers who had taken their cane to Sugar Mill Cepiring in Kendal district and been told that they must use one of thirteen intermediaries designated by the government. Interviewed by *Kompas*, a Cepiring official claimed that the intermediaries had been appointed directly by the provincial *Bimas* development agency. Larger farmers, who have the resources to hold back their crop longer, refused to sell to the intermediaries and appealed to the governor to step in and enforce the regulation (referred to above) to accept cane from farmers.

Sugar mills were also accused of falsifying their transactions with farmers. A TRI farmer in Purworejo district, for example, upon learning that his *rendemen* was only six percent at the mill to which his cane was assigned, took it to another mill where he got nine percent. A TRI farmer in Rembang said that he had weighed his cane on a public scale before taking it to the mill, where he was shortweighted by three *kuintal*.

In Jakarta, the only voice speaking up (or at least being reported) on these events was that of Imam Churmen, member of parliament from the Islamic PPP (*Partai Persatuan Pembangunan*, Development Unity Party). Speaking as vice-chairperson of the parliamentary committee responsible for agriculture, Churmen, whose constituency is in the largest sugar producing province of East Java, urged the government not to avoid its responsibility for the rehabilitation work by blaming the contractors. Both the TRI and TRB farmers were losing income, he said, and so was the government, which had lent Rp. 247 billion in TRI credit, some of which it might now not get back. "If the contractor's at fault, sue him. If it's the project head, he must be prosecuted under the law."

Compared to the rice cases, it is doubtful that the various measures taken by government agencies described above had much short-term impact on cane farmers' income. But it is clear that the farmers' demands produced a crisis to which there was a variety of official responses, some more serious than others, but most recognising the legitimacy of farmers' grievances. In April 1983 the head of the department of agriculture's regional office for Central Java announced the formation of an "*Operasi Manis*" (Operation Sweet) team of officials to monitor the 1983 crushing". All mills were operating at full capacity, he asserted, and TRB production had been inventoried and would be crushed along with TRl cane. KUD officials had been fully briefed and understood their responsibilities. Such statements can hardly be taken at face value (and there were many complaints from farmers to come) but again they are evidence of an expectation that the government must respond to the interests of farmers as well as other groups.

Case Two: Wealthier Sugar Farmers and Local Officials versus the Central Bureaucracy

My second sugar case is the debate leading to a decision taken on August 1, 1983, to raise the price paid by *Bulog* to the farmer by Rp. 1,250 per *kuintal*.[30] The first shot was fired by parliament's Imam Churmen, who urged the government to repeal the excise tax, which adds Rp. 35 to the market price of a kilo of sugar (selling in early 1983 for Rp. 600).

In May, participants in an all-East Java KUD officers' conference (thus representatives for the most part of local officials and better-off farmers) recommended a price boost to the minister of cooperatives and head of *Bulog*, Bustanil Arifin. If the farmer's price goes up it will force up the consumer price as well, responded Bustanil. A weak market will become weaker, and smuggling from abroad will grow. A better way to augment the farmer's income, he suggested, might be to enlarge the 60% share of production received by the farmer compared to the mill's 40%. Minister of agriculture Achmad Affandi, meeting at the same time with officials responsible for TRI implementation in East Java, agreed with the KUD officers that farmers' incomes had stagnated. But he rejected a price hike for the same reasons as Bustanil and proposed instead better implementation of the intensification program. A parliamentary committee, after questioning Bustanil, supported Imam Churmen's proposal to do away with the excise tax. Farmers interviewed by *Kompas* in East Java focused on the *rendemen* rate, down to 6% at many mills, and the division of shares of production as second-best choices for improving their incomes if the price could not be increased.

The August 1 decision to give farmers an increment of Rp. 1,250 per *kuintal*, paid on all production before the division of shares with the mill, was taken at a food coordinating meeting (*Rapat Koordinasi Pangan*) consisting of the senior agriculture and economic ministers. The *Bulog* price remained unchanged, the additional income for farmers being subtracted from existing fees, including—perhaps deliberately, recalling the source of the demand for a price increase—the KUD's management and exploitation fee, which dropped from Rp. 1,400 to Rp. 500 per *kuintal*.

As in the first sugar case, the end product of this conflict between farmers and the central government bureaucracy was only a small improvement in farmers' incomes. And this was despite strong representations by one of the more powerful rural interest groups, the wealthier farmers and village officials who dominate the East Java KUD, backed up by the lobbying of Imam Churmen and other members of parliament from sugar districts. Perhaps a principal reason for these disappointing outcomes is that in sugar policy the array of options is limited and the arrangement of forces too powerful and balanced to be easily reordered. And yet the presence of constraints does not necessarily imply the inability to achieve policy breakthroughs. Presidential Instruction 9/1975 is a telling example, for surely there were more vested interests, and better entrenched ones, in sugar production in the early 1970s than there are now.

Case Three: TRB Farmers and Intrabureaucratic Conflict

The third sugar case suggests comparison with the third rice case, in which the state was shown, in corporatist style, to have a tendency to absorb other interests or even to create them and then define the terms and conditions of their political participation.[31] The specific example had to do with fertiliser distribution and the role of private business and the KUD. My sugar case indicates that there are limits to this process of absorption, that even the relatively powerless have some power, even if they have no control over its use, and that conflict between government agencies can be an obstacle to the growth of Leviathan.

During the 1982 crushing season, as described above, TRB farmers, who grow cane without seeds, fertiliser, pesticides, or credit supplied by the government, were a major source of disruption in the implementation of the TRl program. When the clamour of opposed demands was at its loudest in June, junior minister for cooperatives Bustanil declared that in the future there would be no free cane farmers. All cane growing was to come under TRl and be supervised and coordinated by the KUD. What he had in mind is not totally clear, though I think we can rule out any draconian measures such as prohibiting the growing of cane for brown sugar consumption in the village. More likely, he intended to shut the door on TRB farmers who take their cane to the state-owned mills for conversion to refined sugar by decreeing that only TRI sugar would be eligible for crushing.

If Bustanil's prohibition had been implemented, the scope of government power in the countryside would have expanded. Many farmers would have been forced into joining the TRI program; others would have had their economic options and income reduced as a result of government actions.

The TRB farmers themselves had no direct influence on the decision-making process. At most—and in this case the effect must have been minimal—their voices were heard through the efforts of the press. But the farmers had allies of convenience in the government, high officials in economic/financial and other ministries and on the National Development Planning Board. Their primary concerns were not the bottlenecks at the mills or the hassles confronting the KUD, but rather the levels of sugar production (affecting, among other things, Indonesia's balance of payments) and of rural employment (with implicit consequences for rural-to-urban migration). For them, the solution lay in opening up more opportunities for TRB farmers to participate in the refined sugar economy rather than closing down the few that already existed. The spokesperson for this group was the minister of agriculture (and profarmer Gadjah Mada University professor), Soedarsono Hadisapoetro, who announced on August 18 that TRB farmers' sugar would be welcome at state mills in the next crushing season.

In this particular case, then, the outcome was one in which the state, because of conflicting interests among its own agencies, did not increase its power over society. What it demonstrates is not a general tendency toward balanced private sector-state relationships—the fertiliser distribution case shows the opposite—but rather that within the New Order movement in either direction is possible.

Conclusions

As stated in the introductory section, the history of New Order rice and sugar policy and the six recent cases lead me to two conclusions. The first is that a political system of military and bureaucratic authoritarianism, at least in Indonesia, does not preclude a policy process in which actors outside the central state apparatus play a significant role.

In general terms, the cast of characters on the rice policy stage includes national and local officials, urban consumers, rural producers, and private traders. The first two cases described a decision-making process in which farmers acted directly to voice their grievances against private traders, local and national officials, and, by extension, urban and other consumers, and found a sympathetic ear in the central government. In the second case, they were helped by the corporatist farmers' organisation HKTI, whose leaders would like to have genuine producers' support in addition to official patronage. And business organisations, though constrained by their limited clout compared to the state, appear in the third case. Sugar policy displays the same basic array of participants but adds the role of member of parliament and further differentiates farmers into groups with sometimes conflicting interests.

Journalists and academics are also important participants in both policy areas. New Order authoritarianism severely restricts public discussion of such topics as President Suharto's potential successor or separatist movements in East Timor and Irian Jaya but hardly affects coverage of controversies over sugar cane crushing schedules, fertiliser distribution rights, or even government failure to maintain its floor price for rice. Editorial writers offered strong opinions on many of the cases, as did—though usually between the lines—investigative reporters. Academics writing in the press (the op-ed column is a regular feature in *Kompas* and other papers and in the leading newsweekly *Tempo*) or in the more scholarly *Prisma*, a journal of applied social science, pushed a range of frameworks and explanations as to who was benefiting from particular policies and programs and why. All of this outside commentary became in turn ammunition for the contending sides in each of the policy disputes.

There are many instances in the six cases of direct participation in politics by more or less organised interest groups, and even of representation through parliament, an institution most observers dismiss as the president's rubber stamp. But the cases also demonstrate my second conclusion, which is that much of the influence exerted by groups outside government is indirect and dependent on individuals and groups inside government, where most resources that give weight to political demands are concentrated.

Among these indirect mechanisms of influence, the most important is, as I have labelled it above, second-order or anticipated participation. Governmental anxieties about the possibility of urban riots and rural-to-

urban migration have been critical factors in the shaping of rice policy
in general and in at least two of the cases. In sugar, where the government
has been less responsive to either producer or consumer interests, there
is nonetheless evidence of concern for both TRI and TRB farmers' incentives and of reluctance to push too high the price of refined sugar in
urban markets.

Bureaucratic identification is comparable to anticipated participation in
its dependence on the perceptions and beliefs of others, specifically on
the self-image of bureaucrats as champions of the interests of extra-
governmental constituencies. In both the first and second rice cases, and
perhaps in the third sugar case as well, ministry of agriculture officials
went to bat for farmers.

The concept of allies of convenience refers to situations in which a
group outside government benefits from being on the same side as the
policymakers who win in an internal government dispute, even though
the interests of the two groups are not the same. While there is only one
instance of allies of convenience in the six cases—the parallel desire of
TRB farmers and some high administrative officials for an open milling
policy—it is likely that a more extensive survey of development policy
conflicts would turn up many more examples.

My final mechanism through which governmental outsiders influence
insiders is the pressure of a populist ideological tradition. I will not try
here to untangle interest covered by populist rhetoric from the genuine
expression of populist values but simply assert that both are present in
the behaviour of government officials and in the actions of outsiders.
Officials listen more closely to the demands of certain groups because
they have internalised an ideology that puts the needs of "the people"
first and because the ideology defines the universe of political discourse
in which all Indonesians live. Within the political culture as circumscribed
by the public utterances of leading academics, intellectuals, and government spokespersons themselves, populist justifications are acceptable, and
nonpopulist ones—liberal say, or socialist or religious—are not. Policies
and programs in turn can not help but be shaped to some extent (to what
extent is admittedly the critical question) by the justifications, even if
hypocritical, attached to them.

In the six cases, the impact of populist ideology is most directly apparent
in the fertiliser distribution dispute where it was used by Bustanil Arifin,
the minister of cooperatives, to legitimate a policy decision strengthening
the KUD at the expense of private business. There is little support outside the government these days for the KUD, seen by most observers as
instruments of bureaucratic control and not of popular participation in
development. But they are much closer, at least in spirit, to accepted ideas
of desirable social and economic structure than is the liberal ideology that
lurks below the surface of business leaders' demands for a stronger private

sector. The universities and media therefore gave business virtually no support in the fertiliser debate, leaving Bustanil the ideological winner.

Ideological issues are not so clearly joined in the other five cases, but it is still possible to discern a consistent thread running through them. Officials listened more closely than they would have in a society lacking Indonesia's ideological history to rice farmers' complaints that the KUD set its purchase standards too high and its prices too low, to the complaints of sugar farmers about low rents and the depredations of intermediaries, and to the distress of TRB farmers whose cane was rejected by the mills. Or at least my reading of the cut-and-thrust of policy debate on each of these issues persuades me of the constant presence, if varying impact, of the populist ideological tradition.

Finally, only a Pollyanna would conclude from the evidence I have presented of direct and anticipated participation, bureaucratic identification, allies of convenience, and populist pressure that the politically and economically disadvantaged in Indonesia have potent weapons to carry into political combat. I have not discovered that the image of centralised and concentrated power in Indonesia is wrong, only that it is incomplete. My point, then, is simply that within the system, despite it, and some-times—to recall Albert Hirschman's paradox—because of it, a few tools exist that can be exploited on behalf of the weak. Perhaps further research can expand this initial list and begin to explore strategies and tactics that will maximise their impact.

1. Francine Frankel, *The Political Economy of India* (Princeton: Princeton University Press, 1978).
2. Peter Evans, *Dependent Development* (Princeton: Princeton University Press, 1979).
3. Harold Crouch, "Patrimonialism and Military Rule in Indonesia," *World Politics*, 31: July 1979: 572.
4. Benedict Anderson, "The Idea of Power in Javanese Culture," in Claire Holt, ed., *Culture and Politics in Indonesia* (Ithaca: Cornell University Press, 1972); "Last Days of Indonesia's Suharto?" *Southeast Asia Chronicle*, 63: 1978; "Old State, New Society: Indonesia's New Order in Comparative Historical Perspective." *Journal of Asian Studies*, 42: May 1983.
5. Richard Robison, "Culture, Politics, and Economy in the Political History of the New Order," in Benedict Anderson and Audrey Kahin, eds., *Interpreting Indonesian Politics* (Ithaca: Cornell Modern Indonesia Project, 1982), pp. 131, 144.
6. R. William Liddle, "Soeharto's Indonesia: Personal Rule and Political Institutions," *Pacific Affairs* 58: Spring 1985, reprinted as Chapter One in this volume.
7. Albert O. Hirschman, *Journeys toward Progress* (New York: Norton, 1973), pp. 5 and 6 (Hirschman's emphasis). See also the stimulating article by C.L.G. Bell, "The Political Framework," in Hollis Chenery, ed., *Redistribution with Growth* (London: Oxford University Press, 1974). Though in some ways

a very different approach, I have also found useful for conceptual purposes Warren Ilchman and Norman Uphoff, *The Political Economy of Change* (Berkeley: University of California Press, 1969), and the case study by Robert Bates, *Markets and States in Tropical Africa* (Berkeley: University of California Press, 1981). For Indonesia, the best work along these lines is by Donald K. Emmerson. See especially his "Understanding the New Order: Bureaucratic Pluralism in Indonesia," *Asian Survey*, 23: November 1983.

8. Widjojo Nitisastro, head for most of the New Order of the powerful National Development Planning Board, was recently quoted as saying that Indonesia has experienced four major economic crises since 1966. The second was the rice crisis of 1972–73. Frans Seda, "Catatan-catatan di balik jendela St. Carolus," *Kompas*, June 12, 1985, p. 4.

9. The 1966 figure is from Anne Booth and Peter McCawley, eds., *The Indonesian Economy during the Soeharto Era* (Kuala Lumpur: Oxford University Press, 1981), p. 28; the 1984 figure is from *Kompas*, November 8, 1984, p. 1.

10. Much of the following discussion of the development of rice policy from the mid-1960s to the present is based on Leon A. Mears and Sidik Moeljono, "Food Policy," in Booth and McCawley, eds., *The Indonesian Economy during the Soeharto Era*, pp. 23–61.

11. Article 33, Constitution of 1945. A key proponent of this conception of the KUD is Soedarsono Hadisapoetro, professor of agriculture at Gadjah Mada University and minister of agriculture from 1978 to 1983. See Booth and McCawley, eds., *The Indonesian Economy during the Soeharto Era,* fn. 19, p. 57.

12. Local officials also appear to be major beneficiaries of this program and obstacles to the implementation of a tougher line from Jakarta. In South Sulawesi, according to a *Kompas* story (April 6, 1982) officials owe about Rp. 1 billion of the total Rp. 7 billion in agricultural loans in arrears in the province. The central government has sent special task forces to the provinces to try to raise the repayment rate, but local officials are dragging their feet.

13. *Kompas*, Mar. 30, Apr. 5, 8, 19, 23, 24, May 19, 1982.

14. Although the evidence is patchy, many KUD appear to represent primarily the interests of their own officers, who are members of the village elite and thus officials and/or wealthy farmers, rather than the state, the KUD membership, or farmers as a group. A typical tactic of these KUD officers is to buy from private traders rather than from local farmers, subverting the purpose of using the KUD to replace intermediaries. By buying from private traders and then immediately selling to *Bulog*, KUD officials can make a profit on the transaction while also substantially lowering their administrative costs of collection, storage, etc. The traders, of course, do not observe the floor price in their purchases from farmers. Reports suggest that as much as 80% of KUD purchases in some areas are from intermediaries.

15. *Kompas*, Aug. 31, Sept. 1, 24, Oct. 5, 7, 27, Nov. 16, 17, 1982.

16. *Kompas*, June 1, 8, 17, 1983.

17. See for example interviews with Profs. Sayogyo and Sediono Tjondronegoro of the Bogor Agricultural Institute in *Kompas*, Jan. 5, 1983, and columns by Dr. Loekman Soetrisno of Gadjah Mada University in *Kompas*, Jan. 6 and June 15, 1983.

18. Colin Brown, "The Intensified Smallholder Cane Programme: The First Five Years," *Bulletin of Indonesian Economic Studies*, 18: March 1982: 39. For my general description of the sugar cane industry, I have relied heavily on this article and on three works by Mubyarto, "The Sugar Industry," *Bulletin of Indonesian Economic Studies*, 5: July 1969; "The Sugar Industry: From Estate to Smallholder Cane Production?", *Bulletin of Indonesian Economic Studies*, 13: July 1977; and *Politik Pertanian dan Pembangunan Pedesaan* (Jakarta: Sinar Harapan, 1983), esp. pp. 78–88.

19. Mubyarto. "The Sugar Industry: From Estate to Smallholder Cane Production?," p. 39.

20. Brown, p. 47.

21. J.A. Noertjahyo and A. Suyatna, "Tebu yang Panas dan Pahitsya Gula." *Kompas*, July 27, 1982, p. 4.

22. Brown, pp. 51 and 53.

23. There is an obvious similarity here to the complex structure of interest involved in the fishing industry in Muncar, East Java and described in Donald K. Emmerson, "Orders of Meaning: Understanding Political Change in a Fishing Community in Indonesia" in Anderson and Kanin, eds., *Interpreting Indonesian Politics.*

24. *Kompas* Sept. 20, 1983. A comparison is drawn with the pre-TRI period, when the only participants in sugar production were the mills, the regional government, and the farmers.

25. In the mid-1960s, 58% of the sales proceeds from sugar marketing was taken by government in various taxes. By 1971 the figure had been reduced to 17%. Mubyarto, "The Sugar Industry: From Estate to Smallholder Cane Production?," p. 33. In 1983 there is still a long list of taxes and special funds amounting to a total of approximately Rp. 6,850 per *kuintal* (100 kilos) or 15.6% of the ex-mill price. The excise tax is Rp. 3,500 per *kuintal*, by far the largest item. My calculations from figures in *Kompas* May 23, 1983. This contrasts with a total tax rate of less than 2% for intensified rice production. Brown, p. 58.

26. Under TRI, the mills' share of the refined sugar is 40%, with the remaining 60% returned to the farmer. In the Philippines the split is 25%–75% in the farmer's favour, and in Taiwan it is 30%–70%. *Kompas*, May 23, 1983.

27. An example is the decision taken in 1980 for *Bulog* to buy up all sugar in mill warehouses at the end of each crushing season. The purpose was to prevent speculation by intermediaries who had been buying the certificate of entitlement issued to the farmer by the mill, redeeming them when the price rose. In 1981 the further decision was made for *Bulog* to be given the exclusive right to purchase domestically refined sugar. The purpose here was to prevent wholesale prices from sinking too low at the end of the crushing season, when farmers are most likely to sell their certificates to intermediaries. Brown, pp. 53–54.

28. *Kompas*, July 5, 7, 8, 11, 12, 21, 25, 27, Aug. 4, 24, Sept. 3, 20, 21, 1982, Apr. 26, 1983.

29. TRB is grown for the most part on dry land not competitive with irrigated rice. It is sometimes called "traditional" smallholders' cane, meaning that it is largely consumed as brown sugar within the village economy and not

converted into refined sugar for urban markets. In recent years the price of refined sugar set by *Bulog* seems to have been high enough to entice many TRB farmers to take some of their cane to the mills.

30. *Kompas*, Dec. 2. 1982, May 21, 23, 24, June 9, 16, Aug. 1, 6. Oct. 3, 1983.
31. *Kompas*, June 21, Aug. 24, 1982.

3

Politics and Culture in Indonesia*

Indonesia's 'proper genius has . . . always lain in her ability to work out practicable adjustments among her constituent cultures and to absorb the great host of external influences impinging on her while still, somehow, maintaining a distinct and over-all unique character.'

Clifford Geertz, *Peddlars and Princes* (Chicago: University of Chicago Press: 1983), p. 154.

Indonesia—that is, the modern Republic of Indonesia, which is the only political entity ever to have used the name—is a new state, one of the products of post-World War II decolonisation in Asia. Indonesian nationalism—that is, the European-derived idea that the diverse indigenous peoples of the territory then called Netherlands India constituted a single nation and had a right to independence and a state of their own—dates as a political movement only from the first or second decade of the twentieth century. By the end of the nineteenth century the Dutch had consolidated their control over most of the archipelago stretching 3,500 miles along the equator from Sumatra in the west to New Guinea in the east. Before the Dutch, whose East India company was a local political power from the early seventeenth century, history records many important kingdoms and empires, but none as extensive or as pervasive as today's Indonesian nation-state.

Given the newness of Indonesia as a nation-state, the historical 'proper genius' attributed to it by Clifford Geertz would seem to characterise more

* First published by the Center for Political Studies, Institute for Social Research, University of Michigan, Ann Arbor, 1988.

the working of broadly social than of specifically political institutions. Geertz, however, was writing not as an historian but as an anthropologist primarily concerned with the present and future. His field work in Java and Bali in the 1950s uncovered—as did my own first researches in East Sumatra a few years later—great contemporary cultural and social diversity and rapid recent change, much of it externally induced, in the ways individuals were defining and organising their personal and collective identities and aspirations.

Following a nearly worldwide postwar pattern, the government of the Republic of Indonesia was expected to take responsibility for creating a new kind of order capable of containing and managing this diversity and change, of giving concrete political form to the national idea from which it derived its legitimacy. It failed to do so. Instead, a divided political elite staggered from crisis to crisis, unable to find enough common ground on which to begin to build durable institutions and procedures of governing. By the end of the decade the democratic Constitution of 1950 had succumbed to a radical-sounding but empty rhetoric of continuing revolution and 'guided democracy.'

In these circumstances, Geertz's 1963 claim should perhaps not be read too literally as a scientist's generalisation about ancient social impulses to cohesion. Instead it was at least as much a participant observer's attempt to help find and hold that narrowing patch of solid earth on which integrative political institutions might yet be constructed. His words in the context of their time thus contained more than a little intimation of knocking on wood, of hoping against hope.

It is now a quarter of a century since Geertz wrote, and more than forty years since the nationalist leaders Sukarno and Mohammad Hatta—a Javanese and a Minangkabau from Sumatra respectively—jointly declared Indonesian independence. How have things worked out? What are the basic characteristics and patterns of political culture today? How has government responded to demands arising out of this cultural milieu? Most important, has Indonesia in the 1980s been able to maintain—or to recreate—'a distinct and over-all unique character', and what has been the role of politics and government in this process?

Indonesian Political Culture: Diversity and Unity

The two most important aspects of the new cultural pattern are conveniently summarised in the national motto *Bhinneka Tunggal Ika*, many as one, or, in the standard government translation, unity in diversity. A Sanskrit phrase, *Bhinneka Tunggal Ika* is close in meaning to our own Latin-derived *E Pluribus Unum*, out of many, one. Both semantically and in political practice, however, the Indonesian version reflects more the idea of co-existence or of a permanent balance between the many and the one, each legitimate in its own way, while the American conception—for most of our history, anyway—has stressed the absorption of the many into the one.

One expression of Indonesian diversity is ethnic or linguistic pluralism, comprising: one giant ethnic group, the Javanese, who inhabit the eastern and central portions of the island of Java and make up nearly half the total Indonesian population of 165 million; several large and medium size groups, including the Acehnese, Bataks, and Minangkabaus of Sumatra, the Sundanese of west Java, the Madurese of east Java and Madura, the Balinese, and the Bugis and Makassar peoples of southern Sulawesi; and hundreds of smaller groups scattered throughout the archipelago.

In politics, this highly fragmented pattern has often resolved into a simple dichotomy pitting Java, meaning the ethnic Javanese, against the Outer Islands, that is, all the other indigenous groups. Indonesian Chinese represent about four percent of the population and are a sizeable and economically powerful minority in most cities. Though many have become citizens, as an ethnic category they are not considered to be indigenous by most other Indonesians.

Religious pluralism is also an important dimension of diversity. Nearly ninety percent of the population is Muslim, making Indonesia the world's largest Muslim country. Both culturally and politically, however, the figure is misleading. For as many as two-thirds of the ethnic Javanese, Islamic beliefs and practices are so attenuated and mixed with pre-Islamic Hinduism and indigenous animism as to constitute virtually a separate religion. The Javanese themselves have labels for these groups, *santri* for the devout Muslims and *abangan* for the syncretists. Both groups have been politically important, as have the small but highly educated and strategically placed minorities of Protestants and Catholics. Since most non-Javanese are devout Muslims, there is considerable overlap, though not identity, between the *santri-abangan* religious and the Outer Islands-Java ethnic distinctions.

Differences in ideas about social structure further sharpen this cultural dichotomy. The Javanese *abangan* political elite must be among the most status-conscious and hierarchy-minded in the world. The powerful *priayi* aristocratic class, like the wet rice based Hinduised kingdoms its members once governed, was long ago emasculated by the Dutch. *Priayi* values, however, adapted easily to the bureaucratic administrative style of colonial rule and continue to pervade upper class Javanese thought and culture today.

Independent Indonesia's Javanese bureaucrats, like their pre-colonial and colonial *priayi* predecessors, distinguish sharply between themselves and the *rakyat* (people) or *wong cilik*, 'little people' or common people. The latter have long had a reputation among political observers for extreme deference to the wishes of their social and political superiors. Their behaviour, however—for instance, voting for and joining the communist party in large numbers in the 1950s and 1960s—has not always conformed to their reputation.

In most of the Outer Islands, smaller agricultural surpluses meant less elaborated social structures and cultures. Islamic influence, strongest in commercial port cities throughout the archipelago (including the north coast of Java) after the thirteenth century, was also a powerful equalising force, as was Christianity in the few areas where it took hold in the nineteenth and early twentieth centuries. The resulting contrast—bureaucratic, stratified Java versus the commercial, egalitarian Outer Islands—is very striking.[1]

Indonesia's cultural unity is less obvious, though no less real, than its diversity. Unfortunately, two common misconceptions, like tug-of-war teams at opposite ends of a rope, have directed our and their attention outward to the extremes rather than inward to the centre of the cultural continuum. At one end is the belief that whatever is not recognisably local or is obviously borrowed—the institution of the Presidency, say, or Garuda Indonesian Airways—is foreign, specifically Western, and therefore by definition not part of Indonesian culture. The second misconception is that national culture is the sum of the peaks of the various regional fine arts traditions. Though now largely discredited among Jakarta intellectuals, this idea is still popular in the government's Department of Education and Culture, in provincial capitals, and among educated Indonesians (and foreigners) generally.

A better way to look at Western and regional Indonesian cultures is as reagents in an ongoing chemical reaction. Initially within the crucible of Dutch power, young men (and a few women) went to European-style schools and took jobs in the institutions built or made possible by colonialism: the bureaucracy, the military, schools, newspapers, private businesses. These upwardly mobile men-in-the-middle, products of both the West and their local cultures and therefore different from either, thought the thoughts, led the organisations, and took the actions that created the Republic of Indonesia. They also laid the foundation for the structure of attitudes and beliefs that would constrain and channel future behaviour.

Though still a small minority, those who participate in and shape the national culture today are a much larger percentage of Indonesian society than were their predecessors. Career and educational opportunities exploded with independence and have continued to expand since. In the 1980s virtually every child has access to a primary school, where the medium of instruction is the national language, *bahasa Indonesia*. The number of secondary and tertiary schools has also grown significantly, though at a slower rate.

Independence brought much greater indigenous control—private as well as state, unconscious and unplanned as well as conscious and directed—over culture-shaping activities of all kinds. Socialisation into the national culture through the educational system has been a deliberate policy of all post-independence governments. Virtually all positions of leadership, formal and informal, official and unofficial, above the village level are held by participants in the national culture, as measured by facility in the national language and exposure to the supra-village world. The Indonesian language mass media—state television, which now reaches the most remote villages via satellite, state and private radio, national and regional newspapers and magazines which are mostly privately owned—are a powerful socialising force. Thanks to private radio, cassettes, and cheap entertainment tabloids, even the pop culture of Jakarta teenagers has spread nationwide.

The post-independence growth and spread of *bahasa Indonesia*, originally based on the traders' Malay which has long been the *lingua franca* of the Malay archipelago, is in fact one of the great success stories of cultural integration, both among ethnic groups and between elite and mass, in the Third World. From early in this century, its development has largely been shaped by the needs of the emerging national culture. It is also primarily the language of Indonesian culture: that is, it is not the language of any sizeable traditional Indonesian group or of any larger or more powerful non-Indonesian culture.[2]

Indonesian thus differs fundamentally from, say, Japanese, Chinese, or Thai, which are old languages that, with all their baggage of ancient meanings, must now serve as the vehicle for defining contemporary identity in those cultures. It also differs from the dominant position of English in, say, India or the Philippines, which gives members of those societies easy access to American and world English culture but reduces their ability to control their own cultural development. Low English competence tends to isolate Indonesians from the outside world, but has given them the opportunity to develop a more autonomous culture based on *bahasa Indonesia*.

In the 1980s incompleteness and inbetweenness are still defining characteristics of the national culture. For example, intellectuals frequently complain that the national political culture is only defined by what it is not: not theocratic but not secular, not liberal democratic but not totalitarian, not capitalist but not socialist. It is also true that nearly all Indonesians who participate in the national culture are members of a regional or other less inclusive culture that shapes their values in diverse ways, and that the great majority of Indonesians are less involved in the national than they are in their own local culture.

At the same time, twentieth century events and experiences have clearly settled some problems. New attitudes, concepts, ideas, and institutions have been distilled—in *bahasa Indonesia*—out of the successes, compromises, and failures of the long struggle to create a new society. If Indonesianness is to some extent defined by what it is not, at least some possibilities have been ruled out and the range of choices narrowed and focused. The trend, moreover, has been for cultural development to become more and more a response to the internal tensions and contradictions generated by the increasingly complex and autonomous modern culture itself.

The National Indonesian Culture

What are the ideas, beliefs, and values of the new national culture?[3] At the most general level, to be Indonesian is to be modern and indigenous at the same time. In personal terms, modernity means above all else the aspiration for material prosperity and an urban life style: a Western-type house, a white collar—preferably government civil service—job, and an income level sufficient to purchase the manufactured goods produced by an industrialising economy. Modern Indonesians assume a high degree of social mobility in their society. They believe that most people, regardless of social and economic background, can reasonably aspire to become modern.

They also see Western-style education as the principal, indeed virtually the only, way to begin the climb up the status ladder. Demand for places in the secular, academically-oriented state secondary and tertiary institutions far outstrips supply, though the government has been doing its best to build new schools and to encourage the private sector. Vocational and religious schools are much less popular. It is common knowledge that many Muslim leaders, including heads of well-known traditional and modern Muslim educational institutions, send their own children to the secular state schools.

Becoming modern has its costs, however, at least in the popular perception. Fathers' relationships with children are believed to be more distant than they used to be; aging parents are thought to be neglected by many; unmarried young people are no longer supervised closely; alcohol and drugs are too freely available; neighbours are no longer close; personal safety is threatened by a rising crime rate; and money has become the measure of all worth.

Anxiety over problems such as these has produced a continuing debate about values and a series of skirmishes over particular issues. On both sides of the great cultural divide between Java and Islam, the restoration of traditional and religious values is a widely promoted general solution. Simple nostalgia and lack of imagination explain some of this tendency, but more fundamental is the shibboleth that Indonesianness—modernity plus indigenousness—in practice means combining the best of the West (invariably defined as the 'material') with the best of the East (the 'spiritual'). A perceived crisis caused by new forms of behaviour automatically triggers proposals for a religious or traditional solution.

Restoration of older values is not the only remedy considered, however.

Indonesians feel pulled by what they take to be their past but many also believe that new times require new ideas, borrowed or created for the occasion. The pull and the debate are, in fact, one important aspect of what makes them all Indonesians rather than just Javanese or Outer Islanders, *abangan* or *santri*. They are experienced in common and become part of the context in which the debate continues.[4]

A small but concrete example of this ongoing interaction between modern and traditional values is the hit monthly television drama *Losmen*. The boarding house of the series' title is located in Yogyakarta, a centre of traditional Javanese culture. (Despite its very Javanese setting, the series is extremely popular nationwide.) It is run by the indomitable Bu (Mrs.) Broto, a strongly matriarchal figure (and for that reason alone clearly *abangan* rather than *santri*), with the assistance of her husband and children.

In an episode aired in 1987, Bu Broto's daughter-in-law Linda tries to help her brother-in-law Jarot overcome depression caused by his lack of success as an artist. Linda is a modern woman, not Javanese, probably Christian (religion is never mentioned in *Losmen*), a medical doctor who met her husband, also a doctor, while doing national service in Irian. Linda's ministrations to Jarot are—understandably, in terms of traditional Javanese expectations for such relationships—misunderstood and resented by Jarot's wife and Linda's husband. The crisis is resolved when the traditional Bu Broto takes the side of her modern daughter-in-law, telling the others that they should be grateful to have someone in the family with the medical skills to cure Jarot's illness.

Like the general culture, Indonesia's national political culture is also in part heir to European modernity. The most important borrowed idea has been the nation-state—a three part concept including common peoplehood or nationality, common territory, and popular sovereignty— as the basis of the political community. Indonesian nationality, or the 'desire to be together'—a phrase of the historian Ernst Renan, frequently quoted by the late President Sukarno—has reached across a broad spectrum of political leaders, parties, and ideologies from the 1920s to the present. The phrase sounds romantic and obscure, and in Sukarno's crowd-stirring oratory it was often both. But it expresses a reality that is easy to overlook in a country where diversity is so pronounced that it even provides, as I have argued above, the most common definition of unity.[5]

An important consequence of the desire to be together is a higher degree of national pride and self-confidence than is found elsewhere in the Third World. What makes this possible is an often unconscious but deeply ingrained sense of the autonomy of Indonesian national culture vis-à-vis both domestic ethnic and foreign cultures.

Most Indonesians do not conceive of their ethnic group as a terminal political community in the nation-state sense, even though the majority of members of almost all groups live in well-defined regions, e.g., the

Javanese in central and east Java, the Sundanese in west Java, the Bataks in northern Sumatra, the Bugis in southern Sulawesi. A standard formulation of the relationship, which perhaps oversimplifies matters, is that ethnic culture deals with private life, national culture with public life. Another way Indonesians often put it is that ethnic culture is traditional, national culture modern.

In places like Java, Batakland, and Aceh, where I have lived, it is certainly true that the local culture provides most of what is intimate, warm, and familial, while Indonesianness, which is about getting on in the wider world, tends to be colder, more pragmatic, less personal. On the other hand, there is also considerable inter-cultural penetration as modern ideas about child-rearing, marriage, and other aspects of personal life enter the village and older beliefs about social relations are maintained or revived in upper class urban circles.

None of this activity, however, has altered the basic understanding that the national culture has a monopoly on the nation-state idea. And despite the lack of familial intimacy provided by Indonesianness, there is strong emotional support (at least among the more politically conscious) for the idea of *bangsa Indonesia* (the Indonesian nation), which offers a new form of community as well as an escape from the more oppressive features of ethnic culture.[6]

There are exceptions to this pattern, most notably anti-Indonesian attitudes in the province of Irian Jaya, given up by the Dutch only in 1963, and in the ex-Portuguese colony of East Timor, forcibly annexed to the Republic in 1975–76. Separatist movements in the 1950s in a few provinces, such as Aceh, have also left their mark in anti-Jakarta attitudes and nostalgia for what might have been. And it is true that the farther one gets from urban areas and the lower one descends the socio-economic scale the more local and the less national are the individual cultural experiences.[7] But with these caveats it remains true that the sense of being Indonesian is pervasive and increasingly deeply felt.

Looking outward, the strong identification with Indonesian nationality means an ability to deal with foreigners on relatively equal terms. To be sure, Indonesians recognise the industrial superiority of the West, and sometimes despair that they will ever catch up. But they believe that *as Indonesians*—that is, as people with a modern identity in addition to their ethnic identities—they have the cultural equipment that enables them to compete.[8]

As a fundamental principle, popular sovereignty, the Western-derived idea that government legitimacy ultimately comes from and rests with the people as a whole, is also a settled issue in the national culture, replacing older ideas based on divine or magico-religious conceptions of kingship.[9] In practice, however, it has been more difficult to implement than the principle of national unity. In many Indonesian minds, moreover, the two are closely connected, so that failures in the implementation of popular sovereignty are seen as threatening the very foundation of national unity.

From the beginning of the independent nation the ideal of popular sovereignty has had to contend with problems arising from its interaction with traditional Indonesian culture and social structure. These have included both the instability produced by political parties based on religious and ethnic divisions and the absence or weakness of democratic ideas in traditional, particularly Javanese, culture. Resolution of this conflict has in fact been the single most important problem in the modern political culture.

All of the ideologies of Europe, and a few indigenous ones, have been proposed as principles by which the abstraction of popular sovereignty might be given institutional substance. Actual solutions attempted have included representative democracy (1950–1957), the charismatic personal leadership of President Sukarno (1959–1965), and the current military- and bureaucracy-dominated political system of the New Order. An Islamic state and the dictatorship of the proletariat were once and may again become widely-supported alternatives.

Underlying all of these solutions, not excepting the first, have been strong populist and paternalistic streaks in the national culture.[10] The conceptual apparatus of Indonesian politicians of nearly all ideological persuasions includes both the ideal of 'the people' (*rakyat*) undifferentiated in ethnic, religious, or class terms and the notion of a distinction between the *rakyat* and their *pemimpin* (leaders, in the sense of an all-knowing elite).

The *rakyat* are at once the source of national inspiration and governmental legitimacy and the object of the elite's paternalistic determination to bring them into the modern world. They are also the cause of much anxiety. Probably a majority of elite Indonesians are convinced that without paternalistic leadership Indonesia will dissolve into chaos because of mass backwardness and deep cultural divisions. The image of a 'bunker mentality' among the elite only slightly exaggerates the extent of this fear.

Populism and paternalism are simultaneously indigenous (rooted particularly in Javanese aristocratic culture, but found elsewhere in Indonesia as well), Western (learned from the colonial example and in Western universities), and synthetic, that is, the result of Western-educated Indonesians' interaction with their less-educated countrymen. Level of Western education has in fact for several decades been a primary criterion defining membership in the elite, which helps to explain the vast national hunger for schooling. The New Order's emphasis on state-led development has further strengthened this trend.

How is it possible for Indonesians to have a national culture that is simultaneously modern and indigenous, combining ideas originally associated with the European Enlightenment and Industrial Revolution with very different ideas from their own ethnic and religious pasts? The general answer—applicable across the non-Western world—is that culture change rarely, if ever, wholly replaces one set of values with another. Modernity everywhere is indigenised in the crucible of local understandings and aspirations.

The particular Indonesian answer is that the modern values limned above—individualism, materialism, nationalism, popular sovereignty—entered Indonesia at a high level of abstraction (that is, detached from their European moorings) and have been domesticated by Indonesians' individual and collective struggles with them over the past several decades. Resolutions of particular issues—specific recent examples include the banning of video game arcades and of luxury automobiles, the introduction both of religion and Javanist 'moral education' into the public school system, and the vigilante-style murder of petty criminals by special army units—are experienced in common and become part of the context within which the debate continues. It could hardly have been otherwise, according to the Cornell Indonesianist Benedict Anderson: 'defining what is national can only be a complex project of juxtaposition and separation between the "foreign" and the "indigenous".'[11]

Traditional Cultures and the National Culture

The national political culture stands today in a problematic relationship to both Islam and *abangan/priayi* Javanese culture. For much of the twentieth century, Islam has seemed to many to be outside and in opposition to the developing national culture. Java is also seen as constituting a threat, but from the inside, in the attitudes and values of the Javanese politicians—most especially Presidents Sukarno and Suharto—who have dominated national politics since the early 1950s. During the New Order, both Islam and Javanism appear to have been growing in number of adherents and intensity of commitment, suggesting at least the possibility of greater polarisation and political tension. Non-Javanese ethnic groups and the Chinese minority also have distinctive cultural traditions, but these are much less important politically today than they were in the 1950s and early 1960s.

Islam

Three characteristics of Islamic belief have been sources of conflict between devout Muslims and other Indonesians. Muslims stress their membership in a world-wide community of believers (*umat Islam*), which raises doubts about their loyalty to the less-inclusive Indonesian nation. Second, they believe that their religion provides guidance to the individual adherent and to the leaders of society in all areas of life. There is, therefore, in principle no separation of 'church' and state. And they possess a legal tradition, anchored in the Qur'an and Hadits (lessons from the life of the Prophet Muhammad) and elaborated over the centuries by schools of religious jurisprudence, that is in their minds superior to the Dutch legal codes and procedures that form the basis of national Indonesian law. Perhaps as to be expected of a religion that has no formal hierarchy or other unifying structure, Indonesian Islam has not been monolithic in its application of these tenets. Two large social and educational organisations, Muhammadiyah and Nahdlatul Ulama, have long occupied polar positions—labelled respectively modernist or reformist and traditionalist—on the nature of the religion and its relationship to the nation-state. Muhammadiyah was founded in 1912 under the influence of the Islamic reformism of Mohammad Abduh in the Middle East, Nahdlatul Ulama in 1926 as a conservative reaction to the growing strength of the reform movement.

Islamic reformism, in its Indonesian version at least, has had two goals: to purify the religion by returning to the Qur'an and Hadits, discarding the interpretations of the legal schools and the local beliefs and practices that had grown up during centuries of relative isolation; and to accept the challenge of modernity by adopting Western scientific and technological principles.

Muhammadiyah reformers have shared the second goal with other modernising Indonesians. The first has divided the two groups by linking Indonesian Islam more closely than before to intellectual and political currents in the Middle East. Also divisive has been reformism's combination of a strong interest in the relationship of Islam to the state with a proselytising spirit and an intolerance of other interpretations. Finally, a large proportion of the reformers have come from the Outer Islands, further increasing the social and cultural distance between the reform movement and non-*santri* Javanese.

Nahdlatul Ulama's more conservative Muslims have rejected both the purifying and the modernising aspirations of the reformers. The core of NU's constituency is the Islam of the rural *pesantren*, traditional Islamic schools headed by charismatic *kiai* (Islamic teachers), which dot the landscape of east and central Java. Where the Indonesia-wide Muhammadiyah has aggressively promoted a novel set of universalist aspirations, the Java-based NU was formed to protect an already existing way of life which combined Islamic devoutness with (at least in practice) much narrower religious and political horizons. If Muhammadiyah has been suspect to (and feared by) non-*santri* Indonesians for its supra-national Islamic universalism, NU has been suspect (but demeaned rather than feared) for its sub-national Javanese parochialism.

Muhammadiyah has never been a political organisation, but contributed many leaders and ideas to the Masyumi political party in the 1950s, and was strongly associated with Masyumi's commitment to an Indonesian

Islamic State. With the banning of Masyumi in 1960, Muhammadiyah pulled back from even indirect political activity. NU entered partisan politics in the early 1950s and stayed in until 1984, when its leaders decided, as they said, to follow Muhammadiyah's example and become a purely social and educational organisation. In fact, NU remains active behind the scenes in both partisan and bureaucratic politics.

The two decades of the New Order have been a frustrating but creative period for Indonesian Muslim intellectuals and activists. Initially, the downfall of President Sukarno and the destruction of the communist party raised hopes for a political process more open to Muslim participation, specifically for the resuscitation of Masyumi and for a more substantive, less purely symbolic role for NU. When these hopes were dashed by a new President no less *abangan* (and a good deal less inclined to any kind of popular participation) than his predecessor, Muslims found themselves once again on the outside looking in.

A new political party culturally oriented to the reformists, Parmusi (*Partai Muslimin Indonesia*, Indonesian Muslims' Party), was formed in 1968, but the old Masyumi stalwarts were not allowed to lead the party or to be its legislative candidates. Parmusi was therefore rejected by the reformist constituency, winning only 5.3% of the vote in the 1971 general election, compared to Masyumi's 20.9% in the previous national election, held in 1955.

NU, with 18.7% of the 1971 vote (compared to 18.4% in 1955) retained the support of the traditionalist community. But the government dealt NU two lethal post-election blows: the position of Minister of Religion, held by NU for twenty years, went to a non-partisan modernist; and the party system was reorganised so that both NU and Parmusi became part of a larger Islamic party called PPP (*Partai Persatuan Pembangunan*, Development Unity Party). PPP has been from the first thoroughly penetrated and controlled by the government. Between 1973 and 1984 NU's influence and room to maneuver within PPP, not great to begin with, shrank to the vanishing point.

Reformist Muslim thinkers have responded in three ways to these developments.[12] The best known group, led by the Chicago-trained Nurcholish Madjid, might be called the indigenists. They have attempted to come to an ideological accommodation with the New Order—and with Indonesian national culture—by refocusing their conception of the *umat Islam* and by redrawing the boundaries between Islam and the state. Islam remains a universal religion, they agree, but its practice must be culture-specific. Twentieth century social changes in particular have raised many new questions of interpretation for Islamic law in Indonesia, questions which must ultimately be settled by discussion among Indonesian Muslims. For example, indigenists are currently discussing a reinterpretation, proposed by the Minister of Religion, of the Quranic stipulation that sons inherit twice as much as daughters.

The indigenists' first label for their approach, which provoked a tsunami of criticism from within the reformist community, was secularisation. More recent terms have been desacralisation, also anathema to most Muslims, and 'reactualisation'. The indigenists' view of the state is implied in their slogan 'Islam, yes; Islamic party, no.' There is, in other words, no absolute form of an Islamic state, as there is no clearly definable Islamic political program for which all good Muslims must struggle.

A second group, also more concerned with Indonesian than with universal Islam, might be called NGO (Non-Governmental Organisation) reformists. One of their leading figures is Dawam Rahardjo of the private Institute for Economic and Social Research, Education and Information (in Indonesian: LP3ES, *Lembaga Penelitian, Pendidikan dan Penerangan Ekonomi dan Sosial*), publishers of the respected social science monthly *Prisma*.

NGO reformists are social reformers, concerned with overcoming poverty and inequality. They read *dependencia* and critical theory, neither of which offers an action agenda under current political conditions, and while waiting for more auspicious times attempt to apply a Basic Human Needs approach. For two decades they have made a major effort to turn the traditional *pesantren*, which teaches only religious subjects, into a grass-roots agent of development and cultural transformation. As the name I have given them implies, they also work in and with a wide range of village-level non-governmental organisations. NGO reformists criticise the Nurcholish Madjid-led indigenists for attending to the needs of the newly-rich urban upper and middle classes rather than those of the poor (whom they call the *kaum dhuafa*, an Arabic borrowing, rather than the standard Indonesian *orang miskin*, in a deliberate attempt at developing an Islamic social and political vocabulary).

The third group descends perhaps more directly from the pre-New Order reformists in Muhammadiyah and Masyumi. They are true universalists who believe that Muhammad's message, as contained in the Qur'an and Hadits, is essentially complete and can be applied directly in all Muslim societies. To the universalists, Islam is not in conflict with modern science and technology. A young but increasingly prominent universalist thinker is Amien Rais, who teaches international relations at Gadjah Mada University in Yogyakarta and holds a major leadership position in Muhammadiyah. Like Nurcholish Madjid, Amien Rais earned a Ph.D. at the University of Chicago, where he wrote his dissertation on the Islamic Brotherhood in Egypt.

Islamic universalism is a powerful creed on university campuses, especially at two major national universities in west Java, the Bandung Institute of Technology and the Bogor Agricultural Institute. Campus mosques at both institutions are well-known centres of Islamic study where, many believe, a new breed of religiously-devout *cum* technologically-sophisticated leaders of the *umat* is being created. The universalists have translated the writings of the Iranian intellectual Ali Shariati, and still follow closely the Iranian Islamic revolution. While not in opposition (an impossible stance today), their political attitudes are mostly antagonistic toward a government viewed as hostile to Islamic aspirations.

Traditionalist Indonesian Muslims, particularly of the sort identified with NU in east and central Java, have always been indigenists in the sense that their beliefs and practices reflect local culture. During the Guided Democracy period that preceded the New Order they also developed a reputation as accommodationists or, less politely, opportunists willing to swallow Sukarno's radical rhetoric and encouragement of the communist party in return for government patronage. From 1965 to 1967 they were fierce anti-communists, conducting together with the army a massive witch-hunt of party members and sympathisers. Beginning in the early 1970s they monopolised the political opposition, repeatedly confronting the government in parliamentary and election forums on both religious and social justice issues.

In the 1980s, under the leadership of Abdurrahman Wahid, grandson of an NU founder and son of a prominent 1950s NU leader and Minister of Religion, the organisation has begun to chart a controversial new course. Abdurrahman Wahid's group intends to redirect NU's activities away from political oppositionism and toward village-level development programs. Their objectives, these leaders claim, are to imbue Indonesian Islam with a new social consciousness and to lower the cultural and political barriers separating *santri* from *abangan*.

To these ends NU withdrew from PPP in 1984 and unofficially supported the government party *Golkar* (for *Golongan Karya*, Functional Group) in the 1987 general election, with the result that Golkar gained and PPP lost nearly twelve percentage points in comparison with the previous election in 1982.[13] Abdurrahman Wahid is now a member, representing *Golkar*, of the Working Body of the People's Consultative Assembly, a kind of super-parliament that meets once in five years to elect the President and Vice-President and set the Broad Outlines of State Policy (*Garis-Garis Besar Haluan Negara*). Perhaps most indicative of the new climate, after years of hostility local government officials are now supportive of NU projects and activities and no longer regard NU-affiliated *kiai* as enemies of the state. These developments have, of course, made the NU leadership vulnerable to the charge that, as in the pre-New Order years, patronage and position, not social equality and national integration, are the real goals of their policies.[14]

The old debate between reformists and traditionalists thus continues, but with a number of differences. Like the previous generation in Muhammadiyah and Masyumi, today's universalists do not see the new NU as an improvement on the old. The NGO reformists share the current NU emphasis on social welfare but not its willingness to cooperate closely with the government. The traditionalist Abdurrahman Wahid and the indigenist reformist Nurcholish Madjid are separated by their rural and urban constituencies but have a common commitment to ending the split between *santri* and *abangan*, to removing the stigma of outsider minority so long attached to Indonesian Islam.

As small steps toward integration, Abdurrahman Wahid recently proposed that Indonesian Muslims no longer greet each other with the Arabic *assalamualaikum* but with a simple Indonesian good morning, afternoon, or evening, and Nurcholish Madjid suggested that the Arabic *Allah* for God in the Islamic confession of faith ('There is no god but God, and Muhammad is his prophet') be substituted in the Indonesian translation (as in the English) with the capitalised Indonesian word for God (*Tuhan*).

Both ideas provoked a storm of protest across the *umat*, suggesting that, on these issues at least, the gap between leaders and followers within each camp may be as pronounced as the traditionalist-reformist split that divides the community as a whole. But the latter continues to be deep. In late 1987 the national heads of Muhammadiyah and NU, bringing to mind a U.S.-Soviet summit, formally inaugurated an era of rapprochement by exchanging official visits for the first time in either organisation's history. Muslim elite and intellectual reaction was generally positive, but greater mass acceptance still seems far away.

Javanism

Only a minority—perhaps a third—of the ethnic Javanese are *santri*. The remainder adhere with varying degrees of conviction and interest to an *abangan/priayi* religious tradition that is uniquely Javanese, a hotch-potch of Hindu, Buddhist, indigenous animistic, Islamic, and other beliefs and practices called *kebatinan* (roughly, inner being-ness or the science of the inner being) or *kepercayaan* (literally, beliefs, but as separate from *agama* or religion, the term used for 'world religions' such as Islam or Christianity).

Kebatinan is not a single creed but instead encompasses a wide range of beliefs. Some of these (but by no means all) are organised into several hundred separate associations. The more sophisticated groups—such as Pangestu, which claims more than 100,000 members, is led by the former Minister of Forestry, and has many elite members, including the Minister of Justice—offer codes for righteous living and paths to inner peace that they claim supplement rather than conflict with religion. Others place more emphasis on mystical and magical practices, including numerology (very popular today because of a government-sponsored football pool), fortune-telling, and faith healing.

Kebatinan adherents are Java-centred. Their culture draws on a long local history, much of it expressed in the poetic language of court chronicles, of concern with the inner person and with achieving harmony between the micro-cosmos of the self and the macro-cosmos of the universe. In the national culture, Java-centredness leads to an at least implicit view of Indonesia as Greater Java, as opposed to the Outer Island (and generally *santri*) conception of a pluralist, multi-ethnic nation in which the Javanese are only one among many groups.

Java-centredness also raises among the *abangan* the suspicion that serious Muslims are insufficiently Javanese or Indonesian, too influenced by Arabic culture. For their part, devout Muslims see *kebatinan* as superstition or false religion. They oppose attempts to legitimise it through state action, as in the recent establishment of a directorate for *kebatinan* affairs in the Department of Education and its inclusion in both 1978 and 1983 in the Broad Outlines of State Policy approved by the highest constitutional body, the People's Consultative Assembly. The *santri* position on this issue is particularly intense because most *kebatinan* believers are also at least nominal Muslims.

Kebatinan is by definition non- or anti-rational, so its influence in the national culture tends to be opposed by the most Westernised Indonesians and also by reformist Muslims, who claim to accept the basic principles of Western science and technology.[15] It should quickly be added, however, that non-rationality is not a defining characteristic of *abangan* culture as a whole. Many *abangan* reject *kebatinan*, or are indifferent to it, and many others live comfortably with a split personality as secular rationalists in some aspects of their lives and mystics in others. The very Westernised democratic socialist intellectuals of the Indonesian Socialist Party (banned in 1960, but still influential both as an intellectual and as a political current) are said to be particularly striking examples of this ability to compartmentalise beliefs, but it is a common characteristic of Western-educated Javanese.

Since the early 1950s *abangan* politicians, first under Sukarno and then Suharto, have exercised a near-monopoly over the formation of a vocabulary of national political discourse. Sukarno's best-known slogan, NASAKOM, the idea of an essential unity among nationalists, religious people, and communists, could not be challenged or criticised in public although it was intelligible as ideology only to his fellow *abangan*. Sukarno and the communist party were close political and ideological collaborators, so there was a distinctly mass-oriented (*abangan* proper as opposed to upper class *priayi*) as well as non-Islamic flavour to many of the terms he coined.

President Suharto is less cosmopolitan, more small-town-conservative, more a product of a bureaucratic and military milieu, and more inclined to an *arriviste priayi*-style cultural outlook than was his predecessor. He has used Old Javanese and Sanskrit terms, scarcely understood even by most *abangan*, to label everything from the Parliament building to an annual prize awarded to provincial governments for most successful regional development effort to NASA-launched communications satellites. He is much given to quoting Javanese proverbs and maxims: a recent statement on corruption quoted the nineteenth century court poet Ronggowarsito to the effect that the incorruptible ultimately profit more than those who succumb to the temptations of corruption. In the official government lexicon, there is also much borrowing of English and manufacturing of quasi-English, but virtually no use of Arabic.

The central ideological concept of the New Order, originally put forward by Sukarno in a 1945 speech, is Pancasila, Sanskrit for Five Principles. The principles, deliberately highly abstract, are Belief in God, Indonesian Unity, Humanitarianism, Democracy, and Social Justice. To many of its proponents, secular rationalists and even some Muslims, belief in Pancasila is a means of rising above ethnic and religious parochialism, of identifying what it is that all Indonesians share. Both Presidents have also used it as an ideological weapon to delimit the boundaries of acceptable political contestation, in Sukarno's case against the promoters of the Islamic State idea and in Suharto's for both anti-Islamic and anti-communist purposes. Courses in Pancasila are now required of all government officials and many private groups and are a part of the regular school curriculum from elementary through tertiary levels.

In the New Order Pancasila has taken on mystical and Javanist connotations. In a rare unbuttoned extemporaneous speech to a government youth group in 1982 the President spoke in *kebatinan* terms of the origins of Pancasila, which he said was dug out of the soil of Javanese history, and encouraged the non-Javanese present to study that history. A national holiday, *Hari Kesaktian Pancasila*, the Day of Pancasila Sacred Power, commemorates on 1 October each year the 1965 defeat of the communist party by the army under the leadership of then Major-General Suharto.

To devout Muslims, whether favourably or unfavourably disposed to Pancasila in general, the doctrine can not possibly be *sakti* (holy, possessing sacred power). Describing Pancasila in this way comes close, they say, to giving it the status of a religion, despite the President's frequent denials of such an intention. To secular rationalists, such mystical talk is both an embarrassment and a surface manifestation of deeply anti-modern tendencies in the Javanese elite.

Suharto's insistence that Pancasila is an indigenous product reflects a pervasive *abangan* stance toward the national culture. A high government official recently scolded Indonesian intellectuals for negative attitudes toward tradition. (They were actually opposing the imposition of Javanese hierarchical values.) Citing the similarity between President Reagan's advice to Prime Minister Thatcher after her Falklands victory and an old Javanese expression about not destroying the dignity of a defeated enemy, the official said that 'this proves that our culture is very modern.'[16]

This apologetic attitude is also taken by many Indonesian Muslims, for whom everything in the modern world can be found in the Qur'an. Such an approach offers psychological comfort and is useful for legitimising the unfamiliar, a valuable and perhaps even necessary quality in a society where so much has changed in a few short decades. But the apologetic attitude has its negative side as well: it stunts cultural creativity—or at least raises a barrier between creators and apologists—by denying the need for new concepts and solutions. People who ask hard questions about cultural development are too facilely dismissed as 'overly Westernised' by both the *abangan* and *santri* establishments.

The most important political idea borrowed by the New Order from *abangan* Java—really from the upper class *priayi* culture of the traditional courts—is that of a benevolent ruler and an obedient populace. Like an idealised version of a traditional Javanese king, Suharto projects an image of standing alone at the apex of government. All important national political decisions, as far as outside observers can detect, are made by him. He receives cabinet members and others individually rather than collectively, as petitioners rather than as colleagues.[17]

The president's slightest *petunjuk* (sign, indication) sends lesser officials scrambling to do his bidding. He appears nightly on television and daily on the front page of most newspapers—which never criticise him—and makes frequent inspection trips to the provinces. Born in a village, he has a special interest in agriculture and is often photographed with farmers. Long before the quinquennial sessions of the People's Consultative Assembly session that have elected him President five times since 1968, a chorus of voices is raised in praise of his leadership.

The benevolence-obedience ideal encourages statism in the attitudes of bureaucrats toward society. A small everyday example is the recent obligatory visit of a movie star to the Minister of Transmigration to ask for his blessing (*nyuwun restu*, in the Javanese phrase she used to describe the event) on a proposed film about a transmigrant village.[18] A larger and more institutionalised example is Pancasila Labour Relations, a code describing the paternalistic responsibilities of the government toward labour and management. Most government departments have agencies charged with *pembinaan* (development, building, in the sense of guidance), as in the Department of Education's *Direktorat Pembinaan Penghayat Kepercayaan* (Directorate for the Guidance of Non-Religious Beliefs) or the Department of Information's directorate for the guidance of the press. Newspapers and magazines, mostly privately-owned, are told to behave in a 'free and responsible' way, and are first warned, then shut down if they don't.

Extreme governmental centralisation and uniformity also reflect the benevolence-obedience ideal. Virtually all important policy decisions, for example concerning development, are made in the centre rather than the regions. Implementation instructions rarely take account of regional differences. Typical is a 1979 law on village government. Based on a

Javanese conception of what constitutes a village—its size, subunits, and appropriate activities in society—the law is virtually unintelligible and thus unenforceable in much of the Outer Islands. A less serious but equally telling example has to do with dress codes. Under the New Order there has been a steady increase in the number of groups, from school children to bank tellers, who are expected to wear uniforms. In the Presidential palace, even private women's groups invited to official functions are sent cloth to be made into uniforms for the occasion.

The impulses toward statism, centralisation, and uniformity imply hostility toward those outside the state, which historically meant traders and today means the private business class, many of whose indigenous members (as opposed to the large groups of Chinese and foreign business people) are *santri* and Outer Islanders. European education in the inter-war period, when Lenin's theory of imperialism as the highest stage of capitalism appeared to offer an irrefutable explanation for colonial exploitation, reinforced traditional suspicions, and the bias remains strong today.[19] Culture-based opposition to business must, however, be put in context, since the New Order has undeniably done more to encourage private business, both foreign and especially domestic indigenous, than any of its predecessors.

Since the king can do no wrong, benevolence-obedience implies a tendency toward arbitrary or discretionary government policy-making and implementation as opposed to the development of a structure of law to which all are subject. The most blatant example of arbitrariness is the 'mysterious killings' of the early 1980s, when special army units were used in a number of cities to assassinate well-known criminal gang leaders and petty thieves. There is also much discretion in the form of special favours to officials' relatives, friends, and allies in the implementation, and even occasionally the formulation, of economic development policy.[20]

It is difficult to assess how deeply rooted or pervasive benevolence-obedience is in Javanese, much less national Indonesian, culture. It is certainly a prominent theme in most scholarly accounts by Indonesians or foreigners of Javanese political ideas, especially (but not exclusively) studies based on court culture.[21] It is also found in the moral teachings of the popular *wayang kulit* shadow plays that recount the exploits of Hindu-Javanese gods and mortals. And it is present in the generally accepted Javanese view of the ideal relationship between fathers and children, teachers and pupils, and elder and younger persons.[22] As a concrete political example, the paternalistic and illegal 'mysterious killings' were widely applauded, even by middle-class Indonesians, as an appropriate solution to a rising crime rate.

To politicians of Javanese background (and even many non-Javanese), benevolence-obedience seems to fill a gap in the national political culture. It offers a moral foundation that is reassuring because it is rich in meaning and is one's own, giving today's presidents, ministers, and lesser officials a place in what can at least be construed as a glorious tradition. On the other hand, there is a strong manipulative or self-interested flavour to the concept's broad appeal. It reflects cultural refinement and sophistication and as such is an appropriate ideology for today's *nouveaux* upper classes. Any ruling group of Javanese has a clear political interest in promoting it—not least because it is devoid of any notion of accountability through processes not controlled by the rulers themselves—and it was an important part of Sukarno's self-presentation during Guided Democracy. Other conceptions are likely to be suppressed or at least ignored.

From a subordinate's perspective, benevolence-obedience may also be understood as a political strategy developed by persons with few other resources in a society where wealth, power, and status have long been monopolised by a small minority of aristocrats or officials. Being deferential is one of the few available means of obtaining a share of these goods.

Some evidence for the instrumental quality of deferential behaviour among subordinates is the speed and ease with which, say, ambitious Minangkabaus or Bataks, whose cultures are known for their egalitarianism, have adapted to the Javanist rules of national political life.[23] An important implication of this view is that if the social conditions that produced it change—for example, if economic development disperses the resources of wealth and status more widely—behaviour is likely to change as well.

In the final analysis, perhaps what is most problematic about the benevolence-obedience ideal is the extent of its acceptance by the so-called *wong cilik* or little people of Java. The large vote totals for the government party Golkar (and indeed for the traditional Muslim party Nahdlatul Ulama, which though *santri* is after all also Javanese) in New Order elections are often cited as evidence that most Javanese tend to do what they are told out of respect for established leaders, local and national.

On the other hand, rebellion and more subtle forms of political protest against arbitrary or oppressive rule by court elites are not unknown in pre-colonial and colonial Javanese history.[24] More directly relevant, between 1952 and 1965 the Indonesian communist party gained more than 3 million and its affiliates about 25 million members.

The reasons for the communists' success are controversial, and include the benefits of a close relationship between the party and Sukarno and, in some areas, between it and village elites. But one important ingredient was certainly a willingness to defy the authority of established elites, especially at the local level. Since 1966, however, there has not been a communist party or equivalent organisation, and today it is upper class political ideas, as interpreted by the ruling group, that represent Java in the national political culture.

Non-Javanese Ethnic Cultures

Non-Javanese ethnic or regionally-based political ideas have not offered a serious challenge to the dominance of the *abangan-priyayi* interpretation of the national culture during the New Order. Decentralisation of political decision-making and implementation is probably the main value separating non-Javanese from Javanese, though it is frequently argued that Outer Islanders are also in favour of greater democratic participation in the political process at all levels.

Decentralisation and local democratisation were major issues in the 1950s, and their proponents succeeded in 1957 in passing legislation establishing autonomous executives and legislatures at the province and district levels. This trend was immediately reversed, however, when army rebellions against central government policies in several provinces were put down by the armed forces high command, then in political alliance with President Sukarno. Since that time both Presidents Sukarno and Suharto have been strong centralisers who have not hesitated to repress regional dissidents.

Authoritarianism, while important, is only one reason for the absence of open ethnic or regionalist politics today. The New Order's oil wealth has made it possible for the central government to heavily subsidise regional government budgets and to implement its own welfare programs—agricultural development, small business credits, road, school, and health-centre construction, and so on—directly in villages throughout the country. Upwardly mobile bureaucrats or army officers, the potential leaders of regional discontent, also know by looking at the current incumbents of high office that their chances for personal success at the national level are not diminished by their ethnic origins. And for several reasons, including tourism, the appeasement of provincial middle and upper class cultural pretensions, and its own Javanist inclinations, the government has encouraged the maintenance or restoration of traditional customs and ceremonies, which creates the appearance of local cultural, if not political, autonomy.

The Chinese

The domestic Chinese are a special case of a group at the core of Indonesia's modern economy but outside its formal political and cultural life. Chinese shophouses still dominate the centres of most Indonesian towns. More important, the upper business class in Jakarta and other large cities is overwhelmingly Chinese, a long term condition that has seemingly been little affected by the changing policies of socialist- and capitalist-leaning governments.

Before the New Order there were some Chinese political organisations and even cabinet ministers. There was also much debate about the relationship of Chinese to Indonesian society and culture both within the

Chinese community—divided into several pro-Taiwan, pro-Beijing, and pro-integration factions—and between it and the larger society.

Today there are extremely close and mutually beneficial personal economic relationships between high officials, starting with the president, and Chinese businessmen. Politically, however, the Chinese have been marginalised. One reason is that a too visible Chinese upper class is a political liability. New Order politicians also fear the possibility of left-wing activism and the reemergence of a pro-Beijing fifth column. Culturally, the present government's not-open-for-debate policy has consistently promoted total assimilation through Indonesian-language education and a ban on most Chinese-language media.

The implications of the economic dominance of the Chinese community for Indonesian political culture are largely unexplored. Some writers[25] have argued that the development of the Indonesian language in the latter part of the nineteenth century was strongly influenced by the fact that most producers and consumers of printed Indonesian-language media were Chinese. From the work of Salim Said[26] we know that nationalist film makers since the beginning of their industry before the Second World War until very recently have had to confront the economic reality that the ticket-buying public, theatre owners and financiers were largely Chinese. But in general neither foreign scholars (whose interest is primarily in the Chinese community itself) nor Indonesians have paid much attention to the role of the Chinese in the development of the national Indonesian culture.

Subcultures of the National Culture

In addition to the variations resulting from differing regional and religious cultural traditions, the national culture has produced a number of distinctive subcultures within itself. These include the cultures of the armed forces, the civilian bureaucracy, and the non-official culture of the intellectual and artistic communities.

The Military

The military subculture is the most corporate or caste-like, with its own moral code and, since the early 1970s, a high degree of internal solidarity and loyalty. It is virtually impenetrable by domestic or foreign outsiders, unlike for example the neighbouring Philippine and Thai armies, whose inner conflicts are well known.

In a national culture that generally maintains a certain psychological distance from the outside world, armed forces officers have been the most suspicious of and hostile toward foreigners of all Indonesians. They have also been more inclined than others toward an 'intelligence mentality' that sees politics as basically conspiratorial. In the New Order this has resulted in the proliferation of domestic intelligence gathering organisations, a tendency to concentrate power in the hands of intelligence officers, and a 'security approach' to political activity that severely limits partisan and other forms of popular politics.[27]

Indonesian army officers take great pride in their role over the past four decades, first as liberators of the nation from Dutch rule and then, repeatedly, as its saviours from domestic threats of the 'right' (Islamic and regional rebellions) and the left (communism). They see themselves as more nationalist than the civilian bureaucracy. Regional postings and other appointments, they claim, are unrelated to ethnic criteria. At the same time their doctrines and general self-conception are heavily influenced by *abangan/priayi* warrior ideals, and few *santri* officers have risen to the top military ranks. In east Java, where Javanism seems strongest in the army's Brawijaya division, there is a monument containing a list of the names of the kings of Majapahit (a kingdom that was destroyed in the late 15th century), followed by a list of the Brawijaya commanders.[28] The anti-*santri* bias has been strengthened—to the point of paranoia, some believe—by the history of Islamic rebellions in the 1950s and early 1960s.

Armed forces ideology combines, apparently without tension, the ideal of soldierly discipline with a unique doctrine of *dwi-fungsi*, the 'twin functions' of the armed forces to protect the country from its enemies and to play a 'positive socio-political role' domestically. In the pre-New Order period *dwi-fungsi* justified the army's struggle for power with the communist party. Today it legitimises an army general as president, the appointment of 100 officers to the 500-seat Parliament, and a Defense Department policy of routinely seconding officers to postings in the central and regional civilian bureaucracies. A few retired dissident generals have protested, without apparent impact on the inside, that the President's tight control of the armed forces has drained the content from the original purpose of *dwi-fungsi*, which they argue was to provide an independent check on the power-holders.[29]

During the past fifteen years no issue has been more discussed within the armed forces than the leadership transition from the revolutionary generation of officers, who directly experienced the 1945–49 independence war, to the academy-trained officers who now hold almost all of the senior military positions. The expressed concern has been with 'making permanent the values of 1945'. Exactly what this means has never been very clear, in part because the debate has been closed to outsiders and in part because Suharto and his colleagues rarely speak in more concrete language. Fear that younger officers might turn against their seniors has surely been a major factor, but there is also a genuine desire to perpetuate the New Order as a uniquely Indonesian system of rule superior to other alternatives.

The Bureaucracy

The civilian bureaucracy now numbers about 4 million. Though less cohesive than the 300,000-person military, it too has a caste-like quality.

Where the military's heritage is primarily revolutionary, the civilian officials are descendants more of the colonial and pre-colonial (Javanese) state than of the 1945 Revolution. Bureaucrats, particularly the 150,000 upper level officials, believe that the state (*negara*, a term with powerful resonance for Javanese), which they serve (as *abdi negara*, literally servants of the state), must stand above all other groups in society.

Put slightly differently, the officials believe themselves as the educated elite to be a *noblesse oblige* with a special responsibility for the public welfare. State-led development under the New Order has strengthened this perception. It has also meant that the better-educated bureaucrats tend to see themselves as more modern than the rest of society, including the military. In return for their services to society, officials claim (and exercise) the right to consume a large share of national economic resources.[30]

Civil servants are required to belong to a single professional association, with leadership positions in the association determined by rank in the bureaucracy. Wives are similarly organised in a women's auxiliary, with leadership positions determined by the husband's office.[31] Officials are expected to wear a uniform-like safari suit, and on frequent special occasions don a blue batik shirt decorated with their association's banyan tree symbol. They often live together in housing developments built by their department.

Conflicts within the bureaucracy reflect the cultural cleavages of Indonesian society but are also based on personal competition and the struggles for influence and power among departments and agencies and among points-of-view about policies. The Department of Religion is a *santri* stronghold, which is the principal reason why the directorate for *kebatinan* is not housed there. There is a distinctly non-*santri*—part secular, part *abangan*—flavour to the Department of Education, which has been responsible for building and staffing the essentially secular national educational system. Officials from a particular region or ethnic group, or a particular university, hire subordinates accordingly. Even state university departments' recruitment of junior faculty is affected by ethnic, religious, and similar criteria.

Politics at the ministerial level is characterised by fierce competition among ministers for presidential favour. In a practice called *bapakism* (literally father-ism), ambitious lesser officials seek patrons among their superiors, joining patron-client networks often unrelated to their current positions. For example, the Minister of Home Affairs in the 1983–88 cabinet was regarded as politically weak. His nominal subordinates, the provincial governors, were for the most part clients of one of the two most powerful patrons in the system: the Armed Forces Commander and the State Secretary, a senior official who manages the relationship between the President and the civilian departments.[32]

Prominent examples of inter-agency conflict over turf and policy include a seemingly permanent three-way battle among the Departments of Education, Religion, and Home Affairs for control over education policy-making and implementation and an almost equally well-established fight between the Foreign and Defense Departments over control of foreign policy. More generally, there is resentment among civilian officials of military intervention in civilian affairs, including the pre-emption of key positions in all departments and the military command style of administration found in many offices.

The most central, visible, and continuing policy struggle in the New Order has been over economic issues. The market-oriented, cost- and comparative advantage-conscious professional economists (usually called 'technocrats') at the National Planning Council and the Department of Finance have been pitted against some flamboyant big-project state entrepreneurs and proponents of import-substituting industrialisation (often called 'nationalists') in the State Secretariat, the Department of Industry, and the state aircraft and petroleum companies.

In this debate, the latter have had most of the central concepts of Indonesian nationalism—anti-imperialism, anti-liberalism, pro-statism—as well as the heart of the President on their side. Culturally, the technocrats have been in a very weak position. Though they are nationalists, too, in a broader, Indonesia-first, sense of the term, within Indonesia they are easily dismissed as overly Westernised or even pro-Western.[33]

If the economists are culturally weak, how can we explain their impressive, though admittedly on-again-off-again, influence over twenty years of the New Order?[34] And does their cultural weakness mean that they are likely to be the first casualties of a change in government?

The answer to both questions is probably structural rather than cultural: the economists and their science have been instrumentally indispensable to an economic development strategy that relies heavily on foreign trade and assistance, and their future influence depends primarily on whether that strategy continues or not. But cultural weakness helps to explain the ups and downs of their influence: when the President feels less constrained by foreign exchange scarcity, he listens less to the economists and more to their culturally mainstream opponents. This analysis suggests a severe, though given enough time perhaps not fatal, limitation on the economists' ability to shift the ideological centre to the right, leaving the political economy vulnerable for the foreseeable future to the doctrines of long-dead economic thinkers of the left.

Finally, in any discussion of bureaucratic culture something should be said about corruption, which is a serious problem in bureaucracy-society relations. The government has attempted to defuse the issue by periodic arrests and trials of individuals, invariably low to middle-ranking officials, and by widely-publicised anti-corruption campaigns.

These efforts have not been very successful for at least two reasons:

the ubiquity of corruption, which means that virtually every Indonesian who deals with the state must make under-the-table payments or commit other illegal acts, and the general belief that most high officials misuse their position for private gain. Typical forms of corruption at this level are kickbacks on state contracts, skimming of state company income, and various kinds of rent-seeking arrangements such as import licenses given to friends and family. President Suharto's wife, children, and several other relatives are thought to be among the worst offenders.

In the frequent media discussions of the causes of corruption, cultural explanations are common. For example, in pre-colonial Java and other traditional kingdoms, it is said, the rulers expected gifts from their subjects, and for both giver and receiver the custom has been hard to break in the absence of any modern tradition of bureaucratic discipline. Another explanation links low government salaries with deeper loyalties to family (especially a sense of obligation to children and grandchildren) than to state or society. The pervasiveness of *bapakism* means that personal loyalties between officials are often stronger than institutional ones. And finally, the Javanese habit of deference is said to make it difficult for honest subordinates to blow the whistle on sticky-fingered superiors.

My own explanation for the seriousness of the corruption problem has less to do with culture than with the political needs (also of course financial wants) of the rulers and the lack of popular accountability in the political system. President Suharto's power and that of his New Order government are built primarily on support from the military and civilian bureaucracies. Ministerial competition for power and status within the system also requires material resources.

Corruption has been a critical means of gaining resources and support, to the point that it is now an essential—indeed, normal—aspect of most government decision-making and implementing processes. Foreign advisers, and even Indonesian officials in private conversations, tell a consistent story of informal but highly regularised patterns of obtaining and distributing funds. Contractors kick back so much for a road, so much for a school, and the heads of government offices spread the wealth in predetermined proportions to their subordinates and clients. In the absence of a more open political process, there is little that non-governmental organisations or individuals can do to oppose these arrangements.

The Intellectual and Artistic Subculture

Outside the state the subcultures of the national culture are diverse, lively, and creative. The contrast is between an official culture—the bureaucracy and military described above—whose main concern is defense of the social and political status quo and an unofficial culture pushing for greater freedom and changes in many areas of social and cultural life.[35] I have already described the political and social ideas of the *santri*, who are engaged in quite vigorous debates both within the Islamic community and between it and the larger culture. The *abangan* have fewer new ideas, perhaps because a portion of them are in power and absorbed more in execution than in creation, and perhaps also because the expression of left-wing *abangan* ideas is so dangerous.

Much of the current cultural vigour is in the fine and performing arts, where the search continues for that elusive blend of indigenousness and modernity that constitutes Indonesianness. The seekers tend to be urban, middle or upper class in living standard, and more secular than *santri* or *abangan* in their general cultural orientation (although there is both a *santri* and an *abangan* presence in the arts). In literature they have been writing serious and popular modern novels, poetry, and short stories on themes of cultural conflict and transition for more than half a century. In painting and sculpture a multi-media *Senirupa Baru* (New Visual Arts) group using a super-realist style and commercial art themes currently contends with an abstract expressionist establishment and several other currents, some more and some less Western-influenced.[36] In dance the best national choreographers, such as Sardono W. Kusumo and Bagong Kussudiardjo, are combining the freedom of Western modern dance with the themes and styles of particular local forms.

Indonesian theatre is strongly influenced by the plays of Ionesco, Beckett, Shakespeare, and the Greeks, whose idioms it uses to dissect contemporary Indonesian society, as in the 1987 production of W.S. Rendra's *Panembahan Reso*, a version of the Lear story set in classical Java but speaking to a contemporary concern with the connection between morality and political power. (Rendra seems to be arguing that power is inherently immoral and destructive.)

The very commercially-oriented film industry appeals to a low- and middle- rather than high-art audience, but also addresses social themes. For example, a comedy released in 1987 contrasts lifestyles of the rich and famous with those in a lower middle class housing development. The central character of another recent comedy, a guerrilla leader in the 1945 Revolution, is portrayed sympathetically but unsanctimoniously as an ex-petty thief who is also terrorised by his mother.

There is very little directly political life outside the state and the three established parties, but there are many private activist social groups and institutions. The Jakarta Legal Aid Society, with clones in most major cities and provinces, is a prominent example, as is the LP3ES, mentioned in the discussion of reformist Islam, which promotes modernisation through the traditional Islamic schools. Several non-governmental organisations, some Catholic or Protestant church-related, are active in local-level development projects emphasising intermediate technology and self-reliance.

Much of the national cultural discourse—artistic, social, and political— occurs in the pages of the privately owned *Kompas*, the leading Jakarta and national daily (circulation about 500,000) and *Tempo*, the premier newsweekly (circulation about 150,000), plus a small number of other general and specialised periodicals.[37] There is an influential regional press, particularly in the large markets of Java, north Sumatra, and south Sulawesi. *Kompas* and *Tempo* allot a generous proportion of space to independent columnists, and *Kompas* encourages debate by regularly soliciting specialist opinions on the issues of the day for news articles and special forums.

The attitudes of artists and intellectuals outside the state resist summarisation, but compared to army officers and officials they tend to be more open to new ideas, especially from the West, less fearful that traditional culture is being threatened, more humanist in the sense that they worry about the needs of the individual instead of those of the state or society, more democratic politically and more committed to the rule of law. Though some have spoken or acted against the Suharto government, their approach to politics is more evolutionary than revolutionary. They are also grateful for the social peace and relative prosperity they now enjoy.

A good example of the political views of the non-state intellectuals is the following introduction to a photo feature that appeared in *Tempo* for independence day, 17 August 1987. It is in sharp contrast to official independence day rhetoric, which tends to glorify the state and the collective will of the people and to claim that the Indonesian nation—the implicit definition is racial—has always existed.

> Every 17th of August we hear children singing, about this
> fatherland that they love and will not forget, about the flag that
> flutters bravely above it, about a piece of land that is holy and
> sky that is sacred and sea that is unbroken.
>   Where did all that come from?
>   Not from our plan. At one time, an archipelago enclosing 17,000
> islands was ruled by a colonial power. At another time, that power
> collapsed, and most people in the islands chose to become one.
> With great difficulty, to be sure, but they—or their leaders—
> decided not to be separated. . . . Not because they were of one
> race, not because they were of the same religion, not because they
> spoke with one accent.
>   The will to do this—a nationalist will—at bottom was a desire
> to give meaning to a coincidence: numbers of people, in all their
> diversity, were brought together in the same territory and with the
> same history, and they wanted what had been 'accidental' to have
> a purpose, not to be meaningless.
>   So, we who met along the road in this historical process then
> treated that meeting as though it were the hand of fate. After that
> we told stories about Indonesia that was united many centuries ago
> and Indonesia that will be whole until the end of time. A writer
> said, all that happened because of the magic power of nationalism:
> a nation was born because of our effort to give meaning to the
> fruit of history that fell in the garden of our experience.[38]

The freedoms to speak and work enjoyed by non-state intellectuals, artists, and activists are real but limited. Most newspapers and many magazines have been shut down on occasion and some have been closed permanently. Politically conscious university students, instrumental in the overthrow of Sukarno in the mid-1960s, see themselves as a 'moral force' with an obligation to speak truth to power. But their activism has been effectively curtailed since 1978, when tight political controls were imposed on campus organisations.[39]

Because of his critical stance toward the government, Rendra was not permitted to perform in public for several years. The books of Pramoedya Ananta Toer, Indonesia's best novelist but a prominent activist in the communist party's cultural organisation before 1965 (and a detention camp prisoner from then until 1979), are banned soon after they appear (though copies are in fact easy to obtain). Despite these restrictions, there has nonetheless begun to emerge a small group of cultural critics on the left who charge that contemporary art is elitist and internationally-oriented and does not speak to the needs or concerns of most Indonesians.

The precariousness of intellectual freedom is a result both of the pervasiveness of the officials' culture, with its belief in the state's responsibility to maintain social well-being, and the absence of any countervailing power in the society. A large autonomous indigenous business class— that is, a business class neither predominantly Chinese nor controlled by the state—still seems a long way off. As a result, the income of many intellectuals is indirectly if not directly dependent on the state.

On the other hand, an increasingly educated population is likely to continue to support cultural and social activities outside the state. According to the Central Bureau of Statistics, there were 4.4 million high school and nearly a million university graduates by 1986. Some 200,000 Indonesians are currently enrolled in the 42 state universities, and hundreds of thousands more are in private universities. The number of private lawyers and medical doctors is growing exponentially; according to *Asia Yearbook*, in 1980 and 1986 respectively there were .026 and .1 doctors per 1,000 population.[40] Economic prosperity has also made it possible for many more people to participate in cultural activities than ever before.

The Shaping of the National Political Culture

The origins of contemporary Indonesian political culture can be traced to three widely shared experiences of the first half of the twentieth century: Dutch colonialism, the adoption of Malay as the language of national unity, and the 1945–1949 revolution for independence.

Dutch colonialism in its final phases, from the latter part of the nineteenth century to the beginning of the Second World War, offered Indonesians a bureaucratic and paternalistic model of government. In the first quarter of the twentieth century, its hallmark was implementation of the so-called 'Ethical Policy', Dutch-designed programs for improvement of the quality of native life. Demands for representative institutions met only the most grudging acquiescence to a People's Council with very limited powers and restricted membership, so that among nationalists the idea of democracy remained almost entirely an abstraction. Liberalism was an ideology justifying the dominance of the indigenous economy by Europeans and Chinese. Marxism and the Leninist theory of imperialism better explained to nationalist thinkers the exploitation of Indonesian traders, farmers, and labourers that capitalism seemed to require.

Malay—now called Indonesian—was the first language only of the ethnic Malays, a small group found mainly along the eastern shores of Sumatra and in British Malaya (now Malaysia) across the Straits of Malacca. For many centuries it had been the *lingua franca* of traders throughout the archipelago and the medium through which Islam, the religion of traders, was spread. From the seventeenth to the early twentieth century it also gradually became the language of Dutch colonial administration and of the emerging, largely Indonesian Chinese, modern commercial sector.

There was little opposition from Indonesians of any religious, ethnic, or regional background to the official adoption of Malay as the language of the nationalist movement in 1928. Among its advantages were that its use was already widespread, it gave no large ethnic group a linguistic edge over the others, and it was both indigenous (unlike Dutch or the much less well known English) and at least proto-modern (as the common medium of communication in government administration and commerce). It was also a much more egalitarian language than Javanese, which is lexically two languages, containing extensive separate vocabularies (not just second person pronouns, as in many European languages) for addressing status superiors and inferiors. It thus suited the needs of a new and partially Westernised elite in the awkward position of attempting to promote itself in European nationalist terms as the natural leaders of indigenous society.

In nationalist mythology, the 1945–1949 revolution is the great popular event of modern Indonesian history, the watershed of populist nationalism. The *rakyat* (people, but as I have indicated the connotations evoke by turns elite solidarity with the masses, patronising condescension, and fear) rose as one against the attempt of the Dutch, for a time supported by the British and Americans, to return to the colony seized three years earlier by the Japanese. Among all Southeast Asians, Indonesians believe, only the Vietnamese have an equal claim to be true revolutionaries who fought for their independence. Malaysia and Singapore were given their freedom by the British, while the Philippines and Thailand are even today semi-colonies of the United States.

Revolutionary populism unquestionably had its egalitarian side, as the above image of a *levee en masse* suggests. Autonomous guerrilla forces and political organisations representing *santri*, *abangan*, and various ethnic groups popped up 'like mushrooms in the rainy season.' But in the end,

Indonesia's national revolution was more like the American than the French or the Russian, reaffirming rather than overturning the pre-revolutionary indigenous social structure. A revolution is a transformation of all values, said Mohammad Hatta, but he, Sukarno, and the other conservative leaders who dominated the nationalist leadership were fearful of the consequences of a genuine social revolution. Except in a few areas, notably east Sumatra and Aceh where many traditional rulers and their families were killed, the conservatives largely succeeded in keeping the lid on by lending their support to established Western-educated, relatively secularised local elites.

The Indonesian revolution thus combined fervent populism with conservative elitism. Already combustible, this mixture was further agitated by a number of other factors and events. The unsettled conditions of the period, which included mass evacuations of civil servants to safe areas and scorched earth policies toward advancing Dutch troops, forced postponement of the development of both bureaucratic and representative institutions.

The new national army, a motley collection of ex-Dutch, ex-Japanese, and spontaneously mobilised guerrilla forces, could not organise itself or be brought effectively under civilian control. Repeated internal disputes and policy clashes with the government produced among many officers a growing sense of independent responsibility for their own corporate integrity and for the security of the new nation: in short, a subculture containing their own version of paternalistic populism.

Finally, the idea of federalism, a natural solution to many aspects of Indonesian diversity, was virtually destroyed by association with a last-ditch colonial effort to encircle Republic-held territory with federal states whose leaders the Dutch could control or influence. When the effort failed, loyal regionalists were left without a viable alternative to the powerful centralising tendencies of Indonesian nationalism and Javanese traditional culture.

By the time of independence in 1949, the widespread commitment to the Indonesian language, plus the common experience of revolution, had built a solid foundation for national unity. But the absence of trained administrators and parliamentary politicians, plus the overabundance of leaders with mass mobilisation skills learned during the revolution, foreshadowed an era of political instability.

With the adoption of representative democratic institutions in 1950, a great struggle began among what Clifford Geertz[41] called the *aliran*— 'comprehensive patterns of social integration', that is, political parties and affiliated organisations based on the cultural divisions of Indonesian society—to give content to the ideals of nationalism and popular sovereignty. There were four major *aliran*: the Indonesian Nationalist Party (PNI) and the Indonesian Communist Party (PKI) on the *abangan* side and the reformist Masyumi and traditionalist Nahdlatul Ulama on the *santri* side.

The parliamentary election campaign of 1955, the only genuinely free national election that has ever been held in Indonesia, was a great occasion for political mobilisation. Twenty-eight parties and other organisations won seats, but the four major *aliran* took most of the vote: PNI, 22.3%; Masjumi, 20.9%; NU 18.4%; and PKI, 16.4%. In terms of popular support, PNI, PKI, and NU were all Javanese parties, while Masyumi won 75% of its vote from provinces other than east and central Java. To oversimplify slightly: PNI was the choice of the *abangan/priayi* bureaucracy, PKI of the lesser *priayi* (e.g., elementary school teachers were a major source of cadres) and *abangan* lower classes, NU of rural Javanese Islamic teachers and pious landowners, and Masyumi of urban Javanese and Outer Island merchants and business people.

The years 1955–1965 were a time of cascading crises. Parliamentary institutions had no legitimacy of their own, and no one *aliran* was able to impose its will on the others. During and after the election, *santri* and *abangan aliran* clashed over the issue of whether Indonesia should be an Islamic or a Pancasila state. In the late 1950s several regional military leaders, supported by local civilian groups and abetted by some Masyumi politicians, rebelled against tightening control from the Department of Defense, governmental centralisation in general, growing communist influence in national politics, and a number of other issues. For the whole decade of the 1950s there was little coherence or consistency in government policy-making and implementation in any area.

In the late 1950s the central army leadership and the charismatic President Sukarno, Indonesia's most formidable politician but formally only a figurehead under the parliamentary Constitution of 1950, teamed up to defeat the regional rebels and to take the country away from the parliamentary parties. Of the major parties, only PKI, which provided Sukarno with organised mass support to set against the army's control of territorial government and nationalised industries, was able to increase its clout in national politics. Masyumi was banned in 1960 for involvement in the rebellions, PNI was reduced to begging for favours at the presidential table, and NU settled for continued patronage control of the Department of Religion in exchange for legitimising Sukarno-army rule on behalf of the *santri* community.

Combining populism, paternalism, and Javanist *abangan/priayi* ideas of benevolent absolutism, Sukarno called the new system of rule Guided Democracy. For a few years many Indonesians of nearly all ideological persuasions, disenchanted with representative democracy and without a clear alternative conception of their own, genuinely accepted his claim to be the 'extension of the people's tongue'. By 1963–64, however, it was clear that the Sukarno-army coalition had become a highly unstable army-Sukarno-PKI time bomb, order-minded army and revolution-minded communist party kept apart only by an increasingly frantic president now devoid of genuine political ideas.

The bomb exploded in the early morning of 1 October 1965, when a group of radical young army officers from the presidential palace guard, with some navy and air force backing and the assistance of communist party youth, kidnapped and assassinated six senior army generals. The conspiracy was badly planned and poorly executed, and Major-General Suharto, in command of strategic troops in the Jakarta area, quickly took control of the armed forces and arrested the plotters. Retaliation against the communist party began immediately, and by 1967 perhaps half a million party and affiliated organisation members and sympathisers had been killed.

General Suharto moved more cautiously against President Sukarno, first seizing substantial executive power in March 1966, then accepting appointment, by a People's Consultative Assembly stripped of Sukarnoists, as Acting President in March 1967 and full President in March 1968. General elections, tightly controlled by Suharto through his command of the army and the civilian bureaucracy, have since been held in 1971, 1977, 1982, and 1987. A newly constituted People's Consultative Assembly (40% of its members are chosen in the election, the other 60% by appointment processes controlled by the President) meets after each election. Suharto has been reelected President by this body in March of 1973, 1978, 1983, and 1988.

The New Order and Indonesian Culture

How has the national culture fared under Suharto's New Order government? Reflecting on the consequences of the 1965–66 massacre of communists, Clifford Geertz wrote: 'Emotions surface extremely gradually, if extremely powerfully, in Indonesia: 'The crocodile is quick to sink,' they say, 'but slow to come up.'[42] In a widely discussed article, the Dutch sociologist W.F. Wertheim speculated about the future radicalisation of poorer *santri* as well as *abangan* under the military's jackboot.[43]

Benedict Anderson, in a seminal essay on 'The Languages of Indonesian Politics' written at the end of Guided Democracy, saw Indonesian culture as succumbing to Javanisation. The early revolutionary thrust of the national language, *bahasa Indonesia*, had run out of steam. 'Forming a new and thin topsoil to the cultures of Indonesia, it has proved only too liable to suffer erosion once the winds of change begin to blow.' At the level of elite discourse—comparable to high status Javanese—Indonesian was becoming impersonal, neuter, and formal, weighted down with 'politically polite' Sanskrit and Old Javanese loan words. At the mass level, the earthy and intimate lower class Jakarta dialect of *bahasa Indonesia* had taken on a more positive, deflating or pretension-pricking, role comparable to low status Javanese. In the political climate of late Guided Democracy, what was expressed in Jakarta dialect was 'deepening social conflicts and tensions . . . hatreds . . . turned inward on the society itself . . .'[44]

So far at least, neither Geertz's nor Wertheim's guesses have proved out. At the high status end, Anderson's lexical and structural Javanisation of Indonesian language and culture is still the despair of the intellectuals (including quite a few Javanese), who pepper their critiques of official culture with such epithets as 'feudal' and 'Mataram-complex' (Mataram was the last major central Javanese kingdom). Equally disheartening, in the Andersonian perspective, Jakarta dialect seems no longer to be a lower class weapon against upper class linguistic or political domination, or indeed to be very political at all. Instead, it has become the language of pampered youth, pop culture, and the criminal underclass.

Despite these trends, Anderson's worst fear for the national culture, that it was losing its revolutionary drive, has not been realised. Instead, three things have happened. First, the New Order, albeit in hierarchical Javanist terms, has offered its own version of revolution in the form of *pembangunan* (development), a vast petroleum-fueled program of economic modernisation that has altered for the better the lives of the majority of Indonesians.

Obvious examples of the successful meeting of government policy and popular aspirations for a 'just and prosperous society' (in the common Indonesian populist expression) are the small-holder rice program, which more than doubled output from 12 to 25 million tons in less than twenty years, and the Presidential Instruction Village School program, which has put a primary school within reach of virtually every Indonesian child. New Order-style development has been especially welcomed by military and civilian officials because it combines so well—and so advantageously for their interests—the paternalistic and populist elements of the national culture. It also fits the Javanist benevolence-obedience ideal. But there is very little objection from any group, *santri* or *abangan*, Javanese or Outer Islander, to the principle of *pembangunan*.[45]

Second, the New Order has offered political peace under a single firm, authoritative if authoritarian, leader after two decades of near chaos from the beginning of the Japanese occupation in 1942 to the assassination of the generals and the mass killings and arrests of 1965–66. Many Outer Island groups had suffered from the regional rebellions of the 1950s and were ready to accept any non-communist government. According to Clifford Geertz, Javanese villagers' attempts in the 1950s at reorganising their social lives along political party lines had left them more vulnerable than other groups to the fall-out from partisan clashes in Jakarta.[46] Moreover, among *abangan* Javanese villagers, the idea that a period of chaos will be followed in a cyclical or oscillating pattern by a period of peace and prosperity is thought to be widely accepted, as is the idea of an absolute ruler.

Third, the New Order's Javanism has been open, flexible, and tolerant enough to give other groups room to maneuver within or beneath it.

Sometimes this has been deliberate policy, but often it is an indirect side-effect. A small example of indirection is the impact of the new fashionability of traditional Javanese costumes and customs, including the study of *Javanologi* in government-supported institutes. In response, other groups have seized the opportunity to celebrate their own ethnicity and to establish institutes of *Baliologi, Batakologi,* and so on. Every governor's office now sponsors a traditional (actually very 'nationalised' in style and content) dance troupe which entertains official guests. At least in Sumatra, there is an annual island-wide competition among these troupes.

A larger and more deliberate example of the New Order's flexibility is its Islamic policy. The basic objective has been to support Islam 'as a system of worship and basis for moral living' but not to recognise it as a legitimate political ideology.[47] In the early 1980s all social—including religious—organisations were required to make the state doctrine Pancasila their *asas tunggal* (single fundamental principle). Implementation of this and similar policies has necessarily brought the government into conflict with many Islamic groups, and relations remain tense.[48]

At the same time, the government has shown itself willing to compromise on a number of issues, from the marriage bill controversy of 1973 to the location of the office of non-religious beliefs in the Department of Education to the refusal of Indonesian Catholic requests for a state visit by the Pope. It builds mosques by the tens of thousands, sponsors an official biennial national Qur'an reading competition, gives assistance to Muslim schools, teaches religion in the public schools, and consults regularly with Muslim leaders in the corporatist *Majelis Ulama Indonesia* (Indonesian Islamic Teachers' Assembly), state-sponsored national and regional councils of respected Islamic leaders.

It should also be recalled that Javanism as a religious system is syncretic and so already contains Islamic elements that can be used by the state to approach the *umat.* The *halal bil halal* ritual, when subordinates come to pay their respects to superiors at the end of the fasting month, has become an important New Order institution (though unknown in the Middle East), as has the use of Islamic salutations and prayers at official meetings and ceremonies of all kinds.

Taken together, Suharto's leadership, the generally non-aggressive, non-mobilisational cultural policy, and development-induced prosperity have ironically undermined the hegemony of the New Order's own official version of the national culture. One prominent result of this process is the current creativity of Islamic social and political thought. Another is the subculture of the new non-state intelligentsia, which is not only in opposition to the official culture but holds many of the social and institutional levers directing linguistic and cultural development today.

Twenty years ago, at the end of the Guided Democracy period of rhetorical excess combined with mass mobilisation, it was possible to despair, with Anderson, of the future of the Indonesian language and culture, as one had in the mid-1940s despaired of the cultural future of post-Hitler Germany. Today, a powerful state imposes its hierarchical, high status Javanist version of the national language and culture on the society, but not without significant challenge. To read *Tempo*, *Kompas*, *Prisma*, or a modern novel or short story, to watch a play, a movie, or a dance performance, or to go to an art gallery, is to recognise that there is a vital and dynamic alternative to officialese in the modern culture itself.

Sukarno's Guided Democracy aimed at radical cultural transformation—the creation of *manusia Indonesia baru* (the new Indonesian human being)—but by enforcing conformity to official doctrine across all dimensions of life, totalitarian-style, stifled genuine cultural change. The New Order has a similar goal, though the formulation is characteristically conservative and Javanist: *manusia Indonesia seutuhnya*, the complete, or whole, Indonesian human being.

In that formulation there is perhaps a clue to a cultural explanation—a social vision that is Javanist but also modern and that includes some flexibility, openness, and tolerance—for the New Order's development programs, its absolute ruler, and its policies toward the political and cultural opposition. If the explanation helps us to understand the government's longevity, in contrast to Guided Democracy's brevity, it also locates some of the probable sources of future cultural and political change.

Conclusions

The attitudes and orientations described in this paper constrain, condition, and shape the domestic and foreign political behaviour of Indonesian politicians. But their predictive value in terms of specific policies is limited by their complexity and by the contexts in which they must be placed. The complexity is clear: I have described a national culture still in formation, two major (and many lesser) traditional cultures which influence its development, and three important subcultures within the national culture itself. Two kinds of contexts raise difficulties. Within the individual, cultural variables represent only one element in explaining motivation. Externally, since policy decisions are inescapably tied to time and place, changing domestic and foreign players, circumstances, and opportunities must be taken into account.[49]

With these caveats, it is possible to offer a few general propositions. First, Indonesia's often proclaimed 'free and active' foreign policy slogan rests on a solid foundation of national identity. Within the society some groups (e.g. the army, universalist Muslims) are more and some (e.g., the foreign ministry, the artistic and intellectual community) less suspicious of the outside world, but except for the people of East Timor and Irian Jaya all are Indonesia-firsters.

For this reason, it is in my view simplistic and misleading to see Sukarno as anti-West because of his opposition to Malaysia or his promotion of a Beijing-Jakarta axis, and Suharto as pro-West because of his anti-communism and willingness to accept foreign economic assistance. One of the most interesting questions about Suharto's relations with the West, in fact, has been his much greater reluctance to accept foreign investment in contrast to assistance. At least part of the explanation for this difference lies in the national culture's (and military subculture's) arm's length view of the West and historic belief that foreign capitalists are imperialists, plus the populist commitment to the development of the indigenous economy.

Second, the belief in popular sovereignty combined with the present authoritarian form of government means that the search for genuinely representative political institutions is not yet over. Pancasila Democracy, as Suharto labels the constitutional and political arrangements that have elected him President five times since 1968, is not without its adherents, as I have tried to show, especially from within the *abangan* community. But it has many *santri* challengers, and Islamic devoutness, if not yet political activism, is on the rise in Indonesia as it is everywhere in the Islamic world. Among free intellectuals, there is also very little positive ideological support for the official political culture (as opposed to grudging and partial acceptance of the peace and prosperity the New Order has brought). My point is not to predict upheaval, which I do not think will happen any time soon, but rather a long term struggle of ultimately indeterminate outcome.

Finally, in the short to medium run, and even if there is upheaval, the political system will continue to be dominated by an *abangan* President. The primary reason for this is structural rather than cultural: the army, which happens to be strongly Javanist, commands more political resources than any of its competitors. But some of these resources are cultural. One is the officers' conviction, which shows no signs of lessening, of their right to rule, as expressed in the 'twin functions' doctrine. Another is the intensity with which the *abangan* hold to their beliefs, indeed the growing vitality of mysticism and mystical organisations over the last two decades. A third is the consensual and accommodating tendencies of the New Order's paternalistic populist 'political formula' for governing. Development and Pancasila, as I have described these central symbols, exemplify both the core beliefs of the *abangan* rulers and their genuine effort to define the national political culture in more encompassing terms.

1. It is not absolute, however. Several Outer Island ethnic groups, e.g. the Bugis of South Sulawesi, have aristocratic or quasi-aristocratic traditions that have begun to revive in recent years, in parallel and partially in response to a similar development in Java.

2. The one partial exception to this generalisation is *bahasa Malaysia*, the national language of Malaysia, which is essentially the same language as *bahasa Indonesia*. But Malaysia is a small—and, to Indonesian eyes, provincial—country, and the cultural influences today run almost entirely from Indonesia to Malaysia.

3. The first, and still the only, summary description of the national culture is Hildred Geertz, 'Indonesian Cultures and Communities,' in Ruth McVey (ed), *Indonesia*, New Haven: Yale University Press, 1963, pp. 32–41. Geertz's analysis of what she calls the 'metropolitan superculture', based on observations made in the 1950s, is surprisingly up to date. Perhaps the major change, as the difference in our labels suggests, is the breadth and depth achieved by the national culture today.

4. A recent interview with the writer and educator Budidarma in the Jakarta daily *Kompas* gives a good feel for the perception of a pull between East and West in New Order literary circles. Notice, however, Budidarma's tendency to define what is Indonesian in traditional subcultural terms.

Q. What is the meaning of Indonesianness in your writing?
A. I am happy and proud to be an Indonesian. But in my writing, I can write because I tap the experience and thought of the West. The connection between my Indonesianness and my writing is difficult to formulate exactly. But certainly I feel it.

It's the same with [other Indonesian writers]. I think that if they had not been in contact with Western thought and culture they could not write as they do. But whether we like it or not we are Indonesians. If we were from Samoa, Fiji, or Nauru, we'd be different. So the Western education and way of thinking that we've absorbed has become one with the reality that we're Indonesians, with the result that we produce the works we do.
Q. But that means you're making it a very small factor. The influence of local culture is just the same as the influence of the culture of one's family, for example.
A. We clearly depend on Western culture. That's clear. Is the meaning of Indonesianness as limited as that? Hard to say, isn't it?
Q. What is your attitude toward the great influence Western culture has on our culture?
A. We can't avoid facts. And in this matter Western culture has a very wide influence on life in Indonesia. But we ourselves have an identity. This is not only reflected in our sub-cultures, but also in our desire to reexamine them. So the fact of Western cultural influence can be considered a blessing or a threat.

Now we are beginning to ask who we are. We are beginning to return to the roots of our culture, even though when we talk about it we're very superficial. But nonetheless there's an effort by each of us to know ourselves. Just as America after World War I, seeing a threat, began to look at itself by creating 'American Studies.' They studied their subcultures, their economy, their state in a planned way. A step like this will make us more unified, more knowledgeable about ourselves. And defense against the harmful aspects of outside culture will take place by itself.
Q. As a writer, what's Indonesia's basic problem in your opinion?
A. That our identity is not yet clear. We are still at the formulating stage,

still looking. And up till now we're making decisions based on our instinct. But I don't mean this in a political sense. (*Kompas*, 29 November 1987: 2).

5. Though little discussed today, the basis of Indonesian nationhood is in fact not a settled issue. The Republic of Indonesia is the successor state to Netherlands India, and a historically accurate reading of archipelagic history lets the matter rest there. But such a pragmatic view does not satisfy the emotional need of many Indonesians to deny the Dutch role and to possess an ancient past. Most official pronouncements since independence, especially those for foreign consumption, stress the successor state principle. On some occasions, however—for example, when the 1975–76 takeover of Portuguese Timor is being justified—one hears references to the culture and history of a single race. A few nationalist leaders in the 1940s talked of the 'Malay race' as a political community. See also the section on The Shaping of the National Culture below.

6. I once asked my Javanese language instructor, a small town junior high school English teacher, how he behaved as a Javanese and as an Indonesian. He responded by assuming a hunched-shoulders half-bowing submissive position to demonstrate Javaneseness and then stood erect as an Indonesian. I should add that though at that moment he was expressing his frustration with the demands of Javanese deference, he in fact lived happily in both worlds.

7. At the other end of the scale, in Jakarta and a few other large cities there are individuals without ties to a local culture. Their number is probably increasing (as is the number of Indonesians who are losing their Indonesianness after prolonged stays abroad and/or adoption of a jet-set life style) but is a minuscule part of the total.

8. No other country in Southeast Asia is as blessed with an autonomous modern culture capable simultaneously of incorporating domestic diversity and establishing a secure foundation for external relations. Vietnamese and Thais, who have histories of repelling foreigners, face the outside world confidently enough. But their national identities are indistinguishable from the cultures of the majority ethnic groups, leaving their many minorities with no way to relate to the larger society or to the outside world.

Filipinos suffer from a long history of Spanish and American cultural imperialism. Though there is a distinct national identity which overarches ethnic pluralism, its lack of indigenousness and vulnerability to foreign influences are major weaknesses. Malays in Malaysia have tried unsuccessfully to impose their ethnic culture on a very large Chinese minority, and Singapore is still struggling to escape the cultural implications of its origins as an entrepot with a largely transient population.

9. Earlier ideas nonetheless continue to be influential. In 1976, for example, an obscure former government official with an interest in Javanese mysticism claimed to have been given a divine revelation that he was to replace Suharto as president. The mystic was convicted on a charge of subversion after a trial that received nearly as much press and public attention as the Nixon impeachment hearings in the United States. See David Bourchier, *Dynamics of Dissent in Indonesia: Sawito and the Phantom Coup*, Ithaca: Cornell Modern Indonesia Project, 1984.

10. Herbert Feith, who wrote the classic study of Indonesian politics in the 1950s, called this the 'holistic perspective.' 'Introduction', in Herbert Feith and Lance Castles (eds), *Indonesian Political Thinking, 1945–1965*, Cornell University Press, 1970.
   Feith also saw two other common characteristics in 1950s political culture which in my view are not visible today: an obsession with the moral strengths and weaknesses of individual politicians to the virtual exclusion of concern with institutions and procedures; and an unrealistically optimistic voluntarist view 'that all things could be achieved if men approached them in the right frame of mind.' (p. 20) In 1980s Indonesia an attitude of optimism has certainly been prevalent in official circles, but it is firmly grounded in a history of development successes over more than twenty years. There is necessarily less public debate about leadership and institutions in the authoritarian 1980s than there was in the democratic 1950s. To be sure, much underground criticism focuses on the moral weaknesses of the president and members of his family, but there is also concern with such institutional and structural issues as the power of the military, the impotence of Parliament, and the political consequences of participation in (or dependence on) the world capitalist economy.
11. 'Cartoons and Monuments: The Evolution of Political Communication under the New Order,' in Karl D. Jackson and Lucian W. Pye, *Political Power and Communications in Indonesia*, Los Angeles & London: University of California Press, 1978, p. 295.
12. The best account I have seen of the range of Indonesian Islamic reformist social and political thinking today is Fachry Ali and Bahtiar Effendy, *Merambah Jalan Baru Islam: Rekonstruksi Pemikiran Islam Indonesia Masa Orde Baru*, Jakarta: Mizan, 1987.
13. On the election, see William Liddle, *Indonesia in 1987: The New Order at the Height of its Power*, Asian Survey, 28: 180–191 (1988). As a political party (though the leaders avoid the use of that label, which in the military/bureaucratic culture connotes divisiveness) Golkar was put together in 1969, out of an assemblage of army-led anti-communist organisations first formed in 1964, to contest the 1971 general election on behalf of the government. In 1971 it won 62.8% of the vote and in 1987, 73%. Golkar is not an autonomous party, but rather the electoral face of the New Order's military and bureaucratic rulers.
14. Some of the criticism comes from a still influential group of NU leaders, former political activists (rather than religious teachers) for the most part, who want NU to return to its former role as an independent political party.
15. The struggle for the Javanese soul has been going on for a long time. Here is a powerful passage from a 1938 novel, *Belenggu*, in which a medical doctor is being reproved for neglecting his wife by the wife's traditional Javanese uncle:

> You young kids of today's generation are impatient. Always in a hurry. You want to be dynamic, you say. What's the difference between dynamic and static? Static is the real dynamic, the genuine one. Intellect you say, that's what's highest, you forget, many matters can't be understood with the intellect, but only with intuition. Science, knowledge, logic, you worship, you regard higher than spirit. Doesn't that science you study, medicine, connect the secrets

of nature with mankind, as the basis for medication? You want to use only things visible to the eye, the rest you regard as lies, that which can only be seen with the spirit, you ridicule.

The doctor answers:

No, uncle, you want to take science to the field of magic. You want to follow *dukun* [traditional healers], who act as though they have magical powers, but who knows if they are liars or not? How many of our people have been led astray by *dukun* with magic powers? You want to worship them. You want to let them keep the people ignorant? No uncle, the science that uses the smoke of incense, that intoxicates thought, that carries thought to the world of magic power, to the world of illusion, of genies and fairies, bury that world deep, uncle. Reality, uncle, a little reality, knowing how to choose, knowing how to investigate, our people dream too much, uncle, take them to the world of reality a little, teach them to think in an orderly way, systematically. Don't take them to the world of magic where truth can't be tested, don't take them to the world of dreams, meditating for thousands of years, flat on your back on the ground.

—Armijn Pane, *Belenggu*, Third Edition, Jakarta: Pustaka Rakyat, 1949, pp. 99–100. Available in English as Armijn Pane, *Shackles*. Translated by John H. McGlynn, Athens: Ohio University Center for International Studies.

This passage is as fresh today as when it was written fifty years ago. Indeed, it is echoed in an ironic way by a recent *cause celebre* in the medical profession, in which a prominent Bandung doctor was expelled from the Indonesian Doctors' Association for claiming to be able to cure cancer with a secret medicine prepared in his own laboratory. He had violated the code of ethics of his profession, said a statement from the Association, for refusing to submit his formula to the scientific community for proper testing. The doctor's license was revoked, but he continues to practice as a *dukun*. Some commentators suggested that he had now become a *terkun* (part *dokter*, part *dukun*).

16. *Kompas*, 16 January 1988: 1.
17. In the government's bureaucratese, KISS stands for *Kordinasi, Integrasi, Simplifikasi*, and *Sinkronisasi*; but less reverent Jakartans say it stands for *Ke Istana Sendiri-Sendiri*, To the Palace One-by-One.
18. *Kompas*, 17 January 1988: 7.
19. The *santri* tend to be more hostile toward domestic Chinese business than the *abangan*. In part this is because the devout Muslim traders are in direct competition with the Chinese, and in part it is because in the past as in the present Javanese rulers have used the Chinese, who possess considerable entrepreneurial skills but as 'foreigners' are politically weak, to create wealth for them. Many lower-class *abangan*, however, dislike and resent the Chinese.
20. It is also true, however, that much more attention has been paid to the building of a structure of law in the New Order than during the prior Guided Democracy period. Notable achievements are the marriage law, the criminal procedure law, and new tax laws that are apparently being implemented with much less favouritism than before. Moreover, Suharto's primary public claim to legitimacy as President is legal-rational, that is, that he has upheld the Constitution of 1945. None of this behaviour seems attributable to Javanese ideas.

21. See for example Soemarsaid Moertono, *State and Statecraft in Old Java*, Ithaca: Cornell University Modern Indonesia Project, 1968, and Benedict Anderson, *The Idea of Power in Javanese Culture*, in Claire Holt (ed.), *Culture and Politics in Indonesia*, Ithaca: Cornell University, 1972. There is, however, an alternative tradition of anthropological analysis that stresses corporate and even egalitarian aspects of village Java. See in particular Robert R. Jay, *Javanese Villagers: Social Relations in Rural Mojokuto*, Cambridge: MIT, 1969; Patrick Guinness, *Harmony and Hierarchy in a Javanese Kampung*, Kuala Lumpur: Oxford University, 1986, and Robert W. Hefner, *Hindu Javanese: Tengger Tradition and Islam*, Princeton: Princeton University, 1985. A recent book by Ward Keeler (*Javanese Shadow Plays, Javanese Selves*, Princeton: Princeton University, 1987) describes the tensions caused by Javanese villagers' simultaneous respect for hierarchy and authority and desire for personal autonomy. Anderson's essay—the most original piece of writing in English on Indonesian politics since independence—attempts both to describe traditional Javanese political culture and to show how contemporary Javanese politicians are influenced by it. Its biggest weakness is that it assesses Presidents Sukarno's and Suharto's behaviour directly in old Javanese terms, as though the twentieth century and its cultural consequences for Indonesian politicians who happen also to be Javanese had not occurred. If contemporary Indonesian national culture is both modern and indigenous, as I have argued, then Anderson's analysis offers at best only half an understanding.

22. It is also not totally absent from other Indonesian cultures.

23. A Jakarta newspaper recently published a photograph of a well-known retired Acehnese politician in what appeared to be a submissive Javanese-style bowing position before President Suharto in the president's office. Most Acehnese with whom I discussed the photograph found it embarrassing and demeaning, both un-Acehnese and un-Indonesian, demonstrating that benevolence-obedience is not yet a universal Indonesian norm. (Aceh's own aristocrats were killed or driven into exile in 1946 and have yet to make a comeback.)

24. See for example Sartono Kartodirdjo, *Protest Movements in Rural Java: A Study of Agrarian Unrest in the 19th and Early 20th Centuries*, Singapore: University of Singapore, 1973; and Harry J. Benda and Lance Castles, *The Samin Movement*, Bijdragen tot de Taal-, Land-, en Volkenkunde, 125: 208–240 (1969).

25. C.W. Watson, 'Some Preliminary Remarks on the Antecedents of Modern Indonesian Literature', Bijdragen tot de Taal-, Land-, en Volkenkunde, 127: 427: 417–433, 1971; Claudine Lombard-Salmon, 'Aux origines de la litterature Sino Malaise: un syair publicitaire de 1886', Archipel 8: 155–86, 1974.

26. S. Said, *Profil Dunia Film Indonesia*, Jakarta: Grafiti, 1982.

27. A typical example of the lengths to which this attitude is carried is the restriction on public meetings during the month before the March 1988 People's Consultative Assembly session which reelected Suharto for the 1988–1993 term. University students, always considered a potentially disruptive group, were not allowed to visit each others' campuses or to conduct research in groups. The Department of Education instructed regional officials to search school libraries for subversive books, and a resident of Malang, East Java, was told by the authorities to withdraw a civil suit against a cigarette manufacturer

'to maintain social peace' before the Assembly session. *Tempo*, 6 February 1988: 25.

28. *Tempo*, 19 September 1987: 17.

29. On the dissident generals, see David Jenkins, *Suharto and His Generals: Indonesian Military Politics 1975–1983*, Ithaca: Cornell Modern Indonesia Project, 1984.

30. The former Minister of Home Affairs, Gen. (ret.) Amirmachmud, once claimed in response to public criticism of government development policy that the state had contributed much more to development than the people, who therefore had no grounds for complaint. What he apparently had in mind was the large share of state income generated by the oil tax, which is levied on foreign companies, in comparison with taxes on the population. The remark is typical of official attitudes.

31. The position of women in the bureaucratic variant of the national culture is perhaps best described as 'bourgeois respectability', not so different from the dominant current in the West today. Women are encouraged to educate themselves and seek careers, but admonished to always place their roles as wives and mothers first. Mainstream Islamic thinking on this subject is only marginally more restrictive than *abangan*. At the time of independence, for example, if the *santri* had had control of the national educational system they would have segregated the sexes while still offering modern education to all.

32. In March 1988 the Armed Forces Commander, Gen. L.B. Moerdani, and the State Secretary, Lt. Gen. (ret) Soedharmono, became Defense Minister and Vice-President respectively.

33. On the nationalism of the economists, see Bruce Glassburner, *Political Economy and the Soeharto Regime*, Bulletin of Indonesian Economic Studies, 14: 26–51 (1978).

34. The technocrats dominated economic policy-making from the mid-1960s to the early 1970s, and have been on the ascendance again in the 1980s. They hold most of the key economic positions in the 1988–1993 cabinet appointed in March 1988.

35. Although in defense of the state it should be said that the New Order's economic policies are in the main the very creative product of a group of professional economists, trained in the United States, who work in the National Development Planning Council, the Department of Finance, and other economic agencies.

36. *Tempo*, 27 June 1987: 35–38; and 25 July 1987: 77–78.

37. According to Department of Information statistics, total printed media circulation in 1984 was over 5 million.

38. (*Tempo*, 22 August 1987: 21). Note the extra effort at being completely honest in the phrase 'or their leaders'.

39. Before 1965, the most politically active student groups were *abangan* and leftist. Since 1965, Outer Island *santri*, particularly those affiliated with the reformist HMI (*Himpunan Mahasiswa Islam*, Islamic University Students Association), have dominated student politics at most universities.

40. Far Eastern Economic Review, *Asia Yearbook*, Hong Kong, 1980: 10; 1986: 6.

41. C. Geertz, 'The Javanese Village', in G. William Skinner (ed), *Local, Ethnic, and National Loyalties in Village Indonesia*, Ithaca: Cornell Modern Indonesia Project, 1959, p. 37.

42. C. Geertz, 'Afterword: The Politics of Meaning', in Claire Holt (ed) *Culture and Politics in Indonesia*, Ithaca: Cornell University, 1972, p. 333.
43. W.F. Wertheim, *From Aliran Toward Class Struggle in the Countryside of Java*, Pacific Viewpoint 10: 1–17, 1969.
44. B. Anderson, 'The Languages of Indonesian Politics', *Indonesia* 1: 89–116, 1966.
45. The best overall account of economic development under the New Order is Anne Booth and Peter McCawley, *The Indonesian Economy During the Soeharto Era*, Kuala Lumpur: Oxford University, 1981. The term *pembangunan* was deliberately chosen for its broad appeal, in contrast, say, to *modernisasi*, which for devout Muslims implies *sekularisasi*. There is, of course, controversy over such questions as growth versus distribution and governmental corruption.
46. C. Geertz, 'The Javanese Village', 1959, op. cit., p. 40.
47. Howard M. Federspiel, *The Position and Role of Islam in Suharto's Indonesian New Order at the 21st Year Mark*, 1988, p. 2. Paper prepared for presentation at the 1988 Annual Meeting of the the the Southeast Conference, Association for Asian Studies, Charlotte: North Carolina. This is also, as has frequently been commented on, the basis of the Dutch government's Islamic policy, as recommended by its chief Islamic adviser C. Snouck Hurgronje, in the early twentieth century.
48. Half a decade after the policy was first announced, at least two large organisations with national constituencies are still refusing to change their by laws: the universalist reformist *santri* PII (*Pelajar Islam Indonesia*, Indonesian Islamic [Secondary] Students Association) and the *abangan* GPM (*Gerakan Pemuda Marhaenis*, Marhaenist Youth Movement), currently led by a daughter of the late President Sukarno. 'Marhaenism' was Sukarno's version of populism.
49. An object lesson in the pitfalls of cultural analysis is Benedict Anderson's argument (*The Idea of Power in Javanese Culture*, in Claire Holt (ed.), *Culture and Politics in Indonesia*, Ithaca: Cornell University, 1972, pp. 30–31), that the pattern of Indonesian foreign policy can in part be explained by the Hindu-Javanese concept of *mandala* (circle of influence), according to which 'A state's belligerence is in the first place directed towards its closest neighbour(s), thus making necessary the friendship of the state next to the foe . . .' This explanation works well enough for President Sukarno's hostility toward neighbouring Malaysia, and for his friendship with China, but can not explain Suharto's hostility toward China and support for ASEAN (Association of Southeast Asian Nations, including Thailand, Malaysia, Singapore, Indonesia, Brunei, and the Philippines). The quote is taken by Anderson from Soemarsaid Moertono, *State and Statecraft in Old Java*, Ithaca: Cornell University Modern Indonesia Project, 1968.

4

The Relative Autonomy of the Third World Politician: Suharto and Indonesian Economic Development in Comparative Perspective*

> Scholars should pay more attention to the capacity for autonomous choice on the part of local actors, both public and private, and give greater weight to the importance of these choices in shaping the impact of external environments upon the structure of the local societies.[1]

Introduction: Development, Policies, and Politics

A time line tracing the history of economic growth in independent Indonesia rises gently in the early 1950s, peaks and begins to decline in the mid- to late-1950s, plunges deeply into an abyss of negative growth in the mid-1960s, completely reverses itself in the late 1960s, and begins a steep ascent that slows briefly in the early 1980s before resuming its upward climb. During the boom years, 1969–1982, the annual growth rate averaged nearly 8 percent. By 1989, after a few soft years mid-decade, it had bounced back to 7.4 percent.[2]

Distribution of the benefits of economic growth, the other half of the development package, is not as easily measured as growth. It is also a controversial subject. In the early 1980s, a major study of the Indonesian economy[3] concluded that Jakarta, the national capital, had grown fastest, followed by other cities on Java (by far the most populous island), cities elsewhere, rural Java, and finally rural areas outside Java. The authors also argued, however, that 'real expenditure in both urban and rural

* First published in *International Studies Quarterly*, 35, 4 (December 1991), pp. 403–27.

107

area of Java appears to have increased between 1970 and 1976, for all deciles of the population'.[4] By the end of the decade, though the debate was still lively, positive assessments seemed to be gaining on negative ones.[5]

What accounts for this pattern, particularly for the dramatic growth reversal in the mid-1960s and for the sustained quality of the recovery, which continues even now? Since most Third World countries want development, are the factors responsible for Indonesia's success replicable elsewhere?

At one level, there is a clear answer to the first question: government policies. In a recent study, the economists Bruce Glassburner and Anwar Nasution[6] describe four critical late 1960s–early 1970s policy changes and their consequences. First, liberalisation of the foreign exchange regime, which since 1970 has meant free convertibility of the rupiah, 'facilitated rapid growth of international trade.' Second, interest rate adjustment eliminating negative real rates allowed private investment 'to participate in a vigorous way in residential and business construction, and in creation of industrial and commercial sector fixed capital'.

Third, a program of local government investment decisions supported by direct grants from the central government was 'remarkably successful in fostering the rehabilitation and expansion of basic infrastructure'. Finally, elimination of the previous government's overregulation 'increased the efficiency of the system, raised the rate of return on investment, and thereby contributed to growth'. To this short list of policies with a broad impact could be added a much longer one of more narrowly targeted policies, for example in rice, family planning, and most recently export manufacturing, banking, and the development of a stock market.

Explanation in terms of policy, though often heard from economists, and probably correct as far as it goes, does not put the minds of political scientists to rest. Why, we want to know further, do some governments adopt the right policies while others do not?

My explanation of the Indonesian case—which I suspect has broader Third World implications—centres on the political choices of the key policy maker in the system, President Suharto, in power from 1966 to the present. It argues that Suharto's choices were voluntary or autonomous, not driven by some antecedent determinant. This analysis differs from most studies of the causes of economic success or failure, in Indonesia and elsewhere, which attempt to isolate some powerful forces located in social or political structure or culture, the domestic or international arena, that precede and determine the outcome of the political process.

I will not argue, however, that political choices take place in a vacuum. Indeed, in my view the route to understanding why some governments produce the right policies and others do not is to connect in a concrete, situationally specific way the political considerations of policy makers with the structural, cultural, domestic, and international contexts in which they act. The connective tissues binding the two sides of this equation are the policy makers' perceptions, goals and calculations.

In the Indonesian case, I will try to show how President Suharto's economic policy decisions were conditioned or influenced but not determined by four variables widely cited but often misconceived and misapplied in the Indonesian and comparative literature. These variables are: economic crisis; international economic forces; culture, particularly in the form of leadership ideology; and regime type, specifically patrimonialism. Each, I will claim, has an impact on policy, but only as it has been filtered through President Suharto's perceptions of their nature and impact, goals for himself and his society, and calculations of how best to achieve his goals.

When measured against the common wisdom concerning the typical impact of the four variables, this filtering process produces some surprising findings. Economic crisis does seem to have played a substantial role in changing policy, but only in the context of three other factors—political crisis, the availability of a persuasive (to Suharto) package of promarket economic reforms, and the president's grasp of the linkage between promarket policies and political support—pushing in the same direction.

Related to the impact of crisis is the equally important—but neglected in the comparative literature—variable of the impact of success. Suharto's success in overcoming the first and most serious economic crisis of his regime with promarket policies has been a major factor conditioning his similar responses in subsequent, lesser crises.

International economic forces, conceived as dependence on Western and Japanese capitalism, are the perennial *bêtes noires* of leftist scholarship on the Third World.[7] In my analysis, international capitalism appears in the much tamer guise of Suharto's and other policy makers' perceptions of an opportunity to acquire valuable resources of assistance, investments, and markets. These resources have not been seen as threatening Indonesia's economic independence or its growth potential. To the contrary, their measured utilisation has been an integral part of the policies, recommended by the president's own domestic economic advisers, that have been responsible for the country's remarkable growth record.

Culture has been a heavily relied on *deus ex machina* at least since the publication of Max Weber's *The Protestant Ethic and the Spirit of Capitalism* (1930). In the early postwar years of development theorising, it was frequently cited, perhaps more by economists than by anthropologists, as a major impediment to modernisation.[8] Its recent revival owes much to attempts to use popular or elite beliefs based on doctrines derived from Confucianism to explain the extraordinary economic successes of Korea, Taiwan, Hongkong, Singapore, and even Japan.[9]

In the Indonesian case, most members of the elite and the politically aware public (we know less about the masses) hold pro-state, antiforeign, anticapitalist beliefs and attitudes. How, then, has the government adopted policies that can be construed as antistate, proforeign, and procapitalist? The apparent contradiction is resolved when we look, as I believe Suharto does, at culture not as a fixed set of narrowly defined ideas directly determining policy but as diverse, complex, shifting, and poly-interpretable by a skilful politician whose own values and goals are diverse and complex.

Third World patrimonialism, as a regime type, has suffered from very bad press.[10] Political leaders, it is asserted, tend to adopt antimarket policies in order to satisfy particularist clienteles, with negative results for the economy. In Indonesia, however, patrimonial rule does not seem to have been a significant obstacle to the adoption of market-oriented growth policies. The reason, in my view, is Suharto's discovery that some of the golden eggs produced by growth can be distributed to patrimonial clients without starving the capitalist goose that lays them.

My presentation of the evidence for these arguments is in two sections. The first is an analysis of then Major General Suharto's response to his first economic crisis in 1966. I focus on the ways in which his choices were influenced by political as well as economic crisis, international economic factors, the persuasive power of the ideas of the professional economists, the need for political support, and a culture hostile to capitalism. In the end, I claim, what we see is an autonomous actor who accurately calculated how a commitment to promarket economic policies could be a part of a winning political formula.

The second section examines Suharto's actions in two later crises, the national oil company's near default on its international debt in 1975 and the fall of the world oil price beginning in 1983. The focus here is on patrimonialism, more precisely on the relationship among three powerful constituencies within the government that attempt to shape policy: the professional economists, economic nationalists who have often opposed market-oriented policies, and patrimonialists whose interest is in the distribution of spoils. My main purpose is to show, first, that the economists' early success undergirded their later influence; and, second, that while sticking basically to the economists' line Suharto has also been able to include the other groups in his governing coalition.

A final theoretical point: In recent years much has been claimed for the role of a 'strong state' in explaining Third World economic development.[11] States pursue their own interests, it is asserted, and the result is often development policies benefiting the state and the official class at the expense of society. In comparative Third World terms, and however measured, Indonesia surely has a strong state, and one that has been getting stronger in the quarter century of Suharto's rule.

Yet the heart of my analysis of the Indonesian political economy is that one finds explanations of policy not in the interests of the state *qua* state but in the behaviour of the key actors, particularly President Suharto, as those actors formulate their goals, perceive constraints and opportunities, and calculate appropriate means to deal with them. State presence has been a constant in independent Indonesia, but policies have differed enormously under Presidents Sukarno (1945–1966) and Suharto, and may well change again under a third president. I will return to this point in the conclusion.

The 1965–1966 Crisis and Its Resolution

Among Indonesia-watching professional economists, it is widely accepted as self-evident that the mid-1960s shift from heavily statist to more market oriented policies was crisis determined. In the terrible economic conditions of the time—negative GDP growth, unpayable foreign debts, spiralling inflation—Suharto had little choice, it is said, but to adopt the stabilisation policies of his neoclassically oriented advisers.

The economic crisis of the mid-1960s undoubtedly created a need for change in policy in the minds of many Indonesians. But to understand why change actually took place, and why it took the specific form it did, requires that it be placed in three contexts: the political collapse of 1965; the international economic, domestic, cultural and political regime-type factors shaping policy choice at the time; and the goals, perceptions, and calculations of the leaders, in particular Suharto, who emerged from the 1965 collapse.

The Political Collapse of 1965

From 1950 to about 1957 Indonesia was a competitive parliamentary democracy. A polarised and fragmented party system, the inability of the parliamentary form to incorporate a politically assertive President Sukarno and armed forces, plus a bureaucracy incapable of effective policy implementation led to widespread hostility to the regime, reflected in regional rebellion and central government immobility, in the late 1950s.

From the ashes of parliamentarism arose Guided Democracy, a highly competitive but unstable power triangle. President Sukarno, who had since the 1920s been Indonesia's preeminent nationalist leader, attempted simultaneously to draw strength from and to keep at arm's length an order-minded armed forces and a communist party bent on social revolution.

Sukarno's balancing act collapsed in the early hours of October 1, 1965, when radical younger army officers together with communist youths kidnapped and murdered six senior generals. Major General Suharto, then in command of strategic troops in Jakarta, rallied the army to put down what was immediately perceived as a communist attempt to seize power, beginning a series of events that led to Sukarno's replacement as president by Suharto. Suharto's label for the regime that began in March 1966, when executive authority shifted decisively to him, is the New Order.

During the Guided Democracy period, economic policy was hostage to the army-Sukarno-communist balance and to Sukarno's own political vision of nationalist ideological unity and international activism on behalf of leftist revolutionary causes. Bridges to the West were burned one by one, through expulsion of all Dutch nationals in 1957 and takeovers of British and American businesses in 1963 and 1965. Domestic and international political campaigns were funded by the simple but highly inflationary mechanism of the printing press. No serious attention was paid to the maintenance or improvement of the economic infrastructure, or to developing new areas of economic activity. The president himself repeatedly stated that the laws of economics did not apply to Indonesia's revolutionary conditions.

The 1965 political upheaval was perhaps a necessary condition for economic policy change, freeing the decision-making process from the constraints imposed on it by the political arrangements of Guided Democracy.[12] There is support for this proposition in the comparative literature. As Karen Remmer[13] concludes in a study of the politics of economic stabilisation in Latin America, 'regime breakdowns occurring in conjunction with economic crisis create unusual space for the implementation of stabilisation policies, particularly when regime collapse is attributed to policy inaction rather than to austerity measures'.

More doubtful, however, is Remmer's implication that any particular set of policies is likely to be adopted in such situations. The 'unusual space' created by the conjunction of political breakdown and economic crisis still has to be filled with a new political regime and new economic policies, and at this point any number of other variables may intervene.

Factors Shaping Policy Choice

In the Indonesia case, the adoption of market-oriented and outward-looking economic reforms was not a foregone conclusion. Some factors pushed in that direction, but others did not. Among the former were the persuasiveness of the theories the president's economic advisers used to justify their proposed liberalisation, and behind the theories the existence of a Western and Japanese cornucopia from which immediate assistance and eventual investment could be obtained. Negative factors, or more accurately factors generally considered negative in the Indonesia and comparative literature, included political culture and ideology plus the type of regime that Suharto headed. I will address each in turn.

Foreign assistance and investment and the role of the economists

Critics of Third World economic development on the left[14] have believed that foreign assistance and investment have negative developmental consequences, and therefore should not be adopted as government policy. It is not surprising that their analyses of the reasons why governments seek foreign assistance and investment usually attribute dark motives to domestic political leaders, as is reflected in such terms as 'comprador bourgeoisie' and 'pacts of domination'.

In the Indonesia case, critics of both the left and centre (by centre I mean militant nationalists and/or liberal democrats) have ascribed narrow and unscrupulous motives to Suharto and his military colleagues and have dismissed his professional economic advisers as mere facilitators in a transaction that has exchanged national sovereignty for personal wealth and the political power that comes from well-filled patronage coffers.[15]

Without disputing the personal and political benefits that have accrued to Suharto and his associates, I prefer to start from a different perspective: that what needs to be explained in the Indonesia case is not development failure but success, not a loss of sovereignty but a gain in national wealth and therefore power. From this perspective, Western aid and investment appear primarily not as costs or burdens but as opportunities. To be taken advantage of, however, opportunities have to be perceived and policy instruments forged. It is here that Suharto's domestic economic advisers, acting as 'partisan policy analysts',[16] have made a signal contribution.

From the late 1950s to the mid-1960s, President Sukarno's government had been pursuing economic policies that were increasingly recognised as disastrous. A small group of Western-educated economists, mostly professors at the University of Indonesia in Jakarta, played a key role during this period in explaining the shortcomings of Sukarnoist economics to other intellectuals, officials and politicians. Colonel Suharto heard their lectures when he attended the Army Staff and Command School in Bandung in 1959–1960. In 1966 he asked one of them, Professor Widjojo Nitisastro, recently returned from the University of California at Berkeley, to form a team of economic advisers, beginning a close association that continues to this day.

The economists had, I think, three strengths that made their arguments persuasive to Suharto. First, they were well trained neoclassical and development economists, practitioners of the most advanced of the social sciences, possessors of genuine science in a still very unscientific society. They had analytical tools to explain why Indonesia was experiencing runaway inflation and why economic productivity was so low, and they had already-tested policy recommendations. The real significance of the availability of foreign assistance and investment, I believe, lies here, in that it lent both substance and credibility to the solutions they proposed. In the mid-1960s, no alternative set of policy recommendations had anything like this power to explain and resolve Indonesia's economic difficulties.

Second, the economists were also nationalists, not *deracinée* Westernised intellectuals who approached the Indonesia economy as though it were an abstract model.[17] Professor Widjojo had been a guerrilla fighter in East Java during the independence revolution, and all the economists had spent their formative years in Indonesia during the nationalist and revolutionary periods. They accepted the concept of a mixed economy, with a major role for the state in banking, productive enterprises, and marketing. They were wary of the possible negative political and economic consequences of relying too heavily on foreign investment and assistance, and from the outset found ways to control and limit foreign economic resources.

Finally, the economists were good politicians. From their early public statements, it is evident that they understood how to package their explanations and proposals within a nationalist, populist, collectivist, and even antiimperialist rhetorical wrapper, associating themselves with the mainstream goals of modern Indonesian political culture.[18] Perhaps most important, by all accounts, Widjojo in particular had from the beginning an intuitive understanding of the deferential style that Suharto seems to prefer in his advisers. This knowledge has given him a unique ability to bring Suharto around to his point of view on several crucial issues over the years.[19]

Political culture and ideology
On first examination, Indonesian political culture and ideology would appear to be powerful obstacles to the adoption of liberal economic policies. The current elite, especially its more senior members, tends to be strongly anti-Western, anticapitalist, and pro-state intervention. These attitudes are also widely shared outside the elite.[20]

Suspicion of the West began in the direct experience of Dutch rule, at its most powerful in the first four decades of this century, and deepened during the 1945–1949 popular revolution against a determined Dutch attempt to regain their colony after three years of Japanese occupation during the Second World War. Nationalist movements before the war and independence struggles after were of course commonplace in European colonies in Asia and Africa, but they varied in extent and intensity of popular mobilisation and amount of actual violence between coloniser and colonised. Indonesia belongs to the small group of countries, which includes Vietnam, Algeria, and Zimbabwe, at the top of this scale.

From the early years of this century, in the Western-educated Indonesian mind, capitalism has been closely associated with colonialism via general acceptance of the Marxist paradigm and especially the Leninist idea that imperialism is the highest stage of capitalism. In the West, it is believed, capitalism is an economic system that gives the rich an advantage over the poor and permits the economically strong to dominate the weak. Imperialism allowed Western capitalists to placate the proletariat at home by exploiting the natural and human resources of the colonies.

It follows that the nationalist leaders' vision of the kind of economic system they would create in their own nation-state would, at minimum, not give capitalist entrepreneurs the central role in development. Except for a brief period in the early 1950s, procapitalist policies were in fact rejected by the governments of the first decade-and-a-half after independence.

As a result of the experiences of the last twenty years, the younger members of today's elite are probably much more sympathetic to positive evaluations of capitalism. This is a point on which I will have more to say below. For Suharto's generation, however, and indeed for Suharto himself, who was born in 1921, the old ideas are still deeply held.

Statist attitudes fit very well into an anticolonial and anticapitalist mentality. A powerful state, it is believed, is necessary to maintain hard-won independence in a dangerous and hostile world. In a mixed economy, such as Indonesia has had since independence, a powerful state is required to control and contain the essential motivating force, greed, that drives capitalists. In a developing economy—and development has been the highest priority policy commitment in the Suharto government—a strong state is necessary to plan, regulate, and sometimes own and manage. In Indonesian conditions, it must also inspire, guide, and control a people still backward, poorly educated, and easy prey for false leaders who would inflame religious, class, and ethnic passions.

Statist attitudes are rooted in the colonial period in another sense. The first form of government experienced by the senior members of today's elite was a colonial administration widely praised at home and abroad for its efficiency and also known for its programs of social welfare. The bureaucratic political process that produced these policies provided very few opportunities for participation to the indigenous population, particularly in comparison to such close neighbours as the Americans in the Philippines and the British in India.

The Indonesian nationalists of the prewar period spoke in democratic and participatory terms, but the living model of government with which they were most familiar was bureaucratic and paternalistic. Many of the country's future leaders, including Sergeant Suharto of the Royal Netherlands Indies Army, were in fact a part of that government.[21]

Statism's origins, while strengthened by colonialism, are in precolonial Indonesian, particularly Javanese, political culture. According to the classic study of the subject by Soemarsaid Moertono (1968), the Hinduised Javanese rulers of the later Mataram period (sixteenth to nineteenth century) believed in an absolute state with an absolute monarch at its head. The state had the enormous—we would almost say totalitarian—responsibility for maintaining harmony between the microcosm of the individual human being's world and the cosmic order of the universe, of which it was a replica.[22]

Within the state, 'the king maintained dominance over all persons and goods ... The king, and to a lesser degree his officials as the extension of his power, had to possess might and power commensurate with that of the gods; he had to display the material grandeur and pomp worthy of an image of the gods; and also a lavish beneficence proper to mankind's helper and protector in times of distress.' [23]

The Javanese state was not, however, a developmental state or even one that interacted very much with its own people. Moertono labels its rulers 'conservative traditionalists' who clung 'to established customs and so a distaste for change or for whatever may disturb the regular and predictable flow of events.' [24] Government administration was therefore 'intrinsically primitive in character,' 'neglected people's needs,' and was 'detached from the toils of the common people.' [25]

There is little doubt that President Suharto is deeply influenced by Javanese culture, particularly ideas derived from the Hindu-Javanese mystical *kebatinan* (roughly, inner beingness or the science of the inner being) tradition. [26] The central theme of his recent autobiography [27] is the connection between mastery of oneself and leadership of the nation-state. 'Ojo kagetan, ojo gumunan, ojo dumeh' (don't be easily startled, don't be easily surprised, don't take advantage of others just because you have the power to do so) is only the most frequently repeated of dozens of Javanese aphorisms that dot the book. Overall, and despite references to the president's constitutional subservience to the popularly elected People's Consultative Assembly, the impression is of a ruler who wants to be thought of as supremely in charge, as the epicentre of the Indonesian political cosmos.

Suharto's anticapitalism takes the form in his autobiography of a commitment to the development of cooperatives as the most important economic institution of the future. The idea of the cooperative in Indonesia goes back to the early nationalist movement at the beginning of the twentieth century, and particularly to the 'Father of Cooperatives,' Mohammad Hatta, Indonesia's first vice-president and after Sukarno the most revered leader of the nationalist generation.

Official economic doctrine in the New Order gives prominence to three institutions, which are supposed to coexist in 'family-like' harmony: in order of importance, the state, the cooperatives, and the private sector. According to two key economic provisions in the constitution, 'branches of production that are important for the State and control the basic needs of the people will be controlled by the State', and 'the earth and water and natural riches contained therein are controlled by the State and used to the fullest extent for the prosperity of the people'. [28] In the Indonesian economy today, the state and private enterprise are actually far more developed than cooperatives, which account for only a minuscule portion of economic activity.

Patrimonialism and development

In addition to culture and ideology, regime type is a variable frequently associated with policy. In the comparative cross-national literature, enormous effort has been expended to establish a connection between regime type and policy, but virtually all of the studies have been inconclusive. The principal reason for this may be a failure to draw the appropriate distinctions among regime types or, put slightly differently, to probe more deeply those aspects of regimes that have policy consequences.

In the Indonesian case, the regimes led by Sukarno and Suharto differ greatly in economic policy orientation, though both may be characterised politically as authoritarian, the usual label employed in the cross-national literature, and also as personalistic, a common authoritarian subtype. A more relevant difference for policy, however, may be the degree and type of competition: major, group-based, and polarised in the case of Sukarno's Guided Democracy; minor, patronage- or patrimonially-based, and collegial in Suharto's New Order.

Personal competition within governments, at least as embodied in patronage or patrimonial systems of mobilising power, is a variable typically considered an obstacle to the adoption of liberal economic policies. Joan Nelson, in a valuable essay on the factors that lead governments to resist liberal stabilisation policies, argues on the basis of evidence from Ghana, Zambia, Kenya, Sri Lanka, and Jamaica that 'In countries in which the government relies heavily on patron-client ties, stabilisation (particularly stringent budget discipline) therefore cuts not merely at a government's general popularity but at the resources needed for it to maintain its support base'.[29]

Most students of post-1965 Indonesian political economy agree with this assessment. The Australian political scientist Harold Crouch[30] was the first scholar to identify patron-client relations, or more precisely Weberian patrimonialism, as the principal means by which President Suharto created and maintains his base of political support.

According to Crouch, the patrimonial principle is fundamentally incompatible with the rationality of the economists. The government's 'dependence on economic growth seems to require an administrative system based on the bureaucratic values of predicability, regularity, order, and rationality—in contrast to patrimonial favouritism and arbitrariness.' At the end of the New Order's first decade, Crouch was predicting conflict and instability for the future: 'As a result, basic conflicts over policy and the nature of the regime are becoming increasingly important'.[31]

The Politician's Perspective

I have now reviewed two variables favourable (crisis and the persuasiveness of the technocrat's advice, including the availability of aid and investment) and two unfavourable (culture and patrimonialism) to the adoption of liberal and internationally open economic policies in Indonesia.

Taken together, the causal weight would seem to be on the negative side, particularly if we discount the long-term effects of the immediate political and economic crisis of 1965–1966. That is, the cultural and regime variables might for the moment have been outweighed by the seriousness of the crisis, but after a few years of stabilisation they should have returned with a vengeance.[32] In fact, they have not done so, at least not as predicted. In Part III I will attempt to explain the long-term pattern; here I want to show how the four variables interacted to produce a liberal policy at the outset of the New Order.

In my view, summing variables is the wrong way to approach the problem. This is because there is a crucial intervening variable that makes all the difference for policy outcomes: the goals, perceptions, and calculations of politicians. In the Indonesian case, I believe General Suharto quickly recognised, though perhaps only intuitively at the very beginning, that a system of political stratification built on a core combination of military and civilian bureaucratic forces,[33] with patronage as a chief instrument of reward and punishment, was not incompatible with macro-economic liberalisation. I further believe he had little difficulty assimilating economic liberalisation and political patrimonialism into his more general cultural commitments.

The evidence for these propositions is mostly circumstantial. I will present the core of it in the form of an explicit choice made in 1966 by General Suharto, as the effective head of government at the time, between two alternative models of political economy. In August of that year the army held an important seminar at its staff and command school in Bandung, West Java. The subject was Indonesia's economic and political future and what role the army should play in that future. Suharto himself attended.

Seminar sessions were organised into three sections—military, political, and economic—and chairs and vice-chairs were appointed to organise and direct discussion for each of the sections. Army officers headed all three sections, but the vice-chair positions in politics and economics were given respectively to University of Indonesia economics professors Sarbini Somawinata and Widjojo Nitisastro.

Sarbini, though an economics professor, had long pursued an interest in politics. He was in fact a leading intellectual figure in the Indonesian Socialist Party (PSI, Partai Sosialis Indonesia), a non-Marxist democratic socialist party. The PSI had a reputation for intellectualism and Westernisation, which made its leaders suspect in some quarters, including the army, for being diabolically clever and for lacking sensitivity to Indonesian conditions. In religious terms, most of the PSI leaders were either secular rationalists or adherents to the Javanese mystical *kebatinan* tradition (in some cases, both!). The party had been banned by Sukarno in 1960, but many of its leaders maintained their connections with government officials, including armed forces officers, to whom they were a useful source of ideas and information.

In the first months of the New Order, Sarbini was introduced to one of Suharto's key advisers, Soedjono Hoemardhani, on whom he apparently made a great impression. At Soedjono's urging, Sarbini was appointed vice-chair of the political section of the army seminar.[34] By the end of the seminar, however, it was clear that while Widjojo's star still shone brightly, Sarbini's had been extinguished. Suharto had chosen the economic and political course he would follow.

Sarbini, as a democratic socialist, had offered the general an integrated political and economic plan. The political part called for a restoration of the 1950s multi-party system, including the parties banned by Sukarno, and representative democratic institutions, complete with freedom of the press and association and other limitations on the power of government over society and the individual. The army was to have a role in politics, but on the basis of an 'equal sharing of power' in a civil-military partnership. Sarbini's approach to economic policy, while recognising the short-run importance of foreign assistance to solve the debt crisis and reduce inflation, was basically inward-looking. He called for a massive program of compulsory saving and for assistance to small entrepreneurs, who he believed could become the primary engine of economic growth.[35]

Widjojo, in contrast, offered only an economic plan, the main ingredients of which were seeking Western willingness to reschedule payment of Indonesia's debt, obtaining new foreign loans to enable the government to import basic foodstuffs and production goods, reducing inflation through contractionary money supply and credit policies, and liberalising the foreign exchange regime to stimulate trade. On the face of it, as I have argued above, this plan seemed more likely of success than Sarbini's, which was long on noble goals and short on realistic policies and programs. In particular, how compulsory domestic saving could produce a large amount of investment capital, even in the middle run, and how this could be achieved through a democratic political process, were questions that were never satisfactorily addressed.

Suharto was, I believe, inclined on the merits of the economic arguments to accept Widjojo's plan, but he had to supply his own political strategy to support it. My reconstruction of his thinking emphasises five elements: First, a calculation that a commitment to economic development could be an effective legitimating principle and at the same time a source of support from many groups, including the military, the civilian bureaucracy, and various groups in society; second, a priori hostility to multi-party representative democracy; third, a priori acceptance of the idea of a strong executive; fourth, a calculation that a substantial coercive capacity would have to be a major part of any stable government, not least one led by a soldier; and fifth, awareness that personal political power in Indonesia requires, in addition to military, bureaucratic, and popular support, a system of informal finance.

In Jakarta in late 1965 and early 1966, in all circles except those of the communist party and Sukarno's most faithful followers, it was accepted as obvious truth that the time had come to make economics, not politics, the first priority of government. Sukarno had achieved much as the unifier of an ethnically and religiously diverse people, but he had let 'politics take command,' in the communist party's slogan, at a terrible economic price. It is thus not surprising that the anticommunist Suharto, in a time of economic crisis and general deprivation, and already exposed for some years to the laments of the economists, would see the political possibilities in making economic development the central theme of his government.

It is also not surprising that Suharto rejected out of hand, as he almost certainly did, Sarbini's political program for restoration of representative democracy as a means of creating support for himself and for his development policies. Within the military, it had become an article of faith that many if not all of Indonesia's political problems were caused by a 'too liberal,' 'fifty-percent-plus-one' Western-style democracy that served the individual at the expense of society. In the late 1950s the army had responded to Sukarno's call to bring down the multi-party system, and in the early 1960s had watched in dismay as the president turned for political support to the communist party's more than twenty million members and supporters. Apart from any personal interests or calculations, Suharto thus had a built-in bias against a return to representative democracy.

The idea of a strong executive was also accepted without much thought, I believe, by Suharto. The primary reason for this again lies in Indonesia's most recent history, in which Suharto had participated as a major, though second-rank, player. The grave weakness of parliamentary democracy had been cabinet, or executive, instability. In principle, and initially with army support, this deficiency had been corrected by Sukarno's 1959 declaration of a return to the original revolutionary constitution of 1945. This constitution, which is now central to Suharto's conception of the New Order regime, gives the preponderance of governmental authority to the president, who holds a five-year 'mandate' from the People's Consultative Assembly.

Another reason for Suharto's ready acceptance of a strong presidency may, of course, be his military background. His whole career was spent in that branch of the executive where most emphasis is placed on the obligation of subordinates to follow the commands of superiors. Also worth considering, though we have no evidence, is the possibility that the Later Mataram model of Javanese governance, apparent in Suharto's 1988 presentation of his leadership style, was already a part of his thinking in the mid-1960s.

The fourth element in Suharto's choice of a political strategy was a deliberate calculation that he needed to rely on armed force, that the army would have to be more than an equal partner with civilians. This calculation was probably more political, and informed by recent experience, than economic, and based on future projections, but an element of the latter may have been present as well.

On several occasions in the 1940s, 1950s and early 1960s, the central army leadership had been called upon to put down armed rebellions by communist, Islamic, and regionally-based ethnic groups. In 1965–1966, it was engaged, together with (mostly Islamic) anticommunist groups in society, in destroying the communist party altogether.[36] It is hard to imagine an astute military politician in these circumstances willing to give up unfettered recourse to coercion.

It may also be that Suharto was making a calculation about the necessity of future coercion given the likely social consequences of his economic policies. Reliance on foreign assistance and investment was bound, given Indonesian political culture, to be unpopular regardless of its actual consequences. Contractionary monetary and credit policy was bound to hurt millions of small indigenous traders and manufacturers. Subsequent use of market forces to stimulate growth was bound to give more opportunities to the economically experienced, heavily capitalised, and market-entrenched large Chinese entrepreneurs, further antagonising indigenous Indonesians.

All of these events did in fact come to pass in the 1970s. In my view, however, they were not as obvious in the mid-1960s as hindsight has since made them seem, and thus were probably not important factors in Suharto's initial calculations.

For the army to be an effective instrument of coercion, Suharto first had to dominate it. Though he was the most senior general in a major command position not killed on October 1, 1965, and though the bulk of the officers' corp immediately rallied to his leadership, his permanent control was by no means assured. From the army's founding shortly after independence in 1945 until 1965, no individual or group had been able to master its many conflicting personal, organisational, and territorial divisions.[37] Internal armed forces conflicts were in fact the cause of much of the general political instability of the 1950s. By the end of Guided Democracy there were also many Sukarnoists and procommunists in its ranks.

Between 1966 and 1969 Suharto developed a number of means for gaining and maintaining control of the armed forces, including organisational consolidation, rapid promotion of loyalists and early retirement of opponents, civilian government appointments and foreign diplomatic postings, direct salary supplements to some officers, provision of opportunities for additional income to others, and so on. Together, these

activities—and similar ones involving nonmilitary individuals and organisations—required large cash outlays, for which Suharto needed sources
with deep pockets.[38]

One such source, the critical one at the beginning, was profit-making
state agencies, of which the largest and most successful was the state oil
company headed by Ibnu Sutowo. Sutowo was a very early loyalist,
providing much of the capital for Suharto's initial efforts to replace Sukarno
and to build a solid political base within the army.

A second, and later on more important, source of funds was the so-
called *cukong*, mostly Sino-Indonesian business people who trade a share
in their profits for protection by officials. *Cukongism* has been a prominent
feature of Indonesian political life at least since colonial times. From the
1940s onward, regional military commanders, often left to their own devices
by an impecunious headquarters and central government, have had close
relationships with *cukong*. Liem Sioe Liong, today Indonesia's richest
merchant, industrialist, and banker, got his start in the Central Java
provincial capital of Semarang when Colonel Suharto was divisional
commander there in the late 1950s.

For my argument, the crucial point to be made about these sources
of political funds is that, however illiberal they may appear to the scholarly observer, it is doubtful that Suharto saw them as incompatible in
practice with the economists' macro-economic liberalisation policies to
which he also made an early commitment. An increase in the level of
trust and cooperation between the Indonesian government and the West
could only improve relations between the national oil company and
the foreign companies that pumped and sold most of the oil and had
the capital for further exploration. Where incompatibility existed, Suharto
could cordon off the oil company administratively and financially, allowing it, for example, to borrow internationally when other state agencies
could not.

Similarly, an increase in the level of domestic economic activity and
international trade, which, Suharto was assured by the economists, their
stabilisation policies would ultimately bring, could only benefit the busi-
ness-savvy *cukong* and their official clients. Properly managed, it could
also be made to benefit, and thus bring into the political coalition, a new
class of indigenous entrepreneurs. As to foreign investment, there never
was any intention of allowing it to play more than a small and tightly
restricted role. Indeed, the suspicion has always been strong that the reason
for allowing foreign investment at all was to assuage the foreign bankers
and governments who demanded it as a quid pro quo for their low credit
loans and other economic assistance.

How probable is it that this is an accurate picture of the elements
involved in General Suharto's 1966 decision to blend army-based authoritarianism with macro-economic liberalism? Because the political process

has been closed to outside observation for so long, analysts like myself have been forced to infer motive from behaviour. The results have often been highly speculative.

The autobiography is a helpful but far from conclusive source of new evidence. It is easy to find there (and in many statements over two decades) evidence for Suharto's a priori rejection of parliamentary democracy, support for a strong, paternalistic executive, and belief in the need for a politically active army. Economic development, however, is treated as a national imperative, a highly valued societal goal, not as an opportunity for personal legitimation or political support-seeking. References to political strategy and tactics, perhaps considered beneath presidential dignity, are few.[39]

The president is quite open, however, about the gap between contemporary Indonesian economic reality and the national economy envisioned by the constitution. He is aware of the strength of the private, predominantly Sino-Indonesian, sector, the weakness of cooperatives, and the failures of the public sector. His basic justification for his policies is that to achieve the ideal future, Indonesia must build on the far from ideal present. Moreover, it must do so 'following rational economic laws.' This means, among other things, that the private sector must be given an opportunity to grow now and that cooperatives will be slow to develop.

Suharto also argues that many of his critics misread the constitution's economic passages. The constitution, he claims, does not say that the state must own the basic means of production, just that it must control them, which it can do via laws and policies. His actions in choosing these laws and policies, he naturally assures his readers, are guided by the constitutional commitment to the prosperity of the society as a whole.[40]

What are we to make of these statements, given what we know about Suharto's cultural background and loyalties? To my mind, his account of his policies is evidence of the flexibility or, better, commodiousness of values and beliefs as variables in their effect on political behaviour. This is most emphatically not to say that culture is vacuous or meaningless or, like an overcoat, easily put on and taken off by a cynical politician. It is to say, rather, that its effects depend upon time, place, circumstance, and the individual goals, perceptions, and calculations of politicians. President Suharto is genuinely antiforeign, anticapitalist, prostate, and maybe even procooperatives. But he is also quite capable of adopting policies that are surprising to anyone who knows only his basic values and beliefs. He does not see these policies as proforeign, procapitalist, and antistate, however, and perhaps we should not either.

Policy Making since 1966: Lessons of the Pertamina Default and the Oil Crash

The Triangle of Economists, Economic Nationalists, and Patrimonialists

Since the 1966 victory of the economists, a policy triangle of economists, economic nationalists, and patrimonialists has emerged in Indonesia. In situations of crisis or conflict among these groups, a recurring assumption of domestic and foreign observers has been that the economists are the weakest of the three and likely to lose. Sometimes, in fact, they do lose. On the most important occasions, however, including the near default on its foreign loans of the state oil company Pertamina in 1975 and the downturn and then crash of the world oil market in 1983 and 1986, the economists have won. Why?

The short answer is that Suharto has chosen a political strategy—a base of support, legitimating principles, means of coercion—that is closely linked to the policies of the economists. Just how closely linked was made clear, as I shall show below, by the political and policy challenges presented by the Pertamina affair and the decline in oil revenues. First, however, I want to put those events in the context of a better understanding than we presently have of the exact nature of the relationship among the three sides of the policy triangle.

Who are the economic nationalists and the patrimonialists, and how much of a threat have they been to the influence of the economists? Post-1966 economic policy-making history has frequently been interpreted as a straight fight between the economists and the other two groups combined, though in fact the nationalists and patrimonialists have different interests and goals.

The so-called economic nationalists,[41] like the economists a group of high-level officials, have favoured rapid state-led development, usually involving very large capital investments without much prospect of short- or even medium-term return. Most of them have had little formal training in economics. Their projects have been opposed by the economists, who prefer to limit the direct involvement of the state in production and in general to guide economic activity through manipulation of the price mechanism.

For the first decade of the New Order, the most prominent economic nationalist was Ibnu Sutowo, the president-director of the national oil company Pertamina.[42] Sutowo, born in 1914, was trained as a medical doctor before World War II, and became involved in the oil industry in South Sumatera as an army officer during the independence revolution. Pertamina was created in 1968 as a fusion of three smaller state oil companies with responsibilities in different parts of the country and different aspects of the oil business.

Under Sutowo's leadership, Pertamina pioneered the production-sharing (as opposed to profit-sharing) contract with foreign oil companies, a first step toward greater national control of the industry. He also used his monopoly position and personal bargaining and persuasive skills to pressure the foreign companies into further concessions.

By the mid-1970s, with huge increases in the world price and in Indonesian production, petroleum was earning about three-quarters of Indonesia's total export revenues, accounting for half the government budget and one-fifth of Gross National Product. Pertamina took advantage of this success to expand its interests, investing heavily in liquefied natural gas, fertiliser, petrochemical, refinery, and steel plants, a fleet of oil tankers, and many other projects.

In the 1980s the most prominent nationalist has been B.J. Habibie, Indonesia's czar and apostle of hi-tech.[43] Trained as an engineer in West Germany, Habibie had risen to the post of vice-president for applied technology at the German aircraft manufacturer Messerschmitt Bolkow Blohm before being called home by Suharto in 1974. He believes passionately in the idea that Indonesia can become a leader in world technological development, and that advanced technology can be used to pull Indonesia more quickly into the industrial world.

Habibie is currently Minister of Research and Technology, head of the government's institute for technological development, head of the state aircraft and ship-building industries, coordinator of strategic industries, a director of Pertamina, and active in many other technology-related development projects. The economists oppose most of these projects, especially the very costly Nusantara Aircraft Company, which in cooperation with a Spanish company manufactures a 35–40 passenger plane at a state-of-the-art plant in Bandung, West Java. According to the economists, manufacturing aeroplanes at Indonesia's current level of development squanders very scarce resources. Exactly how much capital is involved is unknown, because financing is mostly extra-budgetary or channelled through Pertamina, but Nusantara admits to a $US one billion government investment since the company was founded in 1976.

Why have the nationalists been so influential? Virtually all observers of Indonesian development policy making have for a long time agreed that Suharto tries to offset the market perspective of the economists with the big-project orientation of the nationalists. Some of this may be calculated to appeal to pro-state sentiments and national security concerns in the military, his primary political constituency, and in the civilian bureaucracy, his second constituency. Much of it, however, appears to come from his own nationalist, statist and military values, that is from culture or ideology rather than interests. Indeed, Suharto's relationship with Habibie has, for reasons of officers' personal and institutional interests, antagonised more than it has pleased the military establishment.

In his autobiography Suharto defended the large investment in aircraft manufacturing for its contributions to national security and to the advancement of local technology, its export potential, and even its labour-absorbing capacity. More emotionally, he writes: 'Indonesia is the largest archipelago in the world. We must continue to develop it as one territorial unit, one political unit, one economic unit, one cultural unit and one defence unit. For that we need to develop strategic industries to free us from dependence on others.'[44]

The economic nationalists have often been confused with the patrimonialists, who are the officials in charge of generating and dispensing patronage. The most important of these officials are located in the State Secretariat, the administrative arm of the presidential office responsible for liaison with the central bureaucracy. Lieutenant General (retired) Sudharmono, vice-president from 1988, head of the State Secretariat from 1973 to 1988, secretary of the cabinet and of the Economic Stabilisation Council for six years before that, and national chair of the state political party from 1983 to 1988, has been the leading patrimonialist.

Suharto's relations with the two groups are very different: he favours the nationalists primarily for ideological and cultural reasons, and perhaps secondarily because they reflect the views of important constituents; the patrimonialists he uses to reward and punish materially those individuals and groups who could threaten his position. The nationalists are in direct and fundamental conflict with the economists over development policy; the patrimonialists have no permanent friends or enemies, only a permanent interest in the continuing flow of funds.

Until the mid-1970s Ibnu Sutowo's Pertamina was the most important source of presidential patronage money, mush of which was funnelled through the State Secretariat. The secretariat's officials were close to Sutowo and tended to defend his interests against the economists. The widespread assumption that the two groups are the same stems in part from this early association. It is also based on the belief, held particularly strongly in the economists' camp, that the true motive of the nationalists is not economic growth but the creation of industrial and financial empires for personal and political purposes.

In the last fifteen years there has been a greater separation between the patrimonialists and the nationalists. In this period patronage funds have come from the (largely Sino-Indonesian) business community's contributions to Suharto's foundations, from state agencies (like the rice procurement board) without nationalist pretensions, and from the State Secretariat's authority (rescinded in 1987) to give final approval on large state contracts. Habibie's agencies and companies are not major sources of patronage outside his own fiefdom. The key patrimonialists in the State Secretariat are now openly supportive of the economists, whose policies promise to raise the general level of business activity, on which fund raising for patronage purposes depends.

From this account, it is clear that the economists have not faced a continuing *alliance méchante* of nationalists and patrimonialists. From the late 1960s to the mid-1970s, because of the influence of Sutowo, the competition did seem to favour the patrimonialists and nationalists as a single group. In the 1980s, however, it was possible for the economists to forge an alliance with many of the patrimonialists against the nationalists, resulting in the reestablishment of the predominant influence the economists enjoyed at the beginning of the New Order.

To their battles with the patrimonialists and the nationalists, the economists have brought a number of strengths that may be summed up in one word: success. In the late 1960s and early 1970s, their policies brought down inflation, reversed the negative growth rate, and began to take effect in agriculture, particularly in the steady growth of the politically critical rice crop. The flow of large amounts of foreign assistance—given annually by the Intergovernmental Group on Indonesia, a consortium of Western countries plus Japan—and of smaller amounts of foreign investment is attributable directly to the economists' policies and the trust that foreign lenders, governments, and investors have in them.

Toward the middle of the 1970s, the economists' prestige dropped when student demonstrators accused them of favouring growth at the expense of distribution, and foreign and domestic Sino-Indonesian entrepreneurs at the expense of indigenous Indonesians, and of being indifferent to corruption in high places. The demonstrations ended in arrests and eventual suppression of all student opposition political activity. The suppression continues in the 1990s, but the public perception of the issues, and with it the evaluation of the economists' policies, has probably changed in favour of the economists. The reason for this is the economists' further successes in overcoming challenges by patrimonialists and nationalists in 1975 and after 1983, as I shall describe below.

As far as Suharto is concerned, the economists have been able to maintain their nationalist credentials throughout the post-1966 period. Though in his heart the president seems to prefer the more glamorous prospects of the projects of the Sutowos and Habibies, the economists have never been entirely out of favour or regarded as an obstacle to the achievements of a strong national economy.

Finally, Suharto appears to have internalised the lessons taught by Widjojo and his colleagues. Sometimes to the chagrin of the economists, the president is now said to believe that he understands the economy as well as they. Suharto's conversion may to some extent make up for the advantage in persuasive technique lost in 1983 when the culturally adept Widjojo was replaced by a colleague more formal in his approach to the boss. Professor Soemitro Djojohadikusumo, the dean of Indonesian economists and Suharto's relative by marriage,[45] has apparently helped to fill this gap.

In concluding this discussion, it is important to be clear that the economists, while on top of the policy heap today, should not be seen as having vanquished the nationalists or the patrimonialists. Rather, the three groups coexist in a sometimes conflictual, sometimes cooperative relationship that has changed over the past two decades and may well change again. From Suharto's point of view, and it is the politician's perspective I am emphasising here, this is the way he seems to want it: the economists are the producers of wealth, the patrimonialists are the distributors of a large portion of it for political purposes, and the nationalists are the embodiment of his dream for more rapid progress toward an industrialised, internationally powerful Indonesia.

The Pertamina Affair and the Decline and Fall of the World Oil Price

The economists' strengths and Suharto's ability to juggle all three sides of the policy triangle have been apparent in the government's responses to the 1975 Pertamina crisis and to the budgetary and overall development strategy crisis brought on by declining oil prices in the 1980s.

The Pertamina crisis was precipitated by the company's inability to make scheduled payments in early 1975 on its loans from two North American banks. Investigations of the company's finances prompted by this disclosure revealed that it had borrowed several billion dollars on its own, against government policy and without approval from the relevant ministries. Prior to this crisis, the total official public foreign debt, including about $US1.5 billion known to have been incurred by Pertamina, was less than $10 billion.

Before 1975 Suharto had allowed Ibnu Sutowo and Pertamina to act independently of the economists, including the Ministers of Mines who were Sutowo's nominal superiors. This was because of Pertamina's big-projects dynamism and its huge patronage contributions, in other words the combined force of the nationalist and patrimonialist sides of the policy triangle.

As the debt scandal unfolded, however, it became clear that Pertamina's activities threatened to bring down the whole edifice of New Order economics. At risk were the good faith of Western and Japanese bankers and governments, the 'balanced' state budget,[46] and vast programs of rural, regional, and indigenous entrepreneurial development made possible by the first OPEC price shock in 1974.

Suharto resolved the crisis by taking the advice of the economists, led by Widjojo. Pertamina was prohibited from further independent borrowing and was brought more closely under the supervision of the Minister of

Mines. Bank Indonesia, the state bank, accepted responsibility for Pertamina's outstanding loans, half of which were then cancelled or reduced through renegotiation. Among the cancelled loans were over $US3 billion that had been borrowed to finance the purchase of oil tankers at well above international market prices. Pertamina's nonpetroleum related projects were either axed or put under the economists' control. In early 1976, Sutowo was himself replaced by an army general respected by the economists.

If Pertamina was the centrepiece of both the patrimonialist and nationalist sides of the policy triangle, why was Suharto willing to allow it to be brought under the control of the economists? As late as 1988, when he completed his autobiography, the president offered the view that Sutowo, who had served him long and faithfully, was not entirely responsible for Pertamina's near default: 'I had to take a just position even though I too know about the tricks in the world of giant businesses, like the oil world. Pertamina has many enemies, who are envious of us'.[47]

Suharto was unwilling to act on these sentiments, however, except to the extent of not immediately firing Sutowo and later protecting him from prosecution. The principal reason was that, counselled by Widjojo, he recognised the seriousness of the threat to the economic policies he had chosen in 1966, and to which he was still committed for political as well as economic reasons. Moreover, no group of advisers other than the economists had a credible or politically acceptable solution to offer. Other patrimonialists and nationalists steered clear of the Pertamina wreckage. Finally, by 1975 Indonesia had began to enjoy the benefits of the first OPEC price shock. With any foresight at all, it was easy to predict that there would be no shortage of economic or political capital to dispense in the near future.

The second challenge won by the economists has been not a one-shot affair like the reining in of Pertamina but rather a series of decisions taken since 1983 to deal with the consequences for development of diminished oil income. It is in the number and consistency of these decisions, and also in their impact on the growth of non-oil exports, that a major victory can be discerned.[48]

The oil boom years 1974–1982 were the heyday of the nationalists and patrimonialists. The government was awash in oil revenues, for which every ministry, state enterprise, political group, and retiring general pressed a claim. Resources were poured into education, agriculture, communications and transportation, the development of import-substituting industries, officials' salaries, subsidisation of agricultural imports and urban consumer goods, and massive capital-intensive projects such as oil refineries, liquefied natural gas plants, and Habibie's aircraft industry.

Many of these policies and programs helped strengthen the president's legitimacy with the general public and laid the foundation for a

performance-related political support base much more extensive than the
core combination of patrimonially-connected army officers and civilian
officials with which he had begun. Urban consumers were wooed with
cheap food and petroleum products; urban and rural indigenous entrepreneurs at all levels were offered subsidised credit; farmers received credit,
seeds, fertiliser, pesticide, and irrigation improvement projects; Muslims
got new mosques and government-sponsored nationwide Quran-reading
competitions; village, district, and provincial governments were given
special development funds; and schools and health centres were built all
over the country.

The economists opposed some of these programs (though not all, for
they are nationalists, too, and recognised the economic, social and political
value of many of them), but their influence was less than it had been
at the beginning of the New Order. To be sure, the Pertamina affair had
served as a salutary warning of the risks of big-project, capital-intensive,
and foreign loan-dependant economic nationalism. The president's new
understanding of these risks undoubtedly strengthened the hand of the
economists in their conflicts with the nationalists and patrimonialists,
particularly the former. The state enterprises were held on a tighter leash
than they had been before, avoiding the problems of over-borrowing
experienced a few years later by Mexico.

In an era of rapidly growing resources, however, the economists were
unable to win many battles against specific big-ticket projects. Instead,
their influence was greatest in the area of macro-economic expertise, that
is, in their ability to persuade the president of the necessity, in their view,
to limit overall spending and maintain a balanced state budget in order
to hold down inflationary pressures. When the supply of resources jumped
again with the second OPEC price shock in 1979, most foreign and domestic
observers believed that the economists were fighting a losing battle for
control of economic policy.

In 1983 Indonesia's economic picture, and with it the influence of the
economists, began to change. In March of that year OPEC members, faced
with a glut in the world oil market, voted to reduce the price of oil from
$US34.50 to $29.50 per barrel. Since roughly 70 percent of Indonesia's
1982 foreign exchange earnings and 60 percent of its budget revenues
were derived from the sale of petroleum products, the OPEC decision was
a sharp blow to the Indonesian economy and to the government's economic policies. But worse was to come. Between December 1985 and
August 1986 the price plunged from $25 to $9 before rising slightly to
$12. In 1987 it rebounded further, but until the Iraqi invasion of Kuwait
in August 1990 it stayed under $20 and sometimes dropped below $15.

Suharto's response to these events, as in the 1975 Pertamina crisis, was
to turn for solutions to the economists. This time, however, the choice
was harder. For one thing, the crisis, at least until the end of 1985 (and

arguably after 1986) was not as immediately pressing as Pertamina's near default. Second, after nearly a decade of riches, the economic nationalists were well entrenched and had many connections with patrimonialists. Third, and perhaps most important, by 1986 the president's children had become major beneficiaries of the protectionist policies of the nationalists and patrimonialists.[49] For all these reasons it was widely believed that Suharto would not follow the advice of the economists.

In the event, he did, although for a long time the final outcome was uncertain, particularly concerning policy changes that would hurt the interests of his children. In 1983 he imposed the first of many austerity budgets, freezing civil servants' salaries and slowing the growth of many programs, rescheduled major high-technology development projects worth $21 billion (representing a saving of $10 billion in foreign exchange), liberalised banking policy, simplified investment and export procedures, and reformed the tax structure. In 1984 the corruption-ridden customs service was virtually shut down, with its responsibilities given to a private Swiss surveying company.

Since 1986, the watchwords have been tax reform, emphasising improved collection, and deregulation, particularly in banking and in the ending of import monopolies on production goods that had been blocking the growth of export industries. Every few months, on average, during the late 1980s the government announced new liberalisation measures, increasing the ability of foreign and domestic businesses to offer their products at competitive world prices. Initial scepticism that these measures were cosmetic has given way, as some of the monopolies (plastics raw materials especially) held by Suharto's children were rescinded and as non-oil exports began to surge,[50] to belief that the commitment is genuine.

The logic behind Suharto's decision to take the economist's advice is by now familiar. In addition to belt-tightening, the economists' proposal was to improve tax collection, improve banking services, raise non-oil export performance, and, at least in the short run until the first three measures could bear fruit, increase foreign borrowing. Like the economists' proposals in 1966 and 1975, this package made good economic sense and was supported by foreign lenders, investors, and governments.

The economists' proposal also made good political sense in terms of Suharto's overall political strategy. If new state revenues could be raised and private business activity restored to its earlier level, legitimation and support would once again flow from the general public and the many groups that had benefited during the salad days. In personal terms, the president's children would have to give up some of their sources of income, but in a large, complex, and state-penetrated economy other wells could surely be tapped.

Despite early foot-dragging, most of the patrimonialists and even many of the nationalists have in the end agreed to the economists' solution. As

in 1966 and 1975, they had no credible economic or political alternative
to offer. They also understood that their prosperity was dependent on the
health of the economy as a whole, and that although they had to accept
retrenchment they were by no means being cut out of the distribution
network.

From the adoption of so many consistent policies over an eight-year
period, it is tempting to conclude that this time the economists have won
not just a battle but the war. The struggle might be seen in two ways:
as a contest for influence among the three sides of the policy triangle,
in which the economists have now accumulated many more political
resources than their competitors; and as a contest for cultural predominance, in which the hearts and minds of Indonesians have been won to
the beliefs that capitalism is good, foreigners are useful, and the state has
a supporting rather than a leading role to play in development.

Expressed either way, the conclusion is undoubtedly premature. In
Suharto's autobiography there is plenty of evidence of his continuing
affection for both the nationalists and patrimonialists, many of whom are
referred to warmly and frequently, in contrast to the economists, who are
rarely even mentioned by name. More to the point analytically, I have
described an economic and political system in which liberal and nationalist
economic policies and patrimonial political arrangements are related in
complex—sometimes antagonistic and sometimes supportive—ways that
suggest that all three groups will be around for some time yet.

On the issue of culture change, the lack of survey data and Indonesia's
authoritarian controls on public expression make it impossible to know
whether popular attitudes have begun to shift or not. My impression is
that they have. A decade and a half—the late 1960s to the early 1980s—
of reasonably effective performance by a mixed state-private economy
brought relative prosperity to millions of Indonesians, urban and rural,
upper, middle, and lower classes. It appears to be understood by many
of these groups that the economists' policies had a lot to do with that
prosperity. In consequence, the downturn of the 1980s was blamed, as
it should have been, on international rather than domestic factors, and
there seems to be considerable public support for the government's efforts
to restart the growth engine via deregulation.

At the elite level, a more tangible straw in the wind is the near uniformity
of proderegulation opinion among intellectuals, particularly but not exclusively economists, in and out of government. Mohammad Sadli, a leading
economist now out of government, has observed that each new generation
of Western-trained Indonesian economists brings home the latest foreign
intellectual fashions, with which it attacks its seniors' policies.[51] His
colleagues, trained in the 1950s, were development economists; their
successors believed in the New International Economic Order, *dependencia*,
and Basic Human Needs; and the newest Ph.D.'s are Reaganite and

Thatcherite free-marketeers who favour deregulation and privatisation. There is much truth in this observation, but in my view it overlooks the extent to which Indonesian economists' and other intellectuals' views are increasingly being shaped by their post-return experiences. Put slightly differently, Indonesian cultural life, including the culture of the intellectuals, is more autonomous today than it was a decade or two ago. With regard to economic policy, there are still a few *dependencia* advocates around,[52] but most members of that generation have become critics of the government's failure to pursue deregulation more vigorously.[53] The centre of gravity of intellectual opinion will undoubtedly move again, but my guess is that in the last two decades there has been a quantum leap to the right that is now unlikely to be reversed.

Conclusions

My central theme has been the autonomous role played by President Suharto in deciding what economic policies to adopt and how to put together and maintain a set of political arrangements compatible with those policies. I have tried to show how, from Suharto's perspective, the persuasiveness of the theories of his economists has interacted with political culture and ideology and with the patrimonial base of the political system to produce an enduring formula that combines liberal economics with illiberal, but not entirely unpopular, politics.

The formula was first chosen in 1966, in a situation of economic crisis, and probably would not have been adopted without the crisis-induced pressure for change. But the fact of economic crisis was not in itself a condition sufficient to determine the political *cum* policy outcome. Similarly, the formula has endured through the 1970s and 1980s in part, but only in part, because of the success of the initial policies. In the final analysis, the impact of both crisis and success has depended on Suharto's perceptions of the problems facing him, his goals for himself and for his society, and his calculations about how to put together an effective political and economic strategy.

In comparative context, this evidence from New Order Indonesia runs directly counter to the currently fashionable institutional or structural argument that state strength is the critical independent variable in development. In my view, the claim that the state is responsible for particular outcomes of growth and distribution has two fatal flaws. One is a too-high level of aggregation. If the Indonesian government today is organised by any single political force, that force is certainly not the vast and itself ill-coordinated state. It is instead the army, whose top leaders meet regularly, formulate political strategies to maintain their control of the government, and create doctrine to legitimate their autonomous power.

To substitute the army for the state does not, however, better explain where development policy comes from. The Indonesian army as such has had little influence on economic policy making, and there is no clear connection between what one might take to be army interests (e.g., for a bigger military budget) and policy decisions (which, certainly in budgetary terms, have never particularly favoured the military). The comparative literature on the relationship between militaries-in-power and development has also been inconclusive.

The second flaw in the state autonomy argument, at least when applied to Indonesia, is the incongruity between the presumed interests of the state and the government's actual economic policies. Self-aggrandisement should mean that the state grows ever bigger and more powerful, but the impact of the market-oriented theory that guides government policy has been to place limits on the bureaucratic imperative to expand. These limits have tightened since the decline of the world oil market beginning in the early 1980s. As the local entrepreneurial class grows large, and given current trends resulting from government policies it almost certainly will do so, the bureaucracy will confront a new player in the political arena with whom it may have to share power.

If 'relative autonomy' rests not with the state and not with the army but with President Suharto, an individual, is analysis reduced to idiosyncratic description? For Indonesia, does this imply that there is no telling what policies and politics the next president, also an individual, will adopt? For comparative political economy, does it imply that there is no telling, period?

Obviously, my answer to these questions is no. In the very final analysis, to be sure, political scientists are hostage to the irreducible humanness—that is, unpredictability—of our subjects. But we are far from that bottom line.

For Indonesia, I believe that my approach has gone further than any other toward resolving the great mystery of the last two decades of politics and policy making: given a hostile culture and a patrimonial political support structure, how have the economists been able to win as many battles as they have? My answers have had less to do with the idiosyncrasies of President Suharto than with the nature of these variables and the relationships among them.

Culture, I have argued, is commodious, flexible, living, not a dead weight smothering political initiative. Antiforeign, anticapitalist, pro-state attitudes did not prevent Suharto from choosing the path of the economists in 1966, 1975, or since 1983. At the same time these beliefs are real. They help to explain the continuing strength of patrimonialism and of economic nationalism as preached and practiced by a Sutowo or a Habibie.

They provide a general direction and purpose for the regime which the economists' policies must be seen to serve, and probably at some point must in fact serve. This is not an insuperable obstacle. Even the economists' minimal (on the Indonesian spectrum) commitment to state intervention can be justified as fulfilling the requirements of the constitution. The key is that their policies must produce growth and distribute benefits, either directly or through compensatory policies, so that most important real or potential political constituencies get (or perceive that they are getting) a fair share. This is in fact what the New Order has so far accomplished.

Patrimonialism in the Indonesian case has turned out not to be a simple matter of a political structure hostile to liberal economics. On the contrary, between the patrimonialists and the economists there is a symbiotic relationship, of which many individuals on both sides are aware. The latter create the wealth that the former consume, and the former generate much of the political support that gives the latter their capacity to make policy. Among the economists there are few who call for a more democratic political system, and among the patrimonialists there are few who oppose the economists' currently great influence. The patrimonialists were once closer to the economic nationalists, which created some tensions between them and the economists, but it was a tension within a larger structure of consensus on goals and means.

Beyond resolution of the great mystery, a second, much more tentative, finding is also relevant to Indonesia's future, when President Suharto is no longer making the policy decisions. It is that policy success may have led to culture change, to a diminishing of the persuasive power of statist ideas of colonial and traditional origin in favour of mixed economy ideas more appropriate to a modern industrialising society. There is hard evidence for this proposition only for a few mid-career economists, but the change may well have reached deep into the society because of the distribution of the benefits of growth. The third president may thus be more naturally—that is, unreflectively—inclined toward market solutions to economic problems than were his predecessors.

For comparative political economy, these findings suggest an approach, a method, and some new research directions. The approach, of course, is to adopt the perspective of the Third World politician who wants to get in power and stay there, and who needs some kind of economic policy. What groups might provide the support necessary for a winning political coalition? What legitimating principle will help him or her win the support of these and other groups at home and abroad? Where can he or she find the means to coerce, or otherwise neutralise, the opposition? What are the available economic policies and how do they relate to these political considerations?

The method is in-depth analysis of cases and complex comparison, preferably of small numbers or even pairs of countries that exhibit interesting similarities or differences.[54] The aggregate data-dependent multi-country method does not seem sensitive enough to discover the patterns of interaction among critical variables in the politics-economics relationship in the Third World.

Finally, two new directions for comparative research are suggested by the Indonesian findings that liberal economics and patrimonial politics have been mutually supportive and that the impact of culture on policy has varied with the goals, perceptions, and calculations of politicians. On the first, we need to look for the causes of development not at type of regime—whether patrimonialism, some other form of authoritarianism, or democracy—but behind it for patterns in the ways in which specific political arrangements may or may not be compatible with specific economic policies.

On the second, we need to rethink our conception of political culture and the role it plays in political life. If we conceive of political culture less as a set of fixed, deeply held values and beliefs, uni-directionally determining behaviour, and more as a loose assemblage of ideas, some of which are flexible and open to change and manipulation by political actors, we will be in a better position to assess its impact on economic policy making in the Third World.

1. R. Bates, *Markets and States in Tropical Africa* (Berkeley, CA: University of California Press, 1981), p. 8.
2. A. Booth and P. McCawley, eds., *The Indonesian Economy during the Soeharto Era* (Kuala Lumpur: Oxford University Press, 1981), p. 4, and M.H. Soesastro and P. Drysdale, 'Survey of Recent Developments,' *Bulletin of Indonesian Economic Studies*, 26:3 (1990), 3–44.
3. Booth and McCawley, *The Indonesian Economy during the Soeharto Era*, pp. 181–217.
4. *Ibid.*, p. 214.
5. C. Manning, *The Green Revolution, Employment, and Economic Change in Rural Java* (Singapore: Institute of Southeast Asian Studies, 1988); H. Hill, 'The Indonesian Manufacturing Sector: Southeast Asia's Emerging Giant?' in A. Booth, ed., *The Oil Boom and After: Indonesian Economic Policy and Performance in the Soeharto Era* (Kuala Lumpur: Oxford University Press, forthcoming).
6. B. Glassburner and A. Nasution, 'Macroeconomic Policy and Prospects for Long Term Growth,' mimeo, 1988, pp. 8–9.
7. R. Mortimer, ed., *Showcase State: The Illusion of Indonesia's 'Accelerated Modernisation* (Sydney: Angus and Robertson, 1973); I. Roxborough, *Theories of Underdevelopment* (London: Macmillan, 1979); R. Robison, 'Culture, Politics and Economy in the Political History of the New Order,' *Indonesia*, 31 (1981), 1–30; V. Randall and R. Theobald, *Political Change and Underdevelopment* (Durham, NC: Duke University Press, 1985).
8. G. Myrdal, *Asian Drama: An Inquiry into the Poverty of Nations* (New York: Twentieth Century Fund, 1968); A.M. Sievers, *The Mystical World of Indonesia: Culture and Economic Development in Conflict* (Baltimore: The Johns Hopkins University Press, 1974).
9. W. Davis, 'Religion and Development: Weber and the East Asian Experience,'

in M. Weiner and S.P. Huntington, eds., *Understanding Political Development* (Boston: Little Brown, 1987), pp. 221–80.

10. H. Crouch, 'Patrimonialism and Military Rule,' *World Politics*, 31 (1978b), 242–58, and J. Nelson, 'The Political Economy and Stabilisation: Commitment, Capacity, and Public Response,' in R.H. Bates, ed., *Toward and Political Economy of Development: A Rational Choice Perspective* (Berkeley and Los Angeles: University of California Press, 1988), pp. 80–130.

11. R. McVey, 'The Beamstenstaat in Indonesia,' in B. Anderson and A. Kahin, eds., *Interpreting Indonesian Politics: Thirteen Contributions to the Debate* (Ithaca, NY: Cornell University Modern Indonesia Project, 1982), pp. 84–91; B. Anderson, 'Old State, New Society: Indonesia's New Order in Historical Perspective,' *Journal of Asian Studies*, 41 (1983), 477–96; P.B. Evans, D. Rueschemeyer, and T. Skocpol, eds., *Bringing the State Back In* (Cambridge: Cambridge University Press, 1985).

12. Another way to put this is to say that the mutually antagonistic and antidevelopmental forces unleashed by the 1945–1949 revolution, including communism, radical nationalism, and militantly political Islam, had to be conquered before development could begin. There is an interesting comparison here with neighbouring Thailand, now widely projected to be the next Newly Industrialised Country in Asia. Thailand has the most conservative social history in Southeast Asia: little colonial influence, no social revolution, and the gradual, controlled development of a modernising elite. At the same time Thailand has had the most surface political instability: dozens of coups and coup attempts since 1932, when the absolute monarchy was overthrown by an alliance of Western-educated civilian officials and military officers. Since at least the late 1950s, however, liberal economic policies have been consistently followed by whoever is in power. What the Thai experience indicates is that given an ideologically and socially uniform elite, political instability does not necessarily imply policy instability. Since 1966, Indonesia may have begun to create its own conservative base for policy stability.

13. K. Remmer, 'The Politics of Economic Stabilisation: IMF Standby Programs in Latin America, 1954–1984,' *Comparative Politics*, 19:1 (1986), 1–24.

14. P. Baran, *The Political Economy of* Growth (New York: Monthly Review Press, 1957); G. O'Donnell, *Modernisation and Bureaucratic Authoritarianism: Studies in South American* Politics (Berkeley: Institute of International Studies, University of California, 1979).

15. R. Mortimer, *Showcase State: The Illusion of Indonesia's 'Accelerated Modernisation,'*; H. Crouch, *The Army and Politics in Indonesia* (Ithaca, NY: Cornell University Press, 1978a); Anderson, 'Old State, New Society: Indonesia's New Order in Historical Perspective.'

16. C.E. Lindblom, *The Policy Making Process* (Englewood Cliffs, NJ: Prentice Hall, 1968).

17. B. Glassburner, 'Political Economy and the Soeharto Regime,' *Bulletin of Indonesian Economic* Studies, 14:3 (1978), 24–51.

18. Kesatuan Aksi Mahasiswa Indonesia, [Action Front of Indonesian Students], *The Leader, The Man and the* Gun (Jakarta: Yayasan Badan Penerbit Fakultas Ekonomi Universitas Indonesia [Publishing Foundation, Economics Faculty, University of Indonesia], 1966.

19. Glassburner, 'Political Economy and the Soeharto Regime'; Suharto, *Pikiran, Ucapan dan Tindakan Saya: Otobiografi* [My Thoughts, Words and Deeds: Autography], Seperti dipaparkan kepada [as told to] G. Dwipayana and Ramadhan K.H. (Jakarta: PT. Citra Lamtoro Gung Persada, 1988).

20. H. Feith and L. Castles, eds., *Indonesian Political Thinking, 1945–1965* (Ithaca, NY: Cornell University Press, 1970); F.P. Weinstein, *Indonesian Foreign Policy and the Dilemma of Dependence* (Ithaca, NY: Cornell University Press, 1976).

21. McVey, 'The Beamtenstaat in Indonesia'; Anderson, 'Old State, New Society.'

22. 'The Javanese, therefore, would not consider the state to have fulfilled its obligations if it did not encourage an inner psychological order (*tentrum*, peace and tranquillity of heart) as well as enforcing the formal order (*tata*). Only then is the state of perfect balance, of perfect harmony, achieved'. S. Moertono, *State and Statecraft in Old* Java (Ithaca, NY: Cornell University Modern Indonesia Project, 1968), p. 3.

23. *Ibid.*, p. 119.

24. *Ibid.*, p. 3–4.

25. *Ibid.*, p. 120.

26. C. Geertz, *The Religions of* Java (Glencoe, IL: The Free Press, 1960); R.W. Liddle, *Politics and Political Culture in* Indonesia (Anne Arbor, MI: Center for Political Studies, University of Michigan, 1988), reprinted as Chapter Three in this volume.

27. Suharto, *Pikiran, Ucapan dan Tindakan Saya.*

28. Republic of Indonesia Department of Information, *The 1945 Constitution of the Republic of* Indonesia (Jakarta: Department of Information, 1989), p. 11.

29. Nelson, 'The Political Economy of Stabilisation', p. 105.

30. Crouch, 'Patrimonialism and Military Rule.'

31. *Ibid.*, p. 251.

32. Nelson, 'The Political Economy of Stabilisation', p. 88.

33. W. Ilchman and N.T. Uphoff, *The Political Economy of Change* (Berkeley and Los Angeles: University of California Press, 1969).

34. Interview with Professor Sarbini Somawinata, Jakarta, November 1986.

35. Sarbini Somawinata, 'Non-Economic Aspects of Development,' in *Five Papers on Indonesian Economic Development* (Jakarta: Jajasan Badan Penerbit Fakultas Ekonomi Universitas Indonesia [Publications Foundation, Economics Faculty, University of Indonesia], 1970; M. Mas'oed, 'The Indonesian Economy and Political Structure During the Early New Order, 1966–1971', Unpublished Ph.D. dissertation. (Columbus: Department of Political Science, The Ohio State University, 1983).

36. The lowest estimate of communists and sympathisers killed is 100,000; the highest, 1,000,000. About 50,000 were held in detention until the late 1970s.

37. R.T. McVey, 'The Post-Revolutionary Transformation of the Indonesian Army, Parts I and II," *Indonesia* 11 (1971), 131–76; 13 (1972), 147–82.

38. Crouch, *The Army and Politics.*

39. One of the most revealing is a discussion of the foundations Suharto has created for patronage distribution, and for which he has been accused of personal corruption. The government party received (in 1985) US$200,000 per month from one of these foundations, he writes, while the other parties are supported from a different foundation. 'Why, this foundation even helps

people to go abroad for medical treatment.' Another interesting reference is
a report of a conflict with a key political adviser who warned that reducing
the kerosene subsidy to consumers, a policy recommended by the economists,
would cause antigovernment protests that could bring the government down.
Suharto says that he knew the people would accept the price increase, because
even at the new price a litre of kerosene would be less expensive than a glass
of tea. Events, he concluded, proved him right. Suharto, *Pikiran, Ucapan dan
Tindakan Saya*, p. 271, pp. 412–13.
40. *Ibid.*, pp. 486–92.
41. I say so-called because the term implies that their opponents, the economists,
are not nationalists in the broader sense of Indonesia-firsters. I have argued
above that one of the political resources possessed by the economists is their
adherence to nationalist values.
42. B. Glassburner, 'In the Wake of General Ibnu: Crisis in the Indonesian Oil
Industry,' *Asian Survey* 16, (1976); 1099–1112; P. McCawley, "Some Consequences of the Pertamina Crisis in Indonesia,' *Journal of Southeast Asian
Studies* 9:1 (1978), 1–27; H. McDonald, *Suharto's Indonesia,* (Blackburn,
Victoria: Fontana, 1980).
43. B.J. Habibie, *Some Thoughts Concerning a Strategy of the Industrial Transformation of a Developing Country* (Bonn: Deutsche Gesellschaft fur Luft und
Raumfahrt, 1983); A. Nasir, "Hi-Tech, Low Yield," *Far Eastern Economic
Review* 136:24, (1987), 110–16.
44. Suharto, *Pikiran, Ucapan dan Tindakan Saya*, pp. 421–23, p. 262.
45. Soemitro's son, an army officer, is married to Suharto's daughter.
46. Since the late 1960s, balancing the budget annually has been an obsession
with the economists and with the president himself. There is a certain artifici-
ality, however, to the concept of a balanced budget in Indonesia. Receipts
from foreign borrowing, always substantial in the New Order, are included
as revenues in Indonesian budgetary calculations.
47. Suharto, *Pikiran, Ucapan dan Tindakan Saya*, p. 286.
48. Survey of Recent Developments, *Bulletin of Indonesian Economic Studies* 18–
25 (1982–1990).
49. Suharto's favouritism toward his six children does not fit well my interpretation of the reasons for his economic policy decisions. Up to the early 1980s
the children, particularly the oldest daughter and the three sons, had been
given shares in the companies and banks controlled by Sino-Indonesian business
interests close to the president but were not themselves significant economic
players. In the 1980s they sought or were given a vast array of import
monopolies, government contracts, and other privileges, angering many business people, nationalists, and patrimonialists, plus the military establishment
and the general public. In political terms, the behaviour of the children has
incurred large costs in group support and legitimacy and produced no benefits
for Suharto.
50. Non-oil exports have increased from $US5.87 billion in 1984 to $8.58 billion
in 1987 and $13.47 billion in 1989. D. Evans, 'Survey of Recent Develop-
ments', *Bulletin of Indonesian Economic Studies* 24:3 (1988), 15; M. Pangestu
and M. Habir, 'Survey of Recent Developments,' *Bulletin of Indonesian
Economic Studies* 26:1 (1990), 16.

51. Interview with Mohammad Sadli, Jakarta, September 15, 1986.
52. M.D. Rahardjo, *Perekonomian Indonesia: Pertumbuhan dan Krisis* [The Indonesian Economy: Growth and Crisis] (Jakarta: LP3ES, 1987).
53. Sjahrir, 'Political Economy of Basic Needs in Indonesia: A Prospective Appraisal', Unpublished Ph.D. Dissertation, (Cambridge, MA: Harvard University, 1983). Published in Indonesia as Sjahrir, *Ekonomi Politik Kebutuhan Pokok* [The Political Economy of Basic Needs] (Jakarta: LP3ES, 1986); D. Kuntjoro-Jakti, 'Konservatisme dalam Anggaran dan Pinjaman [Conservatism in Budgeting and Borrowing],' *Prisma* 14:4 (1986), 47–50; Sjahrir, *Kebijaksanaan Negara-Konsistensi dan Implementasi* [State Policy, Consistency and Implementation] (Jakarta: LP3ES, 1987).
54. An example is the Indonesia-Thailand comparison in footnote 12. Another interesting comparison is Indonesia-Burma. Both are military regimes led by strong figures, patrimonial in their support bases, antiforeign, anticapitalist, and pro-state in ideology, with long histories of strong states. In the mid-1960s, when Suharto adopted outward looking and liberal Economic policies, General Ne Win isolated Burma from the West and nationalised most of the economy. On Burma, see R.H. Taylor *The State in Burma* (London: C. Hurst, 1987).

PART TWO

5

Improvising Political Cultural Change: Three Indonesian Cases*

I

> So long as it is vital, the cultural tradition of a people—its symbols, ideals, and ways of feeling—is always an argument about the meaning of the destiny its members share. Cultures are dramatic conversations about things that matter to their participants.[1]

In the real world, cultures are made up of many, often conflicting, patterns of values, beliefs, and customs.[2] These patterns are dynamic, forever changing in response to and in advance of other movements both within and external to society. Nowhere is this truer than in the old-new nation-states of Asia and Africa, where for a century and more indigenous and imported values, beliefs, and customs have been engaging and disengaging, resolving and dissolving like bits of colored glass in a kaleidoscope.

In the world of social science, however, culture is largely treated as a contextual or independent variable useful to explain variations in behaviour among societies. The political science *locus classicus* of this approach is Gabriel Almond and Sidney Verba's *The Civic Culture*, a five-country comparative analysis of the relationship between popular attitudes toward politics and stable democracy.[3] It was applied to the Third World most influentially in Lucian Pye and Sidney Verba's *Political Culture and Political Development*, where Pye wrote: 'The notion of political culture assumes that the attitudes, sentiments, and cognitions that inform and govern political behaviour in any society are not just random congeries but represent coherent patterns which fit together and are mutually reinforcing.'[4]

* First published in J. Schiller (ed), *Indonesian Culture: Asking the Right Questions*, Athens: Ohio University Southeast Asia Studies, 1996.

In Indonesian political studies, the most celebrated application of this view of the relationship between culture and politics is Benedict Anderson's 'The Idea of Power in Javanese Culture.'[5] Briefly, Anderson identifies four attributes of what he believes to be the traditional Javanese conception of power—its concreteness, homogeneity, constant amount, and amorality—which contrast sharply with, again, as he conceives it, the Western idea of power. He then attempts to demonstrate the merits of the Javanese idea as an analytical tool by employing it to interpret various policy decisions of Presidents Sukarno and Suharto.

Anderson's portrayal is lucid, vivid, and original. It focuses our minds wonderfully on a pattern of beliefs associated with the Javanese *kebatinan* (the science of inner being) tradition, and raises intriguingly the question of its contemporary applicability. As a framework for understanding present day behaviour, however (leaving aside the problem of its historical validity[6]), it is partial in two senses. It describes only one among many threads in the fabric of late twentieth century Indonesian political culture.[7] And it gives us no tools with which to analyse the historical process by which a set of ideas presumably dominant in pre-colonial times maintains its influence in post-colonial Indonesian political thought.

On the first point, compare Anderson's single string approach with Robert Bellah's multi-stranded conception, in *Habits of the Heart*, of American political culture:

> From its early days, some Americans have seen the purpose and goal of the nation as the effort to realise the ancient biblical hope of a just and compassionate society. Others have struggled to shape the spirit of their lives and the laws of the nation in accord with the ideals of republican citizenship and participation. Yet others have promoted dreams of manifest destiny and national glory. And always there have been the proponents, often passionate, of the notion that liberty means the spirit of enterprise and the right to amass wealth and power for oneself.[8]

Bellah's book goes on to examine how these various sub-cultures—biblical, republican, nationalist, and individualist—interact today.

On the second point, the absence of analytical tools with which to understand how cultures change or are maintained over time, we need to examine values, beliefs, and customs not just as ideas but as they relate to concrete domestic and international processes and institutions, the upward and downward movements of powerful social and political forces and currents. Here we must be careful not to succumb to the twin lures of the Scylla and Charybdis of social and cultural determinism.

A good way to begin is to recognise the incompleteness or insufficiency and also malleability of any given cultural inheritance, to be aware that culture is to some extent created anew by every individual in response to the challenges of his or her particular environment. This is not to deny the general stability of cultures, or to exaggerate the effects of the environment, but rather to locate in the individual the mechanism by which cultural change, when it does occur, takes place. Robert Hefner puts the point this way:

In interpretive social science we sometimes assume that individuals simply 'internalize' the values of the group or community of which they are members.... [T]his is for most purposes a much too powerful model of culture. Not all the knowledge we learn in social life is transmitted in such a prepackaged and comprehensive format. A good portion of the knowledge we need to act in the world is, in fact, reconstructed by each of us as individuals. It depends, then, not on the passive internalization of prefigured symbols and meanings, but on *an ongoing improvisation in the face of environmental demands and opportunities.*[9]

Not all individuals count equally in cultural change, of course. In every large-scale modern society, a relative few are endowed with or accumulate resources—intellectual, persuasive, utilitarian, and/or coercive—with which they are able to influence, directly or indirectly, the values, beliefs, and customs of many—sometimes very many—others.

Unfortunately, in the social science theoretical literature there are few helpful guides to analysing how this business of resource-building and resource-deploying works in relation to cultural change. My own most basic assumptions tend toward complexity, catholicity, and indeterminacy. With Max Weber and Clifford Geertz, I believe that cultures are 'at once a product and a determinant of social interaction.'[10] That is, no simple unilinear model can explain why cultures or societies change. Moreover, with Charles Taylor and Albert Hirschman I believe that outcomes are always subject to, and in fact are often affected by, the intervention of previously unidentified variables.[11] I do not therefore aspire to any kind of closed conceptual framework or law-like conclusions.

Given these assumptions, Hefner's formulation of cultural change as 'ongoing improvisation' is a good description both of my own analytical starting point and of my sense of how it is that individuals in a society actually construct their values, beliefs, and customs. In this chapter I will describe the improvisations of three well-known Indonesian intellectuals: Goenawan Mohamad, the editor-in-chief of *Tempo* magazine; Sjahrir, a political economist who heads his own *Sekolah Ilmu Sosial* (School of Social Science) and research and consulting firm, the Institute for Economic and Financial Research; and Nurcholish Madjid, once the chair of *Himpunan Mahasiswa Islam* (Islamic University Students' Association), now a lecturer at the Jakarta *Institut Agama Islam Negeri* (State Islamic Institute) and chair of the private *Yayasan Paramadina* (Paramadina Foundation), a Jakarta-based Islamic studies organisation.

All three of these individuals have engaged in improvisation because they have not found, in the dominant political cultural legacy they have inherited, persuasive answers to the challenges posed by the demands and opportunities of their place and time, the Indonesian nation-state in the last three decades of the twentieth century. The essayist Goenawan has discarded the state-centred collectivism of his national and ethnic past in favor of a more individual-centred conception of society; the economist Sjahrir has rejected his countrymen's belief in the superior morality of the state over the private sector in the economy; and the religious thinker Nurcholish has disavowed the historical commitment of most Indonesian Muslims to a totalistic view of the relationship between religion and society, adopting in its place a render-unto-Caesar secularism toward many questions of social and political life.

What makes these intellectuals interesting is that they are tackling three of the most central, and in my view harmful, beliefs in Indonesian political culture—beliefs that have long impeded progress toward a more participatory polity, prosperous economy, and integrated society—and that their improvisations have taken place in public. All three have written and spoken widely for many years. Their names, ideas, and activities are well known to the newspaper and magazine reading public, in Jakarta and throughout the country. They thus have the potential of shaping the improvisations of other Indonesians as well. Whether they are in fact having much of an impact is, as I have already suggested, a complex matter that I can only begin to examine here.

II

Goenawan Mohamad was born in Batang, a strongly Islamic area on the north coast of central Java, in 1941. He is undoubtedly the most famous dropout from the University of Indonesia's Psychology Faculty, which he entered in 1960. During the Guided Democracy period, he was a member of the *Manifes Kebudayaan* (Cultural Manifesto) group of writers and artists opposed to the communist party-driven politicisation of the arts. In 1965-66 he travelled to and studied in Belgium. His journalism career began with the anti-Sukarno, pro-New Order daily newspaper *Harian KAMI*, after which he founded his own newsmagazine, since 1970 called *Tempo*. Today he is a very successful journalist-business person, and also a highly-regarded poet.

Goenawan's ideas are most fully expressed in his weekly *Tempo* columns, now collected in three volumes.[12] At least in the third volume, whose more than 160 essays I read carefully before writing an introduction, it is clear that his central moral and intellectual commitment is to the individual. The institutions and beliefs of society are useful in so far as they create a context in which individual men and women develop the self-knowledge and social resources that enable them to gain mastery over their own lives.

For example, writing about a dam project from which tens of thousands of villagers were forcibly evicted, Goenawan affirms that what is important is that 'no matter what, the people can not have taken away their right—given to them by God—to choose their own way of life.' After telling the story of a child prodigy who died young without achievements because of his father's overbearing tutelage, Goenawan writes: 'Human beings can be ripened artificially (*dikarbit*), minted (*dicetak*), aimed in a particular direction (*diarahkan*)—who says they can't be. But later on, finally a crisis will hit us as ourselves. Without protection.'[13] In a later essay on the 1940s modernist poet Chairil Anwar, he laments that 'even now, at a time when we often see individuals beaten up by mobs, tortured by the authorities and slandered by the public, we are still afraid of *I* (aku). We feel more secure with *we* (kita).[14]

Accompanying Goenawan's individualism is a cluster of related values and beliefs. He rejects most Indonesian intellectuals' standard dichotomisation of cultures into the 'spiritual' East versus the 'material' West, believing instead that science knows no national or cultural boundaries and that ideas and experiences should be sought from everywhere.

He is hostile to the absolutism of personal rulership ('A country that is governed by one person is not a country at all'[15]), the destructiveness of revolution, the arbitrariness and shackles of bureaucracy, and the fanaticism of ideologues. He is in favor of representative democracy. His columns seek answers to such questions as: What causes democracy? Why are its proponents so often less passionate than its opponents? How can we make choices in a radically uncertain world? How can we reconcile democracy with the selfishness and rapaciousness of human nature?

Goenawan is an autodidact, a born intellectual and a voracious reader who seems to have formed his essential ideas early.[16] In Batang, he read the local press—*Panyebar Semangat* (in Javanese), *Minggu Pagi*, *Suara Merdeka*—which he valued for its high quality editing, non-partisanship, and balanced consideration of issues, unlike the more strident national press of the time. He is an admirer of Albert Camus, and once wrote an introduction to a collection of his essays. If he is heir to any Indonesian intellectual tradition, it is that of the rationalist and Westerniser Sutan Takdir Alisjahbana. But his small-town Javanese upbringing, or perhaps it is his temperament, makes him a less one-sided, more complex and subtle thinker.

Tempo, modelled after *Time* and *Newsweek*, was designed to appeal to a broad educated audience, to bridge many walks of life, unlike its more partisan or specialised predecessors. It has nonetheless had an explicitly political mission, to defend those who can not defend themselves. Goenawan links this mission to his individualism: 'in stressing the individual . . . I actually want to depict the individual as a potential victim, not as a potential disturber of harmony.'[17]

Tempo's linguistic (of course also political, in a broader sense) mission has from the beginning been equally important: to develop a new kind of Indonesian journalistic language, honest and truthful in its reportage, stylistically direct, unpretentious and clear, and free of the cliches and slogans of both ideologues and bureaucrats. It has come very close to achieving these goals, certainly in comparison both to its predecessors and to its current competition.

Sjahrir was born in 1945 in Kudus, central Java, of West Sumatran parents. He was educated at the Faculty of Economics, University of Indonesia, and at Harvard, where he received his Ph.D. in Political Economy and Government in 1983. During the political upheavals of the mid-1960s he was a prominent student activist, becoming chair of the presidium of the national level KAMI (*Kesatuan Aksi Mahasiswa Indonesia*, Indonesian Students Action Front) in 1969. As a young assistant at the Faculty of Economics in the early 1970s, he was a major intellectual force behind the student protest movement that culminated in the anti-Japanese and anti-government riots of January 1974, subsequently labelled *Malari* (*Malapetaka Januari*, the January Disaster).

In Indonesia, Sjahrir studied under the technocrats or so-called Berkeley Mafia, including Professors Widjojo Nitisastro, Ali Wardhana, and Mohammad Sadli. He was also associated with Professor Sumitro Djojohadikusumo, the dean of Indonesian professional economists. At the same time he was strongly influenced by an economist with democratic socialist values, Professor Sarbini Somawinata.[18] Up to 1974, when he was arrested, tried, and convicted for his role in the events leading up to *Malari*, his economics and politics appear to have reflected the ideas of Sarbini more than those of the neo-classical technocrats.

At Harvard, Sjahrir became a convert to the market and a skeptic about the relevance of Western-style democracy for present-day Indonesia. Nonetheless, he remains committed to the goals of broadly-based economic growth and distribution. He also believes that the right kind of government intervention—a mix of neo-classical macro-economic policies, more sectorally-targeted policies to increase competition and thereby enhance market efficiency, plus budgetary allocations for distribution—is crucial to achieving both of these goals.[19]

Since his return to Indonesia in the mid-1980s, Sjahrir's voluminous journalistic writing has been almost exclusively pro-market, anti-regulation and anti-monopoly.[20] Perhaps ironically, this stance aligns him with his former teachers, the reigning technocrats under the leadership of Professor Widjojo, whose policies he once disdained.

To some extent, his current views reflect the temper of the times, as the various non-market alternative approaches to which he was once attracted have been discredited. They are also consistent, however, with his earlier anger at the flagrant abuse—through illegal bribes or legal monopolies—by high officials of public position for private gain. But most fundamentally, in my judgment anyway, they reveal Sjahrir's mature convictions about Indonesian economy and society, and in particular about what government policies will solve Indonesia's economic problems at its present stage of development.

Nurcholish Madjid was born in Jombang, eastern Java, in 1939. Jombang is in the heartland of Javanese Islam, and Nurcholish's father was simultaneously active in the traditional Islamic organisation *Nahdlatul Ulama* (The Awakening of the Religious Teachers) and the Islamic modernism-influenced political party *Masjumi*. When NU broke politically with *Masjumi* in 1952, Nurcholish's father stayed with the latter and transferred his son from a traditional boarding school (*pesantren*) to the famous modernist school at Gontor.

From Gontor, Nurcholish entered the State Islamic Institute in Jakarta, graduating with a degree in Arabic literature in 1968. From 1966 to 1971, a time of great ferment in politics and economics, he was national chair of the Islamic University Students' Association. In January 1970 he gave a speech to a meeting of Islamic student groups that electrified and polarised the Muslim community, and whose impact is still palpable today.

The title of the speech was the rather bland-sounding '*Keharusan Pembaharuan Pemikiran Islam Dan Masalah Integrasi Ummat*' (The Necessity for Renewal of Islamic Thinking and the Problem of the Integration of the Islamic Community),[21] but it contained a concept—*sekularisasi* (secularisation)—that shocked many people. Nurcholish began by asserting that Islam in Indonesia had stagnated. Muslims faced a critical choice: the path of renewal, requiring a thorough rethinking of the meaning of religion in the modern world, at the expense of the solidarity of the community; or the maintenance of that solidarity, at the expense of a freezing of thought and the loss of moral force. Opting for renewal, he proposed a process of *liberalisasi* (liberalisation) which in turn had three dimensions: secularisation, intellectual freedom, and the Idea of Progress and an Open Attitude.

The concept of secularisation Nurcholish borrowed from Robert Bellah, whose paper on 'Islamic Tradition and the Problems of Modernization' he had read on a trip to the United States and the Middle East in 1968.[22] Bellah's paper focused on early Islam, which he considered more 'modern' (in the Western social science sense) than the periods that followed it. Here is what Nurcholish read:

> There is no question but that under Muhammad, Arabian society made a remarkable leap forward in social complexity and political capacity. . . . It is modern in the high degree of commitment, involvement, and participation expected from the rank-and-file members of the community. It is modern in the openness of its leadership positions to ability judged on universal grounds and

symbolized in the attempt to institutionalize a non-hereditary top leadership.[23]

Bellah identified four 'structural elements' of early Islam that made it modern in this sense:

First was a conception of a transcendent monotheistic God. . . . Second was the call to selfhood and decision. . . . *Third was the radical devaluation, one might legitimately say secularization, of all existing social structures in the face of this central God-man relationship.* . . . And finally, there was a new conception of political order based on the participation of all those who accepted the divine revelation and thus constituted themselves a new community, umma. The dominant ethos of this community was this-worldly, activist, social, and political . . .[24]

Nurcholish seized upon Bellah's conceptualisation to articulate his own vision of the proper Islamic society and the shortcomings of Indonesian Islam.

By secularization is not meant the implementation of Secularism, because 'secularism is the name for an ideology, a new closed world view which functions very much like a new religion.' What is needed is every kind of 'liberating development.' This liberation is especially necessary because the Islamic community, due to its own history, is no longer able to distinguish, among values it considers Islamic, which are transcendental and which are temporal.[25]

As a result of this historical process, Islam has lost its 'psychological striking force.' Muslims have become mere traditionalists and can not come to grips with the demands of current and future social change. What needs to be done is to 'make worldly values that should be worldly, and release the Islamic community from the tendency to make them divine.'[26]

These views have implications for politics. Although Nurcholish does not specifically address the issue of an Islamic State, it is clear that he thinks the basic requirement for Muslims is not the form of the state in which they live but the moral character of their political behaviour. The loyalty of Muslims is not to institutions but to Islam itself. They are therefore not obliged to form an Islamic party. Nurcholish uses the phrase 'Islam yes, Islamic party no'[27] for the first time in this speech.[28] An Islamic state is any state in which they can follow the teachings of the Qur'an and *sunnah* (way of life of the prophet). For Nurcholish, these teachings emphasise social justice, egalitarianism, and political participation through democratic institutions.

He also argues for the adoption of useful ideas from outside Islam:

Today, the struggle to improve the fate of the human community is not a monopoly of the Islamic community. The whole human community, staking all of the rationality at its disposal, is involved in efforts to find the best ways to improve the collective life of mankind. Its thoughts in these modern times find expression in such now frequently heard terms as democracy, socialism, populism, communism, and so on.[29]

Nurcholish's views are to some extent a natural continuation of the basic thrusts of nineteenth century Middle Eastern Islamic modernism, especially that of Muhammad Abduh, which were to return to the Qur'an and *sunnah* as the direct sources of inspiration for belief and practice, and to adopt the tools of modern science in order to catch up with the industrialised West. By the 1940s and 1950s, when Nurcholish was growing up in Jombang, modernist ideas were influential throughout Indonesia, especially in the cities, and were being taught at Gontor.

Nurcholish's concept of secularisation, though inspired by a reading of Bellah, seems well within the Islamic modernist principles of his teachers. It nonetheless provoked enormous controversy, almost all of it from within the modernist community itself. One reason was a simple misunderstanding of the word *sekularisasi*, which was taken by many to mean the creation of a non-religious or wholly secular world, despite Nurcholish's explicit disclaimer. More substantively, many modernists refused to part with the shibboleth that Islam is a holistic religion that knows no separation of the things of God from the things of man. In particular, unlike Christianity (they like to say), there is no separation of church and state in Islam.[30]

At the University of Chicago, from 1978 to 1984, Nurcholish read widely in classical and medieval Islamic literature, under the direction of the neo-modernist Pakistani scholar Professor Fazlur Rahman, gaining a new appreciation of non-modernist thought and practice.[31] He had at first intended to specialise in the sociology of religion, but finally wrote his dissertation on the theology and political philosophy of the classical thinker Ibn Taimiya.[32]

Since returning from Chicago in 1984, he has once again become the most prominent intellectual leader of the urban, Western-educated Islamic community. He is a Senior Researcher at LIPI, the Indonesian Institute of Sciences, and a Professor at the Islamic Studies Institute. He is also the founder and head of the private Paramadina Foundation, which conducts religious discussions and in other ways ministers to the spiritual and ethical needs of affluent middle and upper class Muslims.[33]

Nurcholish now calls himself a 'pluralist' or 'inclusivist', by which he means that no single Islamic individual or group can legitimately claim to be in exclusive possession of the truth.[34] Certain knowledge of truth belongs to God, and can only be reached for by man. Intellectual freedom and tolerance for a range of interpretations are therefore basic to a genuinely Islamic society. This approach is of course very compatible, if not identical, with his 1970 views, and he remains a highly controversial figure.

III

So far I have just limned the ideas of three individuals, and elaborated a bit on their origins and characteristics. But the important question is whether something broadly social is going on, whether these individuals are thinking and acting in isolation or are having an impact in changing the values and beliefs of their fellow Indonesians.

This is not an easy question to answer, for both practical and intellectual reasons. The major practical barrier is that Indonesia is not a free society. Fear of government reprisals constrains most people from writing, speaking, or acting authentically in the national political arena. So the observer must sift through the public record for clues as to underlying positions and intentions.

Intellectually, as I stated at the outset, there has been little systematic, cumulative development of conceptual frameworks and hypotheses about the causes of cultural change. There is, however, one fundamental insight on which Karl Marx and Max Weber, together with their respective followers, have been in agreement: that ideas (e.g. Marx's capitalism, Weber's Calvinism) prosper only when they are linked to powerful social forces (e.g. Marx's bourgeoisie, Weber's entrepreneurs).

I accept this insight, and will try to build on it in what follows. At the same time, I am uncomfortable with it, at least when so baldly put, for two reasons. First, it implies that social forces are autonomous of and anterior to ideas, when in fact (or so I believe) ideas often shape both the form and content of social forces in societies under pressure (which is to say all societies in the modern world). Second, it excessively narrows our analytical focus to the two variables of ideas and social forces. What we should be looking for, in addition, are the presence or absence of other variables that help new ideas and forces to come together or that keep them apart.

My way of overcoming these problems is to introduce the concept of resources, the means or 'factors of production' that give weight to the social and political demands of individuals and groups. My definition of resources is broad, indeed infinite (in the sense that new types are always being created), and my approach to them is empirical, inductive, and formative or emergent.

To be specific, for present purposes: what resources are possessed by the defenders of the dominant culture, what resources do my three cultural innovators hold, and how are these resources being shaped—created, expanded, contracted, destroyed—by the political process, that is, by the working out of conflicts among social and political forces in contemporary Indonesia? In what follows, I will focus primarily on the obstacles thrown up by the defenders and the innovators' current and emerging resources, as I see them, but will also try to give some sense of the possibilities for change that emerge from the political process.

The Defenders

The defenders of the dominant values and beliefs enjoy the luxury of the *status quo*. They benefit from four important resources: a supporting cast of tens of millions of believers, many of whom are mobilisable against change; the cultural and social inertia that typically accompanies long-held beliefs; a high degree of 'recoverability' or capacity to adapt to new situations; and powerful networks of social forces and institutions with an interest in their preservation. In the first case, and to a considerable extent in the second, they command the resources of the most powerful institution in Indonesian society, the state, and of the political force that governs the state, the army.

Without a cumulation of survey research or anthropological case studies, it is difficult to gauge just how pervasive and intensely-held, let alone how politically mobilisable, the dominant values of the supporting cast are. My personal impression, derived from long periods of living in both rural and urban Indonesia and a quarter century of reading the daily press, is that they are for sure extremely pervasive.

The intensity with which they are held, and thus their mobilisability and the strength of their inertial force, is another question. To answer it, we need to know something about the extent to which they are a product of each individual's direct experience with the challenges of daily living, which would tend to make them a matter of deeper conviction, rather than a product of the general socialisation process, which I suspect results in more easily toppled beliefs.

Absent such knowledge, here are a few snippets of direct testimony from Indonesians actively involved in the cultural process. Our Muslim innovator, Nurcholish, believes that Islamic intolerance of non-Muslims is pervasive, intense, and easy to mobilise. Arswendo Atmowiloto, editor of *Monitor*, a TV guide and tabloid magazine, and a non-Muslim, was recently mobbed by angry Muslims and subsequently sentenced to a jail term by a Jakarta court. His crime was insulting Islam by reporting that the Prophet Muhammad was not the public figure most admired by Indonesians, according to a poll of *Monitor* readers.

Commenting on the case, Nurcholish said:

> Arswendo did not understand and did not feel how difficult it is to persuade Indonesian Muslims to respect adherents to other religions. I have been involved in polemics, debates, and conflicts for nearly a quarter of a century, and I have felt threats that have made me shudder.[35]

More directly relevant to the issue of the relationship between Islam and the state is a 1990 report from Abdurrahman Wahid, the head of Indonesia's largest Muslim organisation, the traditionalist, rural Java-based *Nahdlatul Ulama* or NU, which claims a membership of 27 million. According to Wahid, Gen. L.B. Murdani, the Minister of Defence and Security, currently the leader of army opposition to President Suharto's death grip on his office, and a Roman Catholic, asked him if NU would support him as Suharto's successor. Wahid's answer was that, though he himself had no objection, NU's members could not yet accept a non-Muslim president.[36]

On the issue of the general relationship between state and society, the young Muslim poet and essayist Emha Ainun Nadjib, known for his closeness to village people, characterised the attitudes of ordinary Indonesians and officials this way in a recent interview:

> All Indonesians I have ever met feel that they are the subordinates (*bawahan*) of the government. Moreover there are very many of our officials in the regions or outlying areas who feel confident that they really are the superiors (*atasan*) of the people. And if you say that popular sovereignty is above the government's sovereignty, you will not only be considered to oppose development, but they will be sure you are really an evil person.[37]

This attitude clearly carries over to the specific relationship between the state and the economy. Perhaps the most worrisome evidence to this effect, worrisome because it shows the extraordinary tenacity of statist views, even among highly-educated and well-informed people, is in a recent paper by the economist Bruce Glassburner.[38] In 1989 Glassburner interviewed thirty-six members of the political and governmental elite on questions of economic policy.

All of these individuals had been asked the same questions in interviews conducted in the late 1960s by Frank Weinstein.[39] Most elite members, Weinstein found, were hostile to free enterprise and markets and believed in the need for state protection of indigenous capitalists and many other anti-market regulations to prevent monopoly and promote more egalitarian distribution. Twenty years later, and despite the enormous success of the New Order's essentially neo-classical macro-economic policy during the intervening period, Glassburner found no change in views.[40]

Concerning the relationship between the collectivity and the individual, army officers and civilian government officials are the most vigorous articulators of the pro-collectivity position. At one level, this is because of the strong belief of officers and officials that their institutions are the only structures in society that can formulate, articulate, and defend the interests of the whole against the special interests of individuals and groups. This belief is reinforced and sustained by their material and status interests, which have been well served by their control of the government.

In the case of the army, belief in the importance of the collectivity is strengthened by the general corporateness that characterises all modern military forces. More specifically Indonesian, the ideology of *dwi-fungsi* (twin functions of defending the country and 'playing a positive socio-political role') legitimises the army, in its own eyes at least, as the central organising and controlling force in Indonesian politics. The general concept of army intervention in politics, for which *dwi-fungsi* is the current name, has a long history going back to the 1945–1949 Revolution.[41] Senior serving officers appear not to debate either its value as basic doctrine or its current implementation. Retired officers, less bound by military discipline and without a need to please superiors, express a range of views about implementation but do not question the doctrine itself. Younger officers, who were socialised into belief in *dwi-fungsi* in military academy and subsequently have been given training in its practice through assignments outside the Department of Defence and Security, may have other views.

In the case of civilian bureaucrats, belief in the collectivity and in the state's role is strengthened by the government's effective building up of civil service associations, particularly Korpri (*Korps Pegawai Republik Indonesia*, Officials' Corps of the Republic of Indonesia), and its wives' affiliate *Dharma Wanita* (Women's Duty). These organisations are imbued with an ethic of public service and at the same time allow officials to display and enjoy their high social status.

New Order government service is also a world unto itself, superior to and isolated from political parties and other organisations of non-civil servants. Promotions and other career ambitions—especially positioning in jobs that enable one to make money on the side—are satisfied largely through the manipulation of internal patron-client networks. Lower-ranking, younger bureaucrats attach themselves to more senior officials, performing various services that raise the status, power, and income of the seniors in return for boosts up the ladder. This pattern helps to solidify officials' sense of their corporateness and separateness from the rest of society.

For the last several years the head of President Suharto's executive office, Minister for the State Secretariat (and a retired army officer) Murdiono, has acted as a kind of official philosopher on behalf of collectivism and statism. In speeches and press conferences, he offers a steady stream of often thoughtful commentary and analysis, typically couched in Javanese aphorisms, anchoring government policy to the collective interest. In the New Order's very hierarchical bureaucratic system, his style and the substance of his views are emulated by other central officials, governors, district, subdistrict, and village heads. Many non-Javanese officials collect books of Javanese sayings to help them understand and participate in this discourse.

All of this seems to work reasonably well as a cultural system. For example, I recall an evening in 1986, when I was watching the national television news in a small hotel in the remote district town of Takengon, central Aceh. I was struck by the fact that I was surrounded by a sea of blue Korpri shirts, with their distinctive *beringin* (banyan) tree motif. They were being worn not only by my fellow hotel guests, but by everyone appearing on the screen as well!

To many non-officials (and even, it must be conceded, to some officials), state television is notorious for its excessive coverage of the doings of officials. But to the people I was with the images on the screen affirmed an important bond, one that most wearers of the shirt care deeply about. For good reason, since it has made a modern life possible for them and at the same time given them a sense of a larger purpose and social commitment.

Though general support for the idea of the collectivity and for the role of the state is widespread within the state itself, there are nonetheless redoubts of individualism. The state universities, especially the best ones like the University of Indonesia in Jakarta and Gadjah Mada University in Yogyakarta, are perhaps the most important. There, even though the lecturers are all of course state officials, the Korpri shirt and the 'safari' daily uniform seen in most government offices are rarer.

The universities provide a kind of protected haven, or atmosphere of relative cultural freedom, where many different ideas are entertained, both in the classroom and in the frequent seminars and conferences that bring in off-campus and foreign speakers. In my experience, mostly at Gadjah Mada, there is a serious attempt at creating an intellectual environment in which faculty and students will not be punished for expressing unorthodox ideas. This intellectual freedom has not gone unchallenged by the government, as the history of repression of student movements and demonstrations attests, but it has never been totally suppressed.[42]

The army's and the bureaucracy's power to defend the ideas of the superiority of the collectivity and the centrality of the state weighs most heavily on the efforts of Goenawan and like-minded intellectuals to raise the dignity and expand the autonomy of the individual. It rests somewhat more lightly on Sjahrir and other pro-deregulation economists, who have at least been able to convince government decision-makers to adopt market-oriented policies. The evidence of Glassburner's article, however, argues that the economists have not yet had much impact on the basic pro-state culture of the political elite, even in regard to economic questions.

The belief that an Islamic society requires an Islamic State has a rather different history. It has never been as pervasively held as the pro-collectivity and pro-state ideas. It does nonetheless appear to have intensive support in certain quarters.

To begin with, its greatest popularity has been among the roughly 50%

of Indonesian Muslims who live outside the Javanese cultural area of east and central Java. Among the Javanese 50%, according to the most widely accepted interpretation, it has been a belief only of devout Muslims or *santri*, and not of the probably larger group of Javanese Muslims called *abangan*, whose actual religious beliefs and practices incorporate Hindu and animistic elements.[43]

Secondly, the self-conscious idea of an Islamic State as an obligation, a goal that good Muslims must struggle to achieve, is largely a development of the late nineteenth and early twentieth centuries and of Islamic modernism. It entered Indonesia via students of the Middle Eastern Pan-Islamism of Jamal al-Din Al-Afghani and Rasjid Rida, and took its first political form in the debates of the 1930s between the *abangan* nationalist Sukarno and the modernist *santri* Mohammad Natsir.[44] Before 1945, perhaps a majority of Indonesian *santri*, and certainly most rural *santri* in Java, had probably never thought about an Islamic State one way or the other.

Third, no Indonesian government has ever been in favor of an Islamic State. The idea's political heyday was the early to mid-1950s, when virtually all Islamic political party leaders were in principle committed to it, though the intensity of commitment varied from party to party.[45] In the national parliamentary elections of 1955, these parties—led by the hotly pro-Islamic State modernist Masjumi and the more lukewarm traditionalist NU, then a political party as well as an educational and social organisation—won nearly half the vote.

Political Islam was defeated in the late 1950s by a coalition of the *abangan* President Sukarno and the *abangan*-led army. Suharto and his army officers are also predominantly *abangan*, and have not allowed it to reemerge. Nurcholish's politics, as I will elaborate below, have paralleled those of Suharto and the army on this issue. His position in relation to the state is thus very different from that of Goenawan, who has few state resources on his side, or even Sjahrir, who enjoys a more narrowly-based rapport with the state.

How powerful is the Islamic State idea today, and where does that power come from? Government repression of pro-Islamic State forces makes the first of these questions hard to answer. Most Islamic intellectuals writing and speaking publicly today, including Nurcholish, say that few Indonesian Muslims still believe in the Islamic State. Their testimony is open to question, however, as they themselves oppose the idea. They are also not closely in touch with what we might call the Islamic underground, would-be Islamic political leaders who work with small groups—most visibly on university campuses, but I suspect among lower middle, working class, and more economically marginal groups as well—and who in the current repressive atmosphere avoid political discussion and especially action.

My own view may be biased by a two-year field experience in Aceh, many of whose people take great pride in their Islamic fanaticism. I nonetheless believe that the automatic, unreflective idea that religion can not be detached from any aspect of life is pervasive in the *santri* community. Specifically concerning politics, most local religious leaders, whatever their present relationship with authority, believe that the *ulama* should be the moral overseers of the *umara* (state leadership, an Arabic term used in Indonesian Islamic discourse). The perceived history of Islam, as described above by Bernard Lewis, combined with the interest of the *ulama* in maintaining their elite status, provides much of the explanation for the idea's staying power. Of course, such a view is not in principle incompatible with moderate and pluralist interpretations of *ulama-umara* relations. But it provides a powerful resource to more radical would-be political leaders.

In the last two decades piety has been a growth industry among urban Indonesians of Muslim background, including many *abangan*. The phenomenon is most visible among the middle class and Western-educated, and is reflected in mushrooming mosque attendance and the now general use of Islamic symbols and rituals by state officials, including non- Muslims.[46]

In general terms, what appears to be happening is that religion is filling an identity gap, enabling individuals to become in their own minds complete persons. It is not that modernity (that is, an urban middle class lifestyle) and nationalism are being rejected, but rather that these ideologies have little to say about either the ultimate or the mundane questions addressed by religion.

The cultural consequences of this new modernity-nationalism-Islam nexus are hard to predict. One possibility, which I describe below, is accommodation with the secular state. Another, however, is a renewed commitment to the idea of the Islamic State, backed by a powerful social force led by intellectuals and middle class people, but given much of its power by its appeal to working class, unemployed, and otherwise marginal urbanites, and by its continued positive resonance for rural *santri*. A large number of the latter live in fact in a kind of permanent uprootedness, back and forth between rural and urban employment and life-style, and may be becoming increasingly susceptible to all kinds of oppositionist, including Islamic State, ideologies.

Finally, I would like just to mention in this discussion of the resources possessed by defenders of the cultural *status quo* Maurice Bloch's concept of the 'recoverability' of ideology. Citing his own work in Madagascar, Bloch argues that the vagueness and alogicality of ideologies make it possible for them to shift from 'one power-holder to another, as an instrument for domination and legitimation.'[47]

In Indonesia, all three of the dominant ideas have been around for a long time and, as in Bloch's Madagascar, have survived many political and social upheavals. The strong state idea in particular, with its deep roots in Javanese political history, seems especially resilient. In another paper, I have attempted to explain how it has been possible for President Suharto to adopt market-oriented macro-economic policies while at the same time promoting (and undoubtedly himself holding) a pro-state ideology.[48] A third example is the long pre-modern association between Javanist kings and Islamic legitimation, broken by Dutch colonialism but restored by Sukarno and Suharto.

The Innovators

What resources do the innovators possess? In general terms I see: small but active social forces, or core constituencies; intellectual prowess combined with rhetorical and political skills; additional constituencies that might be brought into a coalition with the core; support from parts of the state; and both specific and diffuse international backing.

Goenawan Mohamad's core constituency is the Jakarta journalistic, literary, and artistic community, together with its small outliers in other major cities and university towns. This group numbers only in the thousands, but it has been very active in the New Order period. General prosperity and the growth of the educational system and of opportunities to study abroad have expanded the group and also given it a larger and more sophisticated audience than ever before.

I do not want to make too great a claim for this community's capacity to promote cultural change, however. Its members still constitute a tiny and beleaguered minority, isolated from the larger society. As a group, they are in their own minds not very talented, and their audience, despite recent progress, remains small in proportion to Indonesian society as a whole. They have not, with very few exceptions—for example, several stories and novels by the former pro-communist Pramoedya Ananta Toer, whose works are banned by the government and who is also a social pariah, and a few stories by the Yogyakarta-based writer Umar Kayam—produced any world-class literature or other great artistic triumphs so far. The fine arts rubric in *Tempo* is the least popular with readers, the magazine's polls time and again attest.

Goenawan himself has written movingly of this sense of separation. His 'Portrait of a Young Poet as *Malin Kundang*' essay is about a youth who leaves home, becomes rich, denies his mother, is cursed by her, and turns into stone. The implication is of the betrayal by the modern intellectual of his or her cultural heritage, and of the great distance between modern Indonesian and traditional ethnic culture. The essay ends with: 'But if for example there is finally no road home, there is still something that is valuable, that is freedom.'[49] Unfortunately, while Goenawan and many of his colleagues are willing to make this tradeoff, it doesn't point to any means by which the social gap between individualist intellectuals and the collectivist masses might be narrowed.

In its narrowest construction, Sjahrir's core constituency consists of the tiny group of professional economists and the somewhat larger one of educated Indonesians able to understand his sophisticated commentary on economic events that appears in Jakarta newspapers, newsmagazines, and more specialised business publications. Within this group, Sjahrir is not, of course, the leading figure. That title, for more than twenty years, has gone to Professor Widjojo, President Suharto's long time senior economic advisor and for many years head of *Bappenas* (National Planning Board). Several other senior economists, including Professors Sumitro, Mohammad Sadli, Ali Wardhana, Sumarlin, and Radius Prawiro, have also had more policy influence than the still youthful Sjahrir. In addition, Sumitro and Sadli are able academic and journalistic writers.

Sjahrir's uniqueness, and the main source of his possible future influence both in the policy process and on cultural change, is that he straddles two constituencies. He is simultaneously taken seriously by economists, whose litmus test of acceptability is knowledge of and respect for the workings of the market, and by the *Malari* and post-*Malari* generations of anti-Suharto political activists, whose basic commitment is to egalitarian redistribution of the benefits of economic growth.

Sjahrir's recent writings, as I have already indicated, are strongly pro-market. Indeed he often takes the economists in power to task for making too many compromises with anti-market forces. In his public appearances, on the other hand, especially at universities, he frequently reminds his audiences of his own leadership role in the *Malari* demonstrations, the years he served in prison as a result, and his continuing commitment to equality and popular welfare. The lecturers at his School of Social Science are recruited disproportionately from the left of the Indonesian political spectrum. His Harvard dissertation, in both its English and Indonesian versions, also contains references to his previous political activism.

Even this double core, however, does not necessarily make Sjahrir's constituency a major force in future policy-making or cultural change. Intellectually and politically, Sjahrir inherits the tradition of the democratic socialist PSI (*Partai Sosialis Indonesia*, Indonesian Socialist Party), banned in 1960. In the 1950s, the PSI already encompassed both market and anti-market egalitarian orientations. It was nonetheless unable to win many votes in the 1955 elections, the one genuine test of popular support in Indonesian political history.

Of the three innovators, it is Nurcholish who enjoys the largest core constituency, large enough perhaps to be considered a genuine social force, consisting of urban, middle-class, Western-educated, reformist- or modernist-minded devout Muslims. Nurcholish is in fact riding the crest of the general Islamisation of national Indonesian culture that I have already mentioned but not fully described.

Forty years ago Islam was at the periphery of the modern culture, generally considered 'backward' by the best-educated and most culturally sophisticated people. Today, in part as a result of the spread of Western education and of religious instruction in the schools, a new generation simultaneously modern, Indonesian, and Muslim has emerged. Its members are dispersed throughout both the private and the state sectors, and hold many of the most technically and intellectually demanding jobs.

On the available evidence, these people want to be religious but do not want to be led either by the old-fashioned, rural *ulama* who have long dominated much of Indonesian Islamic life or by the newer group of thinkers within modernist Islam, inspired since the 1930s by the one-time Prime Minister and Masjumi leader Mohammad Natsir, who have been committed to the idea of an Islamic State.

Instead, they are looking for a new understanding of their religion that gives them a more realistic set of guidelines, really a code of ethics, for private and family life and for dealing with the outside world. They want to know what are the rights and responsibilities of husbands and wives, how to raise their sons and daughters to be good Muslims and good Indonesians, how to relate to a modern banking system, whether and how to revitalise the concept of *zakat* (religious tax), and even how to deal with such exotica as test-tube babies, organ transplants, and homosexuality.

Many upper and middle class business people are especially attracted to Nurcholish because he preaches accommodation with the New Order state. In this he differs from several other Muslim intellectuals of modernist background, like Dawam Rahardjo of *Lembaga Studi Agama dan Filsafat* (Institute for the Study of Religion and Philosophy), publisher of the quarterly journal *Ulumul Qur'an*, and Adi Sasono of SEAFDA (Southeast Asian Forum for Development Alternatives), who are to a much greater extent partisans of the poor and critics of the government.

Goenawan, Sjahrir, and Nurcholish are all, in their own ways, skilled communicators to large audiences. Partly this has to do with quality of mind and partly with rhetorical skills. *Tempo* magazine is the creation of Goenawan, more than of any other single individual. Its style and content—sprightly Malay—rather than turgid Dutch-based Indonesian prose, coverage of all sides of issues rather than presentation of a partisan point of view, a high level of journalistic competence—are very different from most of its predecessors.

Goenawan's signature contribution, the 600 word weekly column called *Catatan Pinggir* (Marginal Notes), consistently offers the most thoughtful, articulate, and elegant commentary on current events and on Indonesian life in general.[50] *Tempo* sells about 150,000 copies each week. Most of these are bought by Jakarta readers, but enough reach the regions to make *Tempo* (and the daily *Kompas*, circulation about 500,000, whose intellectual and political commitments, if not prose style, are similar to *Tempo*'s) an important molder of elite opinion throughout the country.[51]

In his field of economics, Sjahrir has established himself in his writings as today's most intellectually formidable commentator on and critic of government policy. With a rhetorical style that combines a grasp of economic science, moral commitment, and a light, humorous delivery (not an easy achievement!), he is also a much sought after and persuasive speaker at seminars and conferences.

On first impression, Nurcholish's more straightforward, uncultivated and unassuming style is not as striking as that of Goenawan the poet or Sjahrir the scientist and raconteur. He is nonetheless very effective, both in print and on the podium. Partly this is due simply to the orginality and depth of his ideas and the clarity of his prose, and partly it is because he is articulating an approach to life that is enormously attractive to his constituency. Behind this approach is the moral authority of a modern man with an American Ph.D., an accomplished theologian and religious historian, and—not least—an able preacher who makes a point of regularly giving Friday sermons at mosques throughout the country.

The style and content of Nurcholish's message also has its weaknesses, however. Perhaps his greater visibility as a cultural and even political leader makes these deficiencies more obvious than in the cases of Goenawan and Sjahrir.

Nurcholish's obsession is to persuade Indonesian Muslims to accept his vision of a rational, tolerant, inclusive, 'secular' Islam. He acknowledges, however, that this is a difficult task, because of the deep roots in the community of anti-Westernism, anti-Christianity, indeed intolerance of anything regarded as non-Islamic. In this connection, he often expresses his dislike for certain 'romantic-ideological' Muslim intellectuals who reflect and try to capitalise on the intolerant masses for political purposes.

Nurcholish himself is not worried that these leaders will be able to move Indonesian Islam in a militant or fundamentalist direction, even in the more open and democratic political climate that might follow the Suharto era. To an outside observer, however, it is easy to imagine the middle class appeal of the rational and intellectual Nurcholish being overwhelmed by coarser leaders who know how to inflame the masses.

In terms of reaching out to broader, specifically mass, constituencies, Goenawan and Sjahrir appear to face more daunting obstacles than Nurcholish. Goenawan and his artistic, if not journalistic, colleagues do inhabit a kind of high culture island that appears foreign and forbidding to many, especially rural and lower class, people. To adopt a useful phrase from Herbert Gans, the 'taste cultures' of upper and lower class Indonesians are very different.[52]

How can this gap be overcome? Perhaps one clue can be found in the recent renaissance of *wayang kulit*, the traditional Javanese shadow play, in central Java.[53] In the early 1970s, when I first lived in the Yogyakarta area, the future of *wayang* seemed in doubt. *Dalang* (puppeteers) and their troupes were becoming too expensive for most villagers and even most townspeople to hire. Moreover, young people were said to prefer watching movies, television, and other forms of modern entertainment, and also to be choosing modern occupations over becoming puppeteers. Everywhere one heard dismay expressed at the negative effects on traditional culture of New Order-style capitalist economic development.

Today *wayang* is still expensive, but it is very much alive. Performances are staged frequently all over the Yogyakarta special region. In 1989 and 1990, at the dozen or so plays I attended, the audiences—full houses, even in the cavernous hall where the monthly *Radio Republik Indonesia* performances are broadcast—were predominantly young, male, and middle to lower class. *Wayang* topics—the relative merits of different puppeteers, the selection of particular plays for performance, even innovations in carving—were popular items of discussion in the local press and among a large and active group of aficionados, many of them university lecturers and other professionals.

What explains this resurgence in interest? Partly, of course, it is the continuing strength of *wayang*'s deep connection with traditional Javanese culture, high and low,[54] a resource not available to the modern artists of Jakarta. Of at least equal importance, however, has been the emergence of a new generation of *dalang* who are strongly motivated to succeed— that is, to make money and enjoy high status in the community—and at the same time happen to be tuned in to recent changes in popular culture.

As a result, today's performances tend to be high in 'action', particularly fight and battle scenes, like so many popular foreign movie and TV programs. The flashback—for example, scenes from a character's earlier life introduced to explain a present situation—is also common. To appeal to the young male audience, there is more 'porno' (actually for the most part only mildly risque dialogue) and less philosophy. One *dalang* has even added trumpets to the *gamelan* orchestra!

There are, to be sure, critics of the new *wayang* in Yogyakarta, especially among representatives of the upper taste culture. Their argument is essentially that low entertainment values are replacing high philosophic ones, and that pure Javaneseness is being subverted by Western theatrical concepts. *Wayang* is not being brought up to date, they claim; rather it has lost its heart and soul.[55] My own sense is that *wayang* is as Javanese as it has ever been (which is to say that it has never been purely Javanese, whatever that may mean!) and that its complex appeal endures. Indeed, in another twenty or thirty years, when today's young audience is old, I expect we will all be impressed by the new attention paid to the philosophic side of *wayang*.

To return to my main subject, are such connections possible between high and low taste cultures in Jakarta? One piece of evidence that they are is the popular success of Nano Riantiarno's *Teater Koma* (Comma

Theater), whose plays regularly enjoy long runs in Jakarta's larger theatres.[56] Like the central Javanese *dalang*, Riantiarno wants to be rich and famous. He has also figured out that there is a sizable audience, in this case middle class but relatively unintellectual young men and women, willing to pay thousands of rupiahs to be entertained by a heady mixture of the Broadway musical and low Surabaya and Jakarta folk comedy. Riantiarno's productions have come under heavy fire from Jakarta intellectuals for their purported commercialism, low aesthetic quality, and lack of social message. My own view, again, is rather different. Riantiarno is conducting a conversation, if not yet an argument, with his middle class constituency about issues like social justice (for example in his play *Opera Kecoa*, Cockroach Opera) and political leadership (for example in *Suksesi*, Succession). While it may be true that neither party to this dialogue has as yet achieved any great breakthroughs, Riantiarno at least has found an audience and captured its attention, which is more than can be said for many of his peers.

Sjahrir's main hope for a larger constituency is the entrepreneurial or business middle class, which is believed to be growing rapidly as a result of New Order development policies. As the owner of a financial consulting firm and of a seat on the Jakarta stock exchange, Sjahrir himself can claim membership in this group. Indeed, his firm's clients include some of the largest Sino-Indonesian and indigenous businesses in Jakarta.

Before we can assess the potential of the business class as a social force, however, we need much more information about its size, scope and internal divisions, its racial makeup, and the extent of its autonomy or dependence on the state. By size, scope, and internal divisions, I mean how many entrepreneurs and business people there now are, whether they are concentrated in Jakarta and a few other large cities like Surabaya and Medan or are dispersed more widely throughout the country, in small towns and even rural as well as urban areas, and whether there are significant differences in interest between big, medium, and small businesses, businesses in different sectors of the economy, and so on.

Racially, the common view—which tends to be disputed by both domestic and foreign economists—is that Sino-Indonesians have been much more successful than indigenous or *pribumi* business people in responding to the challenges and opportunities of late 1980s-early 1990s deregulation. This belief creates the potential for conflict between races in addition to or instead of between the business class and statist forces.

On the autonomy question, the common opinion—which few seem to dispute, though I myself take a more optimistic view—is that most prosperous entrepreneurs, of whatever race, at all levels and sectors, owe their success principally to government connections rather than to abilities to meet the challenges of the marketplace. To the extent that this is true, Indonesian business people are not likely to adopt a free market philosophy.

Of the three leaders, Nurcholish not only enjoys the largest core constituency but has also put together by far the biggest and most influential political alliance, combining elements of modernist and traditional Islam with support from the state bureaucracy (to be discussed below). The traditional part comes from *Nahdlatul Ulama*, the village- and rural-centered organisation of religious teachers, concentrated in east and central Java but with large followings in several other provinces as well.

NU, founded in 1926, has been led since 1984 by Abdurrahman Wahid, the grandson of one of the organisation's founders and son of one of its most respected leaders. To this inheritance, of great importance in NU political culture, he brings resources of his own: a will to lead, a politician's sense of how to cultivate and maintain a network of leaders and followers, intellectual and political creativity and daring, and a neo-modernist point of view about the future of Islam and Indonesian society that is very close to that of Nurcholish.

Abdurrahman Wahid's intellectual and political support is a major asset, giving Nurcholish access to the traditional Javanese Islamic community through the leader of its largest organisation. If Nurcholish's own constituency is largely urban and middle to upper class, Abdurrahman Wahid's is a socio-economically broad swath of *santri* villagers. This modernist-traditional alliance is reminiscent of the *Masjumi* political party in the early 1950s, before NU left to become a party on its own. In the 1955 elections, Masjumi and NU combined received nearly 40% of the vote.

This is not to argue that, were Indonesia once again to hold democratic elections, a Nurcholish Madjid/Abdurrahman Wahid-led *Masjumi*-like party would win 40% of the vote. On the modernist side, as I have suggested above, there are more radical alternative leaders, now largely operating beneath the surface because of government repression, who might well attract a large and passionate following if controls were lifted.

Among traditionalists, even NU traditionalists, Abdurrahman Wahid is a unique figure who often leads where his people do not want to go. He bubbles over with unconventional ideas, many of which have to do with concern for the substance rather than the form of religion and with tolerance toward non-Muslims. Many of his constituents respond with incomprehension if not hostility.

In politics, Abdurrahman Wahid claims to be against the idea of an Islamic party. Indeed, under his leadership, NU in 1984 removed itself altogether from the partisan arena. He has condemned as sectarian the recently formed ICMI (*Ikatan Cendekiawan Muslim Indonesia*), Indonesian Muslim Intellectuals' Union), which Nurcholish and many other self-consciously Muslim intellectuals have joined, and founded in response the *Forum Demokrasi* (Democratic Forum), whose members include many Catholic and other non-Islamic activists and thinkers.[57]

Were Abdurrahman Wahid to lead a non-Islamic party in a democratic election, many NU members would undoubtedly refuse to follow his lead. He himself has said that this is as it should be, since every citizen has a right to his or her own partisan affiliation. He is nonetheless an important force for cultural change, bringing new ideas to village Muslims and legitimating those ideas through the traditional authority he holds by virtue of his ancestry and his effectiveness as a political leader.

Of the three intellectuals, Goenawan has the least and Nurcholish the most support from the state bureaucracy. Goenawan's individualism runs directly counter to the state's collectivism. Moreover, government bureaucracy is a frequent target of criticism in his columns. Fearing chaos, bureaucrats construct 'an order that is upright, cold, compact like the wall of a Dutch house.' Bureaucratic rule without accountability leads inevitably to corruption, and 'corruption is a cancer that finally crushes hope and belief.'[58]

Sjahrir's overall approach to political economy, which combines confidence in markets with a commitment to government intervention both to increase competitiveness and to enhance social welfare, is more hospitable to the New Order state. More concretely, he has formed a kind of *de facto* alliance with the technocrats. While he is in a sense their major critic, his criticisms come from inside their paradigm, pushing them to adopt and hold to policies that reflect their best selves.

Nurcholish's support within the New Order state goes further than this. Many bureaucrats are attracted to his ideas, which make it possible for them to be openly proud of their religion without being suspected of pro-Islamic state inclinations. At a more structural level, the label *Tri-Tunggal* (Three-in-One)[59] is sometimes used to describe the similarity in certain ideas and policies among Nurcholish, Abdurrahman Wahid, and Munawir Syadzali, the Minister of Religion, who was educated in Islamic schools but spent most of his government career in the Department of Foreign Affairs before being appointed minister in 1983. Nurcholish is himself widely thought to be a strong candidate to succeed Munawir in 1993, a sign of the degree to which he is accepted within the state bureaucracy.

Perhaps the most important factor that makes me optimistic about the ultimate impact of Nurcholish's ideas is that he represents a new kind of Islamic leader, one who can tap a broad potential constituency of support both within and outside the *santri* community. The historian Taufik Abdullah, in a useful essay on patterns of Islamic leadership, identifies two kinds of leaders in pre-colonial and early colonial Indonesian Islam: the independent *ulama*, usually the head of his own traditional school, and the state Islamic official.[60]

This initial pattern was broken in the early twentieth century with the emergence of a third kind of leader, the Western-style, but Islamic in content and purpose, association activist. The activists did not necessarily know much about Islam—they were Western school-educated and their

skills were organisational and political rather than Islamic-intellectual—
but they nonetheless could make a genuine claim to legitimacy as leaders
of the *umat*.

These leaders were the first to enjoy geographically dispersed influence,
unlike the traditional *ulama* whose support was concentrated in particular
regions. According to Taufik, they were also the first 'crossover leaders',
simultaneously Muslim and national. They emerged primarily within Islamic
organisations, social and educational as well as political, but their membership reach or eligibility was defined in national, Indonesia-wide, terms.

To these three categories Taufik adds a fourth, visible only since the
1970s: new intellectuals like Nurcholish. The new intellectuals have a
deeper understanding of religion than most of their predecessors. At the
same time they are more thoroughly national, because 'more of them have
entered the structure of the national community.' They work as civil servants, teachers, university lecturers, journalists, and business people. Most
of them grew up in devoutly Islamic families and local communities, often
outside Java, becoming modern and national through higher education.

Though they do not have their own *pesantren*, the new intellectuals
are in other ways reminiscent of the old independent *ulama*. They have
acquired status as individuals given respect directly by mass constituencies, not by virtue of holding state office or even in many cases positions
in Islamic organisations. In an era of rapid mass communications, it is
their speaking and writing that makes them known to large audiences.

These are important qualities, because they indicate both high credibility as Islamic leaders and unassailable credentials as full members of
the national political community, i.e. as '*Pancasila*ists'[61] who do not threaten
the foundations of the Indonesian state. To carry the point a little further
than Taufik is willing to, perhaps it can be argued that these intellectuals—Nurcholish foremost among them—have finally bridged the
gap between Islam and secular nationalism that has been at the heart of
the Islamic State versus *Pancasila* controversy since the 1945 constitutional debates.

Finally, all of my cultural figures and their core constituencies extract
resources from outside Indonesia. Sjahrir and Nurcholish have advanced
degrees from American universities, and maintain their connections with
former teachers and friends. Goenawan has recently been a Nieman Fellow
at Harvard and has taken sabbaticals to write and teach in Australia.
These associations become vehicles through which new ideas, and often
money and organisation to support their development, enter Indonesia.

The present international intellectual and political climate is favorable
to the ideas of all three. This is unambiguously so in the cases of Goenawan
and Sjahrir, who enjoy the benefits respectively of the fall of European
communism, which has strengthened the confidence of liberal democratisers
everywhere, and of the Reagan/Thatcher restoration of economic liber-

alism as the reigning political economy philosophy in the West. The influence in Indonesia of world Islam, with its many conflicting strands—including the currently popular radical rejection of the West and call for strict enactment of Islamic law—is more complex and hard to assess. But Nurcholish and his friends have worked hard to introduce and spread a broader range of thinking.

Politics and the Shaping of Resources

Lists of resources possessed by cultural defenders and innovators, such as I have compiled, tend to give a false impression of completeness and permanence. The picture drawn is of a kind of set battle between two armies, each with its social and cultural armour, weapons, and other strengths and weaknesses. But the reality is one of openness and fluidity, the constant decline and disappearance of old resources and creation and deployment of new ones, by multiple participants in a cultural—and ultimately political—process.

The difference is important. The battle metaphor suggests that if we can identify the key resources of the two sides we can predict the winner with some confidence. The process image (which is also a better way to understand battles!) offers no such hope. Rather, it directs us to conceive of culture as history—in the making but not yet made—and to follow closely the development and interplay of social forces and ideas, and the many other variables that may have an impact on the strength and deployability of resources.[62]

Four brief illustrations drawn from current high political maneuvering in Jakarta may give a sense of what I have in mind. The first has to do with how the tides of economic change may affect Sjahrir's store of resources, the second with the way in which the resources of political Islam have been enhanced by President Suharto's struggle to stay in power, the third with how Goenawan's views are benefiting from the army's attempt to push Suharto into retirement, and the fourth with the way in which the recent Timor crisis appears to have ravaged the resources of pro-democratic forces.

Sjahrir's championing of deregulation has a certain tactical appeal for individuals and groups currently threatened by the business activities of the Suharto family. All six of Suharto's children, but most prominently Tutut, the oldest daughter, Bambang, the middle son, and Tommy, the youngest son, are perceived to be getting the lion's share of government 'facilities', in the form of trade monopolies and contracts to build state projects.[63] Sjahrir's public opposition to these projects on market competition grounds makes him a hero to anti-family business people. Put differently, Sjahrir's resources for change are enhanced by the presence in his camp of anti-family business people.

In a few years, when the 71 year old Suharto is no longer president, and many of these same business people are vying for favors from the new government, the climate of opinion may well be less friendly to the pro-market position, and Sjahrir's resources may shrink. My hope, however— and without adequate data, it is admittedly little more than that—is that in the slightly longer run, say in ten to twenty years, presuming continuation of the technocrats' neo-classical influence on policy, a large indigenous, multi-sectoral, autonomous business community will have emerged.

This group will, of course, be strongest in Jakarta but it will also be substantial throughout the more urbanised and industrialised parts of the country, and even in small towns across Java. Many of its members should be very receptive to the ideas of pro-market intellectuals. Moreover, through his consulting and writing, Sjahrir may well have succeeded by this time in gaining the confidence of a large portion of the Jakarta business community. Finally, it is entirely possible that Sjahrir himself will, under Indonesia's third president, be a key policy maker. I see, therefore, the prospect of a net addition of resources to the pro-change side of the equation.

My second and third illustrations come directly from the struggle for the presidential succession.[64] To counter army opposition to a sixth term in office beginning in 1993, Suharto has been cultivating Islamic support. His actions have included: assent to a law strengthening Islamic courts; acceptance of the wearing of the *jilbab* (Islamic headcovering) by female students in state schools; the arrest and sentencing of the *Monitor* editor; approval for ICMI, the new Islamic intellectuals' organisation; and consent to the creation of an Islamic (profit-sharing rather than interest-charging) bank.

Most of these are important issues on which there has been controversy for years or decades. Suharto's shift on each has gained him the support of many *santri* Muslims, though some others have a different conception of their interests as Muslims (and as Indonesians) and have stayed out of the coalition. The latter group includes more radical or militant leaders and intellectuals, who dismiss Suharto's actions as purely self-serving, and also the NU's Abdurrahman Wahid, who has visions both of a more democratic state and of an Islam more autonomous of the state.

The specific cultural consequences of Suharto's opening toward Islam are not clear. One possibility, of course, is the strengthening of Nurcholish's pro-accommodationist position, as more and more urban, educated, middle- and upper-class *santri* become comfortable with a government that responds to their religious as well as non-religious needs.[65]

No less real, however, is the possibility of a growing gulf between the government and the haves, including upper- and middle-class Muslims, on the one hand, and the much larger number of Muslim have-nots, lower-middle, working-class, and economically marginal people whose interests are less well-served by the government and its policies. An important side effect, much feared by Abdurrahman Wahid, may be a slowing down of progress toward democratisation, both of culture and of structure. Many of the best cadres who could be working, in organisations such as his *Forum Demokrasi*, for a more democratic post-Suharto Indonesia have instead been coopted into ICMI.[66]

Interestingly enough, on the other side of the struggle for power, one of the army's principal weapons against Suharto has been support for democratisation. The armed forces fraction occupies the unelected one-fifth of Parliament's 500 seats. Its leadership—probably under the direction of Minister of Defence Murdani—has used this leverage since 1989 to promote a number of popular causes involving defense of the rights of ordinary citizens against specific policies identified with the Suharto government. More broadly, it has argued for democratisation, defined in part as an enlargement of the role of Parliament and a reduction in the power of the executive.

The most recent Suharto-army clash waged on the parliamentary battlefield, as of early 1992, was won by Suharto, who reserved to himself the final screening of candidates for the new Parliament to be elected in June 1992. Several of the most prominent military MPs, including the armed forces' fraction's chair and the chair of Parliament itself, were notified that they would not be reappointed or renominated.

One of the most outspoken ousted MPs was Police Colonel Roekmini, who had often been the focus of newspaper and magazine stories about the new pro-democratic stance of the armed forces. Upon hearing the news, she chose to use the only resource available to her at the moment: irony. In a fine parody of the usual officer's cliched acceptance of collectivity and hierarchy, she said: 'I always say to my superior, the hand of Father [probably implying Suharto] I regard as the hand of God. If he wants to cross my name off, or do whatever else he wants, it's no problem for me. God arranges everything.'[67]

The Suharto-army contest for the presidency is of course not over. While in retreat for the moment, the army is certain to return to the field, and indeed, as an institution, ultimately to triumph over the mortal president. For my purpose, understanding cultural change, what is important is that this competition has provided and is likely to continue to provide resources and room to maneuver to innovators like Nurcholish and Abdurrahman Wahid. It also creates space for Goenawan and the literary and artistic community, whose freedoms to publish, perform, and promote more individualistic and democratic values have been measurably enhanced, in the short term at least.

My final illustration is the recent attack by the government on Non-Governmental Organisations, in Indonesia called LSM (*Lembaga Swadaya Masyarakat*, Community Self-Reliance Agencies).[68] Many observers have seen the growth of LSM in the 1980s as an important resource for political and cultural democratisation.[69]

LSM is an umbrella term covering an array of more than a thousand private, voluntary organisations dedicated to providing a public service. Many LSM contribute to development by bringing small amounts of capital, new technology or organisational skills to bear on local-level projects. Others attempt to modernise traditional institutions, such as the village level Islamic schools called *pesantren*. Still others are advocates for consumers, environmental concerns, access to legal assistance, and so on. One of the best known of the latter is the YLBHI (*Yayasan Lembaga Bantuan Hukum Indonesia*, Indonesian Legal Aid Institute Foundation).

LSM leaders and staff from all over the archipelago form a loose network whose members meet frequently at conferences and seminars. They share a common culture that tends to be suspicious of the New Order government, skeptical of large institutions in general ('small is beautiful'), pro-grass roots, pro-human rights and democracy, and tolerant of religious and ethnic diversity. Much of their funding comes from foreign foundations and governments.

In the 1980s the LSM began in a coordinated way to press the government to allow them greater freedom to operate in the villages and also to change the general direction of development policy toward more decentralised decision-making and more attention to distributive and environmental concerns. A major instrument of this effort was INGI (International Non-Governmental Group on Indonesia), an informal collection of Indonesian and foreign NGOs set up as a deliberate counterbalance to IGGI (Inter-Governmental Group on Indonesia), the consortium of creditor countries that has been giving aid to the Indonesian government since the late 1960s.

Resolutions and aides-memoire drawn up at INGI meetings, held just before IGGI's annual meetings on the level of aid to be given for the forthcoming year, quickly became a thorn in the side of the government. INGI's relative boldness was made possible by its partially foreign membership, the glare of publicity of an international forum, and the support it received from foreign foundations and governments, in particular from the Dutch government in the person of the Minister for Cooperation and Development, J.P. Pronk.

In March 1992, the Indonesian government struck back at INGI and the LSM in circumstances created by the international reaction to the Indonesian army's massacre of nationalist Timorese youth in November 1991. The story is complicated, but in essence President Suharto disbanded IGGI, refused any further Dutch aid, including private foundation aid with funds originally from the Dutch government, and told INGI that it should disband also. YLBHI, which receives 80% of its budget from Dutch sources, was hit particularly hard.

The spur to these actions was an unplanned incident, the November massacre. Without it, and the foreign reactions it provoked, INGI and the

LSM would probably have continued to run up their national and international resources and legitimacy as players in the political and cultural process. With it, they have suffered a setback and the government and other *status quo* forces have scored a victory. As in the other illustrations, however, the contest for Indonesia's future goes on.

IV

Writing at the dawn of independence in Asia and Africa, Edward Shils believed that "the intellectuals will go on playing a large role in the fulfillment of whatever possibilities fortune allots to their societies. . . . as long . . . as they do not disintegrate into tribal and local territorial sovereignties, and as long as they at least aspire to be 'modern.'"[70]

Shils was a close and sensitive observer of Third World intellectuals, particularly in India, and was not generally given to easy optimism or wishful thinking. Nonetheless, reread thirty years later, his view seems too sanguine. Asian and African societies have not disintegrated, and aspirations to be modern are still pervasive. Yet it is hard to argue for the general proposition that intellectuals, of the sort he had in mind and I have been discussing, have played a large role in social and cultural change, large enough at any rate to make a difference.

Why haven't they played a greater role, and how can they be more effective in the future? In search of answers to these questions, this essay has supplied some tools—the concepts of resources and a cultural process driven by intellectuals and other actors acquiring and utilising resources over time—and applied them to three Indonesian cases. I have argued that cultural defenders and cultural innovators alike possess a range of resources, and that both the existence and the value of these resources varies with circumstance and time.

In concrete terms, this approach offers only partial and particular insights, really suggestions for activists in Indonesia and hints to activists elsewhere. It tells them how they might better mobilise and deploy the resources they already have or can create or pick up from their changing social, cultural, political, and economic environment.

This is, to be sure, a limited gain. Nonetheless, it seems to me preferable to the tendency of most social scientists, and certainly of most political scientists, to chase the will o' the wisp of deterministic forces outside the individual human actor. Third World political analysis has accumulated quite a long list of such forces, from the 'system of modernity' of Daniel Lerner[71] in the 1950s to the state capabilities of Theda Skocpol[72] in the 1980s. All of these can better be understood as resources than as determinants, and it is now time to put them into a more analytically productive framework.

1. Robert N. Bellah, et al, *Habits of the Heart: Individualism and Commitment in American Life*, Berkeley: University of California Press, 1985, p. 27.
2. Values have to do with 'how the world should be,' beliefs with 'how the world is,' customs with 'how one conducts oneself under the guidance of a particular set of values and beliefs.' F.G. Bailey, *Humbuggery and Manipulation: The Art of Leadership*, Ithaca: Cornell University Press, 1988, p. 36.
3. Gabriel Almond and Sidney Verba, *The Civic Culture: Political Attitudes and Democracy in Five Nations*, Princeton: Princeton University Press, 1963. For some second thoughts, see Sidney Verba, 'On Revisiting the Civic Culture: A Personal Postscript,' in Gabriel Almond and Sidney Verba, *The Civic Culture Revisited*, Boston: Little, Brown, 1980. Verba writes (p. 399) that in hindsight 'the variations from nation to nation make clear that general sociological processes can easily be modified by political events.'
4. Lucian Pye and Sidney Verba, *Political Culture and Political Development*, Princeton: Princeton University Press, 1965, p. 7. Pye did offer two divisions, between elite and mass culture and between 'those more acculturated to modern ways [and those] who are still closer to the traditional patterns of life.' (pp. 15ff) He did not see these divisions as elements in a dynamic process, however, but rather as dimensions of culture that would help us understand the relative developmental (read: democratic) prospects of different societies.
5. Benedict R. O'G. Anderson, *Language and Power: Exploring Political Cultures in Indonesia*, Ithaca: Cornell University Press, 1990, pp. 17–77. For examples of similar concepts in other traditional societies, see Elizabeth Colson, "Power at Large: Meditation on 'The Symposium on Power'", in Raymond D. Fogelson and Richard N. Adams, eds, *The Anthropology of Power*, New York: Academic Press, 1977, pp. 375–86.
6. For a critique, see M.C. Ricklefs, 'Unity and Disunity in Javanese Political and Religious Thought of the Eighteenth Century,' *Modern Asian Studies* Vol. 26, No. 4 (October 1992), pp. 663–78.
7. As unraveled, for example, in Herbert Feith and Lance Castles, ed., *Indonesian Political Thinking, 1945–1965*, Ithaca: Cornell University Press, 1970.
8. Bellah et al, *Habits of the Heart*, p. 28.
9. Robert Hefner, *The Political Economy of Mountain Java: An Interpretive History*, Berkeley and Los Angeles: University of California Press, 1990, p. 239. Emphasis added.
10. Clifford Geertz, *The Interpretation of Cultures*, New York: Basic Books, 1973, p. 250. H.H. Gerth and C. Wright Mills, eds., *From Max Weber*, New York: Oxford University Press, 1946, esp. 'The Social Psychology of the World Religions,' pp. 267–301.
11. Taylor writes of 'the well-known "open system" predicament, one shared by human life and meteorology, that we cannot shield a certain domain of human events, the psychological, economic, political, from external interference; it is impossible to delineate a closed system.' 'Interpretation and The Sciences of Man,' *Review of Metaphysics* 25 (Fall 1971), p. 49. Hirschman offers the following 'fundamental theorem about the social world. . . . : As soon as a social phenomenon has been fully explained by a variety of converging approaches and is therefore understood in its majestic inevitability and perhaps even permanence, it vanishes.' *Essays in Trespassing: Economics to*

Politics and Beyond, Cambridge: Cambridge University Press, 1981, p. 134.

12. Goenawan Mohamad, *Catatan Pinggir* [Marginal Notes], Jakarta, PT Grafiti, 1982 (Vol. 1), 1989 (Vol. 2), 1991 (Vol. 3). I have also found helpful two collections of essays: *Potret Seorang Penjair Muda Sebagai Si Malin Kundang* [Portrait of a Young Poet as *Malin Kundang*], Jakarta, Pustaka Jaya, 1972; and *Seks, Sastra, Kita* [Sex, Literature, Us], Jakarta, Sinar Harapan, 1980.

13. R. William Liddle, 'Rumah Seorang Penulis' [The Address of a Writer], in Goenawan Mohamad, *Catatan Pinggir 3*, pp. x–xi.

14. Goenawan Mohamad, 'Aku', *Tempo* XXII, No. 29 (19 September 1992), p. 39.

15. R. William Liddle, 'Rumah Seorang Penulis,' p. xii.

16. Much of the information in this and the following paragraph is from an interview with Goenawan in April 1991.

17. '[D]alam mengutamakan individu . . . saya sebenarnya hendak menunjukkan individu sebagai calon korban, bukan sebagai calon pengganggu harmoni.' Personal communication, 23 June 1992.

18. The following paragraph is based largely on an interview with Sjahrir in October 1990. I am also indebted to Peter Timmer and Chris Manning for helping me to see both sides of Sjahrir more clearly.

19. For the balance, see his doctoral dissertation, published in Indonesia as Sjahrir, *Ekonomi Politik Kebutuhan Pokok: Sebuah Tinjauan Prospektif* [The Political Economy of Basic Needs: A Prospective View], Jakarta: LP3ES, 1986.

20. A collection is Sjahrir, *Kebijaksanaan Negara: Konsistensi dan Implementasi* [State Policy: Consistency and Implementation], Jakarta: LP3ES, 1987.

21. The speech was subsequently published in Drs. Nurcholish Madjid, Abdul Qadir Djaelani, Ismail Hasan Metarieum S.H., and H.E. Saefuddin Anshari, *Pembaharuan Pemikiran Islam* [The Renewal of Islamic Thought], Jakarta: Islamic Research Centre, 1970, pp. 1–12.

22. Robert N. Bellah, *Beyond Belief*, Berkeley and Los Angeles: University of California Press, 1970, pp. 146–167. Interview, Nurcholish Madjid, April 1992. I am also indebted to Bahtiar Effendy for helping me to understand Nurcholish and his place in Indonesian Islam.

23. *Ibid.*, pp. 150–151.

24. *Ibid.*, pp. 151–152, emphasis added.

25. Madjid, et al, *Pembaharuan Pemikiran Islam*, pp. 4–5.

26. *Ibid.*, p. 5.

27. *Ibid.*, p. 2.

28. Nurcholish now says that the two figures he most admires among Indonesian Muslims are Mohammad Hatta and Haji Agus Salim, in both cases for their combination of religious and secular knowledge and their nationalism. Interview, April 1992.

29. Madjid, et al, *Pembaharuan Pemikiran Islam*, p. 11.

30. See especially H.M. Rasjidi, *Koreksi Terhadap Drs. Nurcholish Madjid Tentang Sekularisasi* [Correction of Drs. Nurcholish Madjid Concerning Secularisation], Jakarta: Bulan Bintang, 1977. This idea is strong among Islamists as well as Muslims. See for example Bernard Lewis, *The Political Language of Islam*, Chicago: University of Chicago Press, 1988, who writes: 'When we in the Western world, nurtured in the Western tradition, use the words 'Islam' and 'Islamic,' we tend to make a natural error and assume that the religion means

the same for Muslims as it has meant in the Western world, even in medieval times; that is to say, a section or compartment of life reserved for certain matters, and separate, or at least separable, from other compartments of life designed to hold other matters. That is not so in the Islamic world. It was never so in the past, and the attempt in modern times to make it so may perhaps be seen, in the longer perspective of history, as an unnatural aberration which in Iran has ended and in some other Islamic countries may also be nearing its end.' (p. 2) On the political implications of this view, Lewis says: 'At the present time, the very notion of a secular jurisdiction and authority—of a so-to-speak unsanctified part of life that lies outside the scope of religious law and those who uphold it—is seen as an impiety, indeed as the ultimate betrayal of Islam.' (p. 3)

31. For the range of his appreciation, see Nurcholish Madjid, ed., *Khazanah Intelektual Islam* [The Intellectual Treasure of Islam], Jakarta: Bulan Bintang, 1984.

32. Nurcholish Madjid, *Ibn Taimiya on Kalam and Falsafah: The Problem of Reason and Revelation in Islam*, Chicago, University of Chicago Ph.D. dissertation, 1984.

33. 'Para' means 'for' in Spanish, 'madina' is 'civilisation' in Arabic, Nurcholish explained in a speech to the Association for Asian Studies, Washington D.C., 2 April, 1992.

34. See the collection of his post-Chicago essays, *Islam: Doktrin dan Peradaban* [Islam: Doctrine and Civilisation], Jakarta: Yayasan Wakaf Paramadina, 1992.

35. Personal communication, 15 April 1992. Nurcholish's ideas and person are sometimes harshly criticised in the Islamic press, which now reaches even remote areas like the villages of Aceh in either original or photocopy form. Moreover, it is not just Islamic masses that can be mobilised against innovators. The modern dancer Sardono W. Kusumo was once attacked by protestors in Solo and strongly criticised in Bali for his interpretations of traditional dances. Interview, Sardono W. Kusumo, Jakarta, December 1990. See also Goenawan Mohamad, 'Kemerdekaan Kreativitas: Sebuah Pikiran di Sekitar Taman Ismail Marzuki,' in *Seks, Sastra, Kita*, p. 150.

36. Interview, October 1990.

37. 'Mereka Menyangka Saya Kiai' [They Suppose That I Am a Kiai], *Matra*, February 1992, p. 18.

38. Bruce Glassburner, 'Economic Openness and Economic Nationalism in Indonesia Under the Soeharto Government,' paper presented at a conference on Comparative Analysis of the Development Process in East and Southeast Asia, Honolulu: East-West Center, May 1990.

39. The results were published in Frank Weinstein, *Indonesian Foreign Policy and the Dilemma of Dependence*, Ithaca: Cornell University Press, 1976.

40. Though not one of my concerns in this paper, the racial dimension of these attitudes is also reason for worry. Weinstein's and Glassburner's informants blame Sino-Indonesians for much that is wrong with the Indonesian economy. On the positive side, it should be noted that the views of younger elites, whose only experience is of the post-1965 period, may be more pro-market. This point was brought to my attention by Don Emmerson.

41. Salim Said, *Genesis of Power: General Sudirman and the Indonesian Military*

in Politics 1945–1949, Singapore: Institute of Southeast Asian Studies, 1991.

42. I also have a more humorous example of a redoubt of individualism within the state. In the hotel in Takengon, on the same evening that I saw the sea of Korpri shirts there was a no-shirt, soft-porn, program on a closed circuit TV channel. The hotel was owned by the local public prosecutor, who had presumably been given the film after it was seized by the police.

43. Clifford Geertz, *The Religion of Java*, Glencoe: The Free Press, 1960.

44. M. *Natsir versus Sukarno*, Padang: Yayasan Pendidikan Islam, 1968.

45. See the speeches of party leaders in the constituent assembly debates of 1957–59, collected in *Tentang Dasar Negara Republik Indonesia Dalam Konstituante* [Concerning the Foundation of the State of the Republic of Indonesia in the Constituent Assembly], 3 volumes, n.p., n.d.

46. One sign of this general Islamisation is that government officials now routinely begin speeches with the Islamic greeting *Assalamu' alaikum wa rahmatullahi wa barakatuh* (May peace be with you, and the blessing and grace of God). At a conference in 1986 I asked a Christian official of the Department of Education and Culture why he also used the phrase. His answer was that it was not Islamic but national.

47. Maurice Bloch, *Ritual, History and Power: Selected Papers in Anthropology*, London: The Athlone Press, 1989, pp. 131–133.

48. 'The Relative Autonomy of the Third World Politician: Soeharto and Indonesian Economic Development in Comparative Perspective,' *International Studies Quarterly*, Vol. 3, No. 4 (December 1991), pp. 403–427, reprinted as Chapter Four in this volume.

49. Goenawan Mohamad, *Potret Seorang Penjair Muda Sebagai Si Malin Kundang*, p. 20. In personal correspondence (June 23, 1992), Goenawan comments further: 'Malin Kundang only becomes my tragic hero when he becomes a stone, is cursed. Freedom, which for me is a kind of obligation, contains this tragic aspect, because what is confronted is not something that is easy to contradict, indeed on the contrary is something that is often true and powerful.' (my translation)

50. Goenawan's highly intellectual style does have its detractors, however. The weekly *Barata Minggu* (No. 490, April 1987, p. 7), for example, wrote that 'His imagination is high up in the clouds, giving the impression that Goenawan Mohamad is not a real journalist who is oriented to the people.'

51. According to internal marketing surveys, a majority of *Tempo*'s readers are university and high school graduates, live in urban areas, and are employed as civil servants, managers, and other professionals. Interview, Goenawan Mohamad, April 1991.

52. Herbert Gans, *Popular Culture and High Culture*, New York: Basic Books, 1974.

53. The following is based on interviews and observation in the Yogyakarta Special Region from May–October 1971, September–December 1989 and October–November 1990. See also Bakdi Soemanto, *Pergeseran Makna Sakral Dalam Pertunjukan Wayang Kulit* [The Shift of Sacred Meaning in Shadow Play Performance], Yogyakarta, Pusat Penelitian Kebudayaan Lit-UGM, Universitas Gadjah Mada, 1988.

54. See particularly Benedict Anderson, *Mythology and the Tolerance of the Javanese*, Ithaca: Cornell Modern Indonesia Project, 1965.

55. Interestingly, Anderson, writing in the early 1960s, shares some of the concerns of today's high culture critics. Specifically, Anderson perceived a secular trend toward a more simplified view of *wayang* as a contest between Good and Evil, a cinema-influenced emphasis on battle and sentimental boudoir scenes, a declining interest in traditional 'philosophising' and its replacement by the values of Westernised bourgeois culture, a muffling of the social and political criticism voiced by the clowns, and a growing attractiveness of characters who represent uncritical loyalty and patriotism. *Mythology and the Tolerance of the Javanese*, pp. 27–29.

56. R. William Liddle, 'Political Entertainment,' unpublished manuscript, Columbus, Ohio State University, 1990; Barbara Hatley, 'Introduction', in John McGlynn and Barbara Hatley, eds., *Time Bomb and Cockroach Opera*, Jakarta: Lontar Press, 1992; Mary Zurbuchen, 'The Cockroach Opera: Image of Culture and National Development in Indonesia,' *Tenggara*, No. 23 (1989), pp. 124–50.

57. Nurcholish defends ICMI, led by President Suharto's apostle of hi-tech, Minister of Research and Technology B.J. Habibie, as an organisation where previously non-cooperating Muslim radicals are now engaging in a debate with other Muslims and with the government. He hopes this will give them a better sense of the compromises necessary in politics. Interview, April 1992.

58. Quoted in R. William Liddle, 'Rumah Seorang Penulis,' p. xiii.

59. The cultural reference is to the *Dwi-Tunggal* (Two-in-One) of President Sukarno and Vice-President Mohammad Hatta in the early 1950s.

60. 'Pola Kepemimpinan Islam di Indonesia,' in Taufik Abdullah, *Islam dan Masyarakat: Pantulan Sejarah Indonesia*, Jakarta: LP3ES, 1987, pp. 54–87.

61. That is, supporters of the state doctrine *Pancasila*, five principles of belief in one God, nationalism, humanitarianism, democracy, and social justice. In New Order political discourse, Islam from the 'right' and communism from the left are seen as the chief threats to *Pancasila* as the *asas tunggal* (basic principle) of the state.

62. In a related context, his analysis of the 'integrative revolution' in the new states, Clifford Geertz concluded that: 'This may seem like a mere wait-and-see policy, inappropriate to the predictive ambitions of science. But such a policy is at least preferable, and more scientific, to waiting and not seeing, which has been largely the case to date.' *The Interpretation of Cultures*, New York: Basic Books, 1973, p. 310.

63. A recent account is Adam Schwarz, 'All is relative,' *Far Eastern Economic Review*, 30 April 1992, pp. 54–58.

64. For a fuller treatment, see R. William Liddle, 'Indonesia's Threefold Crisis,' *Journal of Democracy*, Vol. 3, No. 4 (October 1992), reprinted as Chapter Seven in this volume.

65. Nurcholish says that he tells Minister for the State Secretariat Murdiono, one of President Suharto's closest advisers, 'Do not let us be defeated by our success.' He means that the New Order has created, and now must share power with, the Islamic middle class. Interview, April 1992.

66. On the other hand, ICMI supporters like Dawam Rahardjo and Adi Sasono argue that working inside the government for causes like more egalitarian distribution of economic benefits is a better path toward eventual democratisation.

67. 'Saya selalu bilang sama atasan saya, tangan Bapak itu saya anggap tangan Tuhan. Mau dicoret, mau diapakan, nggak ada masalah bagi saya. Semuanya Tuhanlah yang mengatur.' *Tempo* XXI, No. 29 (14 September 1991), p. 32. For a more direct statement of her view of the New Order, see 'Calon legislatif di depan tantangan zaman' [Legislative candidates face the challenges of the times], *Eksekutif* 153 (March 1992), pp. 57–58.

68. See the account in *Tempo* XXII, No. 5 (4 April 1992), pp. 13–26.

69. The best account is Philip Eldridge, *NGOs in Indonesia: Popular Movement or Arm of Government*, Clayton, Vic.: Monash University Centre of Southeast Asian Studies, Working Paper 55, 1989. See also Aswab Mahasin, 'NGOs and Political Alternatives: Awaiting Surprises,' Background Paper Untuk Seminar: Pembangunan Masyarakat Desa Yang Berorientasi Kerakyatan Antara Mitos dan Realita [Background Paper For a Seminar: Development of Village Society that is Democratically Oriented Between Myth and Reality], Yogyakarta: Fakultas Ilmu Sosial dan Politik, Universitas Gadjah Mada, 1989.

70. 'Intellectuals in the New States,' *World Politics* Vol. 12, No. 3 (April 1960), p. 364.

71. *The Passing of Traditional Society*, Glencoe: The Free Press, 1958.

72. Peter B. Evans, Dietrich Rueschemeyer, and Theda Skocpol, *Bringing the State Back In*, Cambridge: Cambridge University Press, 1985.

6

Indonesia's Democratic Past and Future*

From 1950 until about 1957, Indonesia was a representative democracy. The country had no democratic experience prior to its 1945 declaration of independence from Dutch and Japanese colonial rule. Since the late 1950s, it has experienced two types of authoritarianism: the personal rule of President Sukarno's Guided Democracy until 1965 and the army-backed New Order of President Suharto from 1966 to the present. At the turn of the 1990s, the New Order's grip on Indonesian society appears, at least on the surface of observable events, as firm as it ever has been.

Under these circumstances, why write about Indonesian politics from a democratic perspective? I have several reasons, but let me highlight three: one broadly theoretical, one methodological, and one concretely empirical. First, as is well known, there is an extremely high correlation between representative democracy and advanced industrial capitalism among contemporary nation-states.[1] Indonesia's economy is far from advanced—it is in fact still below the threshhold of NICdom—but it has made steady progress in that direction for more than two decades.[2] If the capitalist democracies define for the *genus* nation-state a terminus with economic and political dimensions, and if Indonesia is moving along one of these dimensions, it is worth assessing whether and how it might also be moving along the other.

Second, there is a vigorous recent literature on what has been a widespread (if not general) movement toward democratisation in the 1970s and 1980s in southern Europe, Latin America, and East Asia.[3] These new studies examine elites and leaders, and the negotiating and bargaining that have characterised transitions from authoritarianism to democracy.

* First published in *Comparative Politics*, 24, 4 (July 1992), pp. 443–62.

Their approach has several qualities attractive to a student of Indonesian democratisation. It focuses on proximate causes, in the form of the goals, perceptions, resources or capabilities, strategies, and actions of domestic politicians in and out of power. This is in contrast to earlier literatures that emphasised more analytically distant cultural, social, and economic preconditions and, in the *dependencia* framework, the international economic context. It is dynamic, directly examining processes of change in contrast to the static cross-national correlation analyses of the 1950s and 1960s. And it seeks to find patterns through analysis in depth of particular cases, struggling to achieve a better balance than earlier approaches between the uniqueness of historical events and the universality of human experience.

My third reason is that President Suharto is 69 years old. He has held the presidency since March, 1967, and has been elected to the office by the People's Consultative Assembly for five consecutive five-year terms beginning in 1968. Since March 1988, his most recent election, the succession issue has dominated domestic political discussion. Suharto has hinted that he might step down in 1993, but he has also allowed or encouraged others to act, and has himself acted, in ways that indicate he intends to stay on.

Given the apparent solidity of the New Order, succession politics is not identical with democratisation. Nonetheless, succession "has always been the most sensitive internal management problem for authoritarian rulers."[4] A crisis, or even a carefully managed transfer of office, can provide opportunities for presidential candidates and others to take actions that may lead toward or away from a more democratic form of government. It may do this among other things by opening cracks within the elite, a precondition seen by some observers as a *sine qua non* of contemporary transition politics.[5]

While a transition from authoritarianism to democracy in Indonesia does not appear to be imminent, observers and actors alike need, in Robert Dahl's phrase, to "take stock"[6] now of the potential for steps in a democratising direction in the near future. What does taking stock involve? Dahl suggested constructing "country profiles" assessing the extent to which historical sequences, socioeconomic order, level of socioeconomic development, equalities and inequalities, subcultural pluralism, domination by a foreign power, and beliefs of political activists in particular countries constituted conditions favourable or unfavourable to democracy.

Dahl's country profiles have the virtue of wide coverage but the vice of inconclusiveness, since on most of his dimensions it is possible to find countries with unfavourable ratings that are nonetheless democracies. For example, three frequently cited reasons for the absence of democracy in Indonesia are high subcultural pluralism, high inequality between an urban elite and peasant masses, and low level of development. This argument loses force when Indonesia is compared just with its near neighbours, India and the Philippines, who also score poorly on these dimensions but have a far better democratic record.

In this paper, in the spirit of the southern European, Latin American, and East Asian transition studies, I will take stock by assessing the perceptions, goals, strategies, and resources of the politicians in power in the context of the other political forces with which they interact. My assumption is that when and as the potential for transition rises, this is a major part of the knowledge that players and observers will need to have to assess and influence developments.

To summarise what follows, my main argument is in two parts. First, the New Order rulers are firmly convinced that representative democracy is incompatible with two goals they value more highly, national unity and economic development. Second, the political and economic policy strategies chosen in the light of that belief have succeeded in multiplying many times over the elite's political resources relative to those of alternative elites.

For the would-be democratiser, this is a discouraging outcome. Should Indonesian political liberals then turn their attention toward other, more attainable, goals? Or does the comparative literature and Indonesian experience provide us with some guidelines for policies and other actions that can help lay the ground for future democratisation? I conclude with a discussion of some of the vulnerabilities of the New Order, after a quarter-century in power, and ways in which those vulnerabilities might be exploited for democratic ends.

Memories of Democracy

Today's rulers do not have positive memories of the Old Order, their term for the period 1950–1965.[7] Most scholars further subdivide these years into the period of parliamentary democracy, 1950–1957, and the period of Guided Democracy, as then-President Sukarno labelled his attempt at personal authoritarianism, from 1959 to 1965.[8] To the New Order rulers, however, there is an underlying continuity in the pattern of intense mass-based political conflict that led ultimately to the assassination of six senior army generals in 1965. In their minds, what distinguishes the New Order from the Old is the effective quelling of these conflicts, the creation of a political order controlled from the top rather than driven out of control from the bottom.

The conflicts of the 1950s and early 1960s revolved around three axes or dimensions of cleavage in Indonesian society: ethnicity, religion, and social class. Ethnicity in the Indonesian context means cultural, usually language-based, distinctiveness, with each group having a homeland where most of its members still live. Nearly half of Indonesia's 180 million people are ethnic Javanese, most of whom live in the two provinces of east and central Java and the Special Region of Yogyakarta. The remainder include the Sundanese of west Java, about 15% of the total population, smaller groups of Achenese, Bataks, Minangkabau, and Malays on Sumatra, Madurese on Madura, Balinese on Bali, Bugis on Sulawesi, and hundreds of still smaller groups spread across the 3,500 mile archipelagic crescent from the northwestern tip of Sumatra to the southeastern border with Papua New Guinea.

In religion, Indonesia is a largely (about 85%) Muslim society, though it does contain well-educated Protestant and Catholic minorities (about 3% each) whose political influence has been greater than their size. The most important religion-based conflict has been within the Muslim community, however, pitting a nation-wide self-consciously devout group of believers against a Java-centred religious tradition that is a blend of Islamic, Hindu, and animistic beliefs and practices. The self-consciously devout have themselves been split for nearly all of this century between a modernist, reformist (back to the Quran, join the modern scientific world) urban wing and a more traditional rural wing that remains loyal to its *Syafii* heritage within *sunni* Islam.[9]

Concern with social class in the 1950s and early 1960s was largely a Javanese phenomenon. Unlike Latin America or the Philippines, Java (and the rest of Indonesia) has no history of large private landed estates with their socially crippling conflicts between powerful landlords and powerless tenants and farm labourers. In the nineteenth century, export-oriented European privately-held plantations did develop, but their corporate managers did not own land or control their workers' lives in the style of the *haciendas*. After independence, most of the plantations were taken over by the state. Outside the plantations, fragmentation rather than concentration of agricultural land has long been the norm.

In pre-colonial times, Java's Hindu-Buddhist rulers amassed great wealth through taxation of the villagers and spent it on creating "exemplary centres" of court life, splendid microcosmic reflections of the universe.[10] The Dutch, in effective control of most of Java from early in the 19th century, slowly converted the traditional kingdoms into modern administrative polities while retaining much of the earlier conception of an aristocratic (now schooled and bureaucratic) elite with paternalistic responsibility for the welfare of the (unschooled, outside the state) masses.[11] This notion of a two-class society consisting of the *wong gede* (big people)—educated, state-employed, aristocratic in manner if not by birth—in contrast to the *wong cilik*—uneducated, employed in agriculture or petty trade, coarse in manner—was challenged but not vanquished by the populist revolutionary spirit of the 1945–49 independence struggle against the Dutch.

Political conflicts during the Old Order along these three axes of cleavage can conveniently, if only roughly, be divided into three periods: religious conflict from 1950 to 1955; ethnic conflict from 1956 to 1961; and class conflict from 1961 to 1965.[12] During the first period, the political elite and public were obsessed with the prospect of the first general election—held in 1955 after several delays—in independent Indonesian history. By 1950, five years after the independence declaration of August 17, 1945, many parties were in existence but neither players nor observers had a clear fix on mass strength.

The greatest hopes (from within the devout Muslim community) and fears (from outside it) were directed toward Masjumi, a Japanese-era umbrella party containing most of the educational and social organisations of the Islamic community. Many Masjumi politicians favoured the establishment of an Islamic state, though few had any idea what form such a state might take. Because of its ties to pre-existing organisations and its nearly archipelagic-wide reach, Masjumi was touted as the most likely party to win an absolute majority. In the event it did not, in part because one of its constituents, Nahdlatul Ulama (Awakening of the Religious Teachers), a conservative, rural Java-based organisation, decided to contest the elections on its own. Masjumi received 20.9% of the vote, Nahdlatul Ulama 18.4%.

The Islamic threat of the early 1950s was military as well as electoral. In west Java, an Islamic-oriented armed guerrilla group that had been part of the struggle for Indonesian independence proclaimed itself the Islamic State of Indonesia. In Aceh, on the northwestern tip of Sumatra, political leaders unhappy with their incorporation into a larger province formed an alliance with the west Java rebels. Military campaigns were waged in both regions before the rebellions finally ended.

The mid- to late-1950s were characterised by dissatisfaction outside Java with increasing government administrative and political centralisation, pro-Java economic policies, and the growth of the communist party. Local military commanders in several provinces attempted to shift the balance of power by staging local-level coups against the central government and together forming a "Revolutionary Government of the Republic of Indonesia." There was an Islamic element in the regional movements—several Masjumi leaders joined, for example—but Christian ethnic groups and other anti-central, anti-Java, anti-communist forces were also prominent.

The settlement of the regional rebellions set the stage for the last great Old Order struggle, the army versus the communists. Between 1957 and 1959 President Sukarno and the central army leadership formed a coalition that succeeded in both putting down the rebels and overthrowing representative democracy. Sukarno decreed a return to the Constitution of 1945, under which the executive dominates the legislative branch. The victorious generals acquired vast new powers and responsibilities in the economy and regional government and a regularised role in the political process, legitimised by a doctrine of the "middle way" (neither fully military nor fully civilian government).

The four big political parties to emerge from the 1955 elections were Masjumi, Nahdlatul Ulama, PNI (Partai Nasional Indonesia, Indonesian National Party), with 22.3% of the vote, and PKI (Partai Komunis Indonesia, Indonesian Communist Party), with 16.4%. In the upheavals of the late 1950s, Masjumi was banned and the dominant factions of NU and PNI decided to seek favour with the power-holders rather than contest control through mass mobilisation. The PKI, on the other hand, continued to organise from below and, often together with Sukarno, began to challenge the army's political and economic role. It also attempted to burrow within the officer corps.

The climax of this struggle was the kidnapping and assassination in the early morning hours of 1 October 1965 of six senior army generals. The assassinations were followed by an anti-communist pogrom, the repudiation of Sukarno, and the takeover of the government by the army, under the leadership of Major-General Suharto. The question of responsibility for the coup remains a matter of controversy outside Indonesia. In the official army view there is no doubt that it was a communist plot. It is also clear, however, that some of the army's own forces, including the presidential palace guard, were among the conspirators.

The spiralling political tension of the late 1950s and early 1960s was accompanied by economic stagnation, decline, and finally collapse. After a brief boom in the early 1950s, stimulated by the Korean War, the economy grew very slowly for several years before beginning to drop off. In the period of representative democracy the source of the trouble was policy inconsistency caused by a weak executive and sharp differences among the major parties represented in Parliament. In the late 1950s and early 1960s it was the political instability caused by the regional rebellions and the higher priority given by President Sukarno to campaigns against the Dutch over the territory of West Irian and the British over the formation of neighbouring Malaysia. In the aftermath of the 1965 assassinations, economic growth was negative and inflation was running at over 600% per year.

To sum up: in 1965–66, the surviving army leaders were those who had taken up arms against Muslim guerrilla forces in the early 1950s, fought regional rebellions led by their own junior officers in the late 1950s, and been engaged in a struggle to the death with communists—and again with some of their own junior officers—in the early 1960s. They had also witnessed the endless bickering of parliamentary politicians and the loss of control of the economy by the governments of both representative democracy and Guided Democracy. Put briefly, the lessons they learned from these experiences were the primal importance of establishing and maintaining, first, unity among themselves and, second, tight control over others, including most especially Muslims, regionalists, and communists. Without these fundamentals, neither national unity—the goal to which they had been committed since the 1945 independence declaration—nor economic stabilisation and development—the crisis they now faced—could in their view be achieved.

Strategies and Resources of the New Order Rulers

In an essay on "Economic Policies and the Prospects for Successful Transition from Authoritarian Rule in Latin America," John Sheahan argues that democratic consolidation (that is, the period after the transition from authoritarianism) calls for economic policies that

> meet two requirements that pull in contrary directions. One is that they have the consistency necessary for a viable economy, able to function without constant crises and to achieve some economic growth. That requirement implies restraints: the ability to limit claims that would seriously damage efficiency or outrun productive capacity. The other is the ability to answer enough of the expectations of the politically aware groups in society to gain and hold their acceptance. [13]

The transition that took place in Indonesia in 1965–66 was from the personal rule of Sukarno's Guided Democracy to the military-based authoritarianism of Suharto's New Order, not from authoritarianism to democracy. But Sheahan's criteria also apply to the consolidation of the New Order, whose political viability is in considerable part, though not wholly, due to the consistency *cum* responsiveness of its economic policies. This success was achieved through the adoption and maintenance of an illiberal political strategy, with its origins in the Guided Democracy period, and the initial adoption and later reinforcement of a mainly liberal economic strategy, an abrupt departure from Guided Democracy.

These two strategies complemented each other, largely through the effective accumulation and deployment by Suharto of three kinds of political resources: coercive, persuasive, and material.[14] Coercive resources include the capacity of the government to force its citizens to do something they would otherwise not do. Persuasive resources are symbolic or ideological, the capacity to win agreement from others that one's institutions, policies or programs serve those others' interests or the common good. Material resources are the stuff of exchange, the capacity of a government to induce compliance by offering a reward or compensation. Psychic and status resources also fall under this heading.

The central political institutions of the New Order are the strong presidency created by Sukarno and the army-as-a-political-force, also a continuation of Guided Democracy practice. Major-General Suharto was the senior army general in command of strategic troops in Jakarta on the morning of 1 October 1965. As the killing of his superior officers became known, anti-communist officers and troops, the bulk of the army, rallied around Suharto, making him the leader of the forces in opposition to the PKI and its allies, including President Sukarno. Suharto rode this support to the presidency, pressuring Sukarno to grant him extensive executive authority in March 1966, then twice convening a truncated People's Consultative Assembly (without its leftist members) to name him Acting President in March 1967 and finally full President in March 1968.[15]

In these early actions can already be seen two key elements in Suharto's political strategy: reliance on the army as his chief political support base (building his coercive resources), and the attempt to win wider legitimacy by working within a constitutional framework (building his persuasive resources). The Constitution of 1945, which links the New Order to the revolutionary period and at the same time maintains continuity with Guided Democracy, when the army had already acquired a legitimate political role, suited this strategy well. Under its provisions, the presidency is subordinate only to the People's Consultative Assembly, a kind of super-parliament that meets once in five years to name the president and vice-president and set broad goals for state policy. The constitution is vague on the membership of the Assembly, saying only that it is to contain the members of Parliament (People's Representative Council) plus delegates from the regions and other groups. Selection of members of Parliament is to be determined by law.

Since Suharto's elevation to the presidency in 1967, national elections for Parliament have been held on four occasions, in 1971, 1977, 1982, and 1987. Ten political parties, nine from the Old Order and a new government party called Golkar (for Golongan Karya, Functional Groups), contested the 1971 elections. Golkar, representing in essence the mobilisation of the civilian bureaucracy, including village officials, by the army, won 62% of the vote through a combination of effective army/bureaucratic penetration of the villages, harassment of the opposition, and playing on voters' fears and traditional habits of deference to authority.[16]

In 1973 the nine parties were forced by the government to consolidate into two, the Muslim PPP (Partai Persatuan Pembangunan, Unity Development Party) and the nationalist plus Christian PDI (Partai Demokrasi Indonesia, Indonesian Democracy Party). The leaders of both of these parties are screened and their activities monitored by the government. In 1977 and 1982 Golkar again won over 60% of the vote. In 1987 Golkar won 73%, the jump being largely attributable to the decision of the conservative Islamic organisation Nahdlatul Ulama (Awakening of Religious Teachers), one of the four pre-fusion Muslim parties and up to 1982 the biggest single contributor of votes to PPP, to withdraw from partisan politics.[17]

After each general election—in 1973, 1978, 1983, and 1988—Suharto has been reelected president by a People's Consultative Assembly consisting of the members of Parliament plus an equal number of regional and other representatives. These presidential elections have been easy for Suharto to control. His party, Golkar, has always had an absolute majority of the elected members of Parliament. In addition, twenty percent of the members are appointed to directly represent the military. The remaining half of the members of the Assembly are all appointed, and of course are checked for loyalty to the New Order.

Inside the velvet glove of elected offices and institutions has been the steel hand of the army. Army influence is present not only in Golkar, but also in the cabinet (about one-third of its members are serving or retired officers), second and third echelon central bureaucratic positions, the provincial governorships and district heads (one-third to one half), ambassadorships, and so on.[18] Within the Department of the Interior, which oversees regional government, a military dominated directorate-general of social and political affairs watches over local-level organisations throughout the country.

Paralleling the civilian regional government is a system of military commands, charged by the Minister of Defence with liaison with local populations in the event of external attack, but actually used as a monitoring mechanism. Until recently an extra-constitutional security agency, headed by armed forces officers but under the direct control of the president, added yet another layer of military supervision. The agency still exists, but under another name and with apparently reduced powers.

All of these activities are justified by the doctrine of *dwi-fungsi*, the dual functions of the Indonesian armed forces to defend the country and to play an active role in domestic political life.[19] In addition to *dwi-fungsi*, the New Order's principal legitimating symbols are the Constitution of 1945, discussed above, Pancasila (Five Principles), and *pembangunan* (development). The Pancasila are "Belief in the One and Only God, Just and Civilised Humanity, the Unity of Indonesia, Democracy Guided by Inner Wisdom in Unanimity Arising out of Deliberation among Representatives, and Social Justice for All the People of Indonesia."[20]

What the stilted and overblown (also in the original Indonesian) phrases convey most concretely is rejection of the Islamic state (to which it was symbolically opposed in the political-religious conflicts of the 1950s) and of communism (to which it was opposed in the class struggle of the early 1960s). More generally, they represent a search dating back at least to the independence revolution (Sukarno coined the phrase in a speech given on 1 June 1945) for broadly inclusive principles to bind together the diverse groups of an extremely pluralistic society.

Pembangunan or development is the link between a repressive political system and a market economy. It is the vein of gold from which Suharto has mined the material resources that, combined with coercion and persuasion, he has used to increase the New Order's power.

In 1966, General Suharto inherited an economy in crisis, with a declining Gross National Product, skyrocketing inflation, and an unpayable foreign debt. Unlike his predecessor, whose political resources had little connection with the domestic economy, Suharto chose to listen to a group of professional economists led by the Berkeley-educated University of Indonesia academic Widjojo Nitisastro. The economists offered both policy advice, based on the neo-classical and development economics theories in which they were trained, and access to external assistance from Western governments and international lending institutions.

From 1966 to the present Suharto has relied heavily on the economists' advice, particularly in macro-economic policy matters, and on their connections. But the relationship has not been entirely smooth; for much of the 1970s, in particular, they were held at arm's length, only being fully restored to favour in the early 1980s. The reason for these changes has to do with Suharto's political strategy and the relationship of his economic policies to that strategy.[21]

Put simply, Suharto has used economic policy to build support with two kinds of constituencies: personal, or patrimonial, and more general or societal constituencies such as rural producers and urban consumers. Both kinds have required steady growth to increase the quantity of resources available for distribution. Generating growth has been the forte of the economists. Their services were desperately needed in the late 1960s and again since the early and mid-1980s, when the international oil price dropped by two-thirds.

Personal or patrimonial constituency-building has required access to the benefits of growth, which in turn implies policies not favoured by neo-classical economists: the maintenance of financially unaccountable state enterprises, protection for favoured private sector business people, including tariff and non-tariff barriers such as licensing and monopolies, non-competitive state contracts, and so on. The 1970s, the decade of two oil shocks and a top per barrel price of over $30, was the heyday of patrimonialism.

The oil boom in fact allowed the government to formulate policies designed to build support among both types of constituencies. Serving and retired military officers, state officials, Chinese and indigenous businessmen were all able to make use of political ties to advance their fortunes. Rice farmers, as a general category, were an early target of special attention (irrigation rehabilitation, miracle seeds, fertilizer, pesticides, credit), as were the urban consumers of rice and other basic household needs such as kerosene.

Student protests against authoritarianism and corruption in 1973–74, plus an unstable rice price, led to the so-called January Disaster of 1974 in which student demonstrations combined with urban discontent (and some political manipulation from generals at the top of the regime maneuvering for personal advantage), resulting in mass rioting, looting, and burning. The government responded politically with greater authoritarianism (arrests and trials, tightened media controls) and economically with a vast program of local level construction of schools, health centres, markets, roads, and other projects that pumped money into the provinces, districts, and villages. These programs continue to have high priority in the 1980s, despite the government's reduced financial capabilities.

Finally, coercion, persuasion, and material exchange have all been linked together in the New Order's corporatist strategy toward non-state political and social organisations. The forced fusion of the old political parties described above is an example. Golkar, the state party, maintains several organisations active among constituencies it covets, such as youth and Muslims. The government has created Islamic advisory councils at the national, provincial, and district levels. It monopolises labour organisation, controls the national association of business people, and has attempted repeatedly—with varying degrees of success—to penetrate associations of journalists, social scientists, lawyers, doctors, engineers, and so on.

What have been the results of Suharto's political and economic policies for regime consolidation? At the outset of their discussion of 'Opening (and Undermining) Authoritarian Regimes,' O'Donnell and Schmitter argue that since the end of World War II, authoritarian rulers have been unable to 'promote themselves as long-term solutions to the problems of political order and as the best possible modes of governance for their societies. . . . They are regimes that practice dictatorship and repression in the present while promising democracy and freedom in the future.'[22]

The New Order leaders, in contrast to this general pattern, have never promised democracy and freedom in the future. They have instead claimed that their institutions and doctrines—Pancasila, the 1945 Constitution with its strong, indirectly elected president and weak Parliament and People's Consultative Assembly, the dual functions of the army, and the Golkar/PPP/PDI party system—are the permanent solution to Indonesia's political problems, a form of democracy suitable to Indonesian conditions. How successful have they been in making this claim stick?

Precisely because it is an authoritarian system—without free elections, media, or opinion polling—the evidence for judgments about legitimacy is hard to come by. I shall argue here that the regime is genuinely popular in many quarters and at least willingly accepted in others. Some qualifications to this view will be offered in the discussion below of regime vulnerabilities.

The New Order's popularity or acceptance is based on its effective accumulation and deployment, I have asserted above, of political resources of coercion, persuasion, and material benefits. Coercion defines the regime's boundaries, increasing support from insiders while keeping outsiders at bay. It has been applied most brutally to communists, hundreds of thousands of whom were killed or imprisoned in the mid-1960s; then university students, militant anti-government Muslims, and other dissidents who have been suppressed at various times from the 1970s to the present. Coercion is also employed to maintain the three-party system and to limit the freedom of the print and broadcast media. Since the 1965–66 period, terror has not been the hallmark of the regime, but would-be activists are well aware of the government's capacity and willingness to repress them when it feels threatened.

Persuasion is for both insiders and outsiders. Within the core elite of the army there has been a continuing and intense effort to maintain a high level of belief in the regime's basic values, and to transmit these values to the post-revolutionary generation of officers who took power within the army in the 1980s. This effort is reflected in the curriculum of the military academy and the senior staff and command school, and in various internal seminars and other formal discussions sponsored by the government and army leadership. It has been accompanied by a thorough professionalisation of the officer corps, with regular tours of duty, merit promotions, advanced training, and so on.

What evidence there is, in the public statements of officers, reports of seminars and meetings, actions and statements of retired officers, and the gossip of the Jakarta rumor mill, suggests that at the ideological level there is little conflict within the army.[23] The principle of *dwi-fungsi*, in particular, seems well established. Put in comparative terms, a hard-line view prevails.[24] Though there are several dissident retired officers (including some who once held high positions in the New Order), who favour greater democratisation and would like to see the army retreat to a less prominent political role, what is remarkable is that after a quarter century in power the New Order has generated so little opposition from discontented members of the core elite.

Outside the military, the government has also maintained a high level of ideological activity designed to win over the civilian bureaucracy, Islamic, left-of-centre, and regional groups and the general population to the regime's interpretation of Pancasila, the 1945 constitution, *dwi-fungsi*, *pembangunan* and other principles. It is impossible to tell how successful these campaigns have been. In the early days of courses in Pancasila for civil servants there were reports of widespread cynicism mixed with admiration for the climate of open discussion within the closed fora of the courses.[25] More recently, critics within the government have suggested publicly that officials are "*jenuh*" (satiated, implying fed up) and that the courses need to be changed or dropped.[26]

My own, highly impressionistic, sense of the effects of these campaigns is that they have—together with coercion and the providing of material benefits—contributed to a major restructuring of Indonesian political culture. At the very least, what the army considers the "extreme" ends, militant Islam and communism, no longer represent serious threats to what has clearly become a widely-supported centre of agreement on the politics of religion and the economy. Regionalism is more of a puzzle, but here too I think a central area of consensus has been established.

The agreement on the religious issue is that Indonesia has neither a religious nor a secular form of government; all religions are both protected and encouraged by the state. This position has been accepted both by Muhammadiyah, the leading social and educational organisation representing modernist Islam (in the 1950s the major constituent organisation of Masjumi), and Nahdlatul Ulama, the principal representative of rural, traditional Javanese Islam. Muhammadiyah decided early in the New Order to stay out of politics and to concentrate on building schools and hospitals. NU left PPP in 1984, embracing the New Order view that the 1945 constitution is the "final form" of the Indonesian state and that Islamic political aspirations should henceforth be conveyed through non-partisan channels.[27]

On the economy, there is general agreement in support of the principle of a mixed economy. The macro-economic successes of the technocrats' policies have created broad respect for the power of markets and neo-classical theory, a respect that barely existed thirty years ago. At the same time, statist and populist ideas, their roots in the socialist ideology of the pre-war nationalist movement, and nurtured today by concerns over distribution and the rigors of international economic competition, continue to be relevant. In the frequently referred to formulation of Article 33 of the 1945 Constitution (the measure by which all economic policies are assessed in public debate), the state, the private sector, and cooperatives all have a role to play in economic development.[28]

Concerning centre-region relations, the New Order government has been committed to the idea of a unitary, as opposed to federal, state. In practice this has meant extreme centralisation in policy making and implementation in nearly all areas of public life. It has also meant an unprecedented flow of funds, including more than three-fourths of the budgets of most provincial governments, plus many projects implemented directly from the centre and many others channeled through district and village governments, whose budgetary revenues are also largely dropped from the centre. One result of these policies has been a much higher degree of economic integration, measured by growth in inter-regional commerce, population mobility, and national market networks.[29]

There are few supporters of federalism[30] in the regions, but the common sentiment outside Java since the early 1950s has been in favour of greater regional autonomy.[31] During the New Order period, regional enthusiasm for autonomy has been tempered by gratitude for central largesse, and by the participation of many regional business people in the more integrated national economy, but it has not disappeared. Since the early 1970s there have also been many complaints that economic development has been too concentrated in Java generally and the greater Jakarta area especially. A current concern, which may be replacing the Java-Outer Islands focus of previous debates, is with the disparity between fast-growing western (Sumatra-Java-Bali) and slower-growing eastern Indonesia.

Until the mid-1980s the Jakarta government reacted more symbolically than substantively to complaints of over-centralisation. It maintains the legal fiction of first and second level autonomous regions (provinces and districts), whose legislatures are chosen simultaneously with the national Parliament. The regional legislatures also play a symbolic role in nominating district heads and governors, but the actual choices have always been made higher up. In filling these offices, however, the centre has generally been sensitive to the regional and ethnic origins of candidates and to the desires of local elite groups. It has also allowed or encouraged expressions of regional pride, particularly in the preservation of various aspects of traditional culture (good for tourism, too).

Since the mid-1980s the centre-regional power balance has begun to shift toward the regions because of the decline in national revenues that the central government can disburse. Provincial and district-level governments, and other agencies such as the state universities, are being encouraged to seek new sources of revenue and provided with the authority to do so. This has not so far been accompanied by any loosening of political control by the central executive over the local executive, or by any shift in the regional balance of power from the executive to the legislative branch. It is, however, an indication that, in contrast to the unity-threatening politics of the 1950s, the present and future battleground between Jakarta and the regions is likely to be more narrowly focused on issues of money and specific devolutions of authority within the present constitutional framework.

Finally, the increase in material benefits, the third tone in the triad of political resources accumulated by the New Order, has been spectacular. Annual national budget expenditures have increased from the equivalent of about U.S.$500 million at the beginning of the New Order to over $20 billion today.[32] The economy as a whole grew by nearly 8% per year from 1969 through 1981, in contrast to a 1950s rate of 3.2% and negative growth in the mid-1960s.[33] After a drop in the early to mid-1980s, it is now back to a 5% per annum level. Petroleum has led the pace, with the mining sector vaulting from .2% to 22.6% of Gross Domestic Product between 1973 and 1981. But manufacturing also grew by more than 14% per year, and in agriculture the rice crop more than doubled during this period. Today's harvests are three times those of the late 1960s. Trade expanded by 11.7% per year from 1967–73 and 7.4% per year from 1973–1981.[34]

The benefits of this growth have been disbursed both narrowly and widely, as has already been implied in the discussion above of economic policy, and described in the discussion of regional policy. High-ranking military officers, officials and private business people close to Suharto and his circle have been well provided for, but so have officers and civil servants in general (pay raises, legal and illegal opportunities to supplement income), rice farmers, and urban consumers. Tens of millions of Indonesians have gained from the new schools, health centres, roads, markets, and other facilities that have been built in virtually every subdistrict. Even the urban working class and landless labourers in the rural areas have benefited, particularly in the 1970s, from the increased employment opportunities.[35]

In concluding this section, perhaps only one important point remains to be made. The successful accumulation of resources over the last quarter century has made it possible for the New Order government to respond to challenges with changes in substantive policies while maintaining its authoritarian structure intact. In other words, it has not so far had to give in to demands for greater participation. This is most obvious in its 1974 post-January Disaster reforms, when it met calls for democracy with a village development program. One year later, a public outcry against corruption in the state oil company was also resolved without democratisation of the process by which officials are held accountable. Since 1983, the government has reacted to smaller oil revenues by enacting an impressive series of deregulation measures that have boosted non-oil exports and restarted the growth engine.[36] While these policies have gone against some powerful interests close to the government, their adoption did not require President Suharto to bring new actors into the policy process.[37]

Toward A Democratic Future

For the past two decades, I have tried to show, liberal economics and illiberal politics have reinforced each other in Indonesia. Successful economic and other policies have boosted the store of coercive, persuasive, and material resources possessed by the New Order elite. An authoritarian president, controlling society through controlling the army, has provided the political foundation for maintaining a coherent and consistent economic policy strategy. At the same time a combination of responsiveness to critical constituencies and ideological persuasion has kept the role of coercion limited and, much of the time, in the background.

Is there any way to break this connection, specifically to maintain the economic policies while democratising the political system? In this concluding section I will attempt to chip away at (as opposed to resolve) this problem by discussing first some vulnerabilities of the New Order and finally a few courses of action that can be taken to exploit those vulnerabilities. I will leave for another essay the separate question of how a new government might be so constituted as to be both economically and politically liberal and at the same time be stable and maintain national unity.

Despite its successes in building resources, the New Order political system has at least five soft spots: first, an ideological gap between Pancasila democracy and genuine democracy; second, a persistent tension between civilian and military sub-elites; third, a perception-reality gap concerning the nature of mass political cleavage today, as opposed to twenty years ago; fourth, a nagging concern with the distributive consequences of government economic policy; and fifth, some succession-related hairline cracks in the army elite. I shall briefly discuss each of these.

First, only the core members of the New Order elite, particularly those in the military, really believe their own propaganda that "Pancasila Democracy" is intrinsically superior to representative democracy based on free elections and freedom to organise political parties. For many others, Pancasila Democracy is a more-or-less justifiable temporary arrangement until genuine democratisation becomes possible. Despite media restrictions, the democratic ideal is kept alive by a small but sophisticated and internationally-connected intellectual, professional, artistic, and journalistic elite.[38] This elite is most heavily represented in Jakarta and in the national media located there, but a few of its members can be found in even the smaller towns of remote islands.

Second, tension between the two main (but very unequal in power) coalition partners in the regime, the military and the civilian bureaucrats, was very evident at the beginning of the New Order, when the army moved to take control of the government. The material and status benefits provided to the bureaucracy, as the administrators of *pembangunan*, have done much to make the power inequality less irritating. But the sense of we versus they, on both sides, remains. The military still doubt the political abilities and New Order loyalties of the civilians, and the civilians resent the large number of military officers occupying high positions outside the Department of Defence.[39] The conflict is also evident in Golkar, whose leaders describe it as containing three "columns": "A" for the armed forces, "B" for the civilian bureaucracy, and "G" for Golkar itself, meaning the professional politicians (also civilians) who staff the organisation.

Third, I have already alluded to the perception-reality gap in my discussion of the persuasive successes of the New Order elite vis-à-vis its erstwhile religious, class, and regional enemies. The leaders of organised Islam have given up their aspirations for an Islamic state. Communism is no more, in Indonesia or almost anywhere else. Regional groups want more money and more power, but within the present constitutional framework. The implication of these successes is that it has become increasingly implausible for the government to justify denial of participation on the ground that greater freedom to oppose its policies will threaten economic development or national unity.[40]

Fourth, from the beginning of the New Order, domestic (and foreign) critics have assailed the technocrats' economic policies for failing to deal with problems of distribution of the benefits of growth. In 1974 the attacks culminated in the January Disaster riots, followed by a massive development program. In the late 1980s the accusations have swelled again, reflecting the widespread perception that the government's deregulation policies have primarily benefited the wealthy Jakarta few, especially the largest companies, now labelled conglomerates.[41]

These concerns are partly a reflection of underlying socio-economic reality, but they are also driven hard by ideological bias and racial antagonism. On the one hand, there is little doubt that the market-oriented economic policies favoured by the technocrats have contributed to the emergence of a wealthy, urban business class and to the commercialisation of the countryside. Growth has tended to benefit Jakarta first, then urban areas over rural areas and Java over the other islands. The economic power of the conglomerates has indeed become more visible since the deregulation reforms and especially since the development of the Jakarta stock market, with its requirements of financial disclosure, in the past two years.

The most rigorous academic observers offer a more balanced view of distribution, however, arguing that the rising economic tide has lifted all ships. In a 1981 study, Anne Booth and R.M. Sundrum concluded that

> At the moment there appears to be little support for those who argue that the development strategy pursued by the Indonesian government over the last ten years has led to a rapid increase in income disparities and in the number of people in 'absolute poverty' *everywhere* in the country. . . . On the other hand all the available evidence suggests that the number of people in Indonesia, and particularly in Java, living below any acceptable level of material well-being is still extremely large, and if it is declining at all the rate of decline is extremely small. [42]

A more recent analysis of agricultural development edges toward the positive, offering evidence that, contrary to the reports of a decade and a half ago, "rural wage rates have increased significantly, widespread labour shortages have been reported . . ., and many poorer rural households appear to be benefiting especially from employment in urban locations."[43] A study of industrialisation concludes that, in regional terms, "notwithstanding the Jakarta-Surabaya concentrations, a measure of industrial dispersal has been achieved." In terms of scale, annual output of small firms nationwide grew 9.4% (compared to 15.1% for medium and large firms) from 1975–1986; employment growth for the two kinds of firms was similar.[44]

Despite these balanced reports of professional observers, the negative findings tend to be more widely believed in Indonesia for two reasons: the continued appeal of anti-capitalist, anti-foreign ideology among many Indonesians, and the racial anxiety associated with the Chinese complexion of most of the conglomerates. Anti-capitalist, anti-foreign ideology dominated the pre-war nationalist movement and reached a peak during the Guided Democracy years. It is still an undertone in the speeches and private comments of many politicians and officials.[45]

When President Suharto recently invited the heads of 31 of the largest businesses to his ranch outside Jakarta (to pressure them into selling shares to cooperatives), many Indonesians were startled and dismayed to learn that almost all were of Chinese descent.[46] Anxiety associated with Chinese success contributes to what Albert Hirschman has called the tunnel effect, in which tolerance of slow growth is reduced when the non-mobile perceive the mobile to be different from themselves in class or ethnic terms.[47]

Fifth, the succession issue, with which this paper began, does seem to be creating some rifts within the regime. The most obvious is a split between President Suharto and the leadership of the army, which became public at the March, 1988 session of the People's Consultative Assembly. The issue then was the vice-presidency for the 1988–1993 term, which Suharto gave to his longtime patronage chief and Minister for the State Secretariat, Lt. Gen. (ret.) Sudharmono.

For the first time since Suharto brought it firmly under his control in the late 1960s, the army objected publicly and loudly to a presidential decision. Their concern was that Sudharmono might succeed to the presidency, either through the president's death or by accession in 1993. They opposed this possibility for essentially corporate reasons: Sudharmono is an ex-army lawyer, not part of the army inner circle of line generals, who was also known to be cultivating civilian support in the bureaucracy and among Muslims.

After their defeat in the Assembly, the army leaders immediately turned their attention to Golkar, which they had allowed to fall under Sudharmono's control five years earlier. Between March and September they took over the district and provincial branches of Golkar, sending a signal to Suharto that a reappointment of Sudharmono as chairman would have little support at the party's national congress. In the event, the president appointed another retired general, also a former aide but without a political following or ambitions.

In 1989 the army appeared to be attempting to pressure Suharto into stepping down in 1993. Student protests on a variety of local issues were tolerated (and perhaps fanned), the army censor lowered his shield to incoming Western press reports of corruption, the army fraction in Parliament urged greater opennness in public debate, and so on. In September the president struck back, promising to "thrash" anyone who tried to take power unconstitutionally.[48] The issue receded for several months, but in mid-1990 was once again on the front pages of leading newspapers and magazines.

The reasons for military pressure on Suharto himself—as opposed to the hostility toward Sudharmono—are not completely clear. The army's control of the succession process, as the president approaches old age but shows no sign of willingness to lessen his grip, is probably the major factor. Also important is concern with the security (perhaps also patronage) consequences of the growing and increasingly visible business activities of several of the president's children.[49] There are no apparent differences over substantive issues, such as development policy, military budgets, or other aspects of civil-military relations.

Current conflict within the armed forces, succession-related or otherwise, is not as easy to detect as is the Suharto-army dispute. Minister of Defense, formerly Commander of the Armed Forces, Gen. L.B. Murdani, has long been the dominant figure within the army. A Suharto protege as a young intelligence officer, Murdani's power today is based on his still tight hold on the elaborate armed forces domestic intelligence network and the respect accorded his leadership abilities by other senior officers. The current Armed Forces Commander, also a Suharto protege, is sometimes said to take independent positions, but he has no significant following among senior or junior officers. Though a few names pop up in speculations about the next president, the army—perhaps to avoid causing premature conflict—does not appear to have faced this issue. Murdani himself, as a Roman Catholic in a Muslim nation, is said not to be a candidate.[50]

How can these vulnerabilities be exploited by would-be democratisers? Before offering some specific steps that might be taken, three preliminary considerations need to be raised. First, evolution is preferable to revolution. With Dahl, Huntington, Stepan, and others, I believe this generally to be the case.[51] In New Order Indonesia, it is mandated by the enormous imbalance in power between the army and the democratic opposition, and the need to have the cooperation of at least parts of the army if change is to occur. Mass mobilisation of the urban poor or militant Islam, the two most likely revolutionary forces, will lead not to democracy but to military counter-revolution followed by greater authoritarianism.

Second, the group promoting change, at least in the short run, will consist largely of the urban intelligentsia. These people are not revolutionaries, which is another reason for preferring an evolutionary strategy. They are also very small in number and much better equipped to talk, both by professional inclination and by the political context in which they live, than to act. They are not totally unconnected with the masses, however, particularly on the Islamic side, where several democratic intellectuals have large followings in urban and rural areas.[52]

Third, the forms of democracy are already in place and need only be filled with democratic content.[53] President Suharto holds office as president under a democratic constitution, not as the head of a *junta*. Parliament and the People's Consultative Assembly contain unelected members— 20% and 60% respectively—but they are also the product of regular elections. Democratisation will require changes in the role of the army and the nature of the parties, but not in the constitution itself. That there have been throughout the New Order few opponents of the 1945 Constitution, even among the most democratically-minded dissidents, is a good indication that at this level at least the transition can be smooth. Transition negotiations should instead focus on withdrawing armed forces personnel from civilian government positions, reducing the number of armed forces appointees to Parliament and the Assembly, and so on.

Given these considerations, two types of action by democratisers seem most likely to have a positive impact: persuading the ruling group that it is now possible to begin to open up; and improving the political resource position of non-ruling elites. Persuading the elite has in turn two dimensions, changing their beliefs about the role of the executive in a representative democracy, and about the nature of the party system characteristic of representative democracy.

As described in the first section of this paper, the New Order elite's image of democracy was shaped by the experiences of 1950–1959, when Parliament was fragmented by a multi-party system based on cultural, class, and regional cleavages and the executive was as a result extremely weak. Yet there is nothing inherent about weak executives and fragmented party systems in representative democracy, even in representative democracies in pluralistic societies. To the contrary, as Dahl writes in *Polyarchy*, most twentieth-century societies have 'rejected as unworkable the model of assembly government with a weak, subordinate executive.' Particularly in societies with marked subcultural cleavages, 'the executive must have authority that in a realistic sense is beyond the capacities of transitory majorities in parliament to curtail.'[54] In the Third World, India is proof that a strong executive is possible in a democracy.

Changing elite beliefs about the role of the executive is undoubtedly easier than convincing them that allowing political parties to form freely will not necessarily result in a party system like that of the 1950s. What is needed here is a continuing trialogue among the military, intellectuals, and would-be party politicians, plus the further development of the private economy and of civil society as discussed below. The current parties— especially the two non-government parties, PPP and PDI—are probably too discredited (among both the military and intellectuals) to play much of a role in this debate. Golkar on the other hand could be the foundation for a broadly aggregative party of the right, representing much of the civil bureaucracy, the upper business class, and prosperous farmers who are the principal beneficiaries of the New Order.

Actions to improve the resources of non-ruling elites should, where possible, be non-antagonistic and responsive to what the elite considers pressing problems.[55] Three promising examples are: continuing the policy of deregulation, with special attention to the needs of small entrepreneurs; strengthening the legal and court system; and further construction of civil society.

The great benefits of deregulation for democracy are the reduction of state power over and the economic impetus given to the business sector. The underlying logic is the amassing of economic resources, both capital and labour, in the private sector, which can be used to support democratic forces. Recent examples in Asia are Taiwan and South Korea. In Indonesia, the political consequence of deregulation has so far been more negative (both for democracy and for the stability of the New Order) than positive, i.e. the further growth and higher visibility of domestic Chinese business, which simultaneously adds to the private coffers of officials and reduces their legitimacy among indigenous Indonesians. A further negative is that even indigenous big business people have so far been reluctant democrats, because they are able to strike private deals with the power-holders.

One counter to these effects might be to support—Taiwan-style—policies that strengthen small-scale entrepreneurs, who will ultimately be too numerous and various in their policy needs for the government to control by coercion, persuasion, and exchange alone.[56] A straw in the wind is the creation by Nahdlatul Ulama, in cooperation with one of the biggest Chinese tycoons, of a network of rural banks.[57] Such policies are in principle attractive to the government, which needs to counter accusations that deregulation helps only the wealthy and the Chinese, and likely to be more effective than the current approach, which has been to pressure the conglomerates into selling shares cheaply and on low long-term credit to cooperatives.

The rule of law, as a political issue in the Third World, is typically associated with human rights activism. In Indonesia, however, its most influential proponents today are in the business community and in the government itself, making it a prime candidate for coalition-building between powerful New Order elites and not-so-powerful pro-democrats.

Illustrative of the possibilities is a 1989 economists' forum on the need for land reform.[58] What the economists meant by land reform was not redistribution, but rather administrative and legislative action to improve title security. This issue unites foreign and domestic business people, who need clear title to the real estate their offices and factories occupy, government economists, who encourage business growth, and even small landowners, who have nowhere to turn when their property is arbitrarily seized. Tax law reform is another major issue area uniting government officials looking for more revenue, which includes the economists, with business people who want less arbitrariness and unpredictability in collection practices.

Finally, in a civil society, 'certain community and group identities exist independent of the state and . . . certain types of self-constituted units are capable of acting autonomously in defense of their own interests and ideals. Moreover, these identities and interests must not only be dispersed throughout the country, they must also be capable of being concentrated when the occasion demands, that is, they must be organised for coherent collective action.'[59]

Indonesian party politicians in the 1950s tried to build a civil society from the top down. They created a system of national-level parties and affiliated organisations representing farmers, workers, women, youth, students, intellectuals, and other groups. In the pursuit of votes, they then attempted to restructure village life in partisan terms. The attempt failed, mostly because of the unresolvability of conflicts at the national level but also because the effect on local communities—at least in Java—of the introduction of a politics based on ethnicity, religion, and class was more disruptive of traditional relations than it was constitutive of a new social consensus.[60]

The New Order's approach to non-state political and social organisations has been to abolish or control them, another form of construction from the top. Its combination of coercion, persuasion, and exchange has been relatively effective so far in suppressing or coopting most private interests. Yet for all its resources Suharto's government is authoritarian, not totalitarian, and thus limited in its capabilities. In the interstices of authoritarian control a measure of autonomous organisational life—in the press, among private lawyers, doctors, and other professional, artistic, and intellectual groups, churches, Islamic associations, and so on—has been maintained.[61]

In some quarters, like the conservative Islamic association Nahdlatul Ulama and the private development organisations called LPSM (Lembaga Pengembangan Swadaya Masyarakat, Institution for Promoting Self-Reliant Community Development) and LSM (Lembaga Swadaya Masyarakat, Self-Reliant Community Development Institution), it even thrives. NU trades a non-partisan attitude for the right to manage its own internal affairs and the opportunity to fashion its own approach to raising the level of living of its members, for example through its new system of rural banks. Its present national chairman and many younger activists are also working hard to break down the barriers that have long separated traditional from modernist Islam, devout Muslims from non-devout Muslims, and Muslims from Christians.

The LPSMs and LSMs are typically run by urban, educated young people committed to Basic Human Needs and 'appropriate technology' approaches.[62] Ethnicity is not a factor in most of these organisations. Religion often is—many receive funding from churches or have a relationship with Islamic groups—but there is also a common commitment to the idea of development from below that binds them together.

The LPSMs and LSMs supplement—through access to international resources open only to the private sector—official development programs and grant the government a measure of distributional legitimacy at home and abroad in return for organisational autonomy and some room to criticise. A recent study chronicles the 'rapid proliferation of small groups which are playing both developmental and mobilising roles' and holds that this trend "has contributed greatly in its own right toward strengthening processes of democratisation in Indonesia."[63]

It is easy to discount the importance of these and the other private organisations mentioned above in a society currently so dominated by the military and civilian state bureaucracies. Even taken together, they are very small and resource-poor. Yet there is evidence that they have held their own and in some cases, such as the LPSMs and LSMs, and also the regional press, actually grown in size, sophistication, and autonomy.[64] Perhaps most important is that so many of them cut across or combine in new ways the old ethnic, religious, and class cleavages of Indonesian society. In the long run, when economic and elite changes raise the probability of a transition, it may well be the web woven by these non-state organisations that makes democracy work.

1. The best theoretical statement of this link is still Robert Dahl, *Polyarchy*, New Haven: Yale University Press, 1971, Ch. 5. The original locus of the insight is Seymour Martin Lipset, "Economic Development and Democracy," *Political Man*, New York: Doubleday, 1960, pp. 45–76.

2. The fullest study, now dated, is Anne Booth and Peter McCawley, eds., *The Indonesian Economy During the Soeharto Era*, Kuala Lumpur: Oxford University Press, 1979. For more recent partial accounts, see Anne Booth, *Agricultural Development in Indonesia*, Sydney: Allen and Unwin, 1988, and Hal Hill, "The Indonesian Manufacturing Sector: Southeast Asia's Emerging Industrial Giant?" in Anne Booth, ed., *The Oil Boom and After: Indonesian Economic Policy and Performance in the Soeharto Era*, Kuala Lumpur: Oxford University Press, 1992. The *Bulletin of Indonesian Economic Studies*, published three times per year by the Department of Economics, Research School of Pacific Studies, Australian National University, Canberra, has been a superb chronicler of the progress of the Indonesian economy.

3. The benchmark study is the four volume *Transitions from Authoritarian Rule*, under the general editorship of Guillermo O'Donnell, Philippe C. Schmitter, and Laurence Whitehead, published by The Johns Hopkins University Press, Baltimore, 1986.

4. Guillermo O'Donnell and Philippe C. Schmitter, *Transitions from Authoritarian Rule: Tentative Conclusions about Uncertain Democracies*, p. 20.

5. "[W]e assert that there is no transition whose beginning is not the consequence—direct or indirect—of important divisions within the authoritarian regime itself..." O'Donnell and Schmitter, p. 19.

6. The phrase is from Dahl, *Polyarchy*, pp. 216–17.

7. The New Order leaders have not been shy about expressing their hostility to their predecessors. A sampling of the Jakarta daily and weekly press at any time over the past two decades will provide ample evidence, as will perusal of the mountain of K-12 civics books published since the 1970s. A good direct source of top-level military attitudes is President Suharto's autobiography, *Pikiran, Ucapan dan Tindakan Saya: Otobiografi* [My Thoughts, Words, and Deeds: Autobiography], seperti dipaparkan kepada [as told to] G. Dwipayana dan Ramadhan K.H., Jakarta: Citra Lamtoro Gung Persada, 1988. A systematic account of army political ideology, still from the regime's point of view, is Nugroho Notosusanto, ed., *Pejuang dan Prajurit* [Fighter and Soldier], Jakarta: Sinar Harapan, 1984. A more or less official view of the establishment of the New Order, which emphasises its anti-communist origins and the supposed consensus arrived at between the military and civilian political groups, is Nugroho Notosusanto, ed., *Tercapainya Konsensus Nasional 1966 1969* [The Achievement of National Consensus 1966–1969], Jakarta: Bala Pustaka, 1985. Very early New Order statements of army doctrine are Sekretaris Seminar Angkatan Darat Ke-II, [Secretariat of the Second Army Seminar] *Doktrin Perdjuangan TNI-AD 'Tri Ubaya Cakti'* [The 'Three Sacred Efforts' Struggle Doctrine of the Army], Bandung, 1966; and Staf Pertahanan Keamanan [Defense and Security Staff], *Doktrin Pertahanan-Keamanan Nasional dan Doktrin Perdjuangan Angkatan Bersendjata Republik Indonesia 'Tjatur Darma Eka Karma' [The National Defense and Security Doctrine and the 'Four Duties One Destiny' Struggle Doctrine of the Indonesian Armed Forces]*, Jakarta: 1967. An important presentation of New Order political and economic goals is Ali Moertopo, *Dasar-Dasar Pemikiran Tentang Akselerasi Modernisasi Pembangunan 25 Tahun* [Foundations of Thought Concerning 25 Years of Acceleration of Modernisation and Development], Jakarta: Centre for Strategic and International Studies, 1972. The best outside study of the military in the New Order period is David Jenkins, *Suharto and His Generals: Indonesian Military Politics 1975–1983*, Ithaca: Cornell Modern Indonesia Project, 1984. The basics of military ideology are described in the Introduction, pp. 1–12.

8. On the two years in between, see Daniel S. Lev, *The Transition to Guided Democracy: Indonesian Politics 1957–1959*, Ithaca: Cornell Modern Indonesia Project, 1966.

9. On these divisions within Islam, see John L. Esposito, *Islam: The Straight Path*, New York: Oxford University Press, 1988, pp. 4, 86.

10. R. Heine-Geldern, "Conceptions of State and Kingship in Southeast Asia,"

Far Eastern Quarterly 2 (1942): 15–30; Clifford Geertz, *The Interpretation of Cultures*, New York: Basic Books, 1973, pp. 331ff.

11. Heather Sutherland, *The Making of a Bureaucratic Elite*, Singapore: Heinemann, 1979.

12. The classic analysis of the politics of the pre-New Order period is Herbert Feith, *The Decline of Constitutional Democracy in Indonesia*, Ithaca: Cornell University Press, 1962.

13. In O'Donnell, Schmitter, and Whitehead, *Transitions from Authoritarian Rule: Comparative Perspectives*, p. 154.

14. The concept of political resources I have taken from Warren Ilchman and Norman Thomas Uphoff, *The Political Economy of Change*, Berkeley and Los Angeles: University of California Press, 1969. The types of resources are adapted from John Kenneth Galbraith, *The Anatomy of Power*, Boston: Houghton Mifflin, 1983, who distinguishes among three types of power: condign (coercive), conditioned (persuasive), and compensatory (material or exchange). On persuasion as a system of control, see Charles E. Lindblom, *Politics and Markets*, New York: Basic Books, 1977.

15. The politics of this period are described in Harold Crouch, *The Army and Politics in Indonesia*, Ithaca: Cornell University Press, 1978.

16. K.E. Ward, *The 1971 Election in Indonesia: An East Javanese Case Study*, Clayton, Vic.: Monash University, Monash Papers on Southeast Asia, 1974; R. William Liddle, "Evolution from Above: National Development and Local Leadership in Indonesia," *Journal of Asian Studies* 32 (1973), 287–309.

17. R. William Liddle, "Indonesia in 1987: The New Order at the Height of its Power," *Asian Survey* 28:2 (1988), 180–91.

18. The most recent attempt at assessing the extent of military penetration of the civilian government is John A. MacDougall, "Patterns of Military Control in the Indonesian Higher Central Bureaucracy," *Indonesia* 33 (1982), 89–122.

19. An English version is *Republic of Indonesia Armed Forces Manual on the Dual Functions of the Armed Forces*, Jakarta: Department of Defense and Security, 1982.

20. Department of Information, Republic of Indonesia, *Indonesia 1990: An Official Handbook*, pp. 8, 13.

21. I have written at greater length on this relationship in "The Relative Autonomy of the Third World Politician: Suharto and Indonesian Economic Development in Comparative Perspective," reprinted as Chapter Four in this volume.

22. O'Donnell and Schmitter, *Transitions from Authoritarian Rule: Tentative Conclusions About Uncertain Democracies*, p. 15.

23. Conflict within the army up to 1983 is carefully dissected in Jenkins, *Suharto and His Generals*. A more recent analysis is Harold Crouch, "Military-Civilian Relations in Indonesia in the Late Soeharto Era," *The Pacific Review* 1:4 (1988), 353–62.

24. The importance for a democratic transition of a split between hard-liners and soft-liners within the military is stressed by O'Donnell and Schmitter, *Transitions from Authoritarian Rule: Tentative Conclusions about Uncertain Democracies*, p. 16.

25. Personal information based primarily on interviews in Banda Aceh, 1985–87,

and Yogyakarta, 1989. On the Pancasila courses, see Michael Morfit, "Pancasila: The Indonesian State Ideology According to the New Order Government," *Asian Survey* 21:8 (1981), 838–51. An English version of the Pancasila course materials is *P-4: The Guide to the Living and the Practice of Pancasila, and GBHN: The Broad Outlines of the State Policy*, Jakarta: Centre for Strategic and International Studies, 1978.

26. H. Roeslan Abdulgani, "Kejenuhan itu Kadang Terasa," [There are some who feel fed up], *Tempo* 19:47 (1990), 83. *Tempo* is the leading Jakarta newsweekly.

27. Bahtiar Effendy, "Nine Stars and Politics: A Study of Nahdlatul Ulama's Acceptance of Pancasila and its Withdrawal from Politics," M.A. Thesis, Ohio University, 1988. Also S. Sinansari ecip, ed., *NU Dalam Tantangan*, Jakarta: Al Kautsar, 1989.

28. Support for cooperatives, believed to be a counter to the presumed greed inherent in private capitalism, was a pillar of Indonesian nationalism in the pre-war period and is still strong in some circles, including President Suharto's. Suharto, *Pikiran, Ucapan dan Tindakan Saya*, pp. 486–92. The intellectual father of the cooperative idea in Indonesia is Mohammad Hatta, joint proclaimer of independence (with Sukarno) in 1945 and first vice-president of the Republic of Indonesia. See Mohammad Hatta, *The Cooperative Movement in Indonesia*, Ithaca: Cornell Modern Indonesia Project, 1957. The New Order government sponsors an extensive system of sub-district level so-called cooperatives (Koperasi Unit Desa, Village Unit Cooperatives), whose main functions have actually been to purchase rice from farmers for the government and to channel subsidised agricultural inputs from the government to the farmers.

29. Hal Hill, ed., *Unity and Diversity: Regional Economic Development in Indonesia since 1970*, Singapore: Oxford University Press, 1989, p. 53.

30. The term federalism has had few defenders in Indonesia since the aborted Dutch attempt in the late 1940s to maintain influence in the archipelago by setting up "federal states" in the territories under their control.

31. The following analysis does not apply to Irian Jaya (formerly West Irian) and East Timor, two provinces that became part of Indonesia late and unwillingly. Independence movements continue to attract wide support in both provinces. On Irian, see Carmel Budiardjo and Liem Soei Liong, *West Papua: The Obliteration of a People*, Surrey: TAPOL, 3rd. ed., 1988, and Robin Osborne, *Indonesia's Secret War: The Guerrilla Struggle in Irian Jaya*, Sydney: Allen and Unwin, 1985. On Timor, the most recent account is *Human Rights in Indonesia and East Timor: An Asia Watch Report*, New York and Washington: Human Rights Watch, 1989.

32. Current figure from Mari Pangestu and Manggi Habir, "Survey of Recent Developments," *Bulletin of Indonesian Economic Studies* 26:1 (1990), 11.

33. Anne Booth and Peter McCawley, *The Indonesian Economy During the Soeharto Era*, p. 4.

34. Bruce Glassburner and Anwar Nasution, "Macroeconomic Policy and Prospects for Long Term Growth," manuscript, 1988, pp. 8–9.

35. Distribution is actually a controversial issue both in Indonesia and among foreign observers. See the discussion below of distribution as a regime soft spot, and the sources cited there.

36. M. Hadi Soesastro, "The Political Economy of Deregulation in Indonesia,

Asian Survey 29:9 (1989), 853–69; Sjahrir, "The Indonesian Deregulation Policy Process: Problems, Constraints, and Prospects," Jakarta: Yayasan Padi dan Kapas, 1989, mimeo; Bruce Glassburner, "Deregulation in the Indonesian Economy, 1983–90," paper presented at the conference "Indonesia as an Economic Partner for the 90's: An Assessment," Federal Reserve Bank of San Francisco, March 12, 1990.

37. Compare with Terry Lynn Karl, "Petroleum and Political Pacts: The Transition to Democracy in Venezuela," in O'Donnell, Schmitter, and Whitehead, *Transitions from Authoritarian Rule: Latin America*, pp. 196–219. In Venezuela, poor integration of the petroleum sector into the economy as a whole badly hurt domestic and export agriculture, producing changes in social structure that in turn led to demands for democratisation.

38. Direct and indirect critiques of the regime's democratic failings are an everyday occurrence in the media. A recent powerful statement of the effects on the Indonesian personality of the ordinary person's inability to shape events is Putu Wijaya's prize-winning essay, "Wajah Kita" ("Our Face"), *Kompas*, 28 June 1990, p. 4. Yes and no have no meaning in Indonesia, says Putu. "Because no matter what, the plan that's been made can't be changed. What's going to happen must happen, can't be resisted." One says yes or no "just to open one's mouth." "The science of yes-no or no-yes. . . . is the art of how to live. . . . But don't suppose I like it, if I could choose I'd prefer the opposite." (*Kompas* is the leading Jakarta daily.) See also Denny J.A., Jonminofri, and Rahardjo, eds., *Menegakkan Demokrasi: Pandangan Sejumlah Tokoh dan Kaum Muda Mengenai Demokrasi di Indonesia* [Building Democracy in Indonesia: The Views of A Number of Figures and Youth Concerning Democracy in Indonesia], Jakarta: Kelompok Studi Indonesia, 1989.

39. Two recent interviews, one in 1987 with a high provincial official outside Java and one in 1989 with a second-echelon central government department official in Jakarta, have reminded me of the strength of civilian hostility to continued military control. The attitude of both individuals was frustration in their dealings with army counterparts low in administrative capability and high in suspiciousness about security threats.

40. Nonetheless, the military continues to stick to a hard line. In the keynote speech to a recent meeting of high ranking officers at the army staff and command school, a lieutenant-colonel expressed concern that the wave of democratisation sweeping the world not reach Indonesia, "which is still in transition from a traditional-agrarian to a modern-industrial society." *Tempo* 20:14 (1990), 24–25. On July 1 the Minister of Defense, referring to conflict in the Soviet Union, warned of the dangers of "narrow ethnic perspectives." *Kompas*, 2 July 1990, p. 1.

41. Bruce Glassburner, "Economic Openness and Economic Nationalism in Indonesia Under the Soeharto Government," paper prepared for presentation at a conference on Comparative Analysis of the Development Process in East and Southeast Asia, East-West Centre, Honolulu, May 1990; and *Tempo* 19:29 (1989), 92–93.

42. Chapter 7, "Income Distribution," in Booth and McCawley, *The Indonesian Economy During the Soeharto Era*, p. 214.

43. Chris Manning, *The Green Revolution, Employment, and Economic Change*

in *Rural Java*, Singapore: Institute of Southeast Asian Studies, 1988, p. 1.
44. Hal Hill, "The Indonesian Manufacturing Sector: Southeast Asia's Emerging Industrial Giant?", pp. 39, 46.
45. The best study of this subject is Franklin Weinstein, *Indonesian Foreign Policy and the Dilemma of Dependence*, Ithaca: Cornell University Press, 1976.
46. *Tempo*, 20:7 (1990), 22–30.
47. Albert O. Hirschman, *Essays in Trespassing: Economics to Politics and Beyond*, New York: Cambridge University Press, 1981, pp. 39–58.
48. *Tempo* 19:30 (1989). He also appears to be more actively cultivating a Muslim constituency, perhaps as a counterweight to the loss of army support, for example in his controversial backing for a proposed law regulating Islamic courts. See *Tempo* 19:17 (1989), 22–31; and the Jakarta Islamic weekly *Panji Masyarakat* 30:616 (1989), 18–31.
49. For example, one of Suharto's sons owns (with capital provided by domestic Chinese backing and licensing monopolies) one of Indonesia's largest business conglomerates. *Far Eastern Economic Review* 142:47 (1988), 80–82; also the Jakarta business monthly *Swasembada* 5:1 (1989), 8–46. Other Jakarta business people say it is pointless to bid against him for government contracts. Another son controls the domestic clove market, incurring the hostility of manufacturers of the popular clove cigarettes. *Tempo* 20:19 (1990), 80–88. A daughter's company won the contract for building a limited access road around Jakarta, then angered the public by setting the toll for any distance travelled at Rp. 1,500, almost US$1.00. *Tempo* 19:38 (1989), 91–92.
50. Against this view of relatively solid control of the army by Murdani is a recent report in the *Far Eastern Economic Review* by Michael Vatikiotis. Vatikiotis quotes a military source who said that "You can never talk of one military, the army, or such like. There are many camps." "A Stir in the Ranks," *Far Eastern Economic Review*, 5 July 1990, p. 17.
51. Dahl, *Polyarchy*, Ch. 3; Samuel Huntington, "Will More Countries Become Democratic?," *Political Science Quarterly* 99:2 (1984), 193–218; Alfred Stepan, "Paths Toward Redemocratization: Theoretical and Comparative Considerations," in O'Donnell, Schmitter, and Whitehead, *Transitions from Authoritarian Rule: Comparative Perspectives*, pp. 64–84.
52. The two most prominent are Abdurrahman Wahid, head of Nahdlatul Ulama, and Nurcholish Madjid, a former chairman of the influential Islamic Students Association (HMI, Himpunan Mahasiswa Islam) and now active with middle and upper class Islamic business people in Jakarta and other cities. Abdurrahman Wahid, *Muslim di Tengah Pergumulan* [The Muslim in the Middle of the Struggle], Jakarta: Leppenas, 1981; Nurcholish Madjid, *Islam dan Masalah KeIndonesiaan* [Islam and the Problem of Indonesianness], Bandung: Mizan, 1986. For an overview, see Fachry Ali and Bahtiar Effendy, *Merambah Jalan Baru Islam* [Clearing a New Islamic Path], Bandung: Mizan, 1986.
53. The argument of this paragraph is related to two variables discussed by O'Donnell and Schmitter, *Transitions from Authoritarian Rule: Tentative Conclusions About Uncertain Democracies*, pp. 21–23 and 34–36. They argue that less militarised regimes—those in which the civilian role is relatively large—and regimes in which pre-authoritarian representative institutions have sur-

vived are easier to democratise. On the first point, Suharto's Indonesia is not comparable to Franco's Spain in terms of the degree of limited pluralism, but it is clearly less militarised than was the 1976 Argentine government. On the second point, the 1945 Constitution was first adopted as an alternative to genuinely representative democracy, so strictly speaking it can not be claimed that it represents a continuation of pre-authoritarian representation.

54. *Polyarchy*, pp. 220–221.
55. I am much influenced in this formulation by the writings of Albert Hirschman, especially his discussion of "reform-mongering" in *Journeys Toward Progress*, New York: Norton, 1973. Also see Clive Bell, "The Political Framework," in Hollis Chenery, ed., *Redistribution With Growth*, London: Oxford University Press, 1974. Bell's article is about how to get economic redistribution when elites want only growth, but his logic is the same as mine: find policies that will also serve or at least not threaten the interests of significant elite groups.
56. Tun-jen Cheng, *The Politics of Industrial Transformation: The Case of the East Asian NICs*, unpub. Ph.D. dissertation, University of California-Berkeley, 1987, Chapter 3. The next step in Taiwan, which might also be followed in Indonesia, was empowerment of local legislatures. Potential national politicians obtained valuable legislative experience at the local level, especially an understanding of how to push at the walls of the system without having the ceiling collapse on them. Arthur Lerman, *Taiwan's Politics: The Provincial Assemblyman's World*, Washington: University Press of America, 1978. From Japan, Indonesians might borrow the idea of allowing the ubiquitous government-financed rural cooperatives (Koperasi Unit Desa, Village Unit Cooperatives) to be controlled by farmers, instead of local officials as is now typically the case. In Japan, the cooperatives have been a major source of support for the ruling Liberal Democratic Party. Perhaps they could play the same role for Golkar. Ikuo Kabashima, "Supportive Participation with Economic Growth: The Case of Japan," *World Politics* 36:3, 309–38.
57. *Tempo*, 20:15 (1990), 74–83.
58. *Kompas*, 15 August 1989, p. 1.
59. Philippe C. Schmitter, "An Introduction to Southern European Transitions from Authoritarian Rule: Italy, Greece, Portugal, Spain, and Turkey," in O'Donnell, Schmitter, and Whitehead, *Transitions from Authoritarian Rule: Southern Europe*, p. 6.
60. Clifford Geertz, "The Javanese Village," in G. William Skinner, ed., *Local, Ethnic, and National Loyalties in Village Indonesia: A Symposium*, New Haven: Yale Southeast Asia Studies, 1959. For Sumatra, I argued otherwise in *Ethnicity, Party, and National Integration: An Indonesian Case Study*, New Haven: Yale University Press, 1970.
61. Kenneth Young and Richard Tanter, eds., *The Politics of Middle Class Indonesia*, Clayton, Vic.: Monash University Centre of Southeast Asia Studies, 1989. See also *Prisma*, 2 (1984), for several articles on the middle class. *Prisma* is a social science monthly published in Jakarta.
62. *Prisma*, 4 (1988), contains several articles on the LPSM and LSM.
63. Philip Eldridge, *NGOs in Indonesia: Popular Movement or Arm of Government*, Clayton, Vic.: Monash University Centre of Southeast Asian Studies, Working Paper 55, 1989, pp. 57–58.

64. Also in ability to spread the word about government policies and actions that threaten the interests of the poor and even to apply pressure on the government to change its policies. See for example the account in *Tempo* 19:4 (1989), 68–81, of the Kedungombo incident, where a government dam project forced the evacuation of several hundred villagers.

7

Indonesia's Threefold Crisis*

On 8 June 1992, President Suharto celebrated his seventy-first birthday. He has been president of the Republic of Indonesia since March 1967, and is only the second person to hold that office. Indonesia's highest constitutional body, the People's Consultative Assembly, has given him its mandate on six occasions: in March 1967, when he was chosen acting president; in March 1968, when he became full president; and every five years since then.

The four most recent Assembly sessions were preceded by nationwide balloting for the National Representation Council (Indonesia's parliament), whose 500 representatives constitute half the Assembly membership of 1,000 (the other half are appointed in a process controlled by the president). On 9 June 1992, another parliamentary election was won handily by the ruling Golongan Karya (Golkar) party; in March 1993 there will be another Assembly session to select the president and vice president for the 1993–98 term. As of mid-1992, President Suharto is widely expected to win reelection without opposition.

Behind this democratic facade of elections, parliament, and Assembly lies the authoritarian reality of a political system dominated by Suharto, a former general whose power derives from his extraordinarily adept husbanding and shrewd use of a variety of political resources. Suharto's most important resource is his control over the armed forces. He became the army's leader—and the country's saviour—on 1 October 1965, after junior army officers attached to the presidential palace guard and members of the youth organization of the Communist Party of Indonesia (PKI) assassinated six senior generals.

* First published in *Journal of Democracy*, 3, 4 (October 1992), pp. 60–74.

In the wake of these killings, Suharto parlayed his key position as commander of strategic reserves, which brought him ample support from within the military as well as from civilian anticommunist groups, into a successful campaign to ban the PKI and retire President Sukarno, who had been in office since 1945. From about 1963, Sukarno had moved increasingly close to the communists; many thought that he had been complicit in (or at least privy to) the assassination plot. In March 1966, Suharto maneuvered Sukarno into ceding him full executive power, which he then used to orchestrate Sukarno's removal from and his own accession to the presidency.

As president, Suharto quickly became the "Father of Development" (a title subsequently bestowed on him by the Assembly) by adopting the neoclassical economic policies recommended by his advisors, which have led to consistently high rates of economic growth. Economic growth has in turn swelled the accounts of the state treasury and of Suharto's own private foundations, enabling him to buy the support of many key individuals and groups, and to build a bureaucracy that serves the interests of many others.

Suharto is also the beneficiary of Indonesia's strong presidency, which was the creation of the charismatic Sukarno, who dominated the nationalist movement and independence politics from the 1920s until the mid-1960s. It was Sukarno who in 1959 returned Indonesia to the executive-centered Constitution of 1945, thus ending a decade of Western-style parliamentary rule. Some of the first president's charisma still attached to the office, and Suharto, notwithstanding his role in forcing Sukarno to retire, has been careful to maintain a sense of continuity with the past.

The function of elections in this system has been not to choose, but to legitimate. Four-fifths of the members of parliament are elected (the remaining fifth consists of military appointees), but the party organisations and electoral process are closely managed by the government to ensure substantial Golkar victories (from 62 percent in 1971 to 68 percent in 1992).

Suharto's Weakening Grip

After a quarter-century, Suharto's grip on power is beginning to show signs of weakening. The first important evidence of decline came in March 1988, when his nominee for vice-president was publicly and angrily opposed by the military delegates during a tumultuous session of the Assembly. In the end, Suharto got his way, but he had been served notice that the military as a whole and the senior army generals in particular were looking ahead to a time when they, as individuals and as an institution, would still be players but he would not.

The battle between Suharto and the army has been waged on several fronts. In the months immediately after the 1988 Assembly session, army officers—under the discreet direction of their former commander, defense and security minister General L.B. Murdani—moved to take over the district and provincial branches of Golkar, thus cutting into one of the new vice-president's political bases. Reportedly, the generals also began to encourage student activists in Bandung, Yogyakarta, and other cities to engage in protest on local issues, most of which were related to government acquisitions of land for development projects.

In September 1989, Suharto struck back by threatening to 'clobber' anyone—General Murdani seems to have been the main target—who tried to seize power unconstitutionally. Throughout 1990 and 1991, the president maneuvered to recapture the army by putting relatives and former adjutants in key posts. In August 1990, the president's brother-in-law became commander of the army's strategic reserves, the post from which Suharto himself had risen to power.

Suharto has also extended a hand to an old adversary, Indonesia's Islamic political movement, with the apparent goal of offsetting his weakening support from the army.[1] For more than 20 years, Suharto sought to force Muslim political leaders and their organisations into the wings or off the stage entirely. In the last few years, however, their aspirations have met with a far more sympathetic response. Parliament passed a law recognising and strengthening the Islamic courts that adjudicate family-related disputes among consenting Muslims. After long opposition, the Department of Education, a non-Muslim stronghold, now permits female students in state schools to wear Islamic head coverings. Muslim intellectuals were allowed to create a major new organisation, albeit under the chairmanship of one of Suharto's favorite ministers. An Islamic bank has come into being. And finally, in 1991 the president himself (together with a small number of family members and key associates) made the pilgrimage to Mecca.

What is the significance of all this? Are we witnessing just a leadership struggle, specifically a series of defensive maneuvers by President Suharto designed to ensure his reelection in 1993, or is something more fundamental going on? Most intriguingly, might the leadership struggle be a sign of, or an occasion for, a transition from authoritarianism—under which Indonesians have lived since 1959—to democracy, which they knew only from 1950 to about 1957?

A partial answer might be sought by borrowing David Easton's classification of the three levels of a political system: community, regime, and government.[2] According to Easton, a political community is 'a group that seeks to settle differences or promote decisions through peaceful action in common.' In the modern world, the prototypical political community is the nation-state. A regime embodies the rules of the political game, 'all those arrangements that regulate the way in which the demands put into the system are settled and the way in which decisions are put into effect.' And by government Easton meant the holders of state power at any given time, what the British call 'Her Majesty's Government' and Americans refer to as 'the Administration.'

Applying these concepts to Indonesia today, it is hard to deny that the Suharto government confronts a succession crisis. Perhaps more controversially, I will also argue that a crisis of community, of the integrity of the Indonesian nation-state, has now developed and is adding to the weight of the government's burdens. It is harder to evaluate whether the impact of these two crises on the 'New Order' (as Indonesians call the post-1966 regime) will promote democratisation, maintenance of the status quo, or increased repression. Should the crisis of succession and the crisis of community deepen, the interplay (for both regime and opposition) of leadership and specific circumstances will not be easy to predict.

At present, it seems as if the succession crisis is starting to undermine one of the two institutional pillars of the New Order, the strong presidency, while the community crisis has begun to loosen the second pillar, the army's direct role in national political life. Both crises are dividing Suharto from his senior generals, as well as breeding conflict within the army itself. These processes have only just begun, however, and may be reversed if decisive steps are taken soon. On the other hand, if the crises are prolonged, major regime transformation will become an increasingly probable outcome.

The Impending Succession Crisis

There are three basic reasons for the succession crisis that now besets Indonesia's government: the presidency is the most authoritative office under the Constitution; Suharto, the incumbent, is also personally powerful but beginning to lose that power; and the informal rules of the New Order game, as constructed by Suharto himself, provide no means by which a succession can occur without his say-so.

Under the 1945 Constitution, which all political groups now support, sovereignty is held by the people and exercised by the Assembly, which meets once every five years to select the president and vice-president and to determine 'the main lines of state policy.' The president is the chief executive and 'makes laws with the agreement of parliament.' Neither he nor his ministers are responsible to parliament. The president is also commander-in-chief of the armed forces.

Articles 6 and 7 state that the president and vice-president are chosen for renewable five-year terms by a majority vote of the Assembly. Article 8 specifies the formal rules of succession as follows: 'If the President dies, leaves office or cannot carry out his obligations in his time in office, he is replaced by the Vice-President until the end of the period.'

Underlying these formal procedures, however, is the reality of Suharto's personal predominance and his will to power. As long as that will is strong, decisions are made and implemented, even when there is displeasure, as in the case of the vice-presidential selections in 1988. On the other hand, when Suharto's will falters or disappears, there will be a vacuum at the top.

Among Indonesian politicians and observers, there is now a strong belief that should Suharto die or be incapacitated, the incumbent vice-president will not be allowed to become president. The armed forces commander, it is said, will instead declare a state of emergency, and perhaps rule through a committee until a successor is chosen from within army ranks. Most knowledgeable observers do not see the 1945 Constitution, for all the diffuse support it receives, as a serious obstacle to the implementation of this plan.

The succession crisis is not yet acute, but shows signs of becoming so due to Suharto's advancing age and because of some recent policy decisions that have had adverse political consequences. Although Indonesians often say that 71 is 'old for an Indonesian,' leaders in other Third World countries whose people have relatively low life expectancies have lasted well into their eighties.

Suharto's policy decisions in three areas have put him on the defensive, diminishing his political capital and bolstering his opponents. In the mid-1980s his government, in response to the collapse of world oil prices, began to deregulate the economy in order to stimulate the growth of nonpetroleum exports. The new policy succeeded brilliantly, maintaining and even boosting support for the president among several constituencies.

Unfortunately, deregulation has also had the side effect of appearing to benefit the Sino-Indonesian businesspeople who own most of the big domestic corporations much more than so-called indigenous Indonesians. Mass hostility toward Sino-Indonesians has been a frequently erupting volcano in Indonesian history since 1945.

The problem is complicated by the practices of many officials, civilian and military, who provide protection to Sino-Indonesian business interests. Even Suharto himself has taken part in such deals, which have become much more widespread and lucrative under the New Order than at any time previously. The current bad feelings have spurred the president to impose new demands on the Sino-Indonesians—requiring them, for example, to sell shares in their businesses to 'indigenously owned' cooperatives—but the political atmosphere remains thick with anti-Chinese hostility.

The president's fatherly indulgence toward his children's business ventures has probably been even more damaging politically, not least because it has not produced any compensatory support. Three of Suharto's six children are very active in business and appear to win every government contract on which they bid, from road construction in Jakarta to telecommunications systems and satellites. The argument that the children are the leading edge of indigenous business has been hard to sell to other indigenous businesspeople whose tenders consistently fail. Most recently, the miscarriage of an ambitious scheme by Suharto's youngest son to take over the marketing of cloves (used in the manufacture of spiced cigarettes, a major industry) has even begun to threaten the country's financial stability.

The Problem of East Timor

The third policy that has got Suharto into trouble—and perhaps jeopardised the integrity of the Indonesian nation-state itself—is his approach toward the problem of resurgent nationalism on the island of Timor.

With some two hundred separate linguistic and cultural groups spread across its more than 13,000 islands, Indonesia is one of the most ethnically diverse countries in the world. The Javanese, most of whom live in central and eastern Java, constitute a near majority, followed by the Sundanese of western Java, a dozen or so medium-sized groups, and many smaller ones.

For most members of these groups, there is no conflict between ethnic and national identity. Ethnicity is local and family-oriented, nonpolitical in the sense that it makes no claim to sovereign nation-state status. It has been that way at least since the famous 1928 meeting of youth organisations from all over what were then the Dutch East Indies, when delegates declared their loyalty to 'one country, one people, one language.'

There are three exceptions to this pattern: Aceh, the northernmost province of Sumatra, where separatist sentiment has periodically erupted into violence since the early 1950s; Irian Jaya, the western half of the island of New Guinea, incorporated into the Republic of Indonesia only in 1963, a decade and a half after Indonesian independence, where there is today a small but active separatist underground; and East Timor, a vestige of Portugal's East Indian colonial holdings that Indonesia invaded in 1975 and incorporated as its twenty-seventh province in 1976.

Each of these cases constitutes a genuine threat to the integrity of the Indonesian political community, and each is a source of concern to national political leaders. Only the third, however, has the potential to alter the outcome of the succession crisis and foster or intensify a crisis of the regime.

What makes East Timor different, from both the national and the local point of view, is that it was never a part of the Dutch East Indies. The Indonesian army invaded Timor at Suharto's command, not to advance a nationalist agenda, but for the narrowest of security reasons: to prevent a consolidation of power by left-leaning Timorese nationalists who had just declared independence from Portugal. On the Timorese side, there was at that time no sense of a common history with Indonesia, and only a very small number of Timorese favored union with their enormous neighbour.[3]

Since 1976, Indonesian policy has been to pump large sums of development money into East Timor while simultaneously strong-arming proindependence guerrillas and other activists. Despite occasional reversals, this good cop/bad cop approach appeared to many observers (myself included) to be working. By the late 1980s and early 1990s, the guerrillas were thought to number no more than a few hundred—hardly enough to mount a serious offensive. Accelerated development programs had built many roads, schools, hospitals, and health centers. The tight security previously imposed had been relaxed. Timorese had begun to go to other provinces, particularly for higher education, and non-Timorese found it easier to visit or take up residence in Timor.

On 12 November 1991, this apparent progress toward integration was exposed as an illusion. Early that morning, about three thousand mostly young Timorese attended a memorial service in Dili, the provincial capital, for an independence activist who had recently been killed by security forces. As they marched from church to the nearby Santa Cruz cemetery, soldiers fired on them without warning. According to most independent reports, between 75 and 200 Timorese died.[4]

The Santa Cruz massacre was witnessed by several foreign reporters, one of whom was able to film the shooting. The incident quickly became an international *cause célèbre*, particularly in Portugal (which has never accepted the 1976 integration) and Australia (where there is a large Timorese refugee population and substantial sentiment in favor of East Timorese independence). The Dutch and Canadian governments also applied pressure by indefinitely suspending new grants of aid.

President Suharto's actions reaffirmed his reputation as a consummate politician. He first dispatched a National Commission for Investigation (NCI), headed by a Supreme Court Justice and former military judge, to East Timor. The NCI report challenged the army's own initial account. Suharto then cashiered the two most senior commanders responsible for East Timor, directed the chief of staff to appoint a council of generals to investigate further army culpability, ordered the armed forces commander to locate missing bodies, and instructed the attorney general to prosecute civilian instigators of the demonstration.

At the end of February the army chief of staff, acting on his council's report, announced disciplinary actions ranging from discharge to temporary removal from the line of command against six senior officers. In March, the president suspended all further economic assistance from the Netherlands, citing Dutch interference in Indonesian domestic affairs. He also dissolved the Inter-Governmental Group on Indonesia (IGGI), the Dutch-chaired consortium of creditor states that has been giving Indonesia development aid since the 1960s, and replaced it with a new group to be headed by the World Bank. By early July, prison sentences of eight to eighteen months had been handed down in the trials of ten soldiers and lower-ranking officers. Fourteen Timorese nationalists, on trial for their roles in the events leading up to November 12, have been convicted of 'hate-spreading' or subversion and sentenced to prison terms from six months to life, with most in the five-to-fifteen-year range. These events do not appear to foreshadow changes in the government's basic repress-and-develop policy toward East Timor. In Jakarta, government spokespersons, including President Suharto, have apologised for the November 12 killings and promised to redouble development efforts. In Dili, the new field commander has proclaimed an even tougher policy against 'subversives' who favor East Timorese independence.

Many of Suharto's conciliatory actions seem to have been motivated largely by a desire to extinguish the firestorm of international protest that the massacre set off. At the same time, he has balanced the conciliation of foreigners with the dissolution of IGGI, the rejection of further Dutch assistance—an act reminiscent of Sukarno's famous 1964 'to hell with your aid' speech directed at the U.S. ambassador—and the mixing of light sentences for soldiers with heavy ones for Timorese nationalists. Each of these latter moves was applauded by domestic constituencies within and outside the government.

Foreign reactions to Suharto's postmassacre policies have been mixed. By late 1992 most of the world's governments appear to have returned to business as usual with Indonesia, though it is also true that human rights activists in the West now have more support from politicians than they did prior to the massacre. Of greater significance than short-term reaction, however, is the new reality manifested by the demonstration of 12 November: the existence of thousands of Timorese nationalists among young people who are Indonesian-educated, speak Indonesian, and are without personal experience of Portuguese rule. What that signifies is the failure of 16 years of Indonesian policy to win the hearts and minds of a new generation of Timorese, a failure which in turn betokens a crisis of political community deeper than anyone had imagined.

The Presidency and the Army

Now we must ask if the New Order regime itself is also in crisis, and, if so, whether it got that way independently or as a result of the government and community crises. Before an answer to this question can be attempted, it is necessary to describe the regime's defining characteristics. The two most important New Order institutions are the politically active military and the strong presidency. To explain how these institutions operate in Indonesian society, it is helpful to compare them to the Communist Party (CPSU) and the general secretary of the former Soviet Union.

Like the CPSU, the Indonesian army is a corporate, closed organisation with its own history, institutional culture, and ideology. Since its creation in 1945, early in the independence revolution, it has played a prominent and autonomous political role. Since 1966, when it crushed its foremost rival, the Indonesian Communist Party, the army has stood virtually alone as an organised political force.

Its doctrine of *dwi-fungsi*, the 'twin functions' of defending the country and participating actively in domestic politics, justifies a wide range of activities, from choosing a general as president to bureaucratic and legislative appointments of serving and retired officers and the construction of a nationwide surveillance system in the form of regional military commands. The army also dominates the ruling Golkar party and intervenes regularly in the internal affairs of all other important political and social organisations.

The strong presidency, a legacy of the Sukarno era, has become very closely tied to the army since 1966. Suharto rose to power as the army's leader, and has stayed there over the years primarily by cultivating and maintaining the loyalty of the officer corps. To be sure, he has also reached out to nonmilitary constituencies, via economic and other policies—such as the current opening toward Islam—that have given him additional resources and room for maneuver against potential army opponents. But, like CPSU general secretaries from Stalin to Gorbachev, his primary power base is in his own organisation, the army.

I have elsewhere discussed at length the New Order's general strengths and weaknesses, and so will only sketch them here.[5] The rule of president and army appears to have a considerable amount of diffuse popular support because of its achievements in ending the communist threat, creating order, maintaining national unity, and bringing about economic development.

As one would expect, this support is particularly solid from the regime's principal material and status beneficiaries, that is, its military and civilian bureaucratic constituencies. But it extends to nonstate groups as well, in-cluding many upper-class and middle-class people, village elites, religiously syncretic Javanese, pluralistically inclined Muslims, and the Christian and Sino-Indonesian minorities.[6] In this respect Indonesia is not like the Soviet Union, where economic growth stalled after the mid-1970s and the regime's legitimacy—within and outside its own ranks—suffered accordingly.

The regime's weaknesses include an underlying tension between the president and the military establishment, continuing conflict between civilian and military subelites over the division of spoils, a painfully obvious gap between proclaimed democratic values and authoritarian political practices, widespread disbelief in regime propaganda, insufficient sensitivity to regional desires for decentralisation of authority, and a growing number of middle-class groups that are creating their own organisations, defining their own policy agendas, and lobbying for the opening of more political space.

Although the regime's two principal institutions have worked well together for most of the New Order, thanks largely to Suharto's political skills, there is a basic conflict between them. A strong president is naturally likely to see his office as superior to and encompassing other institutions, and will try to expand his sources of support and freedom of action. Similarly, military officers tend to be concerned primarily with their own institution and the maintenance of its dominance over other institutions. Dissatisfaction with the present imbalance is expressed in the frequently heard (softly from serving officers, more loudly from retired ones) complaint that because of Suharto's dominance the twin-functions doctrine no longer operates as it was intended, as a check by the corporate armed forces on the actions of the state.

The officers fear that should their grip on power falter, their sometime allies in the civilian bureaucracy will turn to other political leaders. The gap between the government's rhetoric about 'Indonesian-style' democracy and the reality of heavily managed elections, manipulated political organisations, and subservient legislatures is admittedly no greater than it was in the mid-1970s. What has changed are the circumstances, both international and domestic, that once made thinly masked authoritarianism acceptable.

Emerging Democratic Forces

With the end of the Cold War, the West in general and the United States in particular are likely to press Third World countries to meet higher standards regarding human rights and democracy. International human rights organisations have become more effective as well. In much of East Asia, despite continued Confucianist talk of discipline and collectivism, democratic government is becoming the norm. Heartened by this more favorable international climate, Indonesian democrats have also begun to press their views more vigorously.

The demons against whom government leaders are ever-vigilant come from both the 'extreme left'—the defunct Indonesian Communist Party—and the 'extreme right'—militant Islam. There is also occasional talk of an 'extreme center,' meaning liberal democrats. The ranks of democrats may in fact be growing, but they have never been highly organised and are not militant. The threat from the left has not been credible since the PKI was crushed in the 1960s, and is even less so with the collapse of communism over so much of the world. Political Islam is more problematic, though there is evidence that Indonesia's Muslim intellectuals have for the last two decades been quietly forging a new, nonthreatening conception of the relationship between state and society in Islam.

National-level democrats might well form an alliance with regional groups, who have been among the most disenfranchised Indonesians during the New Order. The regionalists' concern is not that development benefits have failed to flow their way. All provincial budgets are in fact heavily subvened by the centre. Rather it is that central administrative and political controls, designed in part to ensure that outlying regions of the sprawling Indonesian archipelago do not form independent links with neighbouring countries, prevent local interests from pursuing their comparative advantages. This has led to a considerable amount of resentment on the part of regional businesspeople and other interests.

The emergence of an urban middle class of school-educated Indonesians—self-employed or salaried, aspiring to live in single-family homes and to buy motorcycles, automobiles, and other consumer goods—has been among the most prominent effects of the rapid economic growth that began in the late 1960s. The political consequences of this demographic change have been the subject of much speculation but little serious investigation.

On the hopeful side, polls conducted by the Jakarta press show some evidence of middle-class dissatisfaction with government services and a consequent demand for change. We can also see clearly the creation of a capillary structure of prepolitical organisations, a network of more than a thousand nongovernmental voluntary organizations (NGOs) that work in a variety of areas, including village development, environmental protection, labor organising, consumer advocacy, and human rights.

The leaders of the NGOs tend to be critical of the state, and to favour decentralisation of governmental decision making, the self-reliant development of small communities, greater individual freedom, and more democratic participation. They belong to a loosely organized network sharing information and ideas that has also become a lobby with growing access to the state bureaucracy. Internationally, they have been linked with foreign NGOs in the International Non-Governmental Group on Indonesia (INGI), an outfit created specifically to press the IGGI countries to pay more attention to the distributional and environmental issues raised by development.

Nonetheless, there are some drawbacks as well. Indonesia's middle class remains the smallest relative to national population in Southeast Asia, and is disproportionately dependent on jobs in the state bureaucracy. Ethnic Chinese still make up a probable majority of the country's self-employed entrepreneurs (considered a critical group in much analysis of democratisation in the West). Most indigenous entrepreneurs, in small towns as well as in Jakarta, are clients of government patrons, held fast in a web of mutually beneficial exchange. The NGOs receive much of their funding from abroad, which makes them vulnerable to charges of collusion with foreigners against the national interest. When Suharto suspended Dutch aid, many NGOs, including the prominent Legal Aid Institute, were hit hard.

After Suharto

The impending succession crisis may destabilise the regime in two ways: by raising popular awareness of Suharto's political unaccountability, and by weakening the crucial ties that bind the president to his core supporters in the army. It is not exactly news to observers of Indonesian politics that the president is unaccountable to constituencies beyond the army, and for most of his actions most of the time not even to the army. But three issues are tending to produce greater concern: Suharto's apparent determination to stay in office indefinitely, his children's greed, and the economic success of Sino-Indonesians relative to the other groups in the population.

Suharto's unwillingness to yield the presidency after 26 years is an issue all by itself to many Indonesians. This includes of course would-be successors and their entourages and clients, but more importantly the many groups who hope for a new president who will hear them with a more sympathetic ear. Businesspeople and their patrons in both civil and military officialdom who are eager for government contracts understand that there is only one way to rid themselves of competition from Suharto's children. And rivals to the Sino-Indonesian business community are looking for ways to break the mutually beneficial arrangement—political protection for business opportunities—that has brought great wealth to the president and many of his generals.

Senior officers, led by General Murdani and the army chief-of-staff, are known to be unhappy over the first two of these issues; on the third, they have generally spoken out in appreciation of the contribution that the Sino-Indonesian business class makes to the nation's economy. Younger officers, who so far have personally benefited less, may feel differently.

The generals also reportedly oppose Suharto's maneuvering to regain control of the army through the appointment of relatives and adjutants—indeed, many observers now speak of a split between the 'Suharto group' and the 'Murdani group.' Finally, the president's opening to Islam is a source of concern to generals whose own religious background is mostly syncretic Javanese-Hindu-Muslim.

Although some democrats have been proposing a constitutional amendment limiting future presidents to two terms, such a proposal has no chance of passage now. When the succession crisis becomes acute, however, a coalition of forces might be able to wring acceptance of a two-term amendment from one or more of the contenders. Senior officers looking to redress the balance between the army and the presidency might well join such a coalition.

It is also possible that presidential candidates will be willing to make even more concessions than this; the enormity of the gap in resources between Suharto and any of his possible successors suggests that the latter will need to be political horse-traders of a high order. One way to drum up support is to make promises to mass constituencies, as Suharto himself did to many groups in the mid-1960s and is doing with Muslim groups today. In the tougher political climate of the 1990s, a necessary quid pro quo for support from some groups—especially among the middle classes might be greater democracy: freer political parties, more genuine electoral competition, reduced military and civilian bureaucratic interference, and so on.

Less attractive alternatives are possible as well. A younger officer—of either democratic or populist-authoritarian leanings—might exploit the Sino-Indonesian issue against his superiors, in the process bringing down both the regime and the macroeconomic policies that have raised the standard of living of most Indonesians. Alternatively, the army establishment might try to create a monolithic regime, redressing the current president-army imbalance by imposing tighter political controls on the next incumbent. Given the paucity of resources held by any one contender today, this might not be too hard to do, at least at the outset.

The Santa Cruz massacre and its aftermath appear to be having both an indirect impact—via a sharpening of the succession crisis—and a direct impact on regime stability. Suharto's disciplinary measures against the army have sharpened the succession crisis by increasing resentment toward him within the officer corps. His initial removal of two generals from their field commands was highly unusual, and the army council's subsequent recommendation (under presidential pressure, it was widely rumored) of punishments ranging from reassignment to court martial for other involved officers is totally unprecedented in New Order history. The relatively light sentences actually given in the subsequent trials should perhaps be seen as an attempt by Suharto to soften the blow thus dealt to the army's pride.

Santa Cruz and its aftermath may be having a more direct impact on regime stability by calling generally into question the good judgment of army leaders and their 'security approach' to political conflict. Most Indonesian political observers believe that Suharto's original decision to invade and annex East Timor was made at the urging of other officers. Timor policy has since become identified more with the army, and particularly with General Murdani, than with Suharto.

Even the most sympathetic observer would be hard pressed to call the East Timor campaign a success. According to eyewitness journalistic accounts, the 1975 invasion was poorly organised and sloppily executed.

Indonesian troops were often undisciplined and behaved brutally toward the local population. Over the next few years, military action combined with resettlement policies killed more than one hundred thousand people, over a sixth of East Timor's population at that time. Since then, neither armed force nor negotiations have succeeded in destroying the guerrillas. Economic development has also failed to win over the civilian population, or at least the younger members of it who demonstrated in such large numbers last 12 November.

The Indonesian army is trapped—its leaders retain their commitment to the integration of East Timor, but their carrot-and-stick policy of mixing development help with repression has not succeeded after 16 years. Now they face a strong and courageous commitment to independence among the very Timorese youth who are supposed to have been won over by development. The grim prospect is for a rising spiral of violence that will cost more lives and do more damage to the army's reputation.

How might this situation affect the unfolding succession crisis? If the succession does not go smoothly and a power vacuum develops in Jakarta, all sorts of groups, including the East Timorese, will seize the chance to strike deals with one or more of the various contending leaders or groups. With the constraints removed in Jakarta, East Timor's nationalists might find some allies among Indonesian democratisers. Before 1976, Indonesians did not consider East Timor a part of their nation. Even today, the issue is less one of Indonesian nationalism than it is of the armed forces' *amour prope*. Moreover, many politically aware Indonesians recognise how closely the East Timorese struggle for independence mirrors their own revolution against the Dutch nearly half a century ago.

At this point in the succession struggle, events become hard to predict. One outcome might be genuine (but not necessarily stable) democracy for Indonesia combined with immediate independence for East Timor, which would surely entail (or presuppose) an almost total loss of political power by the army. Another possibility is a military crackdown precipitated by the officer corps' fear of national disintegration and its own political demise, ending in a reaffirmation or even heightening of authoritarian rule. Still another possibility is the emergence of a moderate army faction, perhaps led by the current minister of home affairs and army chief of staff, that would advocate both limited democratisation for Indonesia and limited autonomy for East Timor.[7]

Which of these outcomes is most likely? Some observers are convinced that democratisation is imminent. Most prominently, the distinguished political scientist Benedict Anderson has written: '[I]t is, I believe, almost impossible to imagine any successor continuing his rule in the same vein. . . . I have no doubt that the worldwide movement in favor of a certain democratisation is coming to Indonesia, and that there will be astute politicians prepared to take advantage of it.'[8]

My own conclusions, despite the rather apocalyptic tone of my discussion of the regime crisis above, are more cautious. The most I can say is that there will fairly soon be an opening that will furnish an opportunity for democratisation. The democratic forces poised to exploit such an opening are growing in numbers and resources, but foes of democracy, specifically the active leaders of the army, will at that point control the state. In all probability, they will still be as self-confident and sure of their mission as they are now; they will enjoy the support of many others who share their interests and norms; and they will have a virtual monopoly on armed force. We should not underestimate their will and capacity to maintain the regime or, if they think it necessary, to intensify its repressive and authoritarian features.

1. The conflict has basically been between devout Muslims, called *santri*, many of whom have favored an Islamic state for Indonesia, and the *abangan*, Javanese Hindu-Muslim syncretists who favor a more secular state. These two groups together comprise about 85 percent of Indonesia's population. Suharto's own background and beliefs are *abangan*, as are those of most senior army officers.
2. David Easton, 'An Approach to the Analysis of Political Systems,' *World Politics* 9 (April 1957): 383–400. The quotations that follow are from 391–92.
3. The best account of late-colonial Timorese politics and the Indonesian takeover is Jill Jolliffe, *East Timor: Nationalism and Colonialism* (St. Lucia, Australia: Queensland University Press, 1978). The most up-to-date general treatment is John G. Taylor *Indonesia's Forgotten War: the Hidden History of East Timor* (London: Zed Press, 1991).
4. The most thorough and reliable account of November 12 is Asia Watch, "East Timor: The November 12 Massacre and its Aftermath," *Indonesia Issues*, Nos. 17–18, December 1991. For background, see Herb Feith, 'The Origins of the Dili Massacre' (Paper presented to the Asian Peace Research Association Conference, Christchurch, New Zealand, 30 January–4 February 1992). The figure of three thousand demonstrators is from an eyewitness, reporter Alan Nairn, whose story appeared in the *New Yorker*, 9 December 1991.
5. 'Indonesia's Democratic Past and Future,' *Comparative Politics* 24 (July 1992): 443–62.
6. Writing in Jakarta's leading newsweekly, essayist Fachry Ali puts the point this way: 'The legitimacy of Indonesian military leadership, therefore, is not due to the supremacy of their weaponry, but to their ability to solve problems "generally recognized by society."' 'Sipil dan Militer [Civilian and Military],' *Tempo* (Jakarta), 14 March 1992, 93.
7. I am indebted for this last point to Herb Feith. Personal communication, 23 March 1992.
8. 'East Timor and Indonesia: Some Implications' (Paper presented at a Social Science Research Council Workshop on East Timor, Washington, D.C., 25–26 April 1991), 5.

8

The Politics of Development Policy*

First Principles and the State of the Art

> The science of economic policy concerns the search for
> maximizing or satisfying solutions subject to constraints, but those
> constraints are provided not merely by resources and know-how, as
> the elementary economics textbooks teach, but also by ethics,
> culture, history, and politics.[1]

A design for a successful economic development strategy in a contemporary Third World nation-state must include, in my view, specification of three components: goals, or desired outcomes; policies appropriate to those goals; and the societal variables that will lead to the choice by government decision-makers of the right policies.

Each of these components is problematic. The goals of growth and industrialisation, first advanced in the 1940s, have since been complicated by the addition of concerns for distribution or equality and, lately, environmental sustainability. We have today only the most embryonic understanding of how to conceptualise, let alone measure, the tradeoffs required for an optimal combination of these diverse goals.[2]

The policy component is marginally less confused. Decades of experience have led to an emerging consensus on the importance of relying on market incentives in the development process. There nonetheless remain the narrower, but vexing, questions of when and where government intervention is necessary or helpful, and with what policy instruments it is to be carried out.[3]

Analysis of both goals and policies has, with a few exceptions, been the territory of economists. Study of the causes of policy has been a terrain

---

* First published in *World Development*, 20, 6 (June 1992), pp. 793–807.

occupied primarily by other social scientists: political scientists, sociologists, historians, anthropologists. As might be expected from such a motley company, many variables have been advanced in explanation. They include aspects of culture, class structure and other domestic interest-based concepts, the representativeness or coerciveness of governments, world capitalism broadly or dependence on multi-national corporations narrowly, the autonomous state as pursuer of its own interests, the capabilities of bureaucracies, and more.

Many of the hypotheses employing these variables, particularly those that come under the headings of culture and social structure, are in fact not directed at why particular policies were adopted by governments. Instead they are attempts to explain more directly—bypassing the role of government and politics—development success or failure in an economy.

There is a tradition of cultural variables wielded for this purpose, from Max Weber's protestant ethic, as cause of European successes in the sixteenth and subsequent centuries, to the Confucian ethic as cause of post-World War II East Asian growth. Italian familism, African tribalism, Islamic literalism, Indian cow-worship, and Javanese mysticism have all been asserted to explain development failures. A currently popular Gramsci-influenced approach deftly combines culture and class inequalities, arguing that attitudes and behaviour are rooted in, though not strictly determined by, socio-economic position.[4]

In a more orthodox Marxian vein, Latin American class analysts long saw the state or government as epiphenomenal, or at most a useful weapon in the hands of the dominant landed classes. That view was superseded by *dependencia* theory, which in turn has given way to a focus on the state. The *dependencistas* placed most of the blame for lack of development in Latin America on foreigners, particularly U.S.-based multi-national corporations.[5] When, against the predictions of the theory, several Latin American economies began to grow rapidly in the 1960s and 1970s, the concept of an activist, relatively autonomous state was grafted on to the 'classic' dependency idea in a new theory called 'dependent development.'[6] The idea of state autonomy and capabilities as central to development has since been elaborated and extended to other parts of the developing world, notably East Asia.[7]

This is not the place to assess at length the merits of these various approaches. In very general terms, however, they have at least four limitations as theories of the causes of policy. First, as I have already stated, in their search for deeper roots they often do not address the question of the causes of policy at all, or do so only obliquely. A cultural variable like Confucianism is an obvious example. Among other things, this implies that they are unlikely to be of service to reform-minded policy-makers or political activists, who need proximate causes that they can manipulate.

A second limitation is that, even when they do take policy seriously, as in the case of the statists, they look in the wrong place: at the overly-abstracted and overly-aggregated state, presumed to be acting in its corporate interests, instead of at those who control and direct the activities of state agencies. For example, a widely-cited recent study of South Korea, Taiwan, Hongkong, and Singapore attributes these countries' development successes primarily to the policies of societally-insulated state leaderships. It neglects to mention the role of the Korean military under Park Chung Hee and Chun Doo Hwan, the Kuomintang under Chiang Kai-Shek and Chiang Ching-Kuo, the British colonial power in Hongkong, or Singapore's People's Action Party under Lee Kuan-Yew in commanding the state and organising and mediating state-society relations.[8]

Third, they tend to paint with too broad a brush, rendering monochromatic for any given society what I suspect is a rainbow of factors influencing specific policy choices. The claim is that Confucian discipline, *hacendado* or corporate riches, or state strength provide basic explanations for overall success or failure. But what about societies whose birth control programs are acclaimed but whose housing policy has not got off the ground? Or governments that deregulate the banking sector but seem unable to privatise state enterprises? We need independent variables that enable us to distinguish the causes of one policy choice from those of another within a society.

Finally, current approaches are almost invariably locked into a positivist framework of hypothesis-testing and the search for generalisations. This is not in itself a bad thing for policy analysis, because the more variance we can explain the better the design of our strategy. But the desire to generalise can get in the way of the more basic objective of development policy analysis, which is to solve problems facing the economy and society.

Few positivism-inclined political scientists, sociologists, anthropologists, or historians would claim to possess theories that explain much of the variance in their dependent variables. Part of the reason for this is undoubtedly our continuing conceptual and methodological poverty, data-collection limitations, and so on. These weaknesses alone are sufficient reason to be cautious about accepting the conclusions of any current research on development as the sole basis for future policy.

There is a more fundamental explanation for our failings as theoreticians, however: the prodigious capacity for self-willed action of our human subjects. As policy-makers or in other political roles, individuals and groups often act against analysts' expectations. Gorbachev's revolution from the top in the Soviet Union, which caught virtually all Soviet-watchers off-guard, is only the most recent and dramatic proof of this proposition. A less widely-noted example of unexpected behaviour, taken from the country in which I have done most of my own research, is Indonesian President Suharto's extensive deregulation of the economy since 1986.[9]

Any approach to the study of the causes of development policy that does not take this simple but powerful truth into account loses much of its diagnostic and prescriptive potency. What is sacrificed is the sensibility necessary to appreciate the range of possible actions a decision-maker might in fact take, and with it the range of variables or combinations of variables that might influence his or her decision. For the problem solver, the ability to respond flexibly to the unexpected can often make the difference between a win and a loss in the policy game.

The economist Albert Hirschman, who has 'a passion for the possible', puts the general point very well:

Most social scientists conceive it as their exclusive task to discover and stress regularities, stable relationships, and uniform sequences. This is obviously an essential search, one in which no thinking person can refrain from participating. But in the social sciences there is a special room for the opposite type of endeavor: to underline the multiplicity and creative disorder of the human adventure, to bring out the uniqueness of a certain occurrence, and to perceive an entirely new way of turning a historical corner.[10]

In his own policy-oriented work, beginning with the celebrated *Journeys Toward Progress*,[11] Hirschman stresses the need to be constantly on the lookout for paradox. He offers examples of blessings in disguise, unintended consequences of policy actions, and reversible one-way sequences. Blessings in disguise are seeming obstacles or 'fetters' to development that can be turned into assets or 'spurs'. Policies in their implementation typically produce unintended consequences, some of which may in turn shift the balance of political forces in favour of reformers. A supposed one-way sequence, e.g., social consensus as a prerequisite to democratisation, may often work in the other direction, when democracy results from the inability of one group to impose its will on others. 'The essence of the possibilist approach consists in figuring out avenues of escape from such straitjacketing constructs in any individual case that comes up.'[12]

What are the ingredients of a theory of the politics of development policy that avoids these weaknesses of current approaches? What would an alternative approach look like that seeks proximate causes of policies, chooses more pertinent independent variables, recognises the importance of multivariate analysis, and can make sense out of the sometimes surprising behaviour of political actors?

Two research foci, already present but not now occupying the central place in the development literature, seem to me the most promising candidates for our attention: the calculations of politicians and officials when they make policy decisions; and, reversing the causal arrow from politics→economics to economics→politics, the implications for the politics of policy-making of certain economic variables and policies.

The Calculations of Politicians

> Scholars should pay more attention to the capacity for autonomous choice on the part of local actors, both public and private, and give greater weight to the importance of these choices in shaping the impact of external environments upon the structure of the local societies.[13]

What we need to know about the calculations of politicians is how their goals, the strategies they design to achieve those goals, and the resources they possess or can mobilise are related to their policy actions. It is remarkable how little systematic work in political science has been done along these lines. So far, the best attempt—though, as I will argue below, not without its limitations—to provide a conceptual framework is Warren Ilchman and Norman Uphoff's rational choice model, borrowed from economic reasoning, in *The Political Economy of Change* (1969).

Ilchman and Uphoff begin by stipulating that a politician's principal motivation is to gain and maintain power. Power is measured by possession of the resources of authority or legitimacy, economic goods and services, status, information, and coercion or violence. These resources are acquired at the expense of other actors by making policy choices.

Ilchman and Uphoff distinguish policy choices in categories of coping with or inducing social and economic change, remaining in authority in the present or in the future, and building political and administrative infrastructure. Each specific choice is made based on calculations of the balance between the resources one already possesses or can obtain through coalition with others and the resources of opponents.

A typical pattern of interests structured by choices—a system of political stratification—includes: a 'core combination' or ruling coalition; an 'ideological bias' group that favours government policies but does not provide it with concrete support; a 'stability group' that acquiesces in government policies; an 'extra-stability group' that must be coerced into obedience; and 'unmobilised sectors' that are taken into account only as potential allies or opponents. Each group in this pattern possesses its own ideology, propensities to act in certain ways, and time horizons for the achievement of goals that need to be evaluated by politicians seeking to enlist their support.

The best effort to apply this approach empirically is Robert Bates' *Markets and States in Tropical Africa* (1981), which describes the policies of several African governments toward agriculture and explicates the political calculations behind those policies. The book's descriptive chapters discuss policies in three markets in which farmers participate: the market for agricultural commodities, including both food and export cash crops; the market for factors of production, the inputs farmers buy; and the market for consumer goods, particularly commodities manufactured in the city and purchased in rural areas. In each of these markets, Bates shows, government policies discriminate against most farmers. The result is declining agricultural production.

The analytical puzzle for Bates is: 'How do the governments get away with it? In countries that are overwhelmingly rural, as in Africa, how can governments sustain policies that so directly violate the immediate interests of the majority of their constituents?'[14] His answer is in three parts, the first describing the calculations of farmers, the second and third the calculations of politicians. Farmers soften the impact of government policies by using the market defensively: they produce less, thus incurring fewer costs of production; they alter their production mixes, growing less of the lowest priced crops; and they supplement their incomes by entering the labour market.

The ruling politicians rely heavily on powerful urban interests. By choosing non-market rather than market instruments to achieve policy objectives, they create urban clienteles, both business and labour, that support them in several ways, including kicking back a share of the benefits they are given.

They also suppress political protest. Rural demobilisation—banning political parties and organisations that represent farmers' interests—and overt coercion are common techniques. A more sophisticated approach is to make it in the interest of wealthy farmers to support the government and to encourage organisations which they dominate, for example through the promotion of agricultural production schemes. This is a divide-and-rule tactic, deliberately selecting policy measures that can be taken advantage of only by a few, who will then return the favour with political loyalty.

In his conclusion, Bates juxtaposes this coalition pattern—a ruling group allied with the state bureaucracy, urban employers and workers, and wealthy farmers—with two alternative coalitions as possible solutions to the problem of declining agricultural production. The first is an alliance of urban industry and food producers united against a major extractive industry. The food producers in this scenario would gain from taxes on the extractive industry used for agricultural input support, for subsidised transportation of their produce to markets, and for storage and other facilities that would help raise prices; urban industry could benefit from an overvalued currency and tariff protection plus subsidies on urban food prices, again paid for by taxes on the extractive industry.

The second alternative, designed for countries without a major extractive industry, is a coalition between urban industry and producers of export crops. The tradeoff here is one in which measures that reduce the overvaluation of the currency are exchanged for policies that reduce the cost of industrial labour. Devaluation helps exporters, while repressive labour laws, a policy of hiring cheaper foreign labour, and so on are for the benefit of urban industry.

I have limned the Ilchman-Uphoff framework and the Bates argument at some length because I think they are a useful starting point for analysis of the causes of policy. They have three virtues. The assumption that politicians and other decision-makers put political survival interests first is a valuable explanatory tool that, applied sensitively, can carry us some way toward an understanding of why one policy is chosen rather than another in specific situations. The approach lends itself to empirical analysis, as in Bates' description of the responses of African farmers to agricultural policies they did not like.

It also allows us to incorporate many of the factors mentioned in my initial critique of the development literature in an analytically more satisfying way, by treating them as potential allies or opponents of politicians. Classes, other interest groups, state agencies, and foreign economic and political forces create constraints and opportunities to be weighed by decision-makers faced with a policy problem, rather than determinants that overwhelm and deny the individual's capacity for autonomous choice.

I am not, however, advocating that we pursue a rational choice approach to the causes of policy, only that we begin with the idea that decision-makers choose policies in a calculated way, basing their actions on some conceptions of goals, strategies, and resources. Among these goals is surely a desire to attain or maintain power, and equally certainly there are political evaluations of strategies and resources in terms of their contributions to that goal.

Where the rational choice approach is weak is in its economistic assumption that the drive for power is decisive in politics. Hirschman again puts the general point well:

> [T]here are serious pitfalls in any transfer of analytical tools and
> modes of reasoning developed within one discipline to another. As
> the economist, swollen with pride over the comparative rigor of his
> discipline, sets out to bring the light to his heathen colleagues in
> the other social sciences, he is likely to overlook some crucial
> distinguishing feature of the newly invaded terrain which makes his
> concepts and apparatus rather less applicable and illuminating than
> he is wont to think. . . . [T]he distance between reality and
> intellectual schema is here likely to be both wider and more
> difficult to detect than was the case as long as the scheme stayed
> 'at home'.[15]

In the case of the politics of Third World development policy, there are three 'crucial distinguishing features'—vices to balance the three virtues discussed above—that limit the applicability of the Ilchman-Uphoff and Bates approach to the analysis of the calculations of policy-makers.

First, it is too centred on the top leadership and their most basic policies.[16] It thus fails to distinguish between policy issues where the decision-maker's political survival is genuinely at stake and those where it is not, and between policy issues settled at the top of the political system and those decided further down. In the latter, different calculi are presumably at work, sometimes less political and sometimes involving political forces that would not be tolerated in higher or more sensitive arenas. The implication is that, for any given policy issue, the motivation to attain or maintain power should be treated as a variable, not as a constant or assumption.

Second, there is less than meets the eye to the analytical reach of the power-as-overriding-motive assumption, for many strategies and policies may be compatible with the drive for power. Hitler and Stalin wanted power, but so do Kohl and Gorbachev. Southeast Asia in the last half-century has seen many successful power-seeking politicians—Ne Win, Sarit Thanarat, Ho Chi Minh, Mahathir Mohamad, Lee Kuan-Yew, Sukarno, Suharto, Ferdinand Marcos—who have pursued remarkably different economic and other policies. The power motive is thus useful as a conceptual foundation—giving us initial access to the politicians' world view and setting some probable limits to their actions—but there is still plenty of design work for the architect of a theory of the calculations of policy-makers.

Finally, and perhaps most important, the power motive assumption surely offends empirical reality. It must be the case that few politicians anywhere are wholly driven by it, do not have other motives that are constantly interacting with it, balancing or shaping it in their heads in complex ways. Put slightly differently, the very conception of purpose held by an individual is probably best seen as culture-specific, in the sense that one's understanding of the is's and oughts of social relations is shaped by the ideas current in society at the time and by one's own direct experiences in life.

I have just brought culture back into the conceptual framework. But I do not want us to treat it in the simplistic way that most economists have, e.g., Gunnar Myrdal's famous discussion of cow worship,[17] as an attitudinal obstacle, an unfortunate residue of 'tradition' that must be erased from the collective consciousness if economic and social progress is to be achieved. The more positive assessments by other social scientists, e.g., Confucianism as the cause of East Asian success, are equally unpersuasive.

What is wrong with these accounts is that they assume an autonomous mental world, a free-floating universe of ideas, apart from but governing the material world of policy choices and descending through socialisation from generation to generation. I prefer a more balanced conception of the relationship of ideas and interests, in which the selection of beliefs about the nature of social relations is made and remade in the light of each generation's, and each individual's, own needs, experiences, and perceptions of those experiences. 'Man is an animal,' the anthropologist Clifford Geertz has written, 'suspended in webs of significance he himself has spun . . .'[18] Sometimes the spinning is conscious, sometimes not, but it always both reflects and reshapes the social reality of the times.

An example from modern Indonesian political culture is the notion of *ke-Timuran*, 'Easternness'. *Ke-Timuran* has to do with the attitudes necessary to the maintenance of a harmonious society. It contains such ideas as respect for the views of others in general, deference to elders and to authority in particular, a notion that differences of opinion should be expressed privately and non-confrontationally, and so on.

Ke-Timuran has obvious roots in pre-colonial Javanese political culture, and in the beliefs of ordinary Javanese today about how they should relate to each other.[19] But it is also a political resource, especially for holders of high government office, and as such has been consciously cultivated by the contemporary elite. To the extent that non-elites can be persuaded to believe in the principles of *ke-Timuran*, policy-makers can obtain compliance while mobilising and deploying fewer coercive and material resources. *Ke-Timuran* is also to some extent a two-way street: it can be used by non-elites to demand respect and attention to their interests, and to upbraid the elite for high-living and excessive use of force. Without these functions, it is doubtful that it would hold as central a place as it does in the modern culture.[20]

Another example, this one closer to a current policy controversy, is the widespread belief among politically-aware Indonesians that private business people are *serakah* (greedy). A free enterprise economy inevitably means the dominance of the strong over the weak. This belief is rooted in Indonesians' experience of the Dutch colonial economy, and in Marxist interpretations of that experience popular among pre-war intellectuals. It is reinforced by the pre-colonial bias against traders in Javanese aristocratic culture, echoed in today's bureaucratic culture, and by the prominence in the modern private sector of Sino-Indonesians, seen as 'foreigners' by many other Indonesians.

Belief in capitalist greed, unlike *ke-Timuran*, is a political resource held not by the elite, which on the whole promotes free enterprise, but by its opponents. It has become increasingly valuable as a resource since the late 1980s, when deregulation policies have appeared to foster the rapid growth of big Sino-Indonesian businesses at the expense of small non-Chinese firms. Despite mixed evidence as to the true relationship, even many members and close advisers of the government believe the worst of capitalism.[21] In his recently published autobiography, President Suharto apparently felt it necessary to defend his position by arguing for free enterprise only indirectly. He took the pragmatic view that in the short term Indonesia must bet on the strong, taking advantage of the skills and capital of its big business people.[22]

To sum up this section: we need to collect and analyse information about the goals, strategies, resources, and choices of decision-makers and other policy actors. We start with the proposition that they are political animals, evaluating alternative policies in the light of their political survival needs.

But we want to put this proposition in the context of some broader considerations: that political factors weigh more heavily on some issues and in some issue areas than others; that political calculations at the centre of a sovereign nation-state's decision-making processes are different than they are further down; that the power motive does not necessarily imply any particular strategy or policy consequence; that the concept of a power motive needs to be anchored in culture generally and the culture of individual decision-makers specifically; and that culture should be seen not as a set of free-floating ideas but as a product of the complex interaction over time of ideas and interests.

The Political Implications of Economic Variables

> Speculation about connections between economics and politics becomes much more profitable when one focuses not on the roughest outline, but on the finer features of the economic landscape. This can of course best be done by the economist who knows about them; the trouble is that his professional interests do not ordinarily lie in this direction. At the same time, the political scientist who has the motivation to look for such connections lacks the familiarity with economic concepts and relationships that is required.[23]

Hirschman's critique of the focus on the 'roughest outline' of the economic landscape is directed at sociologists and political scientists, both in and outside the Marxian tradition, who have concentrated on 'the most obvious, large-scale features of the economic landscape, such as economic wealth, growth, industrialisation, inflation, mass unemployment, and so on.'[24] The effects of these features are either obvious—e.g., great wealth begets great political power—and therefore uninteresting, or are pitched at such a high level of abstraction—e.g., the impact of economic growth on political stability—as to be unresolvable without further specification.

Hirschman's approach to the problem is to offer not a theory—he admits he doesn't have one—but instead several illustrations of the influence of an economy's 'finer features' on politics. These include: gains from foreign trade as a source of political power; the relationship between the size of the 'consumer surplus' and the probability of political action by consumers; the political impact of the creation of customs unions; the effects of portfolio versus direct investment; the political liabilities of project aid as opposed to program aid; the effects of late industrialisation on the assertiveness and power of the industrial bourgeoisie; and the relationship between the economic and botanical characteristics of coffee and the ability of coffee growers to unite politically.[25]

234   LEADERSHIP AND CULTURE IN INDONESIAN POLITICS

The last two illustrations are worth elaborating for a better sense of Hirschman's analytical strategy. In the initial stages of late-developing (compared to Western Europe and the United States) Latin America, manufacturers typically produced consumer goods with imported machinery for domestic markets. When they began to look for new opportunities to invest, they had a choice of moving into either backward-linking (upstream) or export industries, unlike the earlier European industrialists for whom the former option had already been closed. Mostly they chose to move upstream, with continued government protection, rather than risk the rigors of international competition. The effect was to prevent them from developing the kind of autonomy from state power that might have made them into a more vital political force.

Coffee, on the other hand, according to Hirschman, has a number of special qualities that have tended to lead toward the creation of powerful interest associations of producers. These include the large number of smallholder growers, the long interval between planting and full bearing of the coffee trees (implying supply inelasticity), and the occasional but unpredictable bumper crops, which together result in wide price fluctuations. When prices drop sharply, which they frequently do, there is a strong incentive for growers to join forces in order to apply pressure on the government to provide support.

In his discussion of these and other variables, Hirschman states repeatedly that discovery of the 'finer features' of the economy that have significant political consequences is more likely to be done by economists than by political scientists, since the former have the necessary conceptual and analytical equipment and the latter do not. The point is well-taken, but a political science contribution may also be possible.

What political scientists can do is to give Hirschman's randomly chosen illustrations more systematic form, both in terms of the dependent, political, and the independent, economic, variables. Returning to the concern of the last section of this essay, two kinds of dependent variables are perhaps of most interest to analysts of the political causes of policy. For any specific policy issue or area, we need to know the number and identity of, and the relationships among, the significant players; and we need to know what political resources each brings to the decision-making arena.

On the independent variable side, it may be helpful to make distinctions among relevant characteristics of the macro-economy, sectoral and commodity characteristics, major development problems or challenges, and policy issue-specific qualities. By characteristics of the macro-economy I mean such things as the balance of payments, inflation rate, tax structure, foreign exchange regime, interest rates, the capital market, budgetary balance or imbalance, and so on. Differences among sectors—agriculture, mining, manufacturing, utilities, construction, trade, transportation, the public sector—and commodities and services—staple and non-staple food crops, textiles, leather goods, automobiles, shipping, education, mass media, and so on—could also be an important source of hypotheses about who plays in the policy game and with what resources.

A more forward-looking categorisation might be based on the critical challenges or obstacles to development faced by Third World economies. Richard Doner offers an interesting list: IMF-type structural adjustment (which may invoke the opposition of local manufacturers who rely on an overvalued exchange rate for the import of production goods); reconciliation of the tension between upstream and downstream firm promotion (the former increasing value-added, the latter producing more efficiently in the short-run); standardisation of technologies, which can lead to 'greater scale economies, more rapid cost reduction, and potentially more rapid consumer acceptance,' but tends to be opposed by the firms concerned; reduction of the number of producers in markets burdened with surplus capacity (also likely to be opposed by the firms targeted for extinction); government investment screening to maximise the benefits obtained from foreign capital (a process often influenced by domestic private sector lobbying); and the need to build physical infrastructure and train personnel, collective goods that must be provided by the state.[26]

Some research has already been done by political scientists on the impact of policy-specific variables. Though mostly directed at explaining success and failure in policy implementation, this literature touches on the political aspects of decision-making as well. For example, Peter Cleaves lists several policy variables, including: technical features (simple versus complex); change from status quo (marginal versus comprehensive); target (one-actor versus multi-actor); objective (one-goal versus multi-goal); clarity of goals (clearly stated versus ambiguous or unclear); and duration (short versus long). In each case the former quality is hypothesised to result in more successful implementation. Almost all of these variables have political as well as administrative implications.[27]

Merilee Grindle has a similar list. Policies that produce substantial social and economic change, such as land reform, are, she argues, more likely to be opposed than those that do not. Policies that produce collective benefits are more likely to get broad support than those that produce divisible benefits. Policies that require substantial behavioural change will be harder to implement, because of opposition from the target population, than those that do not.[28]

The variable of policy specificity can be disaggregated in a number of other ways. One possibility is a set of categories offered by Ilchman and Uphoff (1969), which distinguish among policies to cope with or induce social and economic change, to remain in authority in the present or in the future, and to build political and administrative infrastructure. Another is the distinction made by Donald Rothchild and Robert Curry among governing elite policies of accommodation, reorganisation, and transformation of relationships with other political actors.[29]

Finally, Theodore Lowi identifies three major categories of public policies: distribution, regulation, and redistribution. Distributive policies are patronage awards, goods and services given to individuals and groups in the short run 'without regard to limited resources.' Regulatory policies are stated in general terms and affect broader categories of individuals than distributive policies. Though they can be 'specific and individual in their impact, . . . they are not capable of the almost infinite amount of disaggregation typical of distributive policies.' Redistributive policies, like income tax or welfare programs, impact broadly on social classes.[30]

In representative democracies, distributive policies, because they are so tailored to individuals and small groups, tend not to provoke conflict. Regulatory policies pit specific interest groups, the potential regulators and the regulated, against each other, while redistributive policies set the rich against the poor, the elite against the masses. Modified to fit non-democratic politics, Lowi's categorisation may well be applicable to much of the Third World.

To sum up this section, we need to look at the ways in which economic and policy variables affect the politics—who plays, and with what resources—of the policy-making process. Case studies, of the sort conducted by Hirschman, are required to provide data for analysis and a sense of the range of possible connections. But we also should be thinking more systematically about some larger categories into which the cases might fit. A first crack at this problem is to distinguish among macro-economic, sectoral and commodity, critical challenges, and policy-specific variables.

Two Indonesian Illustrations

To illustrate the merits of these research foci, I will now offer two Indonesian cases in point. The first, taken from my own research, shows the value of a voluntarist conception of the political calculations of policy makers. Significant cultural, social, and political structural obstacles to development have been overcome by President Suharto's deliberate choice of a strategy that marries pro-market policies to a powerful and stable political support base.

The second, from a combined case study and comparative analysis by the Harvard economist Peter Timmer, demonstrates the utility of investigating the political implications of economic and policy variables in particular sectoral settings. By placing Indonesian agricultural policy-making in the context of a broader East Asian pattern, Timmer is able to illuminate the choices now confronting Jakarta and the pressures pushing decision-makers down alternative paths of continued stabilisation versus increased protection.

On the whole, economic development in Indonesia over the past quarter century has been a success, certainly in growth but probably in distribution as well.[31] At one level, the reason for this success is clear: the government's adoption in the late 1960s and maintenance since that time of market-oriented macroeconomic policies that have encouraged domestic and foreign private investment. Effective use has also been made of the oil bonanza—for much of this period over half of government revenues and an even larger percentage of hard currency earnings came from petroleum products—to channel funds to local governments for infrastructural rehabilitation and expansion.[32]

What is not so clear is why the government chose these policies, or why it has stuck to them with relative consistency for so long. Much analytical ink has in fact flowed in support of various deterministic propositions that development was not succeeding or could not succeed.

One major obstacle was said to be a culture of mysticism, particularly among the Javanese, who comprise almost half the total population. Another, targeting policy-makers more directly, was a widespread anti-foreign, anti-private sector, pro-state nationalist ideology among the educated elite.[33] I have already described some of the features of this elite culture under the heading of the pervasiveness of the belief in capitalist 'greed'.

Leftist scholars initially emphasised the negative consequences of dependence on foreign assistance and investment for domestic distribution, if not growth.[34] More recently, a strong (relative to other groups in society) and self-aggrandising state official class has been seen, again by scholars in the Marxian tradition, as unwilling to share the fruits of growth.[35] Finally, it has been argued that the government's patrimonial leadership style means reliance on anti-market policies to fill a cash and benefits pool for disbursement to its particularistic clientele.[36]

In a recent article, I have ventured a very different proposition: that the explanation for Indonesia's economic policy choices over the past quarter century lies in the calculations of President Suharto, conceived as a 'relatively autonomous' policy maker.[37] Specifically, I have tried to show that Suharto accepted the pro-market policy recommendations of his Western-educated professional economist advisers for two reasons.

First, he recognised their merits as solutions to the problems confronting Indonesia's economy at the time. Second, he was able to construct a set of political arrangements—legitimating principles, a base of support, and means of coercion—compatible with them. The first of these reasons, I confess, has the ring of obviousness about it, though an intra-regional comparison with Burma under Ne Win or the Philippines under Marcos readily demonstrates its importance as a policy prerequisite. But it is the second reason I wish to emphasise: if Suharto had not seen how liberal economic policies could be made to fit into a supportive political structure, it is highly unlikely that he would have adopted them.

In my analysis, Suharto was initially predisposed to listen to the economists' policy recommendations by the seriousness of the economic crisis—inflation at over 600% per year combined with a negative growth rate—confronting Indonesia in the mid-1960s. In addition, the economists brought several strengths to their relationship with the army general turned national political leader. They were a cohesive group of well-trained professionals, as their sobriquet 'Berkeley Mafia' suggests, in possession of an economic science that had been ignored or contravened, with disastrous results, by Indonesia's first president, Sukarno, for most of the previous decade.

The economists were also nationalists, Western-educated but not Westernised, trained in a foreign science but brought up in colonial Netherlands India and revolutionary Indonesia, and so able to speak the language of their countrymen, and particularly of the politicians. Moreover, their leader, Professor Widjojo Nitisastro of the University of Indonesia's Economics Faculty, was particularly adept at presenting himself as a deferential subordinate, a traditional Java-derived style that Suharto seems to favour in his lieutenants.

Indonesian culture—either in the form of Javanese mysticism or the anti-capitalist, anti-foreign, pro-state ideology pervasive among members of the elite—does not seem to have got in the way of Suharto's relationship with the economists. In his autobiography, Suharto displays attitudes typical of his generation and background. His preferred economic structure puts cooperatives at the centre, relegating private enterprise and the state to supportive roles. Yet he is quite explicit about the need to 'follow rational economic laws', and he recognises that in current Indonesian conditions capitalist growth must precede the development of cooperatives.[38]

Given a propensity to accept the economists' advice on economic grounds, and an ability to overcome cultural constraints, what role did political calculations play in Suharto's ultimate policy decisions? The initial context was a massive political crisis coincident with the economic crisis. For many years President Sukarno had maintained himself in office by balancing the demands of the army and the communist party, the two most powerful political forces at the time. In the early morning hours of 1 October 1965, this power triangle began to collapse. A group of radical younger army officers, together with members of a communist youth group, assassinated six senior generals, leaving Major General Suharto, then in command of strategic troops in Jakarta, at the top of the army's power structure.

In the following months, Suharto used armed force and the support of anti-communist groups in society to destroy the communist party and to erode the power of President Sukarno, who had become (in the army's view) too close to the communists and was even alleged by some to have been involved in the assassination plot. By March 1966 Suharto was in possession of an executive order from the president, authorising him to use whatever force was necessary to restore order.

Suharto was now on the threshhold of power, but he still needed a political formula that would get him through the door and keep him inside. What he chose was an authoritarian 'system of political stratification built on a core combination of military and civilian bureaucratic forces, with patronage as a chief instrument of reward and punishment'.[39] This system has never been seriously challenged, and remains in effect today.

How has it been possible to combine market-oriented economic policies with a political structure based on patron-client ties? The short answer is that Suharto himself has apparently not been impressed by scholarly claims that economic liberalism and political illiberalism are incompatible. At the macroeconomic level he has consistently followed the advice of his professional advisers. The economy has grown steadily as a result. At the same time he has given special opportunities—trade and manu-facturing monopolies, credit facilities, government contracts—in selected areas of the economy to client, for the most part Sino-Indonesian, business people. They have expressed their gratitude by filling the coffers of the president's private foundations. Successful state companies—particularly the national oil company Pertamina, which collects revenues from the foreign companies that actually pump most of the oil, and the food logistics agency Bulog (discussed below), which has an import monopoly on agricultural products—are also believed to set aside some of their profits for presidential political purposes.

When some of the president's policies in specific areas of the economy have been shown to be slowing down or otherwise distorting economic growth, he has been willing to jettison them, even at cost to his patrimonial network. Prominent examples include the reining in of Pertamina's ex-cessive foreign borrowing in the mid-1970s and a series of impressive deregulation measures adopted in the last half of the 1980s. Despite these constraints, he has so far been able to ensure that the flow of political income, from these and other sources, continues at a level sufficient to his needs.

For a complete picture of presidential power in contemporary Indone-sia, patron-clientism must be put in a broader context, as one piece of a complex political strategy. Other important elements include economic performance that has benefited mass constituencies, the deeper legitimacy of his military and national leadership, and the regular use of coercion against opponents. I have emphasised patron-clientism, and anti-developmental elite ideology, here because I want to show that political leaders, desirous of staying in power and maybe even of doing good for their people, are often capable of turning to their advantage what appear to others to be most unpromising materials.

Agriculture, in particular rice, is the sector examined by Peter Timmer in a fascinating paper that combines case study and comparative analy-sis.[40] Who, Timmer asks, is likely to participate, and with what political resources, in the determination of future rice pricing policy in Indonesia?

He addresses this question through an examination of the impact of recent policy history and of the changing structure of the economy, in the comparative context of Japan, South Korea, and Malaysia, three Asian rice economies whose past may foreshadow Indonesia's future.

Timmer first uses a statistical model to demonstrate, against the common wisdom, that the historical rice pricing policy objective of the Japanese, Korean, and Malaysian governments has been stabilisation rather than protection. Policy in these countries has basically been a response to the highly unstable international market. In recent years, however, all three governments—South Korea especially, Japan and Malaysia to a lesser extent—have shifted to more protectionist policies. Their new goal, achieved only with increasing divergence between the domestic and the international market price of rice, has become parity between farm and non-farm incomes.

Why has this shift occurred? Timmer's general argument is that a combination of constituency, institutional, and macroeconomic factors is responsible. In each country, rice farmers have been a large, and politically important, constituency. Industrialisation boosts the incomes of consumers, who then spend proportionally less on rice and other food-stuffs. It also swells the revenues of the state, making budgetary subsidisation of agricultural products relatively cheaper. Rice farmers' interests thus become economically and politically easier to serve.

Institutionally, all three countries have used state rice logistics agencies to maintain acceptable domestic price levels by buying and selling on the world market. These agencies then become powerful lobbies within government for a continuation of the status quo. Macroeconomically, the further industrialisation proceeds, the less effect losses in efficiency in the agricultural sector have on overall growth patterns. Eventually, 'policy for rice prices becomes almost entirely a political rather than an economic issue.'[41]

The Indonesian government, following this general East Asian pattern, has pursued a policy of rice price stability over the past quarter century. It now appears, however, to be at a crossroads, signalled by a slight rise in protectionism for farmers in 1987. This new protectionism is the result of a clash between Indonesia's achievement of self-sufficiency in rice in the early 1980s, or more precisely President Suharto's subsequent determination to maintain self-sufficiency at all costs, and the fluctuating world rice market in the late 1980s. When the world price shot up in 1985, Indonesia sold, depleting its domestic stocks. When there was a domestic shortage in 1987, the government refused to buy from abroad, forcing a sharp price increase to an unprecedented level that has been maintained into the 1990s.

What are the chances that the government is about to embark on a protectionist course, following the lead of its Asian neighbors? Timmer hopes that it will not do so, because Indonesia's level of industrialisation is still far below theirs: 'Many poor consumers would face a lower standard of living and the prospect of malnutrition if Indonesia's rice prices continued to rise signficantly in real terms.'[42]

Unfortunately, both his comparative and case analyses suggest that the urge to protect is likely to grow stronger. The real price of rice in world markets continues to decline, and Indonesia's successful export drive (especially of manufactured goods) is depressing, relatively if not absolutely, agricultural incomes.

In the final analysis, he argues, much will depend on the power position and policy stance of the state rice marketing agency Bulog (*Badan Urusan Logistik*, Logistic Affairs Agency). Since its founding in the mid-1960s, Bulog has had the principal responsibility for implementing government price stabilisation policies through domestic market intervention and purchases from abroad when necessary. Over a quarter century, it has developed a considerable capacity, both analytical and physical (e.g., construction of warehouses for storage, creation of a network of local purchasing agents through a government-sponsored cooperatives program), for surveillance and control.

Bulog and its officials now have a vested interest in policies that allow the agency to continue to play an interventionist role. Because the government's current goal of self-sufficiency implies protectionism, the use of Bulog to implement that goal gives its interest a pronounced protectionist cast as well.

The continuing political importance of rice, and Bulog's past successes in policy implementation, make the agency all by itself a formidable player in the policy game. If it chooses to promote protectionist policies in the future, it may also be able to call on political support from the Department of Agriculture, an agency heretofore without much influence in agricultural policy-making but that now sees itself as the principal defender of farmers' interests.

In Timmer's view, however, for reasons of both growth and equity rice policy for the 1990s should continue to promote stabilisation rather than protection. It should do so, moreover, in ways that tolerate greater price fluctuations and that rely less on Bulog and more on private traders. Higher standards of living throughout the country mean that the share of rice in household expenditures is declining, so consumer tolerance of fluctuating prices is greater. Private sector marketing capabilities are also much improved compared to the 1960s, so that Bulog no longer provides a unique service.

Anti-protectionist forces—chiefly the professional economists or 'Berkeley Mafia'—have been centred in the Department of Finance, Bappenas (the National Planning Agency), and a super-ministerial body called Ekuin, which coordinates the policies of several departments with economic responsibilities. These forces have long dominated macro-economic policy making, and have been particularly effective in the pursuit of trade and financial deregulation in the last half of the 1980s. Their influence in specific sectors, such as industry and agriculture, has been more problematic. National rice and fertilizer prices, however, have been set annually by Bappenas for more than two decades, in a policy process in which Bulog and especially the Department of Agriculture have been lesser players.

The challenge for Bappenas in the 1990s, says Timmer, is to maintain its control of this process. It must do so, his analysis warns us, in the face of a changing political economy and array of political forces, and against a powerful East Asian trend, felt also in Indonesia, toward agricultural protectionism. For these reasons, his conclusion is pessimistic though not despairing. Indonesian policy makers may be severely constrained, but they are 'not entirely . . . captive to broader forces.'[43]

Conclusion

> The course of history depends largely on the daring of those who propose to act in terms of historically viable goals. We do not try to place theoretical limits on the probable course of future events. These will depend, not on academic predictions, but on collective action guided by political wills that make work what is structurally barely possible.[44]

How likely is it that policy-makers in the Third World can be influenced to choose the right economic development policies, assuming that we know what those policies are? To refer to the concrete example just discussed, how likely is it that Indonesian agricultural policy makers can be influenced to continue to follow the path of rice price stabilisation and refrain from embarking on a new protectionist course?

Among Marxian scholars, a popular concern today is with divining the relative importance of 'structure' and 'agency'—read economic determinism and autonomous choice—in human affairs. This essay has given short shrift to determinism, not because I think all things are possible—in fact, I believe with Cardoso and Faletto, and Timmer, that structural constraints are real and formidable—but because few analysts give autonomous choice its proper due.

My focus on agency comes naturally. It has been observed of students of comparative politics that they tend unconsciously to read the characteristics of their country of specialisation into those of a larger universe of nation-states. Thus students of Latin American development see class and international dependency everywhere. Africanists project systems of personal rule and developmental pessimism onto the rest of the Third World and South Asianists universalise electoral and bargaining models of political economy. East Asianists are developmental optimists who advocate a package of Confucian-style culture, monolithic if not authoritarian government, and outward-looking economic policy strategies. What I have seen in Indonesia over the past quarter-century is a considerable though not unfailing governmental ability to choose the right policies. Evidence of success can be found at the macro-level, as in the current deregulation and in the late 1960s steps taken to stabilise and rehabilitate the economy, and at the micro-level, as in the rice production case described by Timmer, school and health centre construction, and family planning policies.

There is evidence of failure among other places in the cooperatives, sugar production, overcommitment to self-sufficiency in rice and over-concentration on rice at the expense of other foods, the creation of trade monopolies by governmental fiat, overprotection of domestic industries, the level of government corruption, and in the lack of decentralisation of government decision-making and administration across a wide range of policies.

If the right policies are sometimes chosen and sometimes not, it follows that economists and political scientists should try to find out, in both situations, the reasons. The potential payoff for policy-makers and political activists, in learning at the minimum 'what is structurally barely possible,' is clear.[45]

In the Indonesian case, my own macro-analysis of the politics of economic policy making suggests that the scope for agency is relatively large, as long as there is a way for the policy-maker to create and maintain a set of political arrangements supportive of the right policies. My concluding hope, therefore, is that this more balanced approach—structure, yes, but of a 'finer features' Hirschmanian sort, with much room for choice by skillful policy-makers—though shaped by one country's experience will turn out to have applicability far beyond that country's borders.

1. J. Bhagwati, 'Behind the Greencard,' *The New Republic*, No. 3830 (14 May 1990), p. 37.
2. For promising attempts at doing so, see R. Repetto, 'Wasting Assets,' *Technology Review*, Vol. 92, No. 1 (January 1989), pp. 40–44; and W. Ascher and R. Healy, *Natural Resource Policy-making in Developing Countries*, Durham, NC: Duke University Press, 1990.
3. For a range of positions, see D. Lal, *The Poverty of Development*, Cambridge, MA: Harvard University Press, 1985; A. Sen, *Resources, Values, and Development*, Cambridge, MA: Harvard University Press, 1984; P. Bardhan, 'Alternative Approaches to Development Economies,' in H. Chenery and T. Srinivasan (eds), *Handbook of Development Economics*, Vol. 1, Amsterdam: Elsevier, 1988, pp. 40–71; and M. Singh, 'Development policy research: The task ahead,' *Proceedings of the World Bank Conference on Development*

244   LEADERSHIP AND CULTURE IN INDONESIAN POLITICS

Economics 1989, Washington, DC: The World Bank, 1990, pp. 11–20.

4. J. Scott, *The Moral Economy of the Peasant: Subsistence and Rebellion in Southeast Asia*, New Haven: Yale University Press, 1976.
5. E.g., A. Frank, *Capitalism and Underdevelopment in Latin America: Historical Studies of Chile and Brazil*, New York: Monthly Review Press, 1967.
6. P. Evans, *Dependent Development: The Alliance of Multi-National, State, and Local Capital in Brazil*, Princeton: Princeton University Press, 1979; F. Cardoso and E. Faletto, *Dependency and Development in Latin America*, Berkeley: University of California Press, 1979.
7. P. Evans, D. Rueschemeyer and T. Skocpol, *Bringing the State Back In*, Cambridge: Cambridge University Press, 1985; F. Deyo (ed), *The Political Economy of the New Asian Industrialism*, Ithaca: Cornell University Press, 1987.
8. S. Haggard and T. Cheng, 'State and foreign capital in the East Asian NICs,' in F. Deyo (ed), op. cit., pp. 84–135. See also S. Haggard, *Pathways from the Periphery: The Politics of Growth in the Newly Industrializing Countries*, Ithaca: Cornell University Press, 1990. Similarly, J. Migdal, *Strong Societies and Weak States*, Princeton: Princeton University Press, 1988, finds that strong states exist in Israel, Cuba, China, Vietnam, Taiwan, North Korea, and South Korea, without mentioning that behind each of these states except the first and the last is a Leninist party. In Israel the organising force is parties in parliament and in South Korea it has been until very recently the army.
9. See R. Liddle, Chapter Four in this volume, and H. Soesastro, 'The political economy of deregulation in Indonesia,' *Asian Survey*, Vol. 29, No. 9 (September 1989), pp. 853–69.
10. A. Hirschman, *A Bias for Hope*, New Haven: Yale University Press, 1971, p. 27.
11. A. Hirschman, *Journeys Toward Progress*, New York: Twentieth Century Fund, 1963. See also the articles collected in Hirschman, *Essays in Trespassing*, Cambridge, Cambridge University Press, 1981, especially Chapter 6, 'Policymaking and Policy Analysis in Latin America—A Return Journey,' pp. 142–66.
12. A. Hirschman (1971), op. cit., p. 29.
13. R. Bates, *Markets and States in Tropical Africa*, Berkeley: University of California Press, 1981, p. 8.
14. *Ibid.*, p. 81.
15. Hirschman (1971), op. cit., pp. 3–4.
16. The first lines of the introductory chapter of W. Ilchman and N. Uphoff, *The Political Economy of Change*, Berkeley: University of California Press, 1969, p. 3, urge us to 'consider the situation of Colonel Yakubu Gowon. What would a political scientist have advised this young African leader who on the first of August, 1966, accepted leadership of the National Military Government of Nigeria?'
17. G. Myrdal, *Asian Drama*, New York: Pantheon, 1968, pp. 103ff.
18. C. Geertz, *The Interpretation of Cultures*, New York, Basic Books, 1973, p. 5.
19. S. Moertono, *State and Statecraft in Old Java*, Ithaca: Cornell Modern Indonesia Project, 1968; B. Anderson, 'The Idea of Power in Javanese Culture,

in Claire Holt (ed), *Culture and Politics in Indonesia*, Ithaca: Cornell University Press, 1972; C. Geertz, *The Religion of Java*, Glencoe, IL: The Free Press, 1960; W. Keeler, *Javanese Shadow Plays, Javanese Selves*, Princeton: Princeton University Press, 1987.
20. See also the discussion in R. Liddle, *Politics and Culture in Indonesia*, Ann Arbor: Center for Political Studies, Institute for Social Research, University of Michigan, 1988, pp. 16–19. Reprinted as Chapter Three in this volume.
21. B. Glassburner, 'Economic openness and economic nationalism in Indonesia under the Soeharto government,' Paper presented at a conference on Comparative Analysis of the Development Process in East and Southeast Asia, East-West Center, Honolulu, HA: May 1990. H. Hill, 'The Indonesian manufacturing sector: Southeast Asia's emerging industrial giant?,' in Anne Booth (ed), *The Oil Boom and After: Indonesian Economic Policy and Performance in the Soeharto Era*, Kuala Lumpur: Oxford University Press, 1994, pp. 43–49, presents data for the 1975–86 period supporting the counter proposition that firms of all sizes have prospered. He argues that 'the most likely explanation for the success of small enterprise is their ability to exploit market niches,' not government protection.
22. Suharto, *Pikiran, Ucapan, dan Tindakan Saya: Otobiografi* [My Thoughts, Words, and Deeds: Autobiography], seperti didpaparkan kepada [as told to] G. Dwipayana dan Ramadhan K.H., Jakarta: PT. Citra Lamtoro Gung Persada, 1988, pp. 486–492.
23. A. Hirschman (1971), op.cit., p. 8.
24. *Ibid.*
25. *Ibid.*, pp. 7–14.
26. R. Doner, 'Approaches to the politics of economic growth in Southeast Asia,' *Journal of Asian Studies*, Vol. 50, No. 4 (November 1991), pp. 836–38.
27. P. Cleaves, 'Implementation amidst scarcity and apathy: Political power and policy design,' in M. Grindle (ed), *Politics and Policy Implementation in the Third World*, Princeton: Princeton University Press, 1980, pp. 281–303.
28. M. Grindle, 'Policy content and context in implementation,' in M. Grindle (ed), *Politics and Policy Implementation in the Third World*, Princeton: Princeton University Press, 1980. See also M. Grindle and J. Thomas, *Public Choices and Policy Change: The Political Economy of Reform in Developing Countries*, Baltimore: The Johns Hopkins University Press, 1991, and R. Ayres, 'Political regimes, explanatory variables, and public policy in Latin America,' *The Journal of Developing Areas*, Vol. 10, No. 1 (October 1975), pp. 15–35. Grindle and Thomas widen the analytical focus to include agenda-setting and policy-making as well as implementation, and emphasise the pivotal role in policy reform of autonomous, complexly-calculating, decision makers. Ayres, who is concerned with the policy process as a whole rather than any particular stage, makes a distinction between 'substance' and 'process' variables and emphasises relationships between the two. An important relationship is 'operational style', a mix of different role orientations, clientele groups, resources, strategies, and patterns of interaction.
29. D. Rothchild and R. Curry, *Scarcity, Choice and Public Policy in Middle Africa*, Berkeley, University of California Press, 1978.
30. T. Lowi, 'American business, public policy, case-studies, and political theory,'

World Politics, Vol. 16, No. 4 (July 1964). Attempts to apply and modify Lowi's categories include: R. Salisbury, 'The analysis of public policy: A search for theories and roles,' in A. Ranney (ed), *Political Science and Public Policy*, Chicago: Markham, 1968, pp. 151–175; T. Smith, 'Toward a comparative theory of the policy process,' *Comparative Politics*, Vol. 1, No. 4 (July 1969); T. Smith, *The Comparative Policy Process*, Santa Barbara: ABC-Clio, 1975; and Francesco Kjellberg, 'Do policies (really) determine politics? And eventually how?,' *Policy Studies Journal*, Vol. 5, Special Issue, 1977, pp. 554–70. Salisbury lists four policy types: distributive, redistributive, regulatory, and self-regulatory. Smith also offers four: distributive, sectorally fragmented, emotive symbolic, and redistributive. Kjellberg replaces Lowi's distributive and regulatory policies with direct and indirect policies, i.e., policies that directly allocate goods and services versus those that set principles and standards.

31. In the peak years, 1969–1982, growth averaged nearly 8%. After a dip in the mid-1980s, it has now returned to about 7%. The most rigorous general analysis of post-1965 Indonesian economic development is A. Booth and P. McCawley (eds), *The Indonesian Economy During the Soeharto Era*, Kuala Lumpur: Oxford University Press, 1981. A very recent assessment is A. Nasution, 'Survey of recent developments,' *Bulletin of Indonesian Economic Studies*, Vol. 27, No. 1 (April 1991), pp. 3–43. The best account of distribution, though now badly dated, is A. Booth and R. Sundrum, 'Income Distribution,' in A. Booth and P. McCawley (eds), op. cit., pp. 181–217. More recent studies that offer basically positive conclusions about distribution are C. Manning, *The Green Revolution, Employment, and Economic Change in Rural Java*, Singapore: Institute of Southeast Asian Studies, 1988; H. Hill, 'Indonesia's industrial transformation: Parts I and II,' *Bulletin of Indonesian Economic Studies*, Vol. 26, Nos. 2 and 3 (August and December 1990; and *Indonesia* (1990).

32. B. Glassburner and A. Nasution, 'Macroeconomic policy and prospects for long-term growth,' Mimeo, Davis: Department of Economics, University of California, Davis, 1988.

33. A. Sievers, *The Mystical World of Indonesia: Culture and Economic Development in Conflict*, Baltimore: The Johns Hopkins University Press, 1974; F. Weinstein, *Indonesian Foreign Policy and the Dilemma of Dependence*, Ithaca: Cornell University Press, 1976.

34. R. Mortimer (ed), *Showcase State: The Illusion of Indonesia's 'Accelerated Modernisation'*, Sydney: Angus and Robertson, 1973.

35. B. Anderson, 'Old state, new society: Indonesia's new order in historical perspective,' *Journal of Asian Studies*, Vol. 42, No. 3 (May 1983), pp. 477–96.

36. H. Crouch, 'Patrimonialism and military rule,' *World Politics*, Vol. 31, No. 4 (July 1979), pp. 242–58. J. Nelson, 'The political economy of stabilization: Commitment, capacity, and public response,' in R. Bates (ed), *Toward a Political Economy of Development*, Berkeley: University of California Press, 1988, makes the argument for the Third World in general.

37. Liddle (1991), op. cit.

38. Suharto (1988), op. cit.

39. Liddle (1991), op. cit., p. 20. The jargon comes from Ilchman and Uphoff (1969), op. cit.
40. P. Timmer, 'How does Indonesia set its rice price? The role of markets and government policy,' Paper presented at the International Conference on the Economic Policy Making Process in Indonesia, Bali, Indonesia: September 6–9, 1990.
41. *Ibid.*, p. 29.
42. *Ibid.*
43. *Ibid.*, p. 4.
44. Cardoso and Faletto op. cit., p. 176.
45. C. Bell, 'The political framework,' in H. Chenery (ed), *Redistribution With Growth*, Oxford: Oxford University Press, 1974; and W. Ascher, *Scheming for the Poor: The Politics of Redistribution in Latin America*, Cambridge: Harvard University Press, 1984, offer some good advice to activists and policy planners on how to maneuver in the tight spaces imposed by structural constraints.

9

Can All Good Things Go Together? Democracy, Growth, and Unity in Post-Suharto Indonesia*

Is authoritarian rule necessary to sustain fast economic growth and/ or the unity of Indonesia?

Alternative Approaches

In comparative political science, there is a substantial body of recent research, much of it East Asia-based, on the relationship between regime type (authoritarian versus democratic) and economic growth. There is no comparable literature on the relationship between regime type and national unity, though current events in East Europe may soon produce one.

The conventional wisdom in the East Asian growth-and-politics literature is that democracy is incompatible with rapid economic development, particularly of the export-led variety. Robert Wade's *Governing the Market*[1] makes the case, mainly with data from Taiwan, that a prime cause of development success in East Asia has been the presence of an interventionist or activist as opposed to a passive-policeman state. An interventionist state in turn must be both authoritarian and corporatist. Stephan Haggard, in his widely-cited *Pathways From the Periphery*,[2] explicitly concludes that authoritarianism is not a prerequisite of successful export-led growth. His substantive argument, however, based on the Korea, Taiwan, Singapore, and Hong Kong cases, puts great weight on the degree of 'insulation' of the state from societal pressures.

In my reading of Haggard's book and many similar studies, the concept of insulation comes close to being a euphemism for authoritarianism.

---

* First published in John Legge and David Bourchier, eds., *Indonesian Democracy: 1950s and 1990s*, Clayton, Victoria: Monash University Centre of Southeast Asian Studies, 1994.

Insulation means the independence of state officials from the demands of social groups, and democracy implies the responsiveness of officials, through the electoral and policy-making processes, to such demands. There is therefore at the very least an inherent tension between the concepts of insulated and of democratic government.

For this reason, insulation seems to me to obscure rather than to clarify the nature of the relationship between regime type and economic growth. I prefer to build instead on the idea that politicians in all systems, democratic and authoritarian, accumulate and deploy in various combinations three basic kinds of political resources: coercive, normative, and utilitarian.[3] This alternative approach offers, I think, a more appropriate frame for examining the connection between the political process and policy outcomes.

Coercive resources, in an authoritarian regime, are the principal stuff of insulation; in sufficient quantity, and effectively mobilised and deployed, they make it possible for government officials to deny and repress popular opinion. In a constitutional democracy, governments also possess and utilise coercive resources, but as the ultimate sanctions behind the judicial process, not as uncontrolled weapons in the hands of the executive.

Coercion in democracies is an instrument of policy enforcement and of protection for officials from individuals and groups who are willing to use illegal or unconstitutional violence to achieve political ends. But it does not protect them from the retribution of interest groups who may mobilise against the government in electoral and other constitutional ways.

Normative resources are attitudes and beliefs like recognition of a state's or a government's legitimacy, identification of state policy with a popular ideology, or the respect or awe accorded to a strong or charismatic leader. They may also be used for insulation, in the limited sense that a government can obtain acquiescence to an unpopular policy if it has wider support for its general policy orientation, its adherence to a constitution, or its leaders' right to make authoritative decisions. But normative resources alone are not likely to provide effective long term support for major policy orientations that are at odds with widely popular demands.

Utilitarian resources are the more tangible, material ingredients of exchange, the policies, programs, appointments, contracts, and awards given by a government in return for political support. They are the predominant component of day-to-day politics in democracies, but can also be important in authoritarian systems (as in fact they have been in Indonesia's New Order).

It is the centrality of utilitarian exchange in democracies that raises fears about their unsuitability for rapid economic growth in developing countries. Many resourceful individuals and social groups may make demands on government for macroeconomic, sectoral, and other policies that run counter to the policies required for growth. If these individuals and groups are sufficiently influential, economic progress will be slowed or even stopped.

This argument is based on the notion of the dilemma of collective action—the proposition that the pursuit by individuals and groups of their private interests does not always or necessarily lead to the realisation of the good of the whole—central to the thinking of public choice theorists. The universality of collective action dilemmas suggests that, in the minds of many public choice theorists and other analysts borrowing from this tradition, like Wade and Haggard, democracy may nowhere be considered a suitable form of government. To my mind, this is a sign for hope rather than despair. For the fact of the matter is that, despite collective action problems, democratic institutions have worked fairly well in most of the industrialised economies of the West for decades, in some cases centuries.

This brief excursus into theory has been designed to counter the mainstream scholarly view that authoritarianism or insulation is a prerequisite for growth, and to replace the conceptual framework of collective action dilemmas that undergirds it with a scheme that will enable us to look more directly at the variables involved. Within this context, how can a democratic government be created that does not threaten either continued rapid economic growth or national unity?

In this chapter I will focus on two major obstacles to successful democratisation of this kind: the nature of politically mobilisable cleavages in Indonesian society and the resource gap between pro- and anti-democratic forces, the latter primarily in the military. I will then offer a distinction, borrowed from the Italian political scientist Giovanni Sartori, between centrifugal and centripetal party systems, and propose that construction of the latter is a *sine qua non* of an Indonesian democracy that does not undermine unity or diminish growth.

In the final section I will discuss a recent statement by Sarwono Kusumaatmadja, a leader of a faction within the state political party Golkar (*Golongan Karya*, Functional Groups) that has long appeared to be genuinely committed to eventual democratisation. My purpose is to begin a debate as to the value of Sarwono's strategy of reform for creating a centripetal party system and thus overcoming the two major obstacles to democratisation.

Groups and the Politics of Growth and Unity in a Democratic Indonesia

In this section I want to single out some key groups in Indonesian society that are potential supporters of democratisation and that might be brought into a new pro-growth, pro-national unity coalition or political formula. I will begin with economic interests, and then discuss ethnic/regional and religious groups.

Domestic and foreign professional economists, no matter how sympathetic personally they may be to democracy, appear to be at one in the view that Indonesia needs to be ruled by an authoritarian government for some time into the future.[4] They believe that to maintain rapid growth the government must continue to pursue an export-led growth strategy, and that the social forces in favor of such a strategy are much less powerful than those in opposition. The latter are said to include both the big conglomerates, most of whose profits still come from sales to domestic markets, and smaller entrepreneurs, who chafe under the restrictions imposed on them by high interest rates and other policies of the economists.

I have several rejoinders to this standard argument. First, there is today something approaching a Third World-wide, certainly an East Asia-wide, consensus on the preferability of the export manufacturing route to development. This consensus is backed up by the ability of the World Bank, the International Monetary Fund, and the Consultative Group on Indonesia to give or deny financial assistance depending on their evaluation of the Indonesian government's policies.

This situation differs considerably from the 1950s, when import substitution policies were advocated by many development economists as the best way to break the vicious circle of underdevelopment. It even differs from the mid-1960s, when it took great courage for General Suharto to adopt the policies of the economists. The current consensus and the World Bank/IMF/CGI institutional backup are powerful resources that can be used to build a winning coalition by either an authoritarian or a democratic politician. Conversely, they make it harder for a politician, again either authoritarian or democratic, to win support by challenging the consensus.

Second, Sino-Indonesians still constitute the large majority of successful business people. If Indonesia becomes a democracy, their way of articulating their political interests is not likely to change very much, at least in the short run. That is, they will still seek a personal relationship with high officials and to a lesser extent work through the business associations described so well by Andrew MacIntyre.[5] They will not form political parties of their own, both because they are suspect as insufficiently Indonesian, and therefore prefer a more private political style, and because political parties led by a 4% racial minority could not hope to attract enough support from the 96% majority to win many parliamentary seats. My point is this: if Sino-Indonesian influence in the New Order is not great enough to overcome the economists' control of macroeconomic policy, it is not likely to do so in a democratic regime either.

Third, fear of capital flight will be just as strong in the minds of the leaders of a democratic Indonesia as it has been to New Order authoritarians. If a new government lowers interest rates substantially, or in other ways destabilises or threatens the business climate, the resulting capital flight to Singapore, Hong Kong, and elsewhere will choke off investment and continued growth, and generate its own political backlash from a range of domestic interests.

Fourth, there is probably a growing number of groups that benefit from deregulation and export-led growth policies and that would therefore constitute a support base for a new democratic government adhering to these policies. Obviously, this base would include all those manufacturers who now export a large percentage of their production, the companies that have made the recent export boom possible. Many of the conglomerates, which contain both export- and import substitution-oriented divisions, are if not pro-export, at least in conflict (and thus politically immobilised or indecisive) on this issue.

The pro-export, pro-democracy base might be much wider than this. It might also include the millions of small farmers who have gained economically from the rice and rural development policies of the past quarter century and who increasingly deposit their savings in the rural banking system.[6] Small-town entrepreneurs may prefer lower interest rates so that they can expand their businesses, and would also probably not mind a mild debt-eroding inflation. But they would be opposed by anti-inflationary, pro-high interest rate savers, who might well be much more numerous today. Organised urban labour—that is, autonomously-formed labour unions replacing the current state corporatist SPSI (*Serikat Pekerja Seluruh Indonesia*, All Indonesian Workers Union)—might also be attracted to this coalition, if it could be demonstrated to union leaders that manufacturing employment in the present and future is dependent on the continued growth of export markets.

Finally, both Ruth McVey and Richard Robison see an increasing regularisation of the Indonesian political process, in terms of the government's relationship with the business community, that may be a first step toward democratisation. McVey writes that 'Increasingly, what determines Southeast Asian policy-makers' strategic decisions will be the interplay of complex interests—bureaucratic, political, and business, national and regional—which will be expressed more and more through agencies, associations, and lobbies rather than through the dyadic relationships of patron-client networks.'[7] Arguably, these relationships are more easily conducted in a Western-style (bourgeois, if you will) democratic political system than in a continuation of the New Order's patrimonial authoritarianism. Robison's analysis focuses more narrowly on the growth of the state, but also stresses a regularisation that includes strengthening the rule of law.[8]

The continuing threat by ethnic/regional and religious groups to national unity is one of the principal New Order justifications for authoritarianism. In a democratic Indonesia, would there be a significantly increased opposition either to the boundaries or to the religious pluralism of the Indonesian nation-state? Alternatively, what regional and religious groups might become major supporters of a democratic regime? One near-certainty is that East Timor, forcibly incorporated in 1975–76, would not long be part of a democratic Indonesia.[9] Irian Jaya, whose modern history sets it apart from the rest of the country, might also see a resurgence of nationalist activity. Aceh, despite recent disturbances, is not a likely candidate for independence. Unlike the people of East Timor or Irian, the Acehnese did participate in the Indonesian nationalist movement. The memory of and pride in that participation remains strong, and there is today a modern, schooled elite solidly rooted in Acehnese culture and society and at the same time fully committed to the Indonesian nation-state. There are also many economic links that bind Aceh to the rest of Indonesia.

Beyond these three regions, separatism is not likely to be an issue at all. The ties of Indonesian nationalism, rooted in the movement and revolutionary years, appear to remain strong. They have been fortified for the elite and for an increasingly educated citizenry by common experiences in school, the spread and growth of modern *bahasa Indonesia* and the all-Indonesia culture whose values and struggles that language expresses and shapes, and by a pervasive political-economic network of institutions.

What is likely to be an issue is decentralisation. While few groups in the regions appear to have any thoughts of seceding, many would like to have a greater devolution of governmental power from the centre to the provinces. This is particularly true for business groups, whose members resent, for example, the restrictions imposed by the centre on exporting directly to foreign buyers (or importing from foreign sellers) instead of having to go through Jakarta or a major regional port like Medan, Surabaya, or Ujung Pandang. More generally, there is a close association between democracy and provincial autonomy in the minds of many members of the politically active or would-be active public who live in the regions.

Finally, there is the question of religious cleavages, and particularly of a politically resurgent Islam. Would Islamic groups in a democratic Indonesia constitute a threat to the maintenance of a religiously plural state? In the last two years much attention has been focused on the formation and activities of ICMI (*Ikatan Cendekiawan Muslim se-Indonesia*, Indonesian Muslim Intellectuals Association) and the opposition to ICMI which has taken shape in Abdurrahman Wahid's *Forum Demokrasi* (Democratic Forum).

My view is that Islamic groups will not constitute a threat as long as they organise as interest groups only. Muslim political parties, however, are likely to be politically destabilising if not genuinely threatening to religious pluralism.

From one perspective, the political calculations of President Suharto, who blessed its creation and anointed its patron, Minister of Research and Technology B.J. Habibie, ICMI is a limited purpose, probably short-term tactical political instrument. It is quite possible, even likely, that both Suharto and Habibie will lose interest in it in the near future.

Muslims outside the government who have joined ICMI appear to have a stronger commitment. They can perhaps be clustered into three groups: clients, with an Islamic (*santri*) social background but without an Islamic agenda, seeking patrons in standard New Order fashion; *santri* social activists who see ICMI as an opportunity to advance an egalitarian agenda; and religious activists who see an opportunity to make Indonesia more Islamic, particularly but not entirely in the formal sense of greater conformity to the symbols of religious observance. Among the latter group there has been much talk about the possibility that ICMI might be the embryo of a new Masyumi in a democratic Indonesia.[10]

The most important Islamic social and political leader who has not joined ICMI is Abdurrahman Wahid, since 1984 the head of *Nahdlatul Ulama* (NU), Indonesia's largest Islamic social and educational organisation, with a claimed membership of over thirty million. Abdurrahman is a social democrat who envisions a democratic Indonesia without religious parties. For that reason he pulled NU out of the Islamic political party PPP (*Partai Persatuan Pembangunan*, Development Unity Party) in 1984. Abdurrahman condemns ICMI as sectarian, as a step backwards toward political divisions based on religion. He believes that it increases the fear of Islam among others.[11] His own *Forum Demokrasi* includes many non-*santri* and non-Muslims.

Is Abdurrahman right? Would a new Masyumi—that is, an Islamic political party competing with non-Islamic parties in genuinely free elections—have a destabilising effect? My own answer is yes, though there are strong arguments on both sides.

Those in favor of an Islamic party (or parties, for surely there would be more than one) say that Indonesians are all now Pancasilaists. They claim that there is no longer a significant group of Muslim political activists or potential activists who favor an Islamic State, as that term was used in the 1950s. Some, indeed, argue that the Islamic State concept was itself never very clear or deeply held in the minds of its protagonists. They assert that a new Masyumi would be like the Christian democratic parties of Europe, a vehicle more of modern middle class than of traditional religious interests.

They also contend that there is a secular trend toward *santrinisasi* or Islamisation, so that the old *abangan-santri* polarisation has lost much of its meaning. And they conclude with the clincher that an Islamic party or parties is what most Muslims want. The issue is therefore not whether there will be Islamic parties in a democratic Indonesia but rather how many there will be, what objectives they will have, how big a share of the vote they will get, and so on.

My sense that Muslim parties are a bad idea is based on two considerations, one elite and near-term, the other mass and long-term. First, demands for an Islamic party made at the time of a democratic transition are bound to be opposed by most army officers, who have been carefully recruited from non-*santri* backgrounds and/or socialised into anti-Islamic State military ideology. Second, Islamic parties will inevitably have a polarising effect at the mass level. This is already apparent in the nervousness of non-Islamic groups concerning ICMI.[12] There is a large constituency potentially mobilisable on issues suspiciously close to the old Islamic State idea. The enormous success of ostensibly apolitical *muballigh* (preachers) like Zainuddin M.Z. is a sign of a popular hunger for guidance in personal life that may be put to political use. During election campaigns there is bound to develop a process of outbidding for the *santri* vote between Islamic and non-religious parties and among competing Islamic parties in which the rhetoric can easily become inflammatory.

On the other hand, persuading Muslims not to form parties in a democratic Indonesia does not mean keeping them out of politics. Like all other groups, Muslims have interests which require channels for articulation to government decision-makers. But these views can be effectively represented by organisations like *Nahdlatul Ulama*, the modernist Islamic social and educational organisation *Muhammadiyah*, and even the currently excessively timorous *Majelis Ulama Indonesia* (the state-created Council of Indonesian Muslim Religious Teachers) without touching the large and dangerous questions to which partisan battles often lead.

Confronting Leviathan

In the previous sections I have argued that despite a scholarly consensus to the contrary, democracy, growth, and unity in countries like Indonesia are probably in principle compatible. I have also tried to show that many groups now exist that might be brought into a pro-growth, pro-unity democratic coalition. There is, however, a Brobdingnagian political force that stands in their way: ABRI, the Armed Forces of the Republic of Indonesia. What are the characteristics and resources of this leviathan, and how might it be induced to withdraw from politics?

Juan Linz and Alfred Stepan propose a useful distinction between hierarchical and non-hierarchical military-based non-democratic regimes.[13] In hierarchical regimes, the military acts politically as an institution under its commanding officers, while non-hierarchical regimes are led by lower-ranking officers who have come to power through coups against their seniors.

In a hierarchical regime, 'the officer corps, taken as a whole, sees itself as a permanent part of the state apparatus, with enduring interests and permanent functions that transcend the interests of the government of the day.' Linz and Stepan draw two important implications from this situation. First, democratic transition may be made easier by the organisational needs of the military, as articulated by its top leaders. Second, however, a hierarchical military poses serious obstacles to the consolidation of a democratic regime, after the transition has taken place. 'Precisely because the military . . . is a permanent part of the state apparatus, and as such has privileged access to coercive resources, it will be an integral part of the machinery that the new democratic government has to manage.'

The New Order is a hierarchically-led military regime in two somewhat different and potentially conflicting senses. First, in a broad sense it is led by Suharto, a general who became *de facto* army commander on 1 October 1965 by virtue of his official position in command of strategic troops and the strong support of his fellow officers, but who has long since retired and is now Commander-in-Chief only *ex officio* as President. Second, ABRI is currently led by officers—the Commander, the Army Chief of Staff, and so on down—appointed by a hierarchical process controlled by seniors. At the top of this hierarchy is of course the President, who directly chooses the Commander and other top officers and who also has final say over virtually all armed forces appointments and promotions of any importance.

What makes this arrangement a potential source of conflict is that two institutional (plus of course many personal) interests are at work: the interest of the presidency and the interest of the armed forces, both of which are seen by incumbents in terms of autonomy from and control over other institutions. Since about 1987 there has been in fact a growing gap between the two institutions. The principal reasons for this are Suharto's advancing age and apparent desire to stay in office until he dies, coupled with armed forces concern to retain control over the presidency and the political system in general in the post-Suharto period. I will pursue the implications of this point below.

What are the political resources with which ABRI has gained and maintained its present dominance over other state institutions and over society? Coercion does not exist in a vacuum. It requires unity within the coercing organisation, in particular a willingness all the way down the line to obey the leadership hierarchy. In the New Order, this obedience has been achieved through a combination of persuasion and exchange.

Persuasion means the promotion of the idea of a moral order within ABRI, emphasising ideals of nationalism, discipline, service, self-sacrifice, and so on, which justify the institution's internal decision processes and also its relationship to the larger society. Exchange means appropriating material and status resources—business opportunities, governmental positions—from society and using them to secure the support of subordinates.

President Suharto and senior ABRI officers have been expert persuaders and exchangers. For the most part, as I have already indicated, the two groups have worked in tandem throughout the New Order to achieve these results. It is probably true, however, that material resources have over time come more and more under the control of the president at the expense of the armed forces.

Effective use of coercion requires organisational networks for intelligence gathering and political supervision. Since the late 1950s ABRI has built four extensive armed forces-society networks: the territorial command system; the appointment of officers to positions within the civilian bureaucracy; appointed membership in the MPR, DPR, and DPRD at the provincial and district levels; and leadership in Golkar by retired officers.

ABRI's relationship with the larger society has not, however, been based entirely on its monopoly over the means of violence, its ability to extract resources from society for internal military consumption, and its surveillance and supervisory capacities. Processes of exchange and persuasion have been at work in other ways as well.

Most armed forces-society exchange has been economic, trading delivery of economic goods and services to many large and politically important civilian groups in return for acceptance of military rule. This practice has motivated the military, under Suharto's leadership, to build an alliance with the professional economists and the civilian bureaucracy. The economists provide the knowledge and skills to make economic growth happen, in return for which they are rewarded with high government positions, respect for their service to the nation, and business opportunities. The bureaucrats provide the organisation and personpower to implement development policies and programs, and they receive similar rewards. In the larger society outside the state, exchange has also probably—without opinion polls or open politics it is impossible to have more than an impression—gone a long way toward persuading people to accept military rule.

What counter forces might induce such a powerful and successful political organisation to withdraw from the political arena?[14] That is indeed a very large question, to which I can sketch only a partial and unsatisfactory answer. A number of forces are now at work that lessen the future tenability of authoritarian rule. These include: the disappearance internationally of the threat of communism, which weakens ABRI's claim to be the chief defender against communism domestically; the growth internationally of pro-democratic forces; the emergence domestically of a network of pro-democratic non-governmental organisations; the absence of Islamic State fervour among members of the now large Muslim middle class; the rise of middle class, professional, and working class groups more generally; and the increasing competence of younger educated civilians to manage the economy, social organisations, and polity, in contrast to the narrower training and experience of their military opposite numbers, who are also many fewer in number.

In the shorter run, the greatest opportunity for reducing ABRI's political role, and perhaps for democratisation, will come with President Suharto's passing from the political scene. The armed forces' unity, internal and external exchange capacity, and especially legitimacy in the larger society are to a large extent the product of, derivative from, the leadership of Suharto. When ABRI is no longer led by Suharto, it will no longer possess these resources in the quantity or quality it does today.

Second, no other individual, military or civilian, possesses anything like Suharto's personal political resources as *Penyelamat Bangsa* (Savior of the Nation), *Bapak Pembangunan* (Father of Development), controller of vast wealth in private foundations, master of the central bureaucracy, skilful political tactician, and so on. Indonesia's third president will have to amass resources of his own, and his control over the armed forces is by no means certain. This situation creates the possibility for change.

Political Parties in a Democratic Indonesia

In the preceding section I have argued that ABRI controls Indonesian politics and government today. In a democratic Indonesia, this role will have to be assumed by a party system—one or more political parties—that represents and mobilises popular demands and support and also holds the offices in which government policy is made. Parties appear to be a *sine qua non* in modern nation-state democracies. So far, at least, no other organisation or institution has been able to fill their role as the critical link between state and society.[15]

How can the creation of a party system be accomplished in such a way as to maintain growth and unity and at the same time to successfully consolidate a democratic transition? Part of the answer, I believe, has to do with a deliberate effort on the part of democratisers to devise a party system with what Giovanni Sartori, analyzing the multi-party system of contemporary Italy in the European setting, has called a centripetal rather than a centrifugal tendency.

Indonesia in the 1950s did not have a large centre party, which Sartori saw as the cause of many of Italy's problems. What it did have was a multi-party system split along three axes—ethnicity/regionalism, religion, and social class—with marked centrifugal tendencies.[16] In the 1955 elections, the only time nationwide free elections have been held in Indonesia, four parties—the nationalist PNI, the modernist Muslim Masjumi, the traditionalist Muslim NU, and the communist PKI—divided almost evenly three-quarters of the total vote, with the remaining quarter fragmented among dozens of tiny parties and other electoral organisations. None of the four major parties had a strong commitment to democratic institutions, and there were deep differences among them as to how to achieve economic growth and national unity.

The centrifugality of the 1950s party system was manifested in the policy incoherence of multi-party coalition cabinets which tried to reconcile too many competing forces, the political instability of relatively rapid cabinet turnover, and the policy inconsistency from cabinet to cabinet. Partisan mobilisation of voters during the election campaign of 1955 and the regional elections of 1957 also led, according to Feith and other standard accounts, to a dangerous sharpening of the tensions among ethnic, religious, and class groups.

What would a party system with centripetal rather than centrifugal tendencies look like in a democratic Indonesia in the 1990s? One implication of Sartori's analysis—which contrasts the 'pathological' multi-party systems of contemporary Italy, Fourth Republic France, and the German Weimar Republic with the 'healthy' multi-party systems of contemporary Sweden, Norway, Denmark, and Switzerland—is that multi-party systems are not centrifugal *per se*. The issue is not the number of parties but whether the parties in the system, especially the major parties, incline toward common positions and compromise of differences or not.

In the 1950s on the religious issue there was polarisation between Masjumi-NU on one side (though NU never took the uncompromising stand that some Masjumi leaders did) and PNI-PKI on the other. On governmental decentralisation, and on many economic policy issues, Masjumi as the party of the Outer Islands was basically in opposition to the Java-based PNI-PKI-NU. On class issues, the lower class-oriented PKI confronted Masjumi-PNI-NU, defenders of several different upper class groups.

The issue today, of course, is not simply how to restructure or recombine the interests of the 1950s, but rather how to respond creatively to the current range of actual and potential, organised and unorganised, interest blocs in Indonesian society. Three possibilities are the East Asian one-party dominant model, the American two-party system, and the European multi-party system.

The East Asian solution, of which Japan is the exemplar but which also includes quasi-democratic Malaysia and democratising Taiwan and Korea, offers the stability and predictability of rule by a dominant party that can count on being returned to office repeatedly by a large majority of the electorate.[17] Comparison with Taiwan, where the KMT is converting itself from a military- and bureaucracy-backed instrument of authoritarian (even Leninist) mobilisation into a broadly-based party capable of genuine contestation, is perhaps most interesting for Indonesians. It suggests the possibility of a similar conversion for Golkar.

The American solution would envisage two major parties divided primarily by economic policy: one adhering more strictly to the kinds of policies followed by the professional economists today, the other to a social democratic or welfare-state set of policies promoting more egalitarian distribution of the benefits of development.[18] The advantage of this arrangement is that conflicts over other issues, particularly religious but also ethnic and regional disputes, would take place within the two major parties and thus not polarise parliamentary debate.

European-style multi-party politics is anathema to New Order officials, who see it as a return to the chaos of the 1950s, and is perhaps thus unlikely to be put into practice. Nevertheless, it might well be the 'natural' outcome of a genuine opening-up of the political process and for that reason would enjoy great popular legitimacy. To the extent that Indonesians really are now all Pancasilaists—that is, reject the Islamic State, communism, and separatism—it would also not be fissiparous in the manner of its 1950s avatar.

A fourth possible model is Thai democracy, also based on a multi-party system. Despite considerable political instability, Thai multi-partyism has not posed a threat either to national unity or to the maintenance of pro-market economic policies. Recent Thai history also suggests two ways to gradually remove the military from politics. One is to reserve an institution for officers—the Senate in Thailand, perhaps the MPR in Indonesia—and then to gradually limit the institution's power. A second is to allow retired officers to become leaders of political parties and members of parliament, where at least some of them are likely to develop an interest in the strength and autonomy of democratic institutions.[19]

Sarwono's Path to Democracy

As there may be many kinds of party system compatible with a pro-growth, pro-unity, consolidated Indonesian democracy, so there may be many possible paths to transition. In this concluding section I want to explore just one of these, the course recommended by Sarwono Kusumaatmadja, long term Golkar activist and currently Minister for Population and Environment, and his colleagues in the G stream in Golkar.[20]

In an interview in the business magazine *Eksekutif*,[21] Sarwono offered his own analysis of the changing character of Indonesian society and the implications of these changes for politics. According to Sarwono, the first quarter century of New Order development has produced a 'new strategic elite' in Indonesian society. This elite consists of four components: the business community, 'which is beginning to emerge politically in the broad sense: people who are able to influence the decision-making process, without having to become a member of a political party or Golkar'; professionals; 'leaders of social organisations (*ormas*) which are active and have a capacity to apply pressure'; and traditional leaders.

The three latter categories are not discussed further in the interview. By professionals Sarwono presumably means the doctors, lawyers, journalists, academics, and other highly educated Indonesians who dominate modern urban life. The social organisations are the non-governmental organisations or LSM (*Lembaga Swadaya Masyarakat*, Self-Reliant Community Development Institution) and LPSM (*Lembaga Pengembangan Swadaya Masyarakat*, Institution for Promoting Self-Reliant Community Development) that have become increasingly active in the past two decades in village-level development, environmental protection, consumer rights, human rights, publishing, and similar areas.

Traditional leaders are a seemingly strange category to be included as part of a 'new strategic elite'. Almost certainly Sarwono is thinking here both of the traditional rural Islamic leaders or *kiai* who frequently pronounce on matters of public importance, and also of the genuinely new phenomenon of Muslim preachers who regularly attract enormous urban audiences. These preachers, as I have said, are so far apolitical, but politicians like Sarwono must be fascinated by their ability to connect with the masses.

Sarwono's central assertion is that Golkar and the political parties must attract these new constituencies if they are to survive into the PJPT II (*Pembangunan Jangka Panjang Tahap II*, Long Term Development Phase II), the second quarter century of development in the government's current jargon. In Golkar's case, which is what Sarwono is primarily interested in, this means expanding beyond the military and bureaucratic streams that have been the backbone of the organisation since the late 1960s. He implies that all four of the new elite groups are potentially part of the Golkar family.

This political change is necessitated by the power of the new groups, which are already influential with government officials and are bound to become more so, especially if deregulation, debureaucratisation, and decentralisation continue. To Sarwono, the new groups do not need the parties so much as the parties need them. If Golkar and the parties do not take advantage of this opportunity and provide a channel for articulation of the new interests, they will become increasingly irrelevant to the political process.

Is this strategy a plausible route to pro-growth, pro-unity democratisation for Indonesia? I see four reasons why democratisers might want to join Sarwono's team, and one why they might not.

First, the strategy's gradualism and top-down quality provide for continuity in a leadership committed to both growth and unity. A major difficulty with more violent, mass-based, crisis-dependent strategies of democratisation is that the values and policies of the new leaders are harder to predict. There is also a higher probability that they will be tempted to rely in the struggle for power on simplistic populist or religious appeals. Once in power, if they deliver on their promises, they will undo the New Order's economic and social progress. If they do not deliver, they will delegitimise the new democratic institutions.

Second, military support for democratisation—a serious obstacle, I have indicated, given the current gap in resources between civilians and the military—might be easier to obtain if army officers have a place in the new system. They might in fact have two places: continuation of the ABRI stream in some form as a part of the Golkar structure from the centre to the districts; and an increased role for retired officers in the more powerful provincial governments that are certain to accompany democratisation. Third, many Muslim groups would be inside the tent, reducing the probability of religious polarisation in parliament. Golkar has in fact a long history of attempting to attract Muslim support.

Fourth, this path also lends itself to a transformation of state, or authoritarian, corporatism into societal, or democratic, corporatism.[22] State corporatism, domination by state officials of the leadership selection and policies of private interest organisations, has been one of the means by which the New Order government has tightened its grip over business, labour, professionals, religious people, students, youth, women, and many other groups. In societal corporatism, on the other hand, interest organisations enter freely into a privileged relationship with the state, trading some autonomy and freedom to challenge state policies for increased access.

Both Stephan Haggard and Robert Wade argue that state corporatism has been an important part of the East Asian development model, and that Korea and Taiwan are now moving in the direction of societal corporatism. Though Sarwono does not mention labour as a new strategic elite, there are several years of evidence, in the form of wildcat strikes and illegal unions, of increasing labour pressure on business, and of the failure of the government's state corporatist strategy to contain this pressure. Indonesia has not yet reached the income level of either Korea or Taiwan. A change in policy from state to societal corporatism may therefore be premature, but it is certainly a possibility in the medium term. A one-party dominant Golkar in a democratic Indonesia might also see the electoral advantage in doing so.

Finally, there are good grounds for skepticism about the Sarwono strategy. Perhaps the most important, to return to Juan Linz and Alfred Stepan, is the nature of the deal that would have to be struck with ABRI in return for any transfer of authority to a democratic government. At some point, Linz and Stepan argue, so many concessions are made to the military during the transition process that democratisation becomes meaningless.

The most powerful military regimes, they say, are led by unified hierarchical armed forces in societies where pro-democratic groups have few political resources. This description sounds very much like Indonesia today. Is it possible to imagine ABRI in this decade willing to give up, to any form of civilian governmental leadership, one or more of the following: autonomy of the Ministry of Defense and Security; the territorial command structure; the quota of appointed members in the MPR and DPR; final-say influence in Golkar; or access to major sources of patronage and position?

If it is not possible, Sarwono's strategy is unlikely to succeed, and we are back to square one. Are there other alternatives for pro-growth, pro-unity democratisers who recognise the tenacity of anti-democratic forces and understand the need for a strong party system?

1. Robert Wade, *Governing the Market*, Princeton: Princeton University Press, 1990.
2. Stephan Haggard, *Pathways From the Periphery*, Ithaca: Cornell University Press, 1990.
3. Edward W. Lehman, 'Toward a Macrosociology of Power,' *American Sociological Review*, 34 (4), August 1969, pp. 453–65.
4. See for example C. Peter Timmer, 'The Political Economy of Rapid Growth: Indonesia's New Development Model,' paper prepared for delivery at the sixteenth graduation ceremony for IPMI (*Institut Pengembangan Manajemen Indonesia*) graduates in business management, December 21, 1992, esp. p. 12.
5. Andrew MacIntyre, *Business and Politics in Indonesia*, Sydney: Allen and Unwin, 1991.
6. See Claudio Gonzalez-Vega and Rodrigo A. Chaves, *Indonesia's Rural Financial Markets*, Columbus: Rural Finance Program, Department of Agricultural Economics and Rural Sociology, The Ohio State University, 1992.
7. Richard Robison, 'The Materialization of the Southeast Asian Entrepreneur,' in McVey ed., *Southeast Asian Capitalists*, Ithaca: Cornell University Southeast Asia Program, 1992, p. 32.
8. 'Industrialization and the Economic and Political Development of Capital: the Case of Indonesia,' in McVey, ed., *Southeast Asian Capitalists*, pp. 65–88.
9. For a discussion, see R William Liddle, 'Indonesia's Threefold Crisis,' *Journal of Democracy* 3, 4 (October 1992), pp. 61–74, reprinted as Chapter Seven in this volume.
10. This idea is also very popular among small town Muslims in east and central Java. Field notes from a trip from Yogyakarta to Surabaya, November 1990.
11. See the long interview, 'Abdurrahman Wahid: Saya Presiden Taxi saja deh' [Abdurrahman Wahid: I'll just be President Taxi], *Detik* No. 563, 2 November 1992, pp. 4–8. It should be noted that many Indonesian observers, not all of whom have an axe to grind, accuse Abdurrahman of acting more out of personal than social motives. He is said to be angry because on a number of occasions he was not invited to join new Islamic organisations and initiatives. And he is said to believe that this exclusion is reminiscent of the condescending way in which Masjumi leaders treated NU leaders in the 1950s.
12. In his *Detik* interview, p. 7, Abdurrahman Wahid says: 'Teman saya itu

macam-macam, ada yang sosialis, nasionalis, atau campuran kedua-duanya, kaki lima, pencakar langit, abangan dan lainnya. Semuanya pada ketakutan. Prihatin semua. Sampai yang konghucu ribut. Bayangkan saja konghucu itu kan tidak pernah tersentuh apa-apa sejak dulu sekarang bingung.' [My friends are of many kinds, some are socialists, nationalists, or a mix of the two, street peddlers, skyscrapers, non-devout Muslims and others. All are scared. They're all anxious. Even the Confucians are making a fuss. Just imagine, the Confucians who have never been touched by anything now are upset.]

13. *Democratic Transitions and Consolidation: Eastern Europe, Southern Europe, and Latin America*, New Haven: Yale University Press, forthcoming, ms. pp. 42-45.

14. In case it needs to be said, the current army leaders have no intention of stepping aside voluntarily. See for example the views of then ABRI Commander, now Vice President, Gen. Try Sutrisno in 'Pangab: Komunis Generasi IV Manfaatkan Isu Hak Asasi Manusia dan Demokratisasi' [Armed Forces Commander: Fourth Generation Communists are Making Use of the Human Rights and Democratization Issues], *Kompas*, 17 November 1992, p. 1, and of then Minister of Defence and Security, now private citizen, Gen. (ret.) L.B. Moerdani in 'Harus Dilawan, Campur Tangan Asing yang Mendorong Gerakan Separatisme' [It Must be Opposed, the Foreign Intervention that Supports Separatist Movements], *Kompas*, 26 November 1992, p. 1.

15. The classic statement of this position is Samuel Huntington, *Political Order in Changing Societies*, New Haven: Yale University Press, 1968, Ch. 7.

16. See Herbert Feith, *The Decline of Constitutional Democracy in Indonesia*, Ithaca: Cornell University Press, 1962. The best study of the 1955 elections is Herbert Feith, *The Indonesian Elections of 1955*, Ithaca: Cornell University Modern Indonesia Project, 1957.

17. On one-party democracies in general, see T.J. Pempel, ed., *Uncommon Democracies: The One-Party Dominant Regimes*, Ithaca: Cornell University Press, 1990.

18. Possible names for these parties are Partai Rakyat Merdeka or PRM (Free People's Party) for the pro-free market party and Partai Rakyat Progresif or PRP (Progressive People's Party) for the welfarist party. For a discussion, see my 'Merekayasa Demokrasi di Indonesia,' in R. William Liddle, *Pemilu-Pemilu Orde Baru: Pasang Surut Kekuasaan Politik*, Jakarta: LP3ES, 1992, pp. 142–53.

19. On this point, see the intriguing analysis of regional 'mafias' led by retired military officers in Indonesia in 'Current Data on the Indonesian Military Elite: July 1, 1989–January 1, 1992,' *Indonesia* No. 53, April 1992, p. 98. To the editors of *Indonesia*, this is a negative development. But it is at least possible that this group, well connected both regionally and nationally, can play a bridging role in a democratic Indonesia. See also Burhan Magenda, *East Kalimantan: The Decline of a Commercial Aristocracy*, Ithaca: Cornell University Modern Indonesia Project, 1991.

20. Journalistic accounts of the decision process within Golkar describe three *jalur* or streams: A for ABRI, B for the civilian bureaucracy, and G for Golkar. G is really a residual category for those party officials who do not directly represent the interests of either A stream (as articulated by the

Commander of the Armed Forces) or B stream (the Minister of Home Affairs). Professional politicians who have made a career in Golkar, like Sarwono, are one important element in the G category.

21. 'Jangan Mengandalkan Aliansi Lama' [Don't Depend on Old Alliances], *Eksekutif*, August 1992, pp. 45–46.

22. The terms are from Philippe Schmitter, 'Still the Century of Corporatism?', *Review of Politics* 85, January 1974, pp. 85–131.

10

Media Dakwah Scripturalism: One Form of Islamic Political Thought and Action in New Order Indonesia*

> Idealism and materialism are dichotomies as abstract concepts, but in everyday life they are facets of the same transaction. Every sign exercises its effect because of the specific context of privilege, disadvantage, frustration, aspiration, hope, and fear in which it is experienced.[1]

I

The convenors of this conference have asked the participants to reflect on opposing scholarly conclusions about Indonesian Islam. The pessimistic view of Clifford Geertz in 1967 that 'scripturalism seems likely to remain in the position of cheering on a modernism whose every advance undermines its own position' is contrasted with the optimistic reading in 1978 of Fazlur Rahman that recent 'feverish educational and intellectual activity ... appears to be heading in the right direction' toward 'a meaningful indigenous Islamic tradition that will be genuinely Islamic and creative.'[2]

In this exchange, Rahman enjoys something of an unfair advantage, for the activity he is praising only began in the late 1960s, at the beginning of the current New Order period in Indonesian state organisation. Geertz has not subsequently written directly about this new trend, although he has reassessed the *santri-abangan* dichotomy in his 1950s east Java field site, Pare, in a 1990 article that seems to confirm his earlier pessimism.[3]

As an observer of the national-level Indonesian intellectual and political

* First published in James Rush and Mark Woodward, *Intellectual Development in Indonesian Islam*, Tempe: Arizona State University Center of Southeast Asian Studies, 1995.

scene from the 1960s to the present, I am more optimistic than Geertz though perhaps not so sanguine as Rahman. This has undoubtedly been a period of great creativity in modernist Indonesian Islam, marked by the emergence of a group of anti- or perhaps a-scripturalist thinkers whom we might call, for lack of a better term, substantialists.[4] Moreover, the new thinkers' ideas unquestionably hold out considerable promise for the revitalisation of the *umat* (Islamic community), a resolution of the decades-long tension over the relationship between Islam and the state, and more mutually tolerant relations with Christians and other non-Muslims. Finally, these ideas have been repeatedly and widely disseminated in the most highly respected national news media, which has certainly helped to make them more influential both within and outside the Indonesian Islamic community.

My optimism is tempered, however, by recognition of the social, economic, and above all political context in which the creativity of the substantialists has taken place. For there is no doubt that they have benefited from that context, and in many instances even consciously used it to strengthen their position. It is also clear that the playing field has been deliberately tilted against other Islamic thinkers and activists, particularly the scripturalists about whom Geertz was so concerned.

This is not to argue that the New Order has been a direct cause of the new creativity in Islamic thought or even that it established the necessary conditions for it. Social life is rarely so simple, and I am sure that in this case a number of other factors are involved as well. But recognition of the presence of the New Order context sensitises us to the possibility that in the post-New Order period this context may change and with it the pattern of incentives and constraints—'the specific context of privilege, disadvantage, frustration, aspiration, hope, and fear'—for different kinds of Islamic thinkers and their audiences.

I shall explore this possibility by discussing three aspects of the problem, after briefly limning the ideas of the substantialists. My first task is to throw some light on scripturalist thought today, a subject that most observers, fascinated by the new thinkers, tend to ignore. Second, I want to describe some of the principal features of the New Order economic, social, and political context, as it has impinged upon Islamic thought and action, during the past quarter century. And finally, I want to speculate about current and possible future changes in context that might tilt the playing field back toward the scripturalists.

II

The views of the substantialists are relatively well publicised within and outside Indonesia, and I will treat them only summarily here.[5] Four key interrelated ideas stand out.

The first and most basic is that the substance or content of belief and practice is more important than the form. Literal adherence to Quranic injunctions, even to such fundamentals as saying the five daily prayers, is less positively valued than behaving morally and ethically in accordance with the spirit of the Qur'an. An outwardly pious Islamic employer who treats his employees unjustly is less praiseworthy than a non-pious or even non-Muslim boss who pays high wages and provides good working conditions.

Second, the message of the Qur'an and Hadits (statements of the Prophet), while timeless in its essence and universal in its meaning, nonetheless needs to be reinterpreted (*ditafsirkan kembali*) by each succeeding generation of Muslims in the light of the social conditions prevailing in their time. The developing world or Third World of today is economically, politically, culturally, and socially a vastly different place from the Arabia of Muhammad's time. Again, literal understanding of the meaning of the Qur'an, or uncritical acceptance of even the most established Hadits or legal principle derived from one of the traditional legal schools (*mazhab*), must give way to modern understanding. Substantialists have deployed a number of terms to describe their application of this concept to late twentieth century Indonesian Islam: *sekularisasi* (secularisation), *desakralisasi* (desacralisation), *reaktualisasi* (reactualisation), and *pribumisasi* (indigenisation).

Third, because it is ultimately impossible for any mere human being to be certain that he or she understands the will and commands of God better than any other person, Muslims must be tolerant toward each other and toward non-Muslims. Some substantialists have accordingly begun to reexamine classical Islamic thought, Shi'ism, and other Islamic traditions outside modernism, while others have attempted to develop and institutionalise a dialogue with Christians.

Finally, substantialist Muslims accept the current structure of government as the final form of the Indonesian state. In particular, the Constitution of 1945, in force originally from 1945 to 1949 and reinstated in 1959, and the pan-religious state ideology of Pancasila, comprising 'Belief in the One and Only God, Just and Civilised Humanity, the Unity of Indonesia, Democracy Guided by Inner Wisdom in Unanimity Arising out of Deliberation among Representatives, and Social Justice for all the People of Indonesia'[6] are said to conform to Islamic political principle.

Briefly, the argument is: the Qur'an does not describe or even mention an 'Islamic State' (*Negara Islam*); the *syari'ah* (Islamic law, considered by scripturalists to be the legal foundation for an Islamic State) can not be turned into positive law; any Indonesian constitution must accept the full legal and political rights of non-Muslims (in this respect the Constitution of 1945 is similar to the Constitution of Madinah); and several Islamic principles, including the most basic of all, *tauhid*, the oneness of God, are incorporated in both Pancasila and the 1945 Constitution. This defense does not necessarily imply political or social conservatism. Many substantialists are in fact critical of the current New Order government on what they consider to be properly Islamic, as well as Indonesian, grounds. Some fault the government for its authoritarian interpretation of Pancasila and the 1945 constitution and call for more genuinely democratic representative institutions. Others contend that the government is not seriously committed to implementing the Social Justice principle.

The paradigmatic statement of the substantialist position is Nurcholish Madjid's 1970 speech, 'The Necessity for Renewal of Islamic Thinking and the Problem of the Integration of the Islamic Community'.[7] Nurcholish was national chair of the Islamic University Students' Association (HMI, *Himpunan Mahasiswa Indonesia*) from 1966 to 1971, a time of great political and intellectual upheaval at the beginning of the New Order. In 1978 he went to the University of Chicago, where he earned a Ph.D. in 1984 under the supervision of Fazlur Rahman.

Today Nurcholish is a Senior Researcher at LIPI, the Indonesian Institute of Sciences, and a Professor at the State Islamic Studies Institute (*Institut Agama Islam Negeri*) in Jakarta. He is also the founder and head of the private Paramadina Foundation, which conducts religious discussions and in other ways ministers to the spiritual and ethical needs of affluent middle and upper class Muslims.[8] He now calls himself a 'pluralist' or 'inclusivist'.[9]

Nurcholish's interests are broadly theological and social in the sense that he is trying to rethink his own beliefs and practices and their relationship to social issues and to encourage his fellow Muslims to do the same. Other prominent substantialists have different interests. For example, Dawam Rahardjo, publisher of the quarterly journal *Ulumul Qur'an*, has worked for many years to help the traditional Islamic village schools called *pesantren* to broaden their curriculum. He is also a social egalitarian and promoter of Latin American *dependencia* and German critical theory. Abdurrahman Wahid is the leader of the non-modernist Nahdlatul Ulama, Indonesia's largest Islamic social and educational organisation, but he is nonetheless an important substantialist figure. Abdurrahman shares Dawam's egalitarian and *pesantren* concerns and is also a powerful voice for democratisation along Western-style representative lines.

III

The scripturalists I shall discuss are those who write for *Media Dakwah* (Preaching Medium) or *MD*, the monthly magazine of the Dewan Dakwah (Preaching Council). The Dewan Dakwah is a Jakarta-based national private organisation, founded in 1967, of religious teachers and officials (*ulama dan zuama*) which sends Islamic preachers (*da'i*) to remote parts of

Indonesia, helps to build mosques, and so on. *MD* is the best-known, and among the most widely-read of the scripturalist publications.[10] It is indeed notorious for its attacks on the substantialists, and is among the most extreme or militant scripturalist organs tolerated by the government.[11]

Both the Dewan Dakwah and *MD* have long been considered to reflect the outlook of Mohammad Natsir, the most prominent Indonesian modernist Muslim intellectual and politician in the twentieth century. In the colonial period Natsir engaged in a famous debate about the relationship between religion and the state with the secular (or syncretist) nationalist leader Sukarno. In the parliamentary period of the early 1950s he was a leader of Masjumi, Indonesia's largest Islamic party at the time, and served for several months as Prime Minister. In the late 1950s he supported a Sumatra-based rebellion against the central government, for which he was arrested and imprisoned until 1966. After an aborted attempt to form a new Muslim party in the late 1960s, his activism was largely restricted to the Dewan Dakwah, and to participation in Islamic organisations outside Indonesia.

Natsir died in early 1993, and had not been directly involved in the editing of *MD* for several years.[12] I emphasise his connection to help the reader locate the magazine in its proper historical, political, and theological context, and not to hold him personally responsible for the specific positions its editors take today.

The contrast between the scripturalists and the substantialists, as displayed in the pages of *MD*, is striking. The main difference is that the scripturalists do not see themselves as engaged primarily in the intellectual activity of adapting the message of Muhammad and the meaning of Islam to the social conditions of the late 20th century. Rather, they believe that the message and meaning are for the most part clearly expressed in the Qur'an and Hadits and need only to be implemented conscientiously. They are thus very *syari'ah*-minded.[13]

The scripturalists are openly hostile to the substantialists, and particularly to Nurcholish Madjid, who comes in frequently for harsh criticism. In October, 1992, for example, in response to a flare-up of Muslim-Christian tension in East Java, Nurcholish spoke out against religious intolerance. 'The religion that is true,' he said, 'is *al-hanifiyyat al-samhah*—seeking truth that is broad-minded and tolerant, without fanaticism, and that doesn't shackle the soul.' Jews, Christians, and Muslims are all part of the 'religion of Abraham,' a continuity (*kesinambungan*) that Muslims have always understood better than others. Moreover, '*al-Islam* is in fact not [originally] the name of a religion, but of an attitude' of submission or surrender (*tunduk, pasrah*) to God which it shares with other religions.[14]

MD reacted to Nurcholish's speech with a cover story entitled 'Did the Prophet fail to Carry Out His Mission? (Examining the thought of Nurcholish).'[15] The story contains an editorial, an account of the speech, an overview of his ideas since the 1970s, a comparison of these ideas with those of the Theosophist Annie Besant (who was influential among some pre-World War II Indonesian intellectuals), and the comments of various prominent and not-so-prominent modernist Muslims. The editors accuse Nurcholish of abandoning all that is central to Islamic belief and practice: Qur'an, *sunnah* (the actions or tradition of the Prophet), and *syari'ah*. In its place he offers only a vague spiritualism, Theosophist-style. 'Nurcholish wants religion only up to the point of surrender, without *syari'ah.*'[16]

MD's critique of Nurcholish is especially interesting for the light shed on who its editors see as the enemies of Islam. Nurcholish himself is regarded as virtually an apostate—'in the end his thinking is outside Islam'[17]—and as an agent, conscious or unconscious, of: CSIS (Centre of Strategic and International Studies), a military-Sino-Indonesian-Catholic influenced think tank and political operations centre important at the beginning of the New Order; 'certain mass media,' a reference to the Javanese Catholic and Sino-Indonesian-run daily *Kompas* and the non-sectarian but Nurcholish-promoting weekly newsmagazine *Tempo*; 'Western imperialism'; and the 'Jewish lobby.'[18]

It is fair to say that the editors of *MD* are obsessed with the idea that Islam, as they understand it, is under siege. Occasionally they contend that Islam is on the rise, in Indonesia and elsewhere, in order to argue that others, non-Muslims and near-apostates like Nurcholish, must accommodate themselves to the new strength of Islam. But mostly they declaim against a long list of enemies.

Prominent on this list are Christians, both Protestants and Catholics.[19] They are seen as well-financed and determined proselytisers who take advantage of the poverty and weak faith of many Muslims, especially the *abangan* Javanese. President Suharto, who has in the last few years responded positively to many scripturalist demands (see my discussion below), is not faulted directly. Many of his policies, however, are condemned as anti-Islamic, including softness toward Christian proselytisation, the national lottery, the ban on Islamic parties,[20] economic policies that are seen as benefiting Sino-Indonesian entrepreneurs and government bureaucrats and hurting indigenous (mainly Muslim) Indonesians, and excessive openness to the West.[21]

The West, particularly the United States, is a target of heavy criticism.[22] Some of the animus has to do with economics, as the U.S. is seen as the major force behind World Bank and International Monetary Fund pressure that has led, in *MD*'s view, to a growing gap between rich and poor, particularly in Jakarta. Some of it is cultural, related to a fear of the attractiveness to many Indonesian Muslims of the secular and materialistic West where individuals have too much personal freedom, which they misuse at the expense of the interest of society as a whole. And some of it is world-political, centering on American support for Israel and opposition to Palestinian nationalism. Behind America's pro-Israel foreign policy are the Jews. 'The support of Clinton for the victory of Israel is a payment he is required to make because of the support of the Jewish lobby in the recent presidential election. As has become a tradition, an American president will not free himself from the Jewish network whose influence is very powerful in determining who is chosen to become the American president. It is said that one of the reasons why George Bush lost was because he neglected Jewish interests.'[23]

Jewish influence is also perceived to be an important factor within Indonesia, despite the fact that Indonesia has no permanently-resident Jewish community. In the cover story on Nurcholish, for example, it is claimed that 'as a practical matter there is nothing new in the thought of Nurcholish, because it has long been developed by the Jews in Indonesia.'[24] Other stories discuss the role of the Jewish community in Indonesia during Dutch colonial times, the Rotary Club (whose members in Indonesia are mostly Sino-Indonesian business people) as a Zionist organisation, the Protocols of Zion and the Jewish conspiracy to control the world, and Quranic commentary on Jews, 'the group that is most mentioned in the Qur'an, because of their behavior and attitude that frequently opposes and manipulates the teachings of God.'[25]

As a late twentieth century liberal American intellectual for whom anti-Semitism is indelibly associated with the Holocaust, I am appalled and offended by the treatment of Jews and Judaism by the editors of *MD*. My point in describing their views, however, is not to associate them with the deeds of the Nazis, which I am sure do not have the same significance for them that they have for me.

It is, rather, first, to portray accurately what I have found (so that others can make their own judgments), and second, to attempt to understand the cast of mind or mentality that it reflects. That mentality is insular, in the sense that 'we' Muslims are seen as a closed, sharply bounded group very distinct from 'they', the rest of the world. It is defensive, in that it regards the rest of the world as opposed to it. It is conspiratorial, in the sense that the non-Muslim world is believed to be organised against them under covert Jewish leadership. And it is naive, betraying a shallow and un-sophisticated understanding of the way in which the world, in fact, works.

The editors of *MD* are not totally absorbed with their enemies. They are also engaged in an effort to define and promote their own conception of what Muslims should believe, how they should practice their religion, and what the role of government and other social institutions should be in Islamic life. One recent concern, for example, is with the revitalisation of *zakat*, the religious tax required by the Qur'an but widely ignored by Indonesian Muslims.[26] Religious education is also a prominent theme, as is the role of women and the restoration of a more traditional or conservative family life.

The proper form of government for a majority Muslim society is a sensitive subject in Indonesia today, for reasons that I shall explain below. To the New Order political leaders, promotion of an Islamic State or any resemblance thereof is strictly taboo. At *MD*, however, the idea is alive and well, though treated with great circumspection. For example, the title of a recent cover story, 'Malaysia Negeri Islami,'[27] represents an attempt at promoting the concept while thrice distancing oneself from the forbidden label. The subject is ostensibly not Indonesia, but neighboring Malaysia. *Negeri* means country, not quite state (*negara*). And *Islami*, while very close in meaning to *Islam*, yet manages to sound softer, to say 'of Islam' rather than Islamic.

The substance of the piece reveals a country where 'the wings of the *syari'ah* are spread wide and firm in all fields of life.' Malaysia's *Bank Islam* (Islamic Bank) is praised as 'not just a symbol, because of the presence of hundreds of branches throughout the country.' The *Tabung Haji* (pilgrimage savings program) has 'triggered popular economic development.' The implicit contrasts are with Indonesia's own fledgling Islamic bank and pilgrimage program, which presumably have little economic impact. There is an International Islamic University, which establishes Malaysia as a Muslim country and 'develops the insights of Islamic science.'

Many Malaysian women, including most female civil servants, wear Islamic clothing (*busana Muslimah*). Signs and public notices are often written in Arabic script. The fasting month is everywhere scrupulously observed. The streets are clean, cars do not blow their horns, and people behave in a disciplined way, obeying 'laws and regulations from the simple to the serious.' Young couples do not hold hands in public, and convicted narcotics dealers are hanged. The story's editorial concludes: 'All of this shows how an Islamic society is able to establish social values that are orderly, disciplined, and civilised. Erased is the view that a Muslim nation is identical with dirtiness, ignorance, injustice, and so on. Islamic Malaysia answers all of this.'

The role of government in creating this exemplary Islamic society is central. 'The upholding of Islam by the Malaysian government is demonstrated in the form of positive laws that reinstate the principles of Islam.' There is a government department of religion, the 'Bahagian Hal Ehwal Islam, something like the Department of Religion in Indonesia, but that only serves and is at the same time responsible for the development of Islam. . . . [It] does not have directorates-general that serve the various religions that exist in Malaysia, as does the Department of Religion in Indonesia where there are directorates-general for Protestantism/Catholicism, Hinduism, Buddhism, and Islam itself.'

Fasting month observance is enforced by a special religious police, 'with heavy sanctions, that represent the legal product of a state modeled on (*mengacu pada*) *syari'ah Islam*.' The government censors anti-Islamic—Christian and secular—foreign and domestic films, television, and other cultural performances, and bans the private ownership of parabolic antennas.[28] It supports preaching activities. It invites foreign Islamic speakers regarded as too controversial by the Indonesian government. It also pays living wages to its employees so that they are not tempted by bribes to allow people to evade the law. Che Mat Che Ali, an Islamic Affairs official interviewed by *MD*, 'himself drives a Mercedes Benz every day.' In the private sector, the government's New Economic Policy has rapidly created a large Muslim Malay entrepreneurial class. Both the *Bank Islam* and the International Islamic University are state-funded.

Malaysia's foreign policy is also singled out for praise. The government is anti-Western, promoting for example the creation of an East Asian trading bloc as a counterweight to American economic power. It is consistently pro-Palestine, as evidenced by its strong criticism of Singapore's decision to open diplomatic relations with Israel. It tends to send its students abroad to schools in non-Western countries. It hosts international Islamic conferences, which appear 'like mushrooms in the rainy season,' not once in a great while as in Indonesia. Concrete financial assistance, not vague verbal support as in the Indonesian case, is given to the Burmese Muslim refugees in Bangladesh.

The image of Malaysia conveyed in the *MD* story is not entirely one-sided. At various points, there are hints that some Malaysian Muslims think that not enough is being done, that the ruling UMNO (United Malays National Organisation) is not as Islamic as the opposition PAS (Parti Islam Se-Malaysia, Pan-Malaysian Islamic Party), and that in some respects Indonesian society is more Islamic than Malaysian. But the general tone is that Indonesia is far from and Malaysia close to being a place where *ulama dan zuama*, religious teachers and state officials, are 'two sides in mutual support.' Finally, in what is perhaps both an excess of wishful thinking and a solid clue as to where the *MD* editors are looking for change in Indonesia, Malaysian Prime Minister Mahathir Mohamad is repeatedly praised for his combination of religious devotion and political brilliance.

IV

What is the societal context, the pattern of privilege and disadvantage, in which substantialist ideas have emerged and appear to a certain extent to have flourished while scripturalist ones have not? Simply put, the New Order government of President Suharto, in power since 1966, has created much of this context through both its direct and its indirect actions.

Directly, the government has consistently opposed all political expressions of scripturalism, in particular the Islamic State idea, and at the same time supported many of the activities of the substantialists. The reasons for this are rooted deep in the political history of independent Indonesia.

In the 1950s, when Indonesia was for several years a European-style parliamentary democracy, there was a great public debate between the proponents of an Islamic State and the defenders of a pan-religious (in some versions, secular) Pancasila State.[29] The modernist-led Masjumi party of Mohammad Natsir was the main protagonist of the Islamic State idea. During the same period there were also several regional rebellions, most of which were led by dissident army officers. Some of these used Islamic State symbols; others, like the Sumatran movement that Natsir joined, were non-Islamic in principle but led by well-known Masjumi politicians.

President Sukarno, Indonesia's foremost nationalist politician and its first president, ended the debate in 1959 by dismissing the Constituent Assembly, which had been popularly elected in 1955 to formulate a permanent constitution, and reinstating the revolutionary Constitution of 1945, which gives the president preponderant power over the legislature. He was able to do this because of the backing of the central army leadership, which he also used to put down the regional rebellions and to ban Masjumi.[30]

Since that time the leaders of the army have been implacably hostile to the idea of an Islamic State, and indeed to all but the most tightly controlled forms of Islamic participation in national political life. They have also been in favor of a strong central government, necessary in their view to combat the fissiparous tendencies of an ethnically as well as religiously diverse society. And they have taken care to recruit, socialise, and promote anti-Islamic State, pro-strong centre officers. Most of these come from *abangan* Javanese backgrounds, though some are Christians, Hindu Balinese, and other non-Muslims.[31]

In addition to religion and region, social class was an important source of conflict in Indonesia in the 1950s. By 1963, the communist party had become the main pillar of President Sukarno's support, and the main challenger to the army's political role and vision. In the early morning of 1 October 1965, six senior officers were kidnapped and assassinated by troops from the presidential palace guard together with members of the communist party's youth organisation. Major-General Suharto, the remaining senior officer in command of strategic troops in Jakarta, quickly moved to put down the challenge. Within weeks the communist party was in retreat, and by early 1966 Suharto had become the effective holder of supreme national political power.[32]

Since 1965 the military leaders have held that Pancasila, that is, their conception of a unitary, pan-religious state and a mixed private-state economy, is under simultaneous attack from the *ekstrem kiri*, extreme left or communism, and the *ekstrem kanan*, extreme right or politicised Islam. Their defense has been repression of communist and Islamic political groups and a general depoliticisation. About half a million communists were almost immediately killed and tens of thousands more were imprisoned for over a decade.

Muslims of all kinds were at first welcomed as partners in the anticommunist crusade, but were soon reined in when they began to press for the rehabilitation of Masjumi, anathema to the military leaders on both religious and regionalist grounds. A new modernist-oriented Islamic party was finally permitted, but without the Masjumi name or the party's old leaders. In 1973, a single omnibus Islamic party, combining the four Islamic parties existing at that time, was created by government edict. This fused party has been steadily drained of Islamic content, and is today at least formally open to members of other religions. Its largest and most principled component, the non-modernist Nahdlatul Ulama led by Abdurrahman Wahid, withdrew in 1984.

In more general terms, the route to power through party-contested elections was shut off by a policy of restructuring election laws and coercing and corrupting opponents behind the scenes, enabling the government's own party, Golkar (Golongan Karya, Functional Groups), to win handily the five general elections held between 1971 and 1992. The two non-government political parties that exist today, one representing Islam, the other a mix of old nationalist and Christian parties, are not allowed to have branches at the local level. Their leaders and legislative candidates are 'screened' for ideological acceptability. Party operating funds are heavily subsidised by the government. Parliament and the People's Consultative Assembly, which under the 1945 Constitution selects the president and vice-president every five years, are rubber stamps controlled by the army-backed president.

The government has also not hesitated over the years to act decisively and forcefully against protest groups, invariably small-scale and localised, that have articulated economic and cultural grievances under the banner of Islam. The point has thus been repeatedly driven home that the extreme right exists, is dangerous, and must be crushed.

To these policies, the substantialists' response, beginning with Nurcholish Madjid's 1970 speech—which contains the phrase 'Islam yes, Islamic party, no'—has been acceptance. In part, this is because of values shared with the government, particularly the common opposition to *syari'ah* as the basis for positive law, but also the common commitment to an incorporative version of Indonesian nationalism that recognises the equal rights of Muslims, Christians, and others as Indonesian citizens.

Partly, too, it is tactical, based on belief that success in the New Order can only come through working within and alongside the government, not by challenging its most vulnerable political institutions, the Parliament and, especially, the legitimacy-granting People's Consultative Assembly. Prominent substantialists can be found today throughout the Department of Religion and other government ministries, in the government-appointed *Majelis Ulama Indonesia* (Council of Indonesian Islamic Teachers), the State Islamic Studies Institutes, the state universities, in the state-controlled and the private press, and in non-partisan organisations outside the state such as Nurcholish's Paramadina Foundation and the thousands of voluntary organisations (*Lembaga Swadaya Masyarakat*, People's Self-Reliance Institutes) engaged in village development, environmental protection, human rights and other activities. Abdurrahman Wahid's Nahdlatul Ulama shares this approach and acts together with the modernist substantialists on many issues.

The scripturalists, on the other hand, have been at a disadvantage from the start because they remain committed to implementation of the *syari'ah*. Government hostility to them has been met by an equal or greater hostility, and few have been willing to adapt even as a tactical matter.

They have continued to press—interestingly, using Western representative as well as Islamic rhetoric—for genuinely democratic implementation of the 1945 Constitution, including most importantly the freedom to form a political party based on Islam. They remain sympathetic to regional demands for greater autonomy. They complain loudly and bitterly whenever the government puts down another rebellious splinter group. And of course their anger has been continuously refreshed by the countless large and small restrictions imposed on their activities, such as the monitoring of mosque sermons for political content and the frequent interrogation of preachers and activists.

Indirectly, the New Order government's economic development and social and cultural policies have also had a significant impact on both the scripturalists and the substantialists. The picture here is more complex, almost certainly less uni-directional, but probably not fully knowable until the New Order politicians have left the scene. I will sketch three general points.

First, steady economic growth at nearly 8% per year from the late 1960s to the early 1980s, and at about 7% since the late 1980s, has raised the level of prosperity, though at different rates, of most Indonesians.[33] One effect of growth has been to create new upwardly-mobile classes of urban entrepreneurs, many tied to the state, which provides them with contracts and various facilities, a private- and state-employed salariat, and professionals (doctors, lawyers, teachers, journalists, and so on).

This success has been disproportionately enjoyed by the Sino-Indonesian minority, only 4% nationally but concentrated in urban areas and in the private business sector and thus well-placed to take advantage of the government's essentially neo-classical growth policies. Nonetheless, indigenous Indonesian business people, including many Muslims, have profited too.

There also seem to be, though this is less clear, large groups of indigenous Indonesians, especially in the urban areas, who have not benefited or have benefited much less than others, and feel deprived as a result. Examples are the residents of Tanjung Priok, the Jakarta port, where a major anti-regime demonstration in the name of Islam occurred in 1984, and increasingly restive factory laborers, especially those who work for foreign companies in the Greater Jakarta area. Many others have achieved some success, but are clinging precariously to the lower rungs of middle class income and status.

Prosperity has also come to the rural areas, as a result of government policies that have strengthened and stabilised the rice economy, financed widely distributed public works projects in agricultural infrastructure, road, school, village hall, and health centre construction, reforestation, and other areas, and created credit institutions and a macro-economic context in which small business people are willing and able to invest. Again, the social and cultural impacts of these changes are not entirely clear, and undoubtedly there have been both winners and losers in the countryside too.

One of the most significant of these groups, I suspect, comprises the millions of small but prosperous rice farmers.[34] These farmers owe their success to government policies, and of course to the good luck of having been born with some agricultural resources with which they could take advantage of the new policies. They are also often closely connected by kinship or friendship to village and supra-village government officials. Necessarily, most of them are Muslims at least in the statistical sense. Given what we know of the *santri-abangan* distribution of the Javanese population, a substantial proportion of them must also be *santri*.

A second general policy of the New Order government has been to promote the idea that all Indonesians, as Pancasilaists, must adhere to a world religion: Islam, Protestantism, Catholicism, Hinduism, or Buddhism, in the government's pantheon of officially accepted religions. This policy got its start in the anti-communist fervour of the immediate post-1965 period, when atheism, syncretic *abangan*-ism, and communism were in many minds indistinguishable.[35] It has continued as a sort of anti-communist vaccination.

In the mid-1970s, it appeared that an organised *abangan* lobby, an association of practitioners of Hindu-Javanese mystical beliefs and practices called *kebatinan* (roughly, the science of the inner being), might broaden the definition of religion to include themselves. President Suharto was at that time widely reported to be a devotee of *kebatinan* and to be sympathetic to the association's demand for a directorate-general in the Department of Religion. In the end, however, the group had to settle for the Department of Education and continued non-religious status. The consequence is that if they are to remain Pancasilaists the *abangan*, most of whom are traditionally nominal Muslims, can not choose to leave Islam for *kebatinan*.

Finally, the public education system, from kindergarten through university, has been vastly enlarged by the New Order government.[36] This is a continuation of policies begun in the early 1950s, and represents a consensus among the Indonesian political elite, and perhaps the public as well, that education is the key to success in the modern world. Thanks to the oil boom, the Suharto government has been able to act on this consensus to a greater extent than any of its predecessors, and elementary school is now within the physical reach of virtually every village child.[37] At the other end of the pipeline, there is a state university in every province.

One effect of this explosion is that there are now many more educated *santri*, both absolutely and as a percentage of the educated population, than there were at independence or even at the beginning of the New Order. Nurcholish Madjid's generation was the first beneficiary of the expansion of educational opportunities, and the numbers have continued to grow in the past two decades. Older government officials frequently remark on the reversal in bureaucratic culture that they have witnessed in their lifetimes. Condescension toward Islamic piety as characteristic of backward villagers has been replaced by an atmosphere in which most officials participate in daily prayers in rooms set aside for the purpose, and all government officials—even Christians!—begin speeches with the Islamic salutation *assalamu' alaikum wa rahmatullahi wa barakatuh* (may peace be with you, and the blessing and grace of God).

A second effect is increased pressure on *abangan* culture. Religious instruction, in the religion of one's choice, is required of all students in the public school system. Fourteen State Islamic Studies Institutes throughout the country turn out religious teachers for the schools. Statistically Muslim *abangan* children now learn, as their parents never did, such basics as how to pray as Muslims. After leaving school, they may revert to earlier beliefs and practices, but it is now much easier for them to become and remain *santri*. At the university level, the growth in the number of pious students, according to long time lecturers at Gadjah Mada University in Yogyakarta, a stronghold of *abangan*-ism, that has been wrought by these changes is extraordinary.[38]

V

What are the implications of these developments for the current balance of political influence between substantialists and scripturalists? How long is this balance likely to endure? Over the past quarter century, the substantialists have been much more influential. Government support, plus repression of the scripturalists, has given them a golden opportunity to develop and disseminate their ideas. Moreover, government, economic and cultural policies have led to the rapid growth of a larger, better educated, and relatively prosperous *santri* community. Perhaps most important, many upwardly-mobile members of this community are sympathetic to the substantialist position, which enables them to be devout and at the same time not incur the suspicion of the government that they are closet 'extreme rightists'.

At least three factors push in the other direction, however, toward a strengthening of scripturalist influence, particularly if a more open political climate follows the Suharto presidency. These are the easier acceptability of scripturalist doctrines to many Indonesian Muslims, the possibility of political alliances with other rising social groups, and the desire of ambitious politicians to build a mass support base.

The substantialist position is at war with many of the hardiest shibboleths in the Islamic world today. For example: the Qur'an is the unmediated word of God and therefore must be read literally; the Qur'an and Hadits provide a set of laws and other clear do's and dont's of personal and social behaviour; unlike other religions, especially Christianity with its willingness to render differently unto Caesar and God, Islam encompasses all aspects of human life, including government.

I have already indicated that the number of *santri* has probably been growing rapidly, both absolutely and as a percentage of total population, during the New Order. A small proportion of these people are urban, well-educated, and middle to upper class, but most continue to live, in small towns and villages, a life style not much different from their parents.

Although there is little evidence one way or the other, it is probably too much to expect that a high percentage of village people would even understand, let alone be attracted to, the ideas of Nurcholish Madjid and friends. These ideas are, after all, sophisticated, abstract, and rather far from the direct personal religious experience of most villagers. When issues are framed narrowly, as in the proposal of the Minister of Religion, supported by Nurcholish, to reinterpret Qur'anic statements on inheritance so that sons and daughters can inherit equally, villagers tend to react with outrage.[39]

Even more educated and upwardly-mobile Muslims are not necessarily attracted to substantialism. That some in Jakarta are is evidenced by the popularity of the religious discussions offered by the Paramadina Foundation and similar organisations. But there are alternatives. Mass-market books on Islamic mysticism or sufism (*tasawuf*) were extremely big sellers in Islamic book stores throughout the 1980s. Sufism also attracts high-culture fiction writers and essayists.[40] Some Indonesian observers laud sufism as a means of gaining a deeper religious experience, while others condemn it as escapism from social concerns.

Another alternative, closer to scripturalism, might be called the *halal/ haram* (permitted/prohibited) complex among secularly-educated young people. Many students at the elite state universities, most famously in Bandung but also in Jakarta, Bogor, Yogyakarta, and elsewhere, are attracted to the Quranic study courses offered by campus mosque groups. These courses tend to focus on issues of personal behaviour of burning concern to adolescents and young adults, particularly those who have left villages and small towns and set their sights on making successful careers in the modern world. They are popular because they provide a strict set of behavioural rules, yes and no answers, within a familiar and reassuring Islamic identity.

In recent years there has been a tendency for students to be drawn increasingly to radical or militant Muslim organisations, some of which ban Western clothing styles for their members, copy Middle Eastern dress and social and religious practices, and in general draw as sharp as possible a line between themselves and non-Muslim society. HMI, the Islamic university students' association that spawned Nurcholish Madjid and many other prominent substantialist leaders, is now said to be considered too moderate and consequently has little appeal among students who identify themselves as devout Muslims.[41]

Sufism, either as a way of plumbing the deepest meaning of religion or as an avenue of escape, is probably not a threat to substantialist influence except in so far as it draws away from political activism people who might otherwise have become substantialists. The *halal/haram* complex is potentially more dangerous. Its ideas are a total rejection of substantialism, offering certainty instead of doubt and further questions. And its appeal is greatest precisely among Indonesia's best and brightest, substantialism's natural and most critical recruiting ground.

A second factor that might lead to greater scripturalist influence is the possibility of forming political alliances with other groups. *MD* cover stories and articles frequently display sympathy to lower class groups, especially in Jakarta, and hostility to a panoply of lower class enemies, including government bureaucrats, their military backers, Sino-Indonesian and foreign, particularly Western, business.

Without greater knowledge of the social background and associations of the *MD* editors, it is hard to know precisely what to make of this sympathy. Much of it reads like boiler-plate populism of the 1950s and 1960s, as close to the Indonesian Nationalist Party as to the socialists and communists. The nationalists of that time, including Sukarno, used populism mostly as a cover for policies that benefited middle and upper class business people, bureaucrats, and themselves personally.

Today's scripturalists may have similar ideas, and may indeed be able to appeal to some disaffected officials and business people, though I suspect the substantialists can hold their own with these constituencies. But we should not dismiss out of hand the more revolutionary possibility that an old dream of the left, the forging of a massive worker-*santri* front, may be closer to becoming a real prospect after a quarter century of capitalist-style development.[42]

Regional interests are another coalition possibility. Apart from Christian and Hindu pockets, the people of Sumatra, Kalimantan, Sulawesi, and the smaller islands of eastern Indonesia are predominantly *santri* and once voted overwhelmingly for Masjumi. Since the late 1950s, when the regional rebellions were defeated and governmental centralisation began in earnest, they have nursed a growing sense of grievance.

One source of anger is process, the fact that no governmental decisions of importance for the regions are made in the regions themselves. Another is content, the fact that so much of the economic growth of the New Order has taken place in the greater Jakarta area and to a lesser extent the Surabaya area in east Java. On the other hand, there have been mitigating factors, including heavy subsidisation of provincial and local government budgets and the centrally-directed but locally implemented public works projects that have blanketed the country since the mid-1970s.

As in the case of class, it is hard to gauge the extent to which scripturalist politicians might develop support in the regions. Some of *MD*'s older editors and sponsors, as I have indicated, were themselves involved in rebellion and do not now appear to regret it. It is possible that this history gives them an edge in obtaining regional support. More likely, the successful regional politicians of the future will try to avoid linking themselves with the past, not least because of the stigma associated with it in the eyes of the military.[43] But there is little doubt, given the social and cultural changes I have alluded to, that their politics will be expressed in a distinctly Islamic idiom.

Finally, in the near future there are likely to be more rather than fewer ambitious politicians contending for power, including supreme power. The occasion for the contestation will be the departure of President Suharto, now 72, from the political arena.

An indication of what might happen is provided by examining Suharto's recent political tactics. From the mid-1960s to the mid-1980s the president relied relatively little on Islamic political support. As I have indicated, his policy from the beginning was to promote Islamic piety while opposing partisan Islamic politics. When great quantities of oil money became available in the mid-1970s, substantial amounts were spent on mosque-building and other religious support activities.

In the late 1980s and early 1990s a new policy of support for many specifically Islamic projects, including at least one that comes close to being political in the partisan sense, has emerged. The impetus for the change appears to have been the growing coldness to the president of the top leaders of the armed forces, who are looking toward a time when they will still be politically active, as individuals and as an institution, and he will not.[44] Suharto has reacted in two ways: by trying to reestablish his grip on the armed forces via a network of generals who are relatives or former adjutants; and by reaching out to Islam.

With regard to Islam, he has: sent to Parliament a law recognising and strengthening the Islamic courts that adjudicate family disputes; reversed long-standing Department of Education policy which prohibited female students in state schools from wearing the *jilbab*, an Islamic head-covering; permitted, after rejecting for many years, an Islamic Bank; allowed the holding of a major Islamic cultural festival in Jakarta; allowed a Catholic entertainment tabloid editor to be sentenced to several years in jail for insulting the Prophet; and, together with his wife and other family members, himself made the pilgrimage to Mecca.

Perhaps the most important evidence of the new relaxation toward political Islam was the formation, in late 1990, of ICMI (*Ikatan Cendekiawan Muslim Se-Indonesia*, All-Indonesia Association of Muslim Intellectuals).[45] From Suharto's point of view, ICMI was probably conceived primarily as a means of gaining support from *santri* intellectuals and social activists prior to the general elections of 1991 and the presidential election of 1993. Its general chairman is Minister for Research B.J. Habibie, a German-trained engineer personally close to Suharto, with no background in Islamic or any other partisan or organisational politics. Measures were taken to ensure that ICMI would be controlled by Habibie's staff.

From the *santri* community—modernists and traditionalists, substantialists and even scripturalists—the reception of ICMI was almost overwhelmingly enthusiastic. To many it looked as though the government, after many years of keeping Islamic intellectuals outside the corridors of power, was finally willing to admit them. Perhaps the largest number were interested more in networking than in promoting any specific Islamic agenda. But virtually all of the major substantialist figures, who do have an agenda, joined, as did a number of individuals previously considered to be opponents of the regime.[46] In some quarters there was talk, subsequently discouraged by the Minister for Home Affairs, that ICMI was the first step in the formation of a new Masjumi.

MD remained a hard nut to crack, but did move in the government's direction. In July 1991 the editors wrote a cover story on ICMI.[47] 'After long years covered with mutual suspicion, we now see a tendency for mutual approach between the government and the Muslims. Is this beneficial or just a puzzle that's hard to solve?' It is true that under the New Order the bureaucracy has been Islamised, they admitted, and in that sense ICMI is a hopeful sign. But it is also true that inside the state Islam has become bureaucratised. The Islamic community should take advantage of this new opportunity but it must remember that 'a solid organisation requires a firm ideological foundation of its own.'

In early 1992 *MD* covered a speech by Deliar Noer, a respected modernist intellectual, attacking the president and ICMI for not paying attention to the growing gap between rich and poor. 'The conglomerates are extending themselves, the cooperatives are weak, middle and small businessmen are weak, whose responsibility is this?'[48] But at the end of the year they published another cover story praising the 'greenness'—the many *santri* members—of the new People's Consultative Assembly, reflecting the political clout of ICMI and of Minister Habibie.[49]

It is important not to make too much of ICMI, or indeed of Suharto's other recent gestures toward Islam. His basic posture of opposition to autonomous and powerful Muslim parties, not to mention an Islamic State, is unaltered. The point is rather that as his power diminishes with age, he is looking around for support outside his principal base in the armed forces, and finding it rather easily in the *santri* community. If Suharto—for so long the absolute master of Indonesian politics—finds it necessary to court support in this way, how much more likely that would-be successors will do the same in the power vacuum that lies ahead?

VI

There is a pessimistic lesson that can be drawn from this analysis of the context of hope and fear experienced by Indonesian Muslims for the past quarter century. It is that the success of the substantialists, a small group of thinkers with a small though growing following, has been too dependent on the support of authoritarian politicians whose needs happen to have coincided with theirs. In a more open or democratic political climate, on a more level playing field, it is probable that the scripturalists would have many more political resources, in mass acceptance of their ideas, organisation, allies, media, and access to politicians, than they have now.

Moeslim Abdurrahman, a young modernist thinker, recently expressed very well my own concern about the strength of the links between substantialist leaders and followers:

> If it may be said that [Nurcholish Madjid's] movement is a movement of ideas, even though it is true that ideas have their own legs, a mechanism is also needed that can more effectively put the legs in motion. . . . Concerning [Abdurrahman Wahid], whose movement may be said to be a movement for the transformation of the umat, the problem is that there is not yet a social machine that understands and can be used effectively in support of his concepts.[50]

Fortunately, my pessimism is allayed by a sense of the complexity of Indonesian Islam and of Indonesian culture and society generally. The advance of the scripturalists will continue to be blocked by three formidable obstacles: the *abangan* population, diminished in size and strength but still vital and unvanquished; the *santri* traditionalists, who have never had the stomach for crusades or absolutes and remain accommodationists to the core; and the modernists themselves, containing as they do a vigorous substantialist as well as scripturalist wing. But the blocking may have to be done in a more open, even relatively democratic, political system, where reawakened fears of the scripturalists' commitments, strengths, and intentions will severely test the nerves and skills of the players.

1. Murray Edelman, *Constructing the Political Spectacle*, Chicago: University of Chicago Press, 1988, p. 9.
2. Clifford Geertz, *Islam Observed*, Chicago: University of Chicago Press, 1971, p. 88; Fazlur Rahman, *Islam and Modernity: Transformation of an Intellectual Tradition*, Chicago: University of Chicago Press, 1982, p. 129. Both of these manuscripts were written several years before their respective publication dates.
3. Clifford Geertz, "'Popular Art' and the Javanese Tradition,' *Indonesia* 50 (October 1990), pp. 77–94. *Santri* are devout Muslims. *Abangan* are syncretists, formally Muslim but in actual belief and practice a mixture of animism, Hindu-Buddhism, and Islam. See Clifford Geertz, *The Religion of Java*, Glencoe: the Free Press, 1960. Self-conscious *abangan* are often adepts of Hindu-Javanese-derived mysticism and are critical of organised Islam, in part for its supposed inability to separate Islamic religion from Arab culture. The *santri* community in Indonesia is conventionally divided into modernist (or reformist) and traditionalist (also called orthodox or conservative) wings.
4. I am borrowing this term from Bahtiar Effendy, who is using it in his forthcoming doctoral dissertation at The Ohio State University.
5. For overviews, see Fachry Ali and Bahtiar Effendy, *Merambah Jalan Baru Islam* [Clearing a New Islamic Path], Bandung: Mizan, 1986, and Howard Federspiel, *Muslim Intellectuals and National Development in Indonesia*, New York: Nova Science Publishers, 1992. My own understanding of substantialism, and of much else about Indonesian Islam, has been shaped by many conversations over the past several years with Bahtiar Effendy. Bahtiar is not, however, responsible for any of the views expressed in this paper.
6. *Indonesia 1990: An Official Handbook*, Jakarta: Department of Information, Republic of Indonesia, 1990. The concept was introduced by the *abangan* nationalist leader Sukarno in 1945 in an attempt to provide a symbolic formulation that would include all groups in the New Indonesia. The 1945 context was conflict between those who wanted a more Islamic and those who wanted either a pan-religious or a secular state.
7. 'Keharusan Pembaharuan Pemikiran Islam dan Masalah Integrasi Ummat', in Drs. Nurcholish Madjid, Abdul Qadir Djaelani, Ismail Hasan Metarieum S.H., and H.E. Saefuddin Anshari, *Pembaharuan Pemikiran Islam* [The Renewal of Islamic Thought], Jakarta: Islamic Research Centre, 1970, pp. 1–12.
8. 'Para' means 'for' in Spanish, 'madina' is 'civilisation' in Arabic, Nurcholish explained in a speech to the Association for Asian Studies, Washington D.C., April 2, 1992. For a further discussion of Nurcholish and his role in Indonesian intellectual and political life, see my 'Improvising Political Cultural

Change: Three Indonesian Cases,' in James Schiller, ed., *Indonesian Political Culture: Asking the Right Questions*, Athens: Ohio University Center for Southeast Asia Studies, forthcoming.

9. For Nurcholish's current views, see the recently-published collection of his post-Chicago essays, *Islam: Doktrin dan Peradaban* [Islam: Doctrine and Civilisation], Jakarta: Yayasan Wakaf Paramadina, 1992.

10. *MD*'s print run in the last months of 1992 was 15,000 per month. In January 1993 it rose to 20,000. Interview, Herry Komar, PT Temprint, Jakarta, March 1993. *MD*'s government printing license restricts it to circulation within the organisation, but it is nonetheless widely available. Interview, Anwar Haryono and Lukman Hakiem, Jakarta, March 1993. For comparison, the best known general circulation Islamic news weekly in Indonesia, *Panji Masyarakat*, has a per issue circulation above 30,000. Interview, Bahtiar Effendy, March 1993.

11. Many other Islamic newspapers and magazines also reflect scripturalist ideas to a greater or lesser extent. For example, the daily newspaper *Pelita* (Islamic, but controlled by the government) and the weekly *Panji Masyarakat* (once the organ of Hamka, one of Indonesia's most famous modernist writers during the late-colonial and early post-colonial periods, and now edited by Hamka's son) sometimes side with the scripturalists and sometimes with the substantialists.

12. In 1991 the principal editors were: H. Buchari Tamam, M. Syah Agusdin, Ona Rahmat Rasyid, and Lukman Hakiem. Buchari was a Masjumi activist in the 1950s, and also joined the Sumatran rebellion. The others are too young to have been involved in pre-1965 politics. In 1992, the magazine did not list its editors. The most famous name, after Mohammad Natsir, associated with *MD* is Anwar Haryono, a Masjumi member of Parliament in the 1950s, who writes a monthly column.

13. This does not mean, however, that they do not recognise the occasional need for *ijtihad* (independent interpretation) to connect Quranic injunctions with twentieth century conditions. See for example the discussion of *zakat* (religious tax) below.

14. 'Mencari Kebenaran yang Lapang' [Seeking Truth that is Broad-minded], *Tempo* XXII, No. 35 (31 Oktober 1992), p. 97. See also Nurcholish's interview, 'Tidak Usah Munafik [We Don't Have to be Hypocritical], *Matra*, December 1992, pp. 13–23. *Matra* is a secular magazine whose editors model it, as far as they can (which is not very far) in today's restricted publishing climate, on *Playboy*.

15. 'Nabi Gagal Menjalankan Missinya? (Menguji pemikiran Nurcholish)', *MD*, December 1992, pp. 41–52.

16. 'Nabi Gagal Menjalankan Missinya?', p. 41.

17. *Ibid.*, p. 47. They do not go so far as to use the term *murtad*, however.

18. All of these phrases are in the editorial, *ibid.*, p. 41, and some are developed elsewhere in the story. Prof. Leonard Binder, for a brief period Nurcholish's Ph.D program adviser at the University of Chicago, is characterised as a 'fanatical Jew' who once 'offered a doctoral degree to an Indonesian Muslim intellectual if he would write a dissertation that denied the role of Islam in Indonesian life in the past and in the future.' Nurcholish

himself does not believe that Binder could ever have made such an offer. Interview, March 1993.

19. See for example the cover story 'Problema Sebuah Kerukunan' [The Problem of Harmony], *MD*, December 1991, pp. 41–52.

20. See for example the cover story 'Pemilu yang Bisu, Sistem Sosial yang Menggeliat' [A Mute Election, an Awakening Social System], *MD*, May 1992, pp. 41–50, and 'Islam Yes, Partai Islam Yes' [Islam Yes, Islamic Party Yes], *MD*, June 1992, pp. 63–66.

21. On the impact of economic policies, see the cover stories 'Ikhtiar Mengaca Diri' [An Attempt at Self-Reflection], *MD*, January 1992, pp. 41–50; 'GBHN' [The Main Outlines of State Policy], *MD*, August 1992, pp. 41–51; and 'Demografi Jakarta Berantakan' [The Demography of Jakarta in Disorder], *MD*, September 1992, pp. 41–50.

22. For example, see the cover story 'Pudarnya Pamor Amerika Serikat' [The Fading Luster of the United States], *MD*, October 1992, pp. 41–50. AIDS is reported to have begun in America.

23. 'Pergeseran Kekuatan Timur Tengah' [Middle East Power Shift], *MD*, December 1992, p. 18.

24. 'Nabi Gagal Menjalankan Missinya?', p. 46.

25. 'Jejak Yahudi dan Baha'i di Indonesia' [The Trail of Jews and Baha'i in Indonesia], *MD*, February 1992, pp. 70–71; DR. GS. Sam Ratu Langi, 'Judaisme', *MD*, October 1992, pp. 24–27 (reprinted from the Japanese-era newspaper *Asia Raya*, 29 April 1943); 'Rotary Club, Perabot Zionis Israel' [Rotary Club, Tool of the Israeli Zionists], *MD*, May 1992, pp. 31–32; 'Membongkar Konspirasi Yahudi' [Exposing the Jewish Conspiracy], *MD*, July 1992, p. 69 (a review of William G. Carr, *Yahudi Menggenggam Dunia* [Jews Grip the World], Jakarta: Al-Kautsar, 1991); 'Yahudi dalam Sorotan Al-Quran' [Jews in the Light of the Qur'an], *MD*, December 1992, pp. 30–31. The quoted material is from p. 30.

26. See the cover story 'Zakat dan Nisbinya Hidup' [Religious Tax and the Relativeness of Life], *MD*, March 1992, pp. 41–50.

27. *MD*, April 1992, pp. 41–51.

28. Two Indonesian artists, the nominally Islamic (formerly Catholic) poet and playwright W.S. Rendra, and the devoutly Islamic but sometimes eccentric poet Sutardji Calzoum Bachri, are mentioned as examples of unacceptable 'coarse poetic language.'

29. *Tentang Dasar Negara Republik Indonesia Dalam Konstituante* [Concerning the Foundation of the State of the Republic of Indonesia in the Constituent Assembly], 3 volumes, n.p., n.d., is a collection of speeches covering the various points of view. Translations of key speeches are in Herbert Feith and Lance Castles, eds., *Indonesian Political Thinking 1945–1965*, Ithaca: Cornell University Press, 1970.

30. Daniel S. Lev, *The Transition to Guided Democracy: Indonesian Politics 1957–1959*, Ithaca: Cornell Modern Indonesia Project, 1966.

31. For data on officers' backgrounds, see the continuing series by the editors of the journal *Indonesia*. The most recent is 'Current Data on the Indonesian Military Elite, July 1, 1989–January 1, 1992', *Indonesia* 53 (April 1992), pp. 93–136.

32. Harold Crouch, *The Army and Politics in Indonesia*, Ithaca: Cornell University Press, 1978.
33. The best general account is Anne Booth, ed., *The Oil Boom and After: Indonesian Economic Policy and Performance in the Suharto Era*, Singapore: Oxford University Press, 1992.
34. My suspicion is based in part on visits to villages and interviews with village heads, east and central Java, 1989 and 1990.
35. See Robert Cribb, ed., *The Indonesian Killings 1965–1966*, Clayton, Vic.: Centre of Southeast Asian Studies, Monash University, 1990, and Robert Hefner, *The Political Economy of Mountain Java*, Berkeley and Los Angeles: University of California Press, 1990, Ch. 7.
36. For a summary, see Barbara Leigh, *The Growth of the Education System in the Making of the State: A Case Study in Aceh, Indonesia*, unpub. Ph.D. dissertation, Sydney: University of Sydney, School of Social and Policy Studies in Education, 1992, Ch. 2.
37. No school fees are collected in the first three grades, but financially school is still a burden for the very poorest families.
38. Interviews, Faculty of Social and Political Sciences, Gadjah Mada University, September–November 1989.
39. My direct personal experience is with villagers and local observers, Banda Aceh and Aceh Besar, 1985–87. Aceh, at the extreme western end of the Indonesian archipelago and with a reputation for both isolation and fanaticism, may of course not be representative of Muslim villagers elsewhere. John Bowen's new book on the neighboring Gayo, *Muslims through Discourse: Religion and Ritual in Gayo Society* (Princeton: Princeton University Press, 1993), suggests that the range of village responses may in fact be quite wide. Jakarta Muslim intellectuals, on the other hand, frequently say that Nurcholish needs someone to translate his views to less sophisticated people. See for example Azyumardi Azra, 'Neo-Modernisme Cak Nur' [The Neo-Modernism of Nurcholish Madjid], *Tempo* XXIII, 5 (3 April 1993), p. 22.
40. E.g., Danarto, *Godlob*, Jakarta: Grafiti, 2nd printing 1987; Emha Ainun Nadjib, *Slilit Sang Kiai*, Jakarta: Grafiti, 1991.
41. *Tempo* XXIII, 3 (3 April 1993), pp. 13–23. Also interview, Wahyu Muryadi, Jakarta, March 1993. Wahyu is a *Tempo* magazine reporter who follows current developments among Muslim students. In the early 1980s he was an Islamic activist at Airlangga University in Surabaya, East Java. Nurcholish Madjid and Imaduddin Abdulrahim, in separate interviews in Jakarta in March 1993, described their own considerable current efforts at weaning the students away from the militants. From the mid-1970s to the early 1980s Imaduddin was himself considered one of the most prominent militant figures at the Salman student mosque in Bandung. Today, his view of Islam and its relationship to society is close to that of Nurcholish.
42. The dream was recalled at the beginning of the New Order by W.F. Wertheim, 'From Aliran Toward Class Struggle in the Countryside of Java', *Pacific Viewpoint* 10 (1969), pp. 1–17.
43. Endang Saifuddin Anshari, son of a 1950s Masjumi firebrand, is quoted in *MD* as believing that the Sumatran-based rebellion of the late 1950s 'tidak salah, tapi kalah' [was not wrong, but lost]. *MD*, December 1992, p. 68. In

a subsequent letter to the editor, Endang denied having made the statement, and *MD* apologised. *MD*, February 1993, p. 7.

44. My general analysis of this situation is R William Liddle, 'Indonesia's Threefold Crisis', *Journal of Democracy*, Vol. 3, No. 4 (October 1992), pp. 60–74, reprinted as Chapter Seven in this volume.

45. The best account of ICMI is M. Syafi'i Anwar, 'Islam, Negara, dan Formasi Sosial Dalam Orde Baru' [Islam, the State, and Social Formation in the New Order], *Ulumul Qur'an*, Vol. III, No. 3 (1992), Supplement, pp. 1–28.

46. Of the figures discussed in this paper, only Abdurrahman Wahid refused to join, on grounds that ICMI was a sectarian organisation that would promote division rather than unity and also coopt intellectuals and activists who should be working for democratisation. Abdurrahman formed his own organisation, *Forum Demokrasi*, with a number of prominent Christians and other non-Muslims.

47. 'Dijamin Halal' [Guaranteed Permitted], *MD*, July 1991, pp. 42–51.

48. 'Belum Menyentuh Akar Persoalan' [Not Yet Touching the Root of the Problem], *MD*, February 1992, pp. 8–9.

49. 'Hijau Mengapa Tidak' [Why Not Green], *MD*, November 1992, pp. 41–52.

50. Moeslim Abdurrahman, 'Dua Pendekar' [Two Champions], *Tempo*, XXII, No. 44 (2 January 1993), p. 108.

Index

End-notes are not indexed.

291